Francis Bacon's Contribution to Shakespeare

A paradigm shift is advocated, away from a single-author theory of the Shake-speare work towards a many-hands theory. Here, the middle ground is adopted between competing so-called Stratfordian and alternative single-author theories. In the process, arguments are advanced as to why Shake-speare's *First Folio* (1623) presents as an unreliable document for attribution and why contemporary opinion characterized Shakspere of Stratford as an opportunist businessman who acquired the work of others. The limitations of current methods of authorship attribution are highlighted, and an entirely new Rare Collocation Profiling (RCP) method is introduced, which, unlike current stylometric methods, is capable of detecting multiple contributors to a text. Using the Early English Books Online (EEBO) database, rare phrases and collocations in a target text are identified, together with the authors who used them. This allows a DNA-type profile to be constructed for the possible contributors to a text that also takes into account direction of influence. The method's facility to identify multiple hands brings powerful new evidence to bear on crucial questions, such as the author of the *Groats-worth of Witte* (1592) letter; the contributors to *3 Henry VI*; the extent of Francis Bacon's contribution to *Twelfth Night* and *The Tempest*; and the scheduling of *Love's Labour's Lost* at the 1594–5 Gray's Inn Christmas revels, for which Bacon wrote entertainments. The treatise also provides detailed analyses of the nature of the complaint against Shakspere in the *Groats-worth letter*, the identity of the players who performed *The Comedy of Errors* at Gray's Inn in 1594, and the reasons why Shakspere could not have had access to Virginia colony information that appears in *The Tempest*, which an insider such as Bacon was privy to. With a Foreword by Sir Mark Rylance, this meticulously researched and penetrating study is a thought-provoking read for the inquisitive student in Shakespeare Studies.

Barry R. Clarke has a variety of interests. He has a PhD in Shakespeare Studies, with peer-reviewed publications on *The Tempest*, and his scholarly publications in quantum mechanics have led to an academic treatise: *The Quantum Puzzle: Critique of Quantum Theory and Electrodynamics* (2017). There are also books on recreational mathematics for Cambridge University Press and Dover Publications, while *Challenging Logic Puzzles Mensa* (2003) has sold over 90,000 copies. He has produced four logic puzzle books for Puzzlewright Press and presently compiles mathematics and logic puzzles for *The Daily Telegraph* and *Prospect* magazine (UK). Viewers in the UK might have seen both his puzzle work and his comedy sketches broadcast on national UK television.

I have only taken upon me to ring a bell to call other wits together.

—*Francis Bacon*[1]

1 Letter "To Dr. Playfere, desiring him to translate the Advancement in Latin." In James Spedding, ed. *The Letters and the Life of Francis Bacon*, Vol. III. London: Longmans, Green, Reader, and Dyer, 1868. p.301.

Routledge Studies in Shakespeare

27 **The Fictional Lives of Shakespeare**
Kevin Gilvary

28 **Jonson, Shakespeare, and Aristotle on Comedy**
Jonathan Goossen

29 **Shakespeare and the Cultivation of Difference**
Race and Conduct in the Early Modern World
Patricia Akhimie

30 **Casual Shakespeare**
Three Centuries of Verbal Echoes
Regula Hohl Trillini

31 **Shakespearean Temporalities**
History on the Early Modern Stage
Lukas Lammers

32 **Rethinking Shakespeare Source Study**
Audiences, Authors, and Digital Technologies
Edited by Dennis Austin Britton & Melissa Walter

33 **Shakespeare and Indian Cinemas**
'Local Habitations'
Edited by Poonam Trivedi and Paromita Chakravarti

34 **Shakespeare and Asia**
Edited by Jonathan Locke Hart

35 **Francis Bacon's Contribution to Shakespeare**
A New Attribution Method
Barry R. Clarke

For more information about this series, please visit: https://www.routledge.com

Francis Bacon's Contribution to Shakespeare

A New Attribution Method

Barry R. Clarke

FOREWORD BY SIR MARK RYLANCE

Routledge
Taylor & Francis Group
NEW YORK AND LONDON

Then Honoures ende vertuously offeres iniurie,
Notus turnes bloud and raises dead
Wherfore inflamed loue, liberty inuites armes.
Morning borne lighte agayn kindles earth,
Certayne enemies of Fortune trouble Honoure,
Earth and Notus choose its ende.

Imagine (6, 1; 1562)

First published 2019
by Routledge
52 Vanderbilt Avenue, New York, NY 10017

and by Routledge
2 Park Square, Milton Park, Abingdon, Oxon, OX14 4RN

Routledge is an imprint of the Taylor & Francis Group, an informa business

Library of Congress Cataloging-in-Publication Data
Names: Clarke, Barry R., author. | Rylance, Mark, writer of foreword.
Title: Francis Bacon's contribution to Shakespeare: a new attribution method / Barry Clarke; foreword by Sir Mark Rylance.
Description: New York, NY: Routledge, 2019. |
Series: Routledge studies in Shakespeare; 35 |
Includes bibliographical references and index.
Identifiers: LCCN 2018052479
Subjects: LCSH: Shakespeare, William, 1564–1616—Authorship—Baconian theory. | Bacon, Francis, 1561–1626—Authorship.
Classification: LCC PR2944 .C56 2019 | DDC 822.3/3—dc23
LC record available at https://lccn.loc.gov/2018052479

ISBN: 978-0-367-13782-3 (hbk)
ISBN: 978-0-429-02854-0 (ebk)
ISBN: 978-0-367-22544-5 (pbk)

Typeset in Sabon
by codeMantra

Contents

List of Figures

List of Tables

Acknowledgements

Without the late Nigel Cockburn's research in *The Bacon–Shakespeare Question* (1998) it is fairly certain that I would not have set out on this path, and an estimate of my debt to him is beyond my capability.

I am very grateful for the continuing support given to this work by Professor William Leahy at Brunel University, UK. His determination to plant a tree of free enquiry, in spite of academia's dogmatic resistance, deserves high commendation. The present scholarly study is one of the branches of that tree.

I am delighted with the generosity that Sir Mark Rylance has shown in donating time from his busy schedule to write a Foreword for the book. His petition for tolerance of the views of others in Shakespeare authorship discussions is a lesson to us all.

At Routledge, Taylor and Francis Group, I should like to thank Michelle Salyga for her unwavering enthusiasm for this project and Bryony Reece for her courteous navigation through the production process. Highly creditable editorial work has also been carried out by Assunta Petrone at manuscript stage.

Professor John Henry at the University of Edinburgh has made several historical points about Francis Bacon that have undoubtedly improved the manuscript. Information on the Virginia Company has been generously provided by Professor Alden T. Vaughan and Tom Reedy, and valuable feedback on attribution methods has been given by Professor David Crystal. I am also indebted to Professor Andrew Gurr for reading significant parts of the manuscript and for his judicious comments on Inns of Court productions.

Those who have expressed encouragement for the project at various stages include Dr Ros Barber, Stuart Birtwistle, Betty Clarke, Peter Dawkins, Norman Denton, Lawrence Gerald, Dr John Killingbeck, Lloyd King, Richard Lea, Susan McIlroy, Simon Miles, Fiona Pocock, Roger Procter, Peter Welsford, Graham Wiltshire, and Nicholas Young.

I very much appreciate the permissions granted by The British Library, Cambridge University Library, The Huntingdon Library, and ProQuest to publish images from their collections.

The Francis Bacon Society also deserves recognition for its generous contribution to the funding of the original university PhD research.

Finally, I am extremely grateful to all those who over the course of my research have offered mean-spirited criticism, placed obstructions in my way, or strained their ingenuity to undermine my self-belief. Their efforts have not passed without compensation. Without their gift of the motivation to succeed, I might not have cared to put in half of the work that this treatise now presents for your gratification.

Notes

The name 'Shakspere' in this work denotes William Shakspere of Stratford, who acted in the Lord Chamberlain's Men, later known as the King's Men. This is a separate notion to the mineral name 'Shakespeare', which is reserved for the 36 plays published in *Mr. William Shakespeare's Comedies, Histories & Tragedies* (1623), which will be referred to as the *First Folio*. Two additional plays are to be included under this name: *Pericles, Prince of Tyre* (1609) and *The Two Noble Kinsmen* (1634), the latter being co-attributed on the title page to John Fletcher. The collection of *Shake-speare's Sonnets* (1609) is also included but not explored in this work.

The Elizabethan New Year began on 25 March, and so, for example, in original documents 20 March 1596 means 1597. The old calendar has been modified to our modern year throughout the text.

Foreword

Sir Mark Rylance

> After making his professional theatrical debut in 1980, Mark Rylance served as the first artistic director of Shakespeare's Globe (1995–2005). He won the Laurence Olivier Award in 1994 for playing Benedick in *Much Ado About Nothing* and the Tony Award in 2014 for his performance as Olivia in *Twelfth Night*. He is an Associate of the RSC and has acted in or directed over fifty productions of plays by Shakespeare and his contemporaries. His roles have included Hamlet which he played over 400 times at age 16, 28, and 40, *Cleopatra*, *Henry V*, *Richard II*, *Romeo*, *Macbeth*, Iago in *Othello*, the Duke in *Measure for Measure*, and nearly all the roles in *The Tempest*. He has written two plays, both in collaboration with others, the first "I am Shakespeare" deals specifically with the authorship question. He is a friend of The Francis Bacon Research Trust, The Francis Bacon Society, The Devere Society, President of The Marlowe Society, an Honourary Bencher of the Middle Temple Hall and a Trustee of the Shakespearean Authorship Trust. In what follows, he explains how interpreting the works of Shakespeare through a Baconian lens has informed his acting career and expresses his wish for greater tolerance of the views of others when considering Shakespeare authorship matters.

I read once of an effort to convert an American Indian tribe to Christianity. The missionaries were welcomed into the Indian village and were attended to for a number of days as they explained the beauty and truth of Christ and the one true God. The Indians nodded and smiled, and the missionaries had the impression that these 'heathen barbarians' truly appreciated Christianity and had been successfully converted and saved. The Indians agreed that all the missionaries had said was true. The visitors departed, thrilled with the success of their conversion.

Imagine their dismay when they returned some months later to find the Indians still carrying on with their old polytheistic practices. How could they, if they appreciated the truth of what the missionaries had told them? But the indigenous people of the First Nation tribes were accustomed to living side by side with other tribes who had their own particular ways of describing the reality of life, particularly the spiritual reality of life. They were accustomed to living side by side with a different expression of truth. One truth did not negate another. Why should the people who lived on the mountain express their truth with the same images as the people who lived in the swampy forest of the valley? When describing the creative genius of the world, the works of that genius are the visible character of the genius at work within them. The Indians had been sincere in their appreciation of the missionaries' understanding of Christ and God. They perceived the missionaries as naturally expounding a vision of creation that was as different to their own as the missionaries themselves appeared different in dress, manner, and language. Each homeland provided its own unique experience and language to describe the creative genius at work within. If only the scholarly homeland of Shakespeare was governed by such respectful people, how much more enjoyable and progressive would our discourse be. For, surely, the creation of the works of Shakespeare is as much of a mystery as the creation of the world they reflect. But sadly, if you are part of an academic community you open these pages at your peril! For God forbid what might happen to you if you find yourself, as I did many years ago, convinced that Francis Bacon had a hand in the works attributed to William Shakespeare.

My mother and father were English teachers who loved Shakespeare, and I had the good fortune to be taken to Shakespeare plays by them and to act with them in these plays from an early age. Miraculously, at the age of 22, I came to live and work for The Royal Shakespeare Company in Stratford-upon-Avon. I read biographies of William Shakespeare and wandered the streets and fields of Warwickshire, imagining the steps of the Bard of Avon.

It wasn't until my return to Stratford to play Hamlet and Romeo at the age of 28 that I first began to doubt the attribution of the plays and poems to William Shakspere, an actor from Stratford-upon-Avon. Francis Bacon was the individual whose life and works filled the 'man-shaped hole' (thank you, Michael Wood) that I discovered between William Shakspere and William Shakespeare, author of the plays and poems I love so dearly.

I was angrily attacked almost immediately at work for my doubt, and now 30 years on I continue to be regularly and passionately attacked (in print, fortunately, not in body) for my doubt about the attribution of the works of Shakespeare to the uneducated man from Stratford-upon-Avon. By the way, a vocabulary of over 30,000 words, as appears in the works of Shakespeare, would be a challenge even for someone as educated as Milton, who only demonstrated 8,000 words in his works. I have read that a Stratford villager would only have used 400 words in Shakspere's day. Bacon, in his works of prose, employs around 30,000 words. He is in fact one of the few in history to come near to Shakespeare.

Yet *The Times* labelled me a 'Heretic at the Globe' (note the religious language) for considering Bacon worthy of consideration in the question of how these wonderful plays were created, a question of importance to me because I am in the business of creating plays and a question that was raised as soon as anyone was writing about Shakespeare, while he was still alive.

How has my interest in Bacon affected my life as a Shakespearean actor? I can't complain. I have a wider and more detailed knowledge than I would have had of the history, personalities, and philosophies of the Shakespearean period. Those who follow the orthodox acceptance of the attribution of the plays to Shakspere tend to contain their appreciation of the plays within the scope of a limited life experience and learning, as life experience and learning are hard to find in the known biography of William Shakspere. To even read about the life of someone like Francis Bacon or Edward de Vere is to risk contamination! I do not exaggerate.

Though I was introduced to the question by The Francis Bacon Research Trust, I am also very appreciative of other candidates. I am fascinated by Oxford's case for involvement in the works of Shakespeare; if he didn't write *Hamlet* then surely it was written with him in mind. I believe he had a hand in writing more than we know and certainly has the strongest case for having authored the sonnets. I am drawn with great curiosity to the possible involvement of the "Swan of Avon", Mary Sidney, the Countess of Pembroke, to whose sons the *First Folio* is dedicated. The female characters within the plays are surely superior to all other women in any drama of that time or since. Was a woman involved in their creation? If so, we have answered the need for a pseudonym and frontman. Most recently, I have been impressed and excited by evidence for the involvement of Emilia Bassano, the Jewish-Italian musician with Moorish background who was the first woman to publish poetry in England and a protégé of Mary Sidney. Derby, Neville, Marlowe … each case opens a different casement window into the nature of the plays. Oh, the dreadful viruses that affected my mental health through those open windows! I was once warned by Professor Stanley Wells, of the Birthplace Trust, to beware, lest I fell into the derangement of Delia Bacon. Poor Delia, the much maligned, pioneering authorship investigator who tragically fell ill towards the end of her life.

I may seem undiscerning in my interest, but the idea of a single author of the Shakespeare works has been much weakened recently, if it ever had strength (see Henslowe's record of payments to authors). The development of computer technology has enabled scholars to compare the use of thousands of words and phrases between possible co-authors. This work was first begun years ago by authorship sceptics. At that time I would have been labelled a heretic by some if I had suggested that any of the plays were collaborations between Shakespeare and another writer, but that idea is now accepted, pursued, and published by leading orthodox scholars and universities. Barry R. Clarke has himself developed a new method of comparison of rare phrases, and, of course, with Bacon's work at hand there is much to compare. It is, unfortunately, very unfair that this is not the case with Shakspere. He only left us six signatures in his own hand, if indeed those few signatures do belong to him. Barry's dissertation, employing his new methodology and completed at Brunel University, was peer-reviewed and accepted: quite a development for Baconian authorship studies. The times they are a-changin'!

Recently, a journalist demanded that I "come to my senses and accept that William Shakespeare the glover's son was William Shakespeare the writer". It was a passionate article, but was the journalist passionate about how such incredible plays were created or rather about some old underlying injustice that has become inextricably linked with the authorship question? The journalist wrote that I have trouble with the "middling sort" being capable of genius. He claims I assert that a "posh boy" must have done it. He named a whole bunch of these 'middling sort', Thomas Cromwell, for one, with whom I have no trouble at all. I also have no doubt that Marlowe wrote the words attributed to him. He had a similar humble origin to Shakspere — a 'middling sort', nothing posh there. He rose to be arguably Shakspere's equal, certainly at the time of his tragic exit from the theatre scene. Isn't it interesting, by the way, that the Shakespeare name first appears on plays after that violent event in a small room in Rotherhithe? Murdered or exiled, I think Marlowe's suppression shocked all the writers, many of whom were listed as anonymous in Henslowe's surviving record of payments to writers for plays presented at the Rose Theatre. Writing plays that questioned religious and political thinking was extremely dangerous at that time.

Marlowe's rise has always interested me, actually. I understand both he and William to have been arguably taught by university graduates in their grammar schools. Unfortunately, we have no proof that Shakspere attended any school, but that's by the by; he wrote great plays, so he must have attended school. Marlowe's teacher seems to have noticed the young boy's genius and promoted him to the University in Oxford, where he subsequently learned all kinds of things that appear in his plays. His trail to creative genius is as clear as Mozart's. Why wasn't young William sent to University? The adult author clearly had the capacity for the highest learning any university could offer. His first plays, *Love's Labour's Lost*, for example, are full of university learning, both book learning and experience of foreign courts, comedia, and even Giordano Bruno's Hermetic Philosophy of the Cabala (thank you, Ted Hughes and Dame Francis Yates).

But the journalist was not really interested or upset about any of this. I doubt the journalist had ever dared to read anything seriously contrary to the orthodox position on the authorship of Shakespeare's works. The journalist, and many others too, don't know anything about it, really.

They don't care. Why should they? What they care about is a very noble defence of the middle classes, the 'middling sort', the humble, normal Englishman inside us all, really. This is a very old and proper wrong to be upset about. It goes right back to William the Conqueror and all the aristocratic families descended from the sell-outs and pirates that sided with that cruel William the Bastard, families who still own almost all the land we live on and work to maintain the appallingly unequal society we all endure. For me to suggest that one of these apparently ruthless villains wrote the works of humble Will Shakespeare is an appalling theft. My critics are deeply concerned for the unwitnessed, hard-working, some would say suppressed part of themselves that fears it will never be capable of remarkable genius, that it will always be in the middle of the crowd and, if it raises its head above that crowd, will be duly robbed. They see those of us who question whether the man from a small midlands town could have written these works of genius as a direct attack and suppression of their own unrecognized genius. I share their fears and recognize their upset in myself as well, but my interest in Francis Bacon as a potential contributing author of the Shakespeare works has nothing to do with whether he is or is not from any middling sort or class. Nor have I ever met anyone sceptical about Shakespearean authorship attribution because they believe the author was of any particular class, aristocratic or otherwise. Everyone curious about the authorship question is curious because what we know about the man Shakspere doesn't match what we find in the plays attributed to him. It is as simple as that. Read Diana Price's excellent *Shakespeare's Unorthodox Biography* and tell me I am wrong. I dare you!

In the case of Bacon, my favourite case, he said he was writing something like the Shakespeare works as the third part of his Great Instauration. He had the ability, the education, the wit, and the life experience to write something like the Shakespeare works. He had the time to write something like the Shakespeare works, and time and again, in his own works he reveals an interest in the very same topics, history, and even words that we find in the Shakespeare works. If the works of Shakespeare had been published anonymously, he would be a prime suspect.

As for the good cause of defending the capabilities of the 'middling sort', I am happy to lend a hand. But if you want me to come to my senses and "accept that William Shakespeare the glover's son was William Shakespeare the writer", it's very simple. You have to go to Doubtaboutwill.org and answer the Declaration of Reasonable Doubt. We took great care to express our reasons for doubt there, and no one has yet bothered to prove us unreasonable. We offered £40,000 to the Birthplace Trust as a donation should they succeed.

But let me return to my exemplary hosts in an unnamed and forgotten Indian village. They did not have a need for one unifying system of definition and worship, one God, one author. The existence of other images bearing witness to a divine creator was not a threat; on the contrary, it added strength to their own images by confirming the presence in many different minds of a divine author. They were not alone in sensing an imaginative spirit within reality.

In the case of the Shakespeare Authorship Question, the insistence that we turn this question of theatrical history into a horse race, where you only look at the horse you have bet on, and only one horse will win, committing all other horses to the knacker's yard, destroys the enjoyment and learning possible. It is such an inhospitable way to host a question in our minds. Yes, Barry is going to investigate and promote the evidence for Francis Bacon's involvement in the creation of the Shakespeare works, but this is not a courtroom, football pitch, or battlefield. This is just history.

No author is separate from their time or the people and culture of their time. The author of the Shakespeare plays didn't just imagine characters out of thin air; they were surely drawn, consciously or unconsciously, from the people of his time. Whether Bacon was involved in the works of Shakespeare or not, his life and works throw such a clear light onto the works of Shakespeare that it is absurd to ignore him. There are 1,100 parallelisms to be found in the writing of Shakespeare and Bacon. Accidental literary coincidences? Commonplaces? Most, but not all. Quite a few, unique in thought and expression to Bacon and Shakespeare. Will I find any of them in my Arden Shakespeare when I rehearse a play? Nope.

When considered in a Baconian light, I have found the plays to be full, as he desired, of accurately observed nature: human, divine, psychological, physical, plant, and animal nature too. I have discovered that the Comedies' enduring strength and humour springs from their underlying Cabalistic structure. The Tragedies have the alchemical understanding of the soul's growth and transformation through elemental processes: dissolving desire, separating thought, and binding action before stillness, death, and rebirth of desire. The Histories have the fascination with good governance and the 'royalty of nature', as the Baconian, Beryl Pogson, so beautifully phrases it. All the plays have a deep passion for justice and mercy, and very enjoyably, when considered in a Baconian light, they are infused throughout with the most remarkable wit, and love for opposites. Sir Brian Vickers writes, "Bacon had in abundance the poet's imaginative energy, that ability to see a resemblance in dissimilars which, according to Aristotle, was a mark of genius in a writer". The plays also profoundly fulfill Bacon's desire to advance learning for all people, entertainingly, sans la canne, especially learning about the effect of the appetites and emotions on the mind, and the subsequent effect of the mind on our eventual actions.

Bacon's love of anonymity and his ambition to be taken seriously in matters of politics and philosophy explain much about a possible cover-up of his poetical works, but how and why would that have been maintained after his death? It is a good question.

This month the television comedian Ben Elton presented me as a character called 'Wolf Hall' in his show *Upstart Crow*. He mocks me for being gullible about conspiracy theories, and I know conspiracy theories can get very wild and overgrown. Nevertheless conspiracies have taken place. We know that Dalton Trumbo, the author of the film *Spartacus*, wrote secretly behind a pseudonym after he was blacklisted by Senator McCarthy. We know many women authors have had to assume male pseudonyms. We know that a President of the United States was able to satisfy his sexual appetite with a new woman almost every evening without the public being aware. Conspiracies of silence have existed.

Then you also have to ask, if the man from Stratford wrote the plays, how did he manage to leave not one trace during his lifetime that he was a writer or even attended school? Why has the evidence disappeared for the years he might have attended grammar school? Did the author of the Shakespeare works really never write or receive a letter? He has been subjected to the greatest literary enquiry of any author's life, but no, there is nothing but the attribution of the *First Folio* to prove that he could write at all. His authorship case may be the greatest conspiracy of them all.

The Stratfordian response to our question about the authorship has usually been to lampoon the questioner, if not worse. It's because they can't answer the question or make it go away, so they try to make us go away. But new evidence continues to be revealed if you don't get stuck in one idea. I don't know who wrote the plays for certain or how they were written. I am not interested in a 'winner takes all' scenario. I enjoy the enquiry, including the work of Stratfordian researchers.

Congratulations to Barry for his excellent concise biography of William Shakspere, fair but stripped of conjecture masquerading as fact. His analysis of the attribution of the *First Folio* to William Shakespeare is a fascinating read; as he introduces us to Bacon, each chapter is full of carefully researched and annotated detail, and yet the whole story unfolds as a page-turner. Thrilling!

Congratulations also to Routledge, the publishers of this book, and institutions such as Brunel University. Time will celebrate those who were not daunted by the fearmongering of the Shakespeare Birthplace Trust and its supporters in the media and academy.

I hope you will read this book not to contradict and confute, not to believe and take for granted, not to find talk and discourse, but to weigh and consider.

Yes, I am a devotee of Francis Bacon. Whatever his role in the creation of the Shakespeare works — and reading Barry's book, and the works of Peter Dawkins and Nigel Cockburn, I would be very surprised indeed if he had no role — I have loved the works of Shakespeare as a manifestation of Bacon's philosophical desires and hopes. His resonant call to observe nature, to serve nature, not to be complacent in our ideas about nature but to try them thoroughly, has helped me enormously as an actor. However, most of all I enjoy Shakespeare in the light of Bacon's praise of goodness and *philanthropia*, the 'affecting of the weal of men', caring for others' welfare as Sir Brian Vickers defines it in his excellent introduction to Bacon's *Essayes*, the absence of which Bacon denounces in his essay 'Of Goodness and Goodness of Nature' as follows:

> This of all virtues and dignities of the mind is the greatest; being the character of the Deity: and without it man is a busy, mischievous, wretched thing; no better than a kind of vermin.

Prologue

> The human understanding when it has once adopted an opinion (either as being the received opinion or as being agreeable to itself) draws all things else to support and agree with it. And though there be a greater number and weight of instances to be found on the other side, yet these it either neglects and despises, or else by some distinction sets aside and rejects; in order that by this great and pernicious pre-determination the authority of its former conclusion may remain inviolate.
>
> —Francis Bacon (1620, XLVI 265)

Despite appearances, this work is much more than just a study of the connections between the philosopher-statesman Sir Francis Bacon (1561–1626), and the Shakespeare canon of plays. It is an investigation into the Shakespeare Authorship Question (SAQ) in general, but more importantly it is a critique of current authorship attribution methods. If our aim is to know as much as we possibly can about the contributors to the Shakespeare canon we need penetrating attribution methods that are not only designed for the detection of multiple hands but can also assess direction of influence. This is not presently the case, and so in Chapter 14 my new RCP method of stylistic analysis is set out. Contrary to current methods, it makes no attempt to reject vital evidence, is far less vulnerable to textual revision than stylometric word counts, and is relatively immune to the charge of 'commonplace' that plagues present phrase-matching techniques.

The main points that arise from the present study are as follows:

1 Due to the unreliability of the *First Folio* (1623) as a record of attribution, and due to the lack of prose work and letters for Shakspere that might inform a stylistic test, it is not possible to detect directly the extent of William Shakspere's contribution to the Shakespeare canon.
2 There is evidence from Shakspere's contemporaries that he employed others to write, added lines of his own which were not highly regarded, then took the credit.

3 Alternative single-originator theories rely on the dubious and pseudoscientific practice of presenting supposed biographical allusions from the Shakespeare work as attribution evidence.
4 A scientific test of style in which a candidate has the possibility of being eliminated is the only reliable approach. This can only be a test of contribution, not origination. If the candidate has insufficient textual data to participate in such a test, as many alternative single-author candidates do, then nothing can be known about their extent of contribution.
5 There is a history of Francis Bacon's interest in drama that is seldom addressed in academic treatises. This includes writing devices for fictional characters presented on royal occasions and at Inns of Court entertainments.
6 There are many hands in the Shakespeare work. Using RCP results, evidence is presented here that Francis Bacon is one of them, particularly in *Love's Labour's Lost* and *The Tempest*.
7 Due to the presence of many hands in the Shakespeare canon, no single-author theory, either for Shakspere or an alternative candidate, can be sustained. Instead attention should be directed to improving stylistic methods of detecting multiple hands in the work.

The present offering mostly relies on my PhD investigation, carried out at Brunel University (Clarke 2014). This has largely been revised here, and new research has been appended. The additional material is as follows. Chapter 5 is a biography of Francis Bacon which has been adapted from my online publication *The Shakespeare Puzzle*. Entirely new material includes an analysis of the second Parnassus play in Chapter 3, an analysis of the First Folio in Chapter 4, and the *Groats-worth* (1592) letter in Chapter 6, which contains the first known reference to Shakspere. In Chapter 7, an original study of *Vertues Commonwealth* (1603) is presented, a pamphlet that alludes to the *Groats-worth letter* and to which Francis Bacon has some interesting stylistic connections. The arguments for *Twelfth Night* being a Middle Temple play, although developed during my PhD research, were not included in the final thesis. The complete study is given in Chapter 10. The inclusion of Chapters 12 and 13 provides a new survey and critique of historical and modern authorship attribution methods. These chapters are technical in nature, demand a greater application from the reader than the earlier ones, and are intended mainly for practitioners of stylometry and matching-phrase searches. Finally, Chapter 14 provides a greater clarity of exposition of the RCP method than that given in the 2014 PhD thesis.

Academics have historically been reluctant to address any investigation into the claim that William Shakspere of Stratford did not originate the plays in the *First Folio* (1623) collection. This is partly due to the circumstance that a different single-originator is usually proposed in the context of a conspiracy theory. Such presentations struggle in vain to achieve the standard of evidence that orthodox researchers demand of their academic journals. The present work claims that single-originator theories in general cannot be corroborated and that only contributors to the Shakespeare canon can be tested. It is hoped that this work contributes to the dissolution of what currently stands as a fractious war between competing single-author (originator) theories, including those for Shakspere, which, as inflexible ideologies, are only a parody of scientific method, and encourages researchers to adopt a more productive focus on arguments for contribution. Not only does this appear to me to be a more reliable path to the truth of the matter, but it can only result in a greater spirit of cooperation.

Bibliography

Bacon, Francis. *Novum Organon Scientiarum*. London: Johannen Billium, 1620.

Clarke, Barry R. "A linguist analysis of Francis Bacon's contribution to three Shakespeare plays: *The Comedy of Errors*, *Love's Labour's Lost*, and *The Tempest*." PhD thesis. Brunel University, 2014.

1 Introduction

> For the wit and minde of man, if it worke vpon matter [...] is limited thereby [...] but if it work vpon it selfe, as the Spider worketh his webbe, then it is endlesse, and brings forth indeed Copwebs of learning, admirable for the finesse of thread and worke, but of no substance or profite.
>
> —Francis Bacon (1605, 29)[1]

1.1 A New Method of Attribution

To the best of our current knowledge, William Shakspere of Stratford was not the sole author of the collection of plays *Mr. William Shakespeare's Comedies, Histories, & Tragedies* (1623). One need not be a conspiracy theorist to reach this conclusion. It is accepted by most academic practitioners of stylometric and phrase-matching tests. In fact, *All's Well That Ends Well*, *1 Henry VI*, *3 Henry VI*, *Henry VIII*, *Macbeth*, *Timon of Athens*, and *Titus Andronicus* are just a few of the works in which other hands have been strongly indicated (see Chapter 4). However, the only man to receive credit in the *First Folio* eulogies is the actor William Shakspere of Stratford, who played in the Lord Chamberlain's Men, later known as the King's Men. So, the *First Folio* collection of 36 plays cannot possibly be an accurate record of attribution of the Shakespeare work. Once one is aware of this fact one is entitled to ask just how much Mr Shakspere wrote. The best method of identifying the contributors to a text is through a stylistic test, but Shakspere has no independent prose works or extant letters to make a comparison with. So, his style is unknowable.[2] Nevertheless, if the several contributors to a play detected by stylistic tests take up most of the text then this can only restrict his contribution to it. This eliminative method appears to be the only way that the extent of Shakspere's exclusion can be placed within approximate limits. His inclusion is untestable.[3]

In the absence of documentary evidence, it is not possible to assert who originated any of the plays in the *First Folio*. For example, it is not beyond the bounds of possibility that a manuscript draft by some unknown dramatist was acquired by some author—later detectable—who inserted topical allusions and revised it into a complete play. For this reason, no play can ever be dated with certainty. What *can* be detected in a play are the rare locutions of writers that already exist in a database of contemporary texts, for example, Chadwyck–Healey's Early English Books Online (EEBO) database, and what *can* be dated are topical allusions and themes.

If other hands have been revealed, then they are usually regarded as grateful collaborators, playwrights who conspired with Shakspere to work on separate scenes. Practitioners of stylometric tests are careful not to consider these other hands as later revisers—writers who alter the work of others—for then the assumption necessary for their method to work, that their text segments are uniform in a single hand, would be violated. In July 2017, in a lecture delivered at the Oxford Festival of the Arts, Professor Jonathan Bate provided his own interpretation of the presence of other pens, characterizing William Shakspere as a superior script doctor who improved the work of lesser wits. Unfortunately, Professor Bate neglected to provide any evidence for his conjecture, and without presenting evidence from a test that might delineate Shakspere's contribution to the canon it remains an uncorroborated one.

In reaction to the untenable assumption of Shakspere as single-originator, a number of conspiracy theories have arisen, mainly out of the fact that the work relies on a knowledge of classical literature that the non-university-educated Shakspere cannot be shown to have had. So, instead, an enlightened courtier must have composed the work under the pseudonym Shake-speare (hyphenated).[4] Such theories differ only in the identity of this courtier—although some have proposed a collaborating group of concealed writers.[5] Now, the same arguments apply here as for Shakspere. There are many hands in the Shakespeare canon, so there cannot be a single author. One need only use EEBO to analyze *3 Henry VI*, with Greene, Marlowe, and Munday implicated as contributors, to realize this (see Appendix A).[6]

The main method employed in establishing the identity of this concealed courtier usually consists of extracting assumed biographical allusions to the supposed candidate from the Shakespeare text. A case made in this way can only gain force if the equally ingenious constructions for other supposed candidates are dismissed. Then, with all other possibilities rejected, the argument for the favoured candidate is confidently exhibited as the only alternative. Unfortunately, it is not a practice that submits any writer to the possibility of failing a critical test. In other words, hoarders of biographical allusions can take comfort in the knowledge that their candidate can never be ruled out. This single-minded gathering of connections is pseudoscience, and, in this regard, we cannot ignore Karl Popper's caution:

> I shall certainly admit a system as empirical or scientific only if it is capable of being tested by experience. These considerations suggest

> that it is not the *verifiability* but the *falsifiability* of a system that is to be taken as the criterion of demarcation. In other words: I shall not require of a scientific system that it shall be capable of being singled out, once and for all, in a positive sense; but I shall require that its logical form shall be such that it can be singled out, by means of empirical tests, in a negative sense: *it must be possible for an empirical system to be refuted by experience.*
>
> (2002, 18)

This gathering of autobiographical allusions in the Shakespeare canon has been carried out for Shakspere too, although more to expand his biography than to reinforce his claim for single authorship, which his proponents already assume to be beyond question. William Leahy has noted that "biographers who together produce the works that make up the sub-genre of Shakespearean biography look to the plays and poems for biographical detail. In short, they build a life of Shakespeare from his surviving literary works" (2016, 40).

Some of this detail clearly misses the mark. For example, Ros Barber has shown that "Not a single claim that Shakespeare used Warwickshire, Midlands or Cotswold dialect can be upheld" (2016, 116). Nevertheless, new biographies regularly crave for space on store bookshelves, claiming to possess an accurate account of Shakspere's life from cradle to grave. On closer inspection, they are nothing but a recycled mythology, a patchwork of invention stitched together by mercenary blotters who find factual evidence hanging on every syllable of the Shakespeare canon. Negligent thinkers swallow it whole for without sufficient independence to interrogate the facts, all they are digesting is a work of baseless fantasy. In response, Kevin Gilvary (2017) has provided a detailed study of modern Shakspere biographies, pointing out how they create a 'biografiction' through their unjustifiable interpolation of conjectural material.

The Renaissance philosopher-statesman Sir Francis Bacon (1561–1626) of Gray's Inn is one candidate who has been proposed as the secret single author of the Shakespeare canon. However, the only claim set out in these pages is that he is one of several contributors. With 27 works in Chadwyck–Healey's Early English Books Online (EEBO) database, it is possible for a stylistic test to either suggest or—and the following is what makes his test scientific—contraindicate him as a contributor to a Shakespeare play. If Bacon seems an unlikely candidate for dramatic contribution, it is only because most academic treatises neglect his role as producer for the Inns of Court players and have passed over the several examples of fictional devices he wrote for contemporary entertainments. Here our English polymath, who served as Solicitor General (1607), Attorney General (1613), and Lord Chancellor (1618), shall be revealed as a man active in the production of plays and masques at the Inns of Court law schools. There is documentary evidence that he assisted in writing dumb shows for *The Misfortunes of Arthur*, a play performed by the Gray's Inn players before the queen at Greenwich in February 1587–8. He wrote speeches for the mock Privy Councellors at the 1594–5 Gray's Inn Christmas revels, where *The Comedy of Errors* received its first known performance, and there is also strong evidence that *Love's Labour's Lost* was planned for enactment there but was cancelled. The play almost certainly contains allusions to Bacon's speeches at the revels proceedings (see Tables D.1 and D.7, Appendix D). There are also the Queen's Day celebrations in 1592 and 1595, for which he again wrote entertainments. So, as Bacon had a clear interest in drama it seems appropriate to run stylistic tests on the Shakespeare plays with Bacon included as one of the possibilities for contribution. Unfortunately, stylometric tests restrict the possible contributors to a small group of well-known dramatists.

To bring more evidence to the argument, the present author has developed the new technique of Rare Collocation Profiling (RCP), which adopts a more forensic approach than stylometry. Here, individual phrases and collocations in a target text are systematically and exhaustively checked to identify which ones are rare in relation to a contemporary database of texts. The search engine for the EEBO database (which contains thousands of searchable pre-1700 texts) is well suited for this task. A locution that appears in less than, say, 0.2% of the texts dated before that of the assumed target text date is defined as rare, and the authors that are returned for these locutions in the EEBO search, both before and after the target date, are recorded. In this way, a DNA-type profile for rare locutions can be constructed for those authors who appear frequently in the significant returns.[7] For those alternative single-originator candidates who have insufficient works in EEBO to participate in such a test, the conclusion must be similar to that for Shakspere: if they made a contribution, the extent of it cannot be known. However, this need not be final. Should sufficient textual data for a candidate be obtained in the future their access would become feasible.

The RCP method has several major advantages over stylometry:

i RCP's forensic focus on individual phrases and collocations rather than a word count reduces dependence on the requirement that a text must be uncorrupted by later revision. It is assumed here that scribes and compositors would alter an individual word with greater abandon than a complex phrase or collocation, which carries a greater meaning and authorial preference.

ii The phrases and collocations used are 'rare' so that there can be no charge of 'commonplace', that is, many possible sources.

iii In using the EEBO database, any of the thousands of authors are afforded the possibility of being a source or contributor, not just the few well-known dramatists which stylometric methods are restricted to.

iv Attention is paid to the direction of influence of a rare return, that is, whether or not the target text sourced or was a source for a returned author in EEBO. If both directions of influence occur for this author from other searches (mutual borrowing) then this is an argument for contribution to the target text.

v No vital evidence is rejected. There is no forced reduction of an author's corpus (to equalize genre, time period, corpus size) in order to give all candidates an equal chance. There is no equal chance. The confidence that is to be placed in a claim for contribution is proportional to the number of rare matches obtained. If an author has insufficient textual data to run a test then the conclusion is that nothing can be decided for that candidate until further data is presented.

An example of the data logging of rare returns from Act 1 of *Pericles* is given in Appendix G. Examples of profiles for authors with frequent returns constructed from such a log for other plays are shown in Appendices A–F. So far, five Shakespeare plays and three pamphlets have been subjected to the new RCP method. Supported by the availability of this new evidence, the connections between Francis Bacon and some of the Shakespeare canon are now set out in detail.

1.2 Overview of the Work

In Chapter 2, a document-based biography of Shakspere is given. Although the extent of his education is unknown, it seems that there is insufficient justification for concluding he could perhaps read but not write as some have suggested. As well as acting in productions around London, he is known to have engaged in business deals involving malt, property, and moneylending. However, there is no evidence that he was acquainted with the nobility, and there is not the slightest hint that he owned or had access to even a small percentage of the books that the Shakespeare canon used as sources (Muir 2009).

Contemporary opinion of Shakspere is explored in Chapter 3. The 'War of the Theatres' was punctuated by attacks on various dramatists, delivered through the lines of characters on the stage. On the one side was Ben Jonson, while John Marston was one of several protagonists on the other. Since the victim was usually confronted with his own defects, we can expect to obtain an insight into contemporary opinion of his real character. These were serious attacks on real theatre personalities that usually elicited a response in kind. In the second Parnassus play acted at Cambridge University (c.1600), Shakspere comes under scrutiny in the character of Gullio. Here he is characterized by Ingenioso as an employer of scholars who wrote plays that Gullio put his own name to. Ben Jonson's testimony in his Epigrams lends weight to this view.

There are several quartos bearing Shakspere's name that were not his. Chapter 4 surveys a selection of these before examining the integrity of the *First Folio* (1623) as a record of attribution. It soon becomes clear that those who supplied eulogies to Shakspere for the collection, praising his authorship, were misinformed; concealing the reality; or, when their conscience gave them pause, ambiguously refraining from assigning him credit.

An account of Francis Bacon's life is the subject of Chapter 5. Here, his problems with debt; his political battles with Edward Coke; and the obstruction of his advancement in government by his cousin Robert Cecil, Lord Salisbury, are dealt with in detail. Here, we also learn that he wrote dumb shows and mock speeches for Gray's Inn entertainments, had control over the Inns of Court playing companies, and gave lines to fictional characters for Queen's Day devices. His fall from high office is also examined, an event that seems to have been motivated more by Parliament's attempt to disempower King James than by doubts as to Bacon's integrity.

A careful analysis is carried out in Chapter 6 of the open letter to Marlowe, Nashe, and Peele in Robert Greene's *Groats-worth of witte* (1592). By referring to Greene's previous publications, the nature of the complaint against 'Shake-scene' in the letter is clarified. A new RCP analysis of the letter gives Greene priority over Nashe and Chettle, two candidates who have previously been proposed as its author. A new analysis of both the Octavio and Folio versions of *3 Henry VI*, to which Greene's complaint alludes, identifies Robert Greene as a contributor to this play. The conclusion reached is that his complaint against Shakspere was that although Greene was paid for his contribution to *3 Henry VI*, Shakspere took all the credit and profit, while Greene was abandoned to poverty.

Vertues Common-wealth (1603) by Henry Crosse (for whom no biography exists) contains several strong allusions to the *Groats-worth* letter and the pamphlet in general. Chapter 7 examines these and suggests that Crosse reinforces the letter's claim that Shakspere could write but not very well. A table of rare apophthegms is given that appears both in *Vertues* and Bacon's work, showing that both Francis Bacon and Henry Crosse had similar modes of thought. There is also a table of rare phrases that their works share. Although Bacon's usage occurs after 1603, suggesting that he borrowed from the pamphlet, a more complete study is required before deciding on his status as a contributor. At the very least, it appears that his connection to *Vertues* suggests that he knew of the *Groats-worth* charge against Shakspere.

Two Shakespeare plays, *The Comedy of Errors* (*CE*) and *Love's Labour's Lost* (*LLL*), appear to have been scheduled for the 1594–5 Christmas revels at Gray's Inn. The *Gesta Grayorum* (*GG*) exists as a contemporary account of proceedings at the revels, and it refers to "a Comedy of Errors (like to Plautus his Menechmus)". In Chapter 8, an analysis is made of past Inns of Court performances to bring evidence to bear on identifying the players at the revels. It transpires that there is more evidence in favour of the Gray's Inn players enacting *CE* than of Shakspere's company, the Lord Chamberlain's Men, enacting it. In contrast, *LLL* appears to be a play that was planned for the festivities but was cancelled. Chapter 9 looks at the rare parallels between the *GG* and *LLL*, many of which arise in fictional speeches that Francis Bacon wrote for the revels. These suggest that the play contains allusions that mirror the revels' proceedings. A new RCP analysis is given, providing strong evidence that Bacon contributed to both *LLL* and *GG*.

Since Francis Bacon was a producer for the Inns of Court players, it seems reasonable to look at his contribution to other plays that appeared at the Inns of Court. In Chapter 10, there is evidence that *Twelfth Night* (*TN*) was a play designed for the Middle Temple. Dating evidence for *TN* is explored: in particular, a strong argument is presented to counter Leslie Hotson's view that its first known performance was at Whitehall on 6 January 1601. It appears instead that the play was especially designed for presentation at the Middle Temple on 2 February 1602. However, there are also good correspondences between the mock arraignment of the "discontented lover" at the 1597–8 Middle Temple revels and Malvolio's predicament in *TN*, suggesting that an earlier version might have been played. The subplot of misrule involving Sir Toby in *TN* is appropriate for an Inns of Court Christmas revels, and the performance of a play called *Twelfth Night* on Candlemas (2 February) is shown to have been particularly relevant for the Inn. The Inns of Court records are reviewed to see how far they support the view that it was a professional company that gave the first known performance of *TN*. Having found no such evidence, precedent suggests that Inns of Court players performed the play. Finally, since Bacon produced the Inns of Court players, a new RCP analysis of the play is carried out to examine the extent of his contribution.

Just before 1611, when *The Tempest* received its first known enactment at King James's court, there was a sensational event in the news. This was the shipwreck of the Virginia Company's supply ship the *Sea Venture* at Bermuda, with the unprecedented survival of all its crew. Allusions are to be found in the play, and Chapter 11 sets out the reasons why it would have been difficult for William Shakspere to have had access to them. The Solicitor General, Sir Francis Bacon, was on the Virginia Company Council, and there is evidence that Bacon managed to inspect a source for *The Tempest* that few could have seen, a confidential Company report, 'True Reportory', that was only published 14 years after the first known performance of the play. An RCP analysis of *The Tempest* shows that Bacon made a significant contribution.

The last three chapters are reserved for a more technical treatment, involving analyses of authorship attribution methods. Chapter 12 looks at the defects of hapax legomena (a word that appears only once in an author's canon) as authorial markers, pointing out that they give a deceptive impression of rarity. The problems involved in counting methods are pointed out, not least the dubious assumption that segment lengths are uniform in a single contributor. In Chapter 13, two modern methods of attribution are explored: the stylometric counting of individual words and phrase-matching. The Zeta and Delta methods of stylometry are examples of the former, and their single-contributor assumption is shown to be their weakness. For the latter, *Pericles*, Act 1, is analyzed to show that the use of commonplace phrases and collocations has led to George Wilkins having been unjustifiably proposed as a contributor. A new RCP analysis shows that Thomas Dekker is a stronger candidate. Finally, in Chapter 14, the new method of RCP is set out, showing how it relies on the identification of rare phrases and collocations in a target text. Not only does this allow the possibility of suggesting several contributors, which stylometric methods are unable to do, but the defect of using commonplace locutions that plague the treatment of *Pericles* is avoided.

Notes

1 Note also "Aristo Chius the Stoic (saith Diogenes) compared Dialectic Dissertations to a Spiders Web, which is artificially made but yields no profit" in Gale (1677, 29).

2 Those who use stylometric tests usually fall into the error of assuming that certain scenes in Shakespeare plays in which other hands have *not* been detected must contain *only* Shakspere's work and style. They cannot possibly know this, nor the extent of revision carried out.

3 In my view, Michel Foucault's essay "What is an author?" is an unfortunate intervention in the field of authorship attribution. Couched in ill-defined technical jargon, which only serves to delay interrogation of the text, he focusses entirely on the social consequences of a piece of text, and rejects any investigation into the operational chain of authorship. While it contains pertinent objections to identifying an originator, it is clear that it is aimed at contributors in general. By his failure to address the confrontation of conjecture with experiment, the essence of the scientific method, Foucault's concluding remark "What matter who's speaking?" (1995, 245) seems to betray a lack of interest in scientific enquiry in general.

4 Even a researcher as thorough as Diana Price leans towards the alternative single-author position, suggesting, "the theory that Shakespeare was the pen name of a gentleman of rank could explain the trail of unauthorized or corrupt Shakespeare plays" (2012, 141). Also, "the spelling 'Shakespeare' designated the dramatist whoever *he* [my italics] was" (Price 2018, 25n).

5 I began my investigations many years ago as one of these single-author theorists, initially holding the view that Francis Bacon acted alone under the pseudonym Shake-speare. However, access to the EEBO database and later consideration of the implications of my PhD study has caused me to modify my view of Bacon from a secret originator to one of several contributors.

6 Alternative single-author theorists are a prisoner to delusion. Their constructions are only a mirage of an objective truth, a belief system entirely in the service of the will, designed to avoid and obfuscate the judgement of

a critical test. If true scientific progress is to be made, the ego must be banished from the judgement. In the words of G. K. Chesterton, "angels can fly because they take themselves lightly" (1908, Chapter VII).

7 Here I define 'frequently' to mean at least three rare locutions.

Bibliography

Barber, Rosalind. "Shakespeare and Warwickshire dialect." *Journal of Early Modern Studies* 5 (2016): 91–118.

Chesterton, Gilbert K. *Orthodoxy*. London: John Lane, 1908.

Foucault, Michel. "What is an author?" In Sean Burke, ed. *Authorship from Plato to the Postmodern*. Edinburgh: Edinburgh University Press, 1995.

Gale, Theophilus. *The Court of the Gentiles, Part III: The Vanity of Pagan Philosophy Demonstrated*. London: Printed by A. Maxwell and R. Roberts for T. Cockeril, 1677.

Gilvary, Kevin. *The Fictional Lives of Shakespeare*. Routledge Studies in Shakespeare. New York: Routledge, 2017.

Leahy, William. "The dreamscape of nostalgia: Shakespearean biography: Too much information (but not about Shakespeare)." *Journal of Early Modern Studies* 5 (2016): 31–52.

Muir, Kenneth. *The Sources of Shakespeare's Plays*. New York: Routledge, 2009.

Popper, Karl. *Logik der Forschung*. Austria: Verlag von Julius Springer, 1935. English translation, *The Logic of Scientific Discovery*. New York: Routledge, 2002.

Price, Diana. *Shakespeare's Unorthodox Biography: New Evidence of an Authorship Problem*. Shakespeare-authorship.com, 2012.

Price, Diana. "My Shakespeare: 'A conjectural narrative'." In William Leahy, ed. *My Shakespeare, the Authorship Controversy*. Edward Everett Root, 2018.

Part I

Shakspere and Bacon

2 A Shakspere Biography

The extant documents for the actor William Shakspere reveal him to be an entrepreneur in the London theatre world, as well as a money-lender, a dealer in malt, and a property speculator. However, there is no evidence that he had access to the books that are known to have provided background material for some of the Shakespeare plays.

2.1 Birthdate

The baptism of "Gulielmus filius Johannes Shakspere"[1] is recorded in the Stratford parish register under the year "1564" and against the marginal date "April 26" which fell on a Wednesday. The original document does not endure as the record was copied from the original paper sheet into a more substantial parchment book around 16 September 1600 by the vicar Richard Bifield, who signed his name along with the four churchwardens at the foot of the page. Three crosses in thick black ink at the right end of the line draw attention to the entry and seem to have been added later. There is no record of a birthdate, but Queen Elizabeth's *Book of Common Prayer* (1559) indicates that the christening had to be performed not later than the first holy day or Sunday after birth. Assuming that this transpired, this places the earliest birth date on Sunday 23 April 1564.[2] Young William was fortunate to survive. The plague struck Stratford that summer, carrying away 250 of its 2,000 inhabitants (Schoenbaum 1991, 8).

For 25 April 1616, there is an entry in the Stratford parish register recording the death of "Will Shakspeare gent". The monument in Holy Trinity Church, Stratford, claims he expired on 23 April 1616, age 53. If this age is correct, then Shakspere must instead have been born between 24 April 1562 and 23 April 1563. Since there is no known birthdate, only a date of baptism, was the ceremony delayed for over a year? Or had the monument engraver suffered a fit of dyscalculia? Whatever the explanation, modern society now presumes his birthdate to be 23 April 1564. As we shall see, this is only the first of many anomalies surrounding the life of William Shakspere of Stratford.

2.2 Education

There is no evidence that young William went to school. If he *did* go, then from the age of four or five, he would have been educated by an usher at a petty school (Baldwin 1943). Each child brought a hornbook consisting of a sheet of paper framed in wood and covered with transparent horn. The paper had both the capital and lower-case letters of the alphabet, syllables, and the Lord's Prayer. The hornbook was followed by 'The ABC with Catechism', a series of questions and answers from the *Book of Common Prayer*, together with graces to expound at meal times. Finally, 'The Primer and Catechism' taught the Calendar, Almanac, and the seven penitential psalms. These instruments of learning allowed instruction in prosodia (reading), orthographia (writing), and sometimes numeration.

After two years, the student was suitably prepared for grammar school. The Kings New School at Stratford-upon-Avon would have had the *Short Introduction to Grammar* (1534) by William Lily as the standard textbook, one which Edward VI decided should be used in all schools (Melchiori 2000, 7). In addition to the principles of grammar, there were Latin sentences to be memorized by rote, usually from *Sententiae Pueriles* by Leonhardus Culmannus, *Cato* by Erasmus, and the fables of Aesop. The works of Terence and Plautus might be used for practising translation from Latin to English, and the Latin works of Horace, Juvenal, Ovid, and Virgil were often studied for sense before the student left school at 14 years old. Whether or not young Shakspere was acquainted with these texts is unknown, but these were the standard texts of the day. However, there would have been no history of the British islands, no modern languages, and little instruction in the writing of English. John Brinsley, headmaster of Ashby-de-la Zouch grammar school in Leicestershire, gives an insight into the state of contemporary English teaching in grammar schools in his book *Ludus Literarius* (1612):

> There seems vnto mee, to be a verie maine want in all our Grammar schools generally, or in most of them [...] That there is no care had in respect to train vp schollars so, as they may be able to expresse their minds purely and readily in their owne tongue, and to increase the practice of it, as well as in the Latine or Greeke. (Brinsley 1612, 22)

If Shakspere had been educated at Stratford Grammar School, then he would have fallen far short of the comprehensive learning that the Shake-speare *First Folio* (1623) later exhibited. He would undoubtedly have needed a programme of self-education and almost certainly access to a substantial library, one that had works such as Holinshed's *Chronicles* and Plutarch's *Lives*, used by several of the Shake-speare plays.

There is no record that William Shakspere had the university education of leading dramatists such as Francis Beaumont (Pembroke College, Oxford), John Dryden (Trinity College, Cambridge), Christopher Marlowe (Corpus Christi College, Cambridge), John Marston (Brasenose College, Oxford), Thomas Nashe (St. John's College, Cambridge), and Edmund Spenser (Pembroke College, Cambridge), although this did not hinder playwrights such as Ben Jonson and Thomas Kyd. These two *did*, however, have the advantage over Shakspere of attending the prestigious Westminster School.

2.3 Literacy

As to the extent of Shakspere's literacy, the matter cannot be concluded from his family background alone. In Elizabethan Stratford, 13 of the 19 men who ran the town's affairs made a mark instead of signing a name (Twain 1909). William's father, John, was a glover,[3] wool trader,[4] constable,[5] and town bailiff[6] (Schoenbaum 1987, 30–36). His signature does not survive, although there are several examples of his mark on official documents. William's mother, Mary Arden, was the daughter of Robert Arden of Wilmcote, a yeoman farmer. When her father died, she was left Asbyes, the estate in Wilmcote. She too employed a mark (Schoenbaum 1987, 21). On the other hand, on 5 March 1610, when Margery Lord decided to sell the tavern in Middle Row to the Stratford-upon-Avon Corporation, Gilbert Shakspere, one of William's younger brothers, managed to provide a strong signature as witness to the deed (SBT, ER27/9).

2.4 Access to Source Material

In an attempt to create a biography of Shakspere's teens, the will of Alexander Hogton, a Catholic squire of Lea Hall, Preston, Lancashire, has been used to speculate that Shakspere had high-level acquaintances to assist him in his self-education (Baker 1937; Chambers 1944, 52–56; Hamer 1970, 41–48). In his will dated 3 August 1581 and read on 12 September 1581, Hogton instructed his half-brother Thomas to:

> be friendly unto Folk Gyllome and William Shakeshafte now dwelling with me, and either to take them unto his service or else to help them to some good master.

As a reward, Thomas could expect:

> instruments belonging to musics and all manner of play-clothes, if he be minded to keep and do players. (Schoenbaum 1987, 112)

Assuming that Shakeshafte was Shakspere of Stratford, this appears to be evidence that the 17-year-old had already began life as a player in a private household and was benefitting from a substantial library where he could absorb the necessary play sources. In this environment, Shakspere could be associated with various earls and patrons familiar to the Hogton family who could assist the advancement of the young man's writing career. There was also a Stratford connection. John Cottam, master of Stratford grammar school from September 1579, returned to his family home at Tarnacre near the Hogton's home in 1581, an event that mythos supposes must have occasioned Shakspere's introduction to the Hogtons (Honigmann 1998, 15). Fairy tale porkies in straw houses are always hostage to the wind, and Samuel Schoenbaum duly obliged with gusto in playing the wolf. Even though Stratford saw several variant spellings of Shakspere, Schoenbaum pointed out that Shakeshafte was not one of them, but it *was* a spelling used around Lancashire, and there are known to have been many William Shakeshaftes resident there at the time (1987, 114). It is also far from certain that the "play-clothes" were those of actors, and they could with greater justification have been those of musicians who played the "instruments belonging to musics". We must also consider that Shakspere needed time to court Anne Hathaway for she was already pregnant less than 12 months after Hogton's will was read. The facts are too weak to corroborate the Hogton scenario, and so, the notion that the teenage Shakspere had access to either a substantial library or powerful patrons falls short as evidence.

2.5 Marriage

Nothing more is known about Shakspere until 28 November 1582, when as William Shagspere, he married Anne Hathaway (or Hathwey), the daughter of a local farmer, who was eight years his senior (Schoenbaum 1987, 76–79). To do so, the unusual step was taken of travelling 21 miles to Worcester to acquire a common licence from the consistory court. The licence would have been addressed to the minister assigned to preside over the wedding in Stratford and would have been issued to waive the customary regulations governing marriage in order to hasten its completion. The privilege came with a penalty. Two friends of Anne's family took up a bond against which £40 was forfeit, should the marriage fail. One wonders if a pregnant Miss Hathaway, or her family, had forced the issue because six months later, once again as Shakspere, William baptized his first child Susanna at Holy Trinity Church. It would be another three years before the twins Hamnet and Judeth completed the family, receiving their baptisms on 2 February 1585.

There is no evidence that Shakspere ever sent or received a letter, although there are no surviving letters either for Marlowe, Webster, Fletcher, or Beaumont. Someone who *did* send a letter was John Dowdall, who, on 10 April 1693, dispatched one to his cousin Edward Southwell from Butler's Merston, six miles from Stratford-upon-Avon and eight miles from Warwick. It describes his travels around Warwickshire, one of his visits being to Holy Trinity Church at Stratford where Shakspere had been buried almost 77 years earlier. There he reports that:

> The clerk that showed me this church was above eighty years old. He says that this Shakespeare was formerly in this town bound apprentice to a butcher, but that he ran from his master to London, and there was received into the play-house as a servitor [servant], and by this means had an opportunity to be what he afterwards proved. (Dowdall 1838, 11–12)[7]

Unfortunately, the clerk neglected to reveal what this was. The seventeenth-century antiquarian John Aubrey regurgitates this account of young Shakspere's apprenticeship:

> His father was a Butcher, and I have been told heretofore by some of the neighbours, that when he was a boy he exercised his father's trade, but when he kill'd a calfe he would doe it in a high style, and make a speech. (Clark 1898, 225–226)

However, according to Aubrey, Shakspere had a rival:

> There was at that time another butcher's son in this towne, that was held not at all inferior to him for a natural wit, his acquaintance and coetanean, but dyed young. (Clark 1898, 226)

Aware of the implications for Shakspere's wit, Samuel Schoenbaum tersely dismisses Aubrey's anecdote, claiming that it "belongs not to biographical record proper but to mythos" (1987, 72). However, when Aubrey reports William Beeston's view that Shakspere:

> understood Latin pretty well: for he had been in his younger years a schoolmaster in the country. (Brit Lib, MS Arch. F.c.37)

then Schoenbaum seems unable to apply the same level of scepticism. As far as teaching the older students is concerned, "in the country" could not have been Stratford because an Oxford or Cambridge degree was a prerequisite, but it might have been possible to find a position in a smaller community without a degree.

Aubrey also estimates the age at which Shakspere moved to London:

> This William being inclined naturally to poetry and acting, came to London, I guesse, about 18; and was actor at one of the playhouses, and did act exceedingly well.

How Aubrey obtained this 'act-fact' is far from transparent. Given that Shakspere's twins, Hamnet and Judeth, were baptized when he was 21 years old, was he dividing his time between Stratford and London, or was this estimate incorrect? Aubrey continues:

> He began to make essayes at dramatique poetry, which at that time was very lowe; and his playes took well.

Aubrey claims this information came from "some of the neighbours". Were there witnesses that saw Shakspere writing these early plays—which would have been valuable testimony—or had the integrity of Aubrey's report been seduced by his rhetorical ardour?

2.6 Shakspere the Businessman

Shakspere was also involved in several business dealings. In May 1592, a loan of £7 was delivered on a bond to John Clayton of Willington in Bedford under the name of "William Shackspere". Eight years later, Shakspere moved to sue Clayton, now in the Marshalsea Prison, for the full amount (NA, KB 27/1361/1, rot. 293). In May 1597, Shakspere purchased New Place for £60 in silver from the lawyer William Underhill of Idlicote in Warwickshire (NA, PROB 11/90/176). Built in 1483 by John Mercer, later to be Lord Mayor of London, this single dwelling house, with its ten fireplaces, two gardens, and two barns, no longer survives. There is yet more evidence of usury. In October 1598, Richard Quiney from "the Bell in Carter Lane" composed for Shakspere's eye an unsent letter requesting a £30 loan, with the enticement that Shakspere act as paymaster in any future transactions. He omitted to inform Shakspere that the money was intended for his friend Abraham Sturley to assist with his debts (SBT, ER27/4). In May 1602, Shakspere bought 107 acres of Stratford land for £320, and in September that same year he took a lease on Chapel Lane Cottage, which sat on a quarter of an acre behind New Place (SBT, ER28/1). Two years later, we find Shakspere as a litigant suing the Stratford apothecary, Philip Rogers, at the Court of Record for 35 shillings and 10 pence plus 10 shillings damages. On at least six occasions, Shakspere had sold him several measures of malt (SBT, ER27/5). Four years later, in August 1608, he sued John Addenbrooke of Tanworth-in-Arden in the Stratford court for £6 with 24 shillings damages (SBT, ER27/6). When Addenbrooke could not be found "within the liberty of the borough", Shakspere (recorded as Shackspeare) chased his surety, the blacksmith Thomas Horneby, for the full amount. Whether or not he succeeded is unknown, but his persistence forced the whole affair to run in court from August 1608 to June 1609 at least. It should be clear from these records that throughout the period that Shakspere was meant to be composing five-act dramas, he was an active businessman who traded in malt, purchased property, and profited from moneylending.

2.7 The Ben Jonson Model

It might be instructive to compare William Shakspere with Ben Jonson, whose background most closely resembles that of the Stratford man, for this might enlighten us as to what one might reasonably expect from a man with humble beginnings. Jonson began in his stepfather's trade as a bricklayer and joined the English army in the Netherlands before becoming an actor with the Earl of Pembroke's Men around 1597. It was about this time that he wrote his earliest known play, *The Case is Altered* (published in 1609), graduating the following year to write plays for the Lord Admiral's Men. His third comedy, *Every Man Out of His Humour* (acted in 1599), draws from Plautus, Terence, Persius, Horace, Juvenal, Cicero, Seneca, Plutarch, and Lucien, demonstrating the fact that he had access to a good private library (Riggs 1989, 58).[8] Despite hindering his own prospects of securing noble patronage—he killed a player with Pembroke's Men in a quarrel and adopted the Catholic faith—by 1605, Jonson had written a Twelfth Night masque for King James and boasted the Earls of Pembroke, Salisbury (Robert Cecil), and Montgomery among his friends. By 1609, about 12 years after his first play, he had secured the patronage of Prince Henry, King James's eldest son, for his published learned commentary on *The Masque of Queens*. This suggests that objections levelled against Shakspere's ability as a dramatist on the basis of inferior class and the absence of a formal education are insufficient. However, evidence that Shakspere had the opportunity to study the required sources would certainly assist in dissolving the growing doubt that now surrounds his claim to have contributed substantially to the Shakespeare canon.

2.8 Shakspere the Actor

There can be little doubt that the Stratford man was also the London player. At the Herald's College are two preliminary drafts dated 20 October 1596, by the Garter King-of-Arms, Sir William Dethick, of a document granting William's father, John, a family coat of arms. When John Shakspere died in September 1601, William inherited it, and since he also owned land, he was entitled to be known as a 'Gentleman', that is, a member of the landed gentry. In 1602, the York Herald, Ralph Brooke, accused Dethick of "elevating base persons". Of the 23 cases Brooke cited, Shakspere was fourth on the list, and below Brooke's rough drawing of his coat of arms is written "Shakespear the Player by Garter" (FL, MS V.a 350). By 1602, there were over 20 Shakespeare plays in existence, so one wonders why Shakspere was not recorded as a dramatist. In November 1596, a court order named "Willelmum Shakspere" amongst others in a petition for sureties of the peace. To obtain such an order, the complainant, in this case William Wayte, a known criminal, would have had to swear before a judge of the Queen's Bench that he was in danger of death or bodily harm, although the matter more likely concerned an unrecovered debt. The accused would have had to post bond to keep the peace, on pain of forfeiting the security (NA, KB 29/234). The appearance of Robert Langley on the document, a man who had helped finance the Swan Playhouse in Paris Garden, strengthens Shakspere's connection to the theatrical world.

We know that William Shakspere appeared in plays by Ben Jonson. *Every Man in His Humour* (performed in 1598) and *Sejanus* (1603), respectively, name "Will. Shakespeare" and "Will. Shake-speare" in the cast list, alongside "Ric. Burbadge, Aug. Philips, Hen. Condel, Joh. Hemings, Will Sly" and others from the Lord Chamberlain's Men, later the King's Men (Jonson 1616, 72, 438). However, Jonson's *Workes* (1616) inform us that after *Sejanus* (1603), the King's Men enacted his plays *The Foxe* (1605), *The Alchemist* (1610), and *Cataline* (1611) without Shakspere in the cast.

In December 1598, in a clandestine operation, the Lord Chamberlain's Men relocated their home from The Theatre in Shoreditch, south across the Thames to Bankside, using materials from the original building to construct the Globe. On 21 February 1599, Shakspere was listed with John Heminges, William Kempe, Augustine Phillips and Thomas Pope on a document leasing land upon which the new Globe was built. Three parties were involved: Nicholas Brend leased it out, and the Burbage brothers, Cuthbert and Richard, shared the acquisition of the lease with a group of five from the Lord Chamberlain's Men (Chambers 1930, II 58–63).[9]

When the final draft of Shakspere's will was completed on 25 March 1616, he left property, household goods, a yearly allowance to his younger daughter Judeth, and a second-hand bed. He left no books in his will (although this was not unusual) and neither has any book owned by Shakspere ever been traced (which is less unusual). If the Shakespeare canon had risen out of a single mind, there is one certainty: books would have occupied the centre of this person's life. In contrast, several of Ben Jonson's books have been found, signed and annotated by him (Ridell and Stewart, 183), and even Edward Alleyn, a player in the Lord Admiral's Men, left evidence of book ownership (Collier 1843, xxix).[10] In a will dated 4 May 1605, Augustine Phillips, an actor in the King's Men, bequeathed "to my ffellowe William Shakespeare a Thirty shillings peece in gould" (Honigmann and Brock 1993, 72–75).[11] For his part, Shakspere left money to John Heminge and Henry Condell, who were actors in the King's Men and authors of a commendatory verse that appears in the *First Folio*. This again identifies Shakspere of Stratford as a London actor.

There are other facts connecting Shakspere to the theatre world. When Queen Elizabeth died on 24 March 1603, James VI of Scotland was crowned King of England. James, who enjoyed the stage, took over the patronage of The Lord Chamberlain's Men, then London's premier acting company, with its new name the King's Men. William Shakspere's name appears on the patent creating the new company:

> Wee [...] doe licence and authorize these our Servauntes Lawrence ffletcher, William Shakespeare, Richard Burbage, Augustine Phillippes, Iohn Henninges, Henry Condell, William Sly, Robert Armyn, Richard Cowlye, and the rest of theire associates freely to vse and exercise the Arte and Facultie of playinge Comedies, Tragedies, Histories, Enterludes, Moralles, Pastoralles, Stageplaies and such other like as they haue alreadie studied or hereafter shall vse or studye as well for the recreation of our loving Subiectes as for our solace and pleasure when wee shall thinke good to see them during our pleasure. (NA, C 82/1690)

2.9 Shakspere's Exit

Shakespeare's *Venus and Adonis* (1593) and *The Rape of Lucrece* (1594) both contain dedications to the Earl of Southampton, but Shakspere's will gives not the slightest hint of acquaintance with the aristocracy. Neither does it express the slightest concern about the 18 still unpublished Shakespeare plays some of which were also unperformed. We can contrast his will with that of the philosopher and statesman Sir Francis Bacon, who, in April 1621, was confined to bed and believed himself near to death. Although his will was produced in haste, his unpublished work was sufficiently important to him to merit inclusion:

> My compositions unpublished, or the fragments of them, I require my servant Harris to deliver to my brother Constable, to the end that if any of these be fit in his judgment to be published he may accordingly dispose of them. And in particular I wish the Elogium I wrote *In felicem memoriam Reginae Elizabethae* may be published. And to my brother Constable I give all my books. (Spedding *et al.* 1861–74, VII.228–230)

Bacon survived to make a further will four years later, which ran into even greater detail about his intentions for publication (Spedding *et al.* 1861–74, VII.539).

On 23 April 1616, Shakspere died. His funeral was just an ordinary event unlike those of Ben Jonson, Edmund Spenser, John Dryden, Michael Drayton, and Francis Beaumont, who were all honoured by a place in Westminster Abbey. Perhaps Shakspere's wish was for a hometown burial. Shortly after they died, John Fletcher, George Chapman, Philip Massinger, Francis Beaumont, and Ben Jonson all received eulogies from their illustrious contemporaries. Apart from a sonnet written in the hand of William Browne of Tavistock, a friend of the minor poet William Basse, Shakspere received no such honour (Brit Lib, Landsdowne MS 777 fol.67v).[12] In fact, it was not until seven years later in the *First Folio* (1623) that any organized tributes were expressed. Mark Twain admirably sums up the incongruency in *Is Shakespeare Dead?*

> Has it ever happened before — or since — that a celebrated person who had spent exactly half of a fairly long life in the village where he was born and reared was able to slip out of this world and leave that village voiceless and gossipless behind him — utterly voiceless, utterly gossipless? And permanently so? I don't believe it has happened in any case except Shakespeare's. And couldn't and wouldn't have happened in his case if he had been regarded as a celebrity at the time of his death. (Twain 1909, 34–35)

Apart from six surviving William Shakspere signatures, which are inconsistent, there is no record of his handwriting. No original Shakespeare manuscript for a sonnet or play has ever been found, but neither do any survive for the work of Christopher Marlowe, Ben Jonson, John Fletcher, Francis Beaumont, Robert Greene, Thomas Heywood, Thomas Dekker, or Thomas Middleton. In fact, Diana Price has given a comprehensive checkbox list of 24 leading dramatists of the period, indicating whether or not they leave evidence of an education, a record of correspondence on literary matters, documents that indicate payment for plays, evidence of a direct relationship with a patron, surviving handwritten letters, and so on. While each of them scores on at least one of these characteristics, Shakspere is the only one who fails to register (Price 2012, 310–322). It should be clear from all this that rather like Philip Henslowe, who had a variety of business interests and a financial stake in several London theatres (Foakes 2002), William Shakspere of Stratford exhibits all the characteristics of a theatre-wise entrepreneur who dealt in property, commodities, and loans. Of course, there is the *First Folio* (1623) with its references to Shakspere as an author, but in Chapter 4 we shall discover the extent of its unreliability. For the present, we shall now examine how contemporary dramatists, who were familiar with the London theatre world, viewed Shakspere.

Notes

1 'William son of John Shakspere'.
2 The holy day on Tuesday 25 April, St. Mark the Evangelist's Day, was not used possibly because it was considered unlucky.
3 Thomas Siche lost his law suit against "Johannes Shakspere de Stretford [...] glover" in 1556.
4 John Shakspere sued the clothier John Walford for failing to pay £21 for 21 tods (448 lb) of wool in the Court of Common Pleas in Trinity Term 1599.

5 He was sworn in as one of four constables in autumn 1558.
6 1 October 1568 was the first day of his year in office, which permitted him to preside over Court of Records sessions.
7 The letter entitled "Description of Severall places in Warwickshire" came into the hands of the publisher when Lord de Clifford's papers were sold at auction in 1834. It now resides in the Folger Shakespeare Library, MS V.a.74. Dowdall's *Traditionary Anecdotes* also reports that Sir Walter Scott was told the story by Mr Lucy that the park from which Shakspere had stolen a buck "belonged to a mansion at some distance where Sir Thomas Lucy resided [... and] that they had hid the buck in a barn". Sir Walter evidently did not believe the story for he states that "After that we went to the Castle [of Carlisle] where a new showman went through the old trick of pointing out [Sir Walter Scott's imaginary hero] Fergus MacIvor's *very* dungeon".
8 There is also an inventory of Ben Jonson's private library (Ridell and Stewart 1994, 183).
9 From the court plea of Thomasina Ostler listing Shakespeare as shareholder in the Globe and Blackfriars property (Ostler v. Heminges 1615, Coram Rege Roll 1454).
10 In a will dated 13 December 1626 he states, "I give and bequeath to the Corporation of God's-Gift College [Dulwich College ...] my books and instruments".
11 According to his will, seven players were of the first rank in the King's Men in May 1605: Christopher Beeston, Richard Burbage, Henry Condell, John Heminges, Augustine Phillips, William Shakespeare, and William Sly. Five others were of the second rank.
12 The poem, which has been dated 1618–23, urges the deceased Spenser to make room for Shakespeare in his tomb alongside Chaucer and Beaumond [sic] but if this is not possible "Under this carved marble of thine own / Sleep, rare Tragedian, Shakespeare sleep alone".

Bibliography

Baker, Oliver. *In Shakespeare's Warwickshire and the Unknown Years.* London: Simpkin Marshall Ltd, 1937.

Baldwin, Thomas W. *William Shakespeare's Petty School.* Urbana: University of Illinois Press, 1943.

Bodleian Library, MS Arch. F.c.37 formerly Aubrey MS. 6, f.106.

Brinsley, John. *Ludus literarius.* London: Printed for Thomas Man, 1612.

British Library, BL Landsdowne MS 777, fol.67v.

Chambers, Edmund K. *William Shakespeare: A Study of the Facts and Problems.* 2 vols. Oxford: Clarendon Press, 1930.

Chambers, Edmund K. *Shakespearean Gleanings.* London: Oxford University Press, 1944.

Clark, Andrew, ed. *Brief Lives chiefly of Contemporaries, set down by John Aubrey between the years 1669 and 1696.* Oxford: Clarendon Press, 1898.

Collier, J. Payne, ed. *The Alleyn Papers.* London: Printed for the Shakespeare Society, 1843.

Dowdall, John. *Traditionary Anecdotes of Shakespeare Collected in Warwickshire in 1693.* London: Thomas Rodd, 1838.

Foakes, Reginald A., ed. *Henslowe's Diary*, second edition. Cambridge: Cambridge University Press, 2002.

Hamer, Douglas. "Was William Shakespeare William Shakeshafte?" *The Review of English Studies* 21, No.81 (January/February. 1970): 41–8.
Honigmann, Ernst Anselm Joachim, and Susan Brock, eds. *Playhouse Wills, 1558–1642*. New York: Manchester University Press, 1993.
Honigmann, Ernst Anselm Joachim. *Shakespeare the 'lost years'*. New York: Manchester University Press, 1998.
Jonson, Ben. *The Workes of Beniamin Ionson*. London: William Stansby, 1616.
Melchiori, Giorgio, ed. *Merry Wives of Windsor*. The Arden Shakespeare. London: Thomas Nelson, 2000.
Price, Diana. *Shakespeare's Unorthodox Biography: New Evidence of an Authorship Problem*. Shakespeare-authorship.com, 2012.
Ridell, James, and Stanley Stewart. "Spenser's House of Alma in the early seventeenth century." *The Ben Jonson Journal* 1 (January 1994): 183–200.
Riggs, David. *Ben Jonson: A Life*. Harvard University Press, 1989.
Schoenbaum, Samuel. *William Shakespeare*. Oxford: Oxford University Press, 1987.
Schoenbaum, Samuel. *Shakespeare's Lives*. Oxford: Clarendon Press, 1991.
Spedding, James, Robert Leslie Ellis, and Douglas Denon Heath. *The Letters and Life of Francis Bacon*. 7 vols. London: Longmans, 1861–74.
The Folger Library, Washington DC, MS V.a 350.
The National Archives (UK), C 82/1690, no. 78 recto.
The National Archives (UK), KB 27/1361/1, rot. 293.
The National Archive (UK), KB 29/234 (1).
The National Archives (UK), PROB 11/90/176.
The Shakespeare Birthplace Trust, Stratford upon Avon, ER27/4, recto.
The Shakespeare Birthplace Trust, Stratford upon Avon, ER27/5, recto.
The Shakespeare Birthplace Trust, Stratford upon Avon, ER27/6, recto.
The Shakespeare Birthplace Trust, Stratford upon Avon, ER27/9.
The Shakespeare Birthplace Trust, Stratford upon Avon, ER28/1, recto.
Twain, Mark. *Is Shakespeare Dead?* New York: Harper & Brothers, 1909.

3 Contemporary Opinion

The second Parnassus play acted at Cambridge University during the 'War of the Theatres' (1598–1602) hints at the idea that Shakspere hired scholars to write plays, to which he added his own name, and even took lines from other writers. Additional testimony from John Marston and Ben Jonson reinforces this interpretation.

3.1 Shakspere the Dramatist

There are several documents that are suggestive of Shakspere of Stratford being a dramatist. Francis Meres, in *Palladis Tamia: Wits Treasury* (1598), places "*Shakespeare*" alongside Sidney, Spencer, Daniel, Drayton, Warner, Marlowe, and Chapman, with the declaration that because of them "so the English tongue is mightily enriched". Also we find "the sweete wittie soule of *Ouid* liues in mellifluous & hony-tongued *Shakespeare*, witness his *Venus* and *Adonis*, his *Lucrece*; his sugred Sonnets" as well as "the Muses would speak with *Shakespeares* fine filed phrase, if they would speake English". However, Meres gives no finer tribute than that shown in Figure 3.1 (Meres 1598, 282). Since Meres uses 'his', he is evidently referring to a person 'Shakespeare' rather than just a body of work.

Both *Venus and Adonis* (1593) and *Lucrece* (1594) appeared with the name "William Shakespeare" at the foot of the dedication to the Earl of Southampton, and a quarto edition of "A PLEASANT Conceited Comedie CALLED, Loues labors lost" (1598) sported a title page that declared "Newly corrected and augmented By W. Shakespere". Since Shakspere of Stratford was the highest profile 'Shakespeare' in the theatre world, this undoubtedly makes the claim, and quite a serious one, that he was the originator of the above-mentioned works.

However, our intention here is to examine the conjecture that the work was not singly authored by Shakspere. One scenario is that he might have asserted ownership of various works acquired from anonymous writers and stamped his name on them in the process, and that is not the same as authoring them. For all we know, Meres could

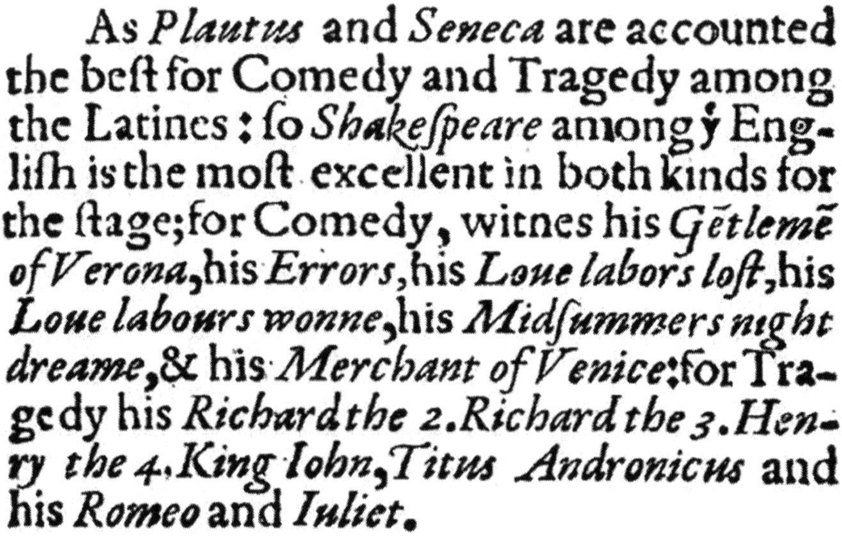
As *Plautus* and *Seneca* are accounted the beſt for Comedy and Tragedy among the Latines : ſo *Shakeſpeare* among ẏ Engliſh is the moſt excellent in both kinds for the ſtage; for Comedy, witnes his *Gẽtlemẽ of Verona*, his *Errors*, his *Loue labors loſt*, his *Loue labours wonne*, his *Midſummers night dreame*, & his *Merchant of Venice*: for Tragedy his *Richard the 2. Richard the 3. Henry the 4. King Iohn, Titus Andronicus* and his *Romeo* and *Iuliet*.

Figure 3.1 An opinion of several Shakespeare plays. Francis Meres, *Palladis Tamia* (1598).

be referring to Shakespeare the rights owner rather than Shakespeare the dramatist. Alternatively, Meres might sincerely have believed that Shakspere was a dramatist. It certainly appears that there were contemporaries that *did* believe this, and Alan Nelson gives several examples (Nelson 2018, 1–24). For example, Sir Richard Baker (1568–1645), author of *A Chronicle of the Kings of England* (1643), states that "For Writers of Playes, and such as had been Players themselves, *William Shakespeare*, and *Benjamin Johnson*, have specially left their Names recommended to posterity" (Baker 1643, 422). This, no doubt, refers to the two major collections that appeared under these names, Jonson's *Workes* (1616) and Shakespeare's *First Folio* (1623). Edmund Tilney, Master of the Revels, kept a performance notebook in the hand of William Honnyng, his secretary, with the heading "The poets which mayd the plaies", under which for the 1604–5 season appears the name "Shaxberd" for the plays "Mesur for Mesur", "The Plaie of Errors", and "The Marchant of Venis" (Nelson 2018, 9). Another illustration arises from the occasion when Leonard Digges and James Mabbe took a tour of Madrid in 1613. Digges's mother had married Thomas Russell of Alderminster, who, three years later, was to act as overseer to Shakspere's will. Mabbe bought a book of sonnets by Lope de Vega Carpio, which he sent to his friend William Baker in Oxford. On the flyleaf, Digges had written, "Will Baker: Knowinge that Mr Mab: was to send you this Booke of Sonets, which with Spaniards here is accounted of their Lope de Vega as in Englande wee sholde of our Will

Shakespeare [...]" (Nelson 2018, 18). However, Professor Nelson only presents a unilateral view, selecting favourable quotes from the third Parnassus play (Nelson 2018, 8–9), and Ben Jonson's 'Timber' (Jonson 1641, 97–98),[1] without addressing the sustained attack on Shakspere's credentials in the second Parnassus play and without including the serious doubts that Jonson expressed about Shakspere's literary talent in his 'Timber' (1640); see Section 3.4.

So, there is a need to redress the balance and afford the reader the opportunity to examine the objections that were actually levelled against Shakspere by some of his contemporaries. To this end, we turn to the 'War of the Theatres', a series of satirical poems and plays running from 1598–1602, in which several writers attacked each other. Although no dramatist is mentioned explicitly, there are sufficient clues to identify the victims, and the lack of restraint should offer a crucial insight into their unmitigated opinions of each other. It is interesting to note that although Ben Jonson came under particularly heavy fire, with accusations against him ranging from intellectual deficiency to short-tempered narcissism, not once was his priority of the works under his name brought into question, while, in contrast, serious objections were raised against Shakspere's authorship. There is a good reason why we should take these attacks seriously—because the intended victims responded in kind.

3.2 The "War of the Theatres"

There is a degree of scholarly consensus as to the earnestness with which writers attacked each other on the stage at the turn of the seventeenth century. Simons characterizes the 'War of the Theatres', or 'Poetomachia' as Dekker called it, as a display of "personal attacks and professional criticism that Jonson, Marston, and Dekker levelled against each other" (2018, 11). In this acting out of "animosity", it seems that "Jonson thought of Marston as verbally obtuse" and "Marston took issue with [... Jonson's] apparently self-aggrandizing satiric authority" (Simons 2018, 11–12). According to Bednarz, John Marston's opening salvo *Histriomastix* (1599) was "symbolically whipping, as a class, all common players" and with "unmitigated sarcasm, *Histriomastix* travesties the professional actors and their outmoded repertoire through his depiction of Posthaste, the poet-player, and Sir Oliver Owlet's Men, the clownish company of former tradesmen" in a demonstration of "unprovoked cultural aggression" (1993, 103). *Westward Hoe* (1604) was a satire resulting from a collaboration between Thomas Dekker and John Webster. Hirschfeld (2004, 29) sees *Eastward Hoe* (1605), written the following year by George Chapman, John Marston, and Ben Jonson, as "a form of aggressive parody [of *Westward Hoe* ...] a snub at Dekker and Webster [...] a malicious mockery". Not only did it imitate the title of its progenitor, but it was played out on the stage by the rival boy company (Hirschfeld 2004, 37).[2] By this time, Marston and Jonson had evidently built bridges.

The three Parnassus plays, *The Pilgrimage to Parnassus*; *The Return from Parnassus, Pt. 1*; and *The Return from Parnassus, Pt. 2*, otherwise entitled the *Scourge of Simony*, were performed at St. John's College, Cambridge, from 1599 to 1601.[3] Here, the 'War of the Theatres' reached its highest intensity, as Ben Jonson on the one hand, and John Marston, Samuel Daniel, Henry Chettle, Anthony Munday, and Thomas Dekker on the other, delivered veiled attacks on each other in the lines of characters on the stage. In the middle of this war, and particularly in the Gullio–Ingenioso exchanges in the second Parnassus play (Part 1), we find Shakspere portrayed. The comments against him will be examined in detail.

The main antagonists in the dispute were Jonson and Marston, and the conflict began with Jonson's attack on Samuel Daniel in the speeches of the character Master Matthew in *Every Man in his Humour* (1598). Marston was a friend of Daniel, and so in the former's *Scourge of Villainy* (1598) there is a prefatory piece "To those that seem judicial Perusers" in which Marston refers to Jonson as "Torquatus", that is, 'one who wore something around the neck'. The offending lines are as follows:

> I wrote the first Satire in some places too obscure [...] Yet when by some scurvy chaunce it shall come into the late perfumed fist of judicial Torquatus (that, like some rotten stick in a troubled water, hath got a great deal of barmy[4] froth to stick to his sides) I know he will vouchsafe it, some of his new minted epithets [...] when in conscience he understands not the least part of it.

In 1598, Jonson had killed one Gabriel Spenser in a duel and had only narrowly escaped the rope by invoking a right called 'neck shrift', which granted him his freedom if he could read verse from the Holy Writ. 'Torquatus' appears to be a reference to this. In Satire XI of the *Scourge of Villainy* (1598), Marston blasts Torquatus with "his very intellect, Is nought but a curvetting sommerset [a leaping horse]" (Bullen 1887, 375). This was no idle banter between friends. In a conversation between Ben Jonson and his contemporary, the Scottish poet William Drummond, Jonson confessed that he "beat him [Marston ...] took his pistol from him, [and] wrote his Poetaster [1601] on him; the beginning of them were, that Marston represented him on the stage, in his youth given to venerie" (Drummond 1842, 20–21). Drummond also informs us that Jonson was

> a great lover and praiser of himself, a contemner and scorner of others, given rather to loose a friend than a jest, jealous of every word and action of those about him [...] thinketh nothing well but what either he himself or some of his friends and countrymen hath said or done. (1842, 15)

In Satire III of his *Scourge of Villanie* (1598), Marston turns his attention to Shakspere (1598, sig. D2). Here, he makes use of sexual metaphors

Shall broking pandars ſucke Nobilitie?
Soyling fayre ſtems with foule impuritie?
Nay, ſhall a trencher ſlaue extenuate,
Some *Lucrece* rape? and ſtraight magnificate
Lewd *Iouian* luſt? Whilſt my ſatyrick vaine
Shall muzled be, not daring out to ſtraine
His tearing paw? No gloomie *Iuvenall*,
Though to thy fortunes I diſaſtrous fall.

Figure 3.2 An attack on Shakspere. John Marston, *The Scourge of Villanie* (1598, Satire III). Key: 'pandars', pimp or procuror; 'sucke', attract; 'trencher slave', player or villain who feeds off others; 'extenuate', make light of; 'Lucrece rape', theft with possible allusion to Shake-speare's *The Rape of Lucrece*; 'magnificate', praise; 'Juvenall', Roman satirist whose work Marston parodied.

while citing Shakespeare's *Lucrece* (1594). In referring to the Roman satirist "gloomie Juvenal" and his disastrous fortune, Marston seems to be directing his protest at Shakspere the actor (Figure 3.2):

In other words, could a "foule impuritie" such as Shakspere the actor, who is drawn as a broker and procurer, have attracted the patronage of such fair noble blood as the Earl of Southampton? Lines 3 and 4 might also be claiming that Shakespeare the "trencher slave" has made light of his abduction [rape] of the *Lucrece* work. According to Davenport:

> M. [Marston] is clearly thinking of the tradition, deriving from the scholiast, about Juvenal: that he lampooned Paris, an actor, whom Domitian was in love with, and that the emperor in revenge appointed the satirist to a minor post in Egypt where he ended his days in miserable exile. (1961, 117, 300–301)

The "nobilitie" can only be the Earl of Southampton to whom *Lucrece* is dedicated. In stating that his "satyrick vain" would not be silenced, Marston must also have anticipated disastrous consequences for himself, and, in fact, his satires were destroyed by order of the Archbishop of Canterbury and the Bishop of London less than a year later. With a blanket ban on verse satire, Marston saw drama on the stage as a useful vehicle for his impulse and so began the 'War of the Theatres'. Table 3.1 shows how the conflict evolved.

Table 3.1 The order of events in the 'War of the Theatres'

Year	*Author*	*Victim*	*Play*
1599	John Marston	Jonson as Chrisoganus	*Histriomastix*
1599	Ben Jonson	Marston as Carlo Buffone "a public, scurrilous, and profane jester" whose style is "fustian"; Dekker as Orange.	*Every Man Out of His Humour*
1600	Thomas Dekker	Jonson as Emulo "the lath, lime, and hair man, with his absurd gallimaufry of language"	*Patient Grissil*
1600	John Marston	Jonson as Brabant Senior	*Jack Drum's Entertainment*
1600	Ben Jonson	Marston or Dekker as Anaides	*Cynthia's Revels*
1601	Ben Jonson	Marston as Crispinus, an inferior poet and plagiarist, Dekker as Demetrius, an inferior playwright	*Poetaster*
1601	Thomas Dekker	Jonson as Horace, a short-tempered buffoon only interested in praise	*Satiromastix*[a]
1602	John Marston	Jonson as Lampatho Doria, his weight lampooned "I'll make Greatness quake, I'll tan the hide of thick'skin'd Hugeness"	*What You Will*

[a]This was acted by the Lord Chamberlain's Men, with Shakspere in the cast, at the newly built Globe Theatre.

3.3 The Parnassus Plays

The first Parnassus play, *The Pilgrimage to Parnassus*, appears to have been written in three days before being performed at the Christmas or New Year's revels 1598–9 (Smeaton 1905, xiii). Two youths, Philomusus and Studioso, make a pilgrimage to "green Parnassus Hill" through Trivium, or "Logic Land", where they must beware of two robbers Genus and Species who try to acquire "every true man's invention". When they pass into "the Land of Rhetoric" they meet a disillusioned Ingenioso on his way back from Parnassus, who complains that he was cozened [tricked] and that his writing brought him no fortune. The play seems not to anticipate the two sequels, and it reveals nothing of direct interest about Shakspere.

The second play, *The Return from Parnassus, Pt. 1*, picks up the story seven years later with Philomusus and Studioso, now as scholars, fortuitously meeting Ingenioso again. He has since been invited by a patron Gullio to supply him with verses that he intends to advertise as his own. According to Ingenioso, Gullio "braggs, when he comes abroade, of his liberalitie to schollers and what a rewarder he is of wittie devises: but indeed he is a mere man of strawe, a great lump of drowsie earth" (Lines 228–231). Gullio eventually appears in Act 3, Scene 1, and informs us that "pretty sleightie apparel, stood mee not paste in two hundred pounds" (Lines 912–914). The allusion can be explained as follows. In Robert Greene's *Groats-worth of Witte* (1592) there is an attack on a player referred to as "Shake-scene" [Shakspere] who "supposes he is as well able to bombast out a blanke verse as the best of you [dramatists]". This will be examined in more detail in Chapter 6. For the present, it will suffice to mention 'Robertoes Tale' in the same *Groats-worth*, in which Roberto [Greene himself] is approached by a player who says "I suppose you are a scholler, and [I] pittie men of learning should liue of lack". The player declares that he "was a country Author [...] and for seuen yeers space was absolute Interpreter to the puppets [actors]". Roberto asks "how meane you to vse mee?" The player responds "Why sir, in making Playes [...] for you shall be well paid, if you will take the paines". Significantly, the player reveals that "my very share in playing apparel will not be sold for two hundred pounds". Let us for the moment work with the possibility that Gullio represents Shakspere, that is, 'Gulielmus [Gullio] Shakspere'.

Now let us see what Gullio reveals about himself. Here the Shakspere allusions come thick and fast. In one section of dialogue, Gullio informs us that while Sidney's *Arcadia* was pretty, "soe are my sonnets" (Lines 959–960), and at his Oxford inn he is congratulated by Genus and Species, the two unsavoury characters from the first Parnassus play who purloin the inventions of others. He also tells us that "I am verie latelie registered in the roules of fame in an Epigram made by a Cambridge man, one weaver fellow". This is another allusion in need of clarification. In 1599, John Weever, who was educated at Queens' College, Cambridge, published a collection of epigrams, one of which was headed "Ad Gulielmum Shakespeare". It begins "Honie-tong'd *Shakespeare* when I saw thine issue / I swore *Apollo* got them and none other" (Weeuer 1599, fourth week, Epigram 22).[5] So now the idea that Gullio represents Shakspere is gaining force.

Ingenioso responds with "youre bodye is nothinge but a faire inne of fairer guests that dwell therin" (Lines 987–988). If there is any doubt that Gullio is Shakspere, it is quickly extinguished when Gullio brags about his skill at impressing a lady with his oration. In the process, he pretends that Ingenioso is a lady to be wooed, and proceeds to recite a line from Stanza 1 of *Venus and Adonis* "and like a bould-faced sutore 'gins to woo thee".[6] In an aside to the audience, Ingenioso protests, "We shall have nothinge but Shakespeare and shreds of poetrie that he hath gathered at the theators! (Lines 1009–1010) [...] Marke, Romeo and Juliet! O monstrous theft!" (Line 1015). Whether or not Gullio is Shakspere, Ingenioso's opinion of Shakspere is now abundantly clear. At this point, Gullio pours out the whole of Stanza 2 in *Venus and Adonis* (Lines 1018–1022),[7] to which Ingenioso responds

INGENIOSO: Sweete Mr. Shakespeare!

GULLIO: As I am a scholler, these arms of mine are long and strong withal, Thus elms by vines are compast ere they falle.

INGENIOSO: Faith, gentleman! Youre reading is wonderfull in our English poets!

GULLIO: Sweet mistris, I vouchsafe to take some of there words, and applie them to mine owne matters by a scholasticall invitation.

A couple of lines later Ingenioso echoes Francis Meres's praise of Shakespeare, and Weever's epigram, when he mockingly complements Gullio with "never was so mellifluous a witt joynet to so pure a phrase" (Lines 1024–1035).[8] Gullio invites Ingenioso to compose some verses, "and when thou hast done I will peruse, polish, and correcte them" (Lines 1046–1047). However, just when we seem to have identified Gullio as Shakspere, Gullio specifies that he wants the verses in the style of "Chaucer's, Gower's, and Spencer's and Mr. Shakspeare's" (Lines 1052–1053), and declares, "O sweet Mr. Shakespeare! I'le have his picture in my study at the courte" (Lines 1054–1055). This, of course, suggests that Shakspere is a different man from Gullio, and his reference to himself as a 'scholler' supports this (unless he is delusional); yet, whether or not Gullio is Shakspere, Ingenioso's portrait of Shakspere as a player who passes off the work of others as his own is transparent.

In Act 4, Scene 1, Ingenioso and Gullio return, with Gullio boasting that he has been entertained by aristocracy. "I think he meanes to poison mee with a lie!" exclaims Ingenioso. "Why he is acquainted with nere a lorde" (Lines 1130–1131). Further muddying of the waters occurs when Gullio declares "I'le worship sweet Mr. Shakespeare, and to honoure him will lay his Venus and Adonis under my pillowe" (1223–1225). Again we are being invited to doubt that Gullio is Shakspere. Clearly enraged, Ingenioso declares Gullio to be a "post put into a sattin sute, this haberdasher of lyes, this bracchidochio" (Line 1235).

Their final interaction takes place in Act 5, Scene 1. Gullio, who is now whimsically unimpressed with Ingenioso's literacy, provokes the scholar into a volley of invective. In the process, Ingenioso accuses Gullio of being "the scorne of all good witts [...] that never spokest wittie thinge but out of a play" (Lines 1466–1467). The scene ends with Ingenioso revealing that Studioso and Philomusus intend "to call on mee at Gullio's chamber in Shoreditch" (Line 1496). The Theatre, which opened in 1576 at Shoreditch, was the base of Shakspere's company, the Lord Chamberlain's Men, from 1594–8. In October 1598, "William Shakespeare" was named on a certificate compiled by the London tax commissioners as living in St. Helens Bishopsgate, near Shoreditch, while having defaulted on paying 13 shillings and four pence in tax. Apparently, he had left the parish (LTC, E179/146/369). So 'Shoreditch' might be yet another Shakspere allusion. Disillusioned by the exploitation of scholars, Studioso, Philomusus, and Ingenioso decide to leave Parnassus Hill, presumably with their tax bill settled.

Despite the questions raised against Shakspere's dramatic activity, William Macray is unable to see anything but Gullio's respect for "Mr. Shakespeare", characterizing his quotations from Shakespeare as "signs of the popularity which had already been won" (1886, x). However, to Ingenioso, and presumably to the *Parnassus* author who invented the character, Shakspere was a boasting social climber in a satin suit, who lied about his connections to the nobility, and who hired poverty-stricken scholars to write pieces that he passed off as his own. To quote Nelson "The Parnassus plays, to be sure, are fiction; but, as with any satire, the humour depends on real and recognised circumstances" (2018, 9). Francis Bacon aptly summarizes the power of considering the whole rather than individual parts of the evidence in his *Advancement of Learning* (1605): "For [we should realize that] the harmony of science, supporting each part the other, is and ought to be the true and brief confutation and suppression of all the smaller sort of objections" because "were it not better to set up one large light in a noble room, than to go about with a small one, to illuminate every corner, thereof?" (*The Works of Francis Bacon* 1815, XI l[roman]).

The third Cambridge play, *The Return from Parnassus, Pt. 2*, was performed for the Christmas revels of 1601–2, and contains references to the Jonson–Dekker exchange. It was printed twice in 1606 by G. Eld for John Wright, with some differences of expression between the texts. Here, there is a hint that the character Amoretto represents Shakspere. Recall that Ingenioso depicts Gullio in the second Parnassus play as a "post put into a sattin sute". Ingenioso's diatribe against Amoretto in Act 4, Scene 2, evolves as follows:

> And you Maister *Amoretto*, that art the chiefe Carpenter of Sonets, a priuileged Vicar for the lawlesse marriage of Inke and Paper, you that are good for nothing but to commend in a sette speech [...] it's fine when that Puppet-player *Fortune*, must put such a Birchen-lane post in so good a suite, such an Asse in so goode fortune. (Lines 1722–1729)

Ingenioso even addresses Amoretto as "fond gul", which again might be an allusion to Gullio (Line 1761).

In this third play, the two scholars, Philomusus and Studioso, have now returned from Italy to Parnassus Hill and are desperate for employment, having learned that their university education offers them little prospect. The dialogue wastes no time in attacking Jonson, with the character Iudioso abusing him as "a bould whoreson" (Line 301). In Act 4, Scene 3, after trying several professions, Philomusus and Studioso approach Dick Burbage and Will Kempe of the Lord Chamberlain's Men with the aim of becoming actors "and must the basest trade yield us relief". While Burbage remains civil, Kempe cannot conceal his disdain for university-educated playwrights nor for classically educated non-university ones, such as Ben Jonson:

> *Kempe.* Few of the vniuersity men pen plaies well, they smell too much of that writer *Ouid*, and that writer *Metamorphosis*, and talke too much of *Proserpina & Iuppiter.* Why heres our fellow Shakespeare puts them all downe, I and *Ben Ionson* too. O that *Ben Ionson* is a pestilent fellow, he brought vp *Horace* giuing the Poets a pill, but our fellow Shakespeare hath giuen him a purge that made him beray his credit. (Lines 1806–1813)

In fact, the only sense in which Shakspere—who is portrayed as a non-university man—gives Jonson a metaphorical purge is by acting in Dekker's *Satiromastix*, a play that satirizes Jonson. One is tempted to interpret "pen plaies well" as confirmation that Shakspere had dramatic talent; however, in Act 5, Scene 1, overcome with disillusionment, Philomusus and Studioso leave the acting company and become travelling fiddlers:

> Studioso (going aside sayeth).
> Fayre fall good *Orpheus*,
> that would rather be King of a mole hill, than a Keysars slaue:
> Better it is mongst fidlers to be chiefe,
> Than at [a] plaiers trencher [service] beg reliefe.
> But ist not strange [these] mimick apes [actors] should prize
> Vnhappy Schollers at a hireling rate.
> Vile world, that lifts them vp to hye degree,
> And treads vs downe in grouelling misery.
> *England* affordes those glorious vagabonds [actors],
> That carried earst their fardels [bundles]on their backes,
> Coursers to ride on through the gazing streetes,
> Sooping [sweeping] it in their glaring Satten sutes [suits],
> And Pages to attend their maisterships:
> With mouthing words that better wits haue framed
> They purchase lands, and now Esquiers are [named]. (Lines 1953–1968)

This appears to be a general reference to the exploitation of scholars by players. Shakspere had inherited his father's coat of arms in September 1601, only three months before this play was performed, "and now Esquires are named".[9] However, it is not even necessary for this to be particular to Shakspere. Even if all actors were the target, the speech implies that every actor that has land and is a "Gentleman", including Shakspere, speaks the words of better wits, presumably university-educated ones. That is to say, none of the plays he speaks in are his own. As for Philomusus and Studioso, they finally decide to become shepherds and end the play attending flocks of sheep on the downs of Kent.

3.4 Ben Jonson's View

Ben Jonson's *Epigrams* (1616) were largely written between 1598 and 1601 while the 'War of the Theatres' was still raging. In Epigram LVI, he borrows the term 'poet-ape' from Philip Sidney to describe an unidentified actor,[10] the only piece in the collection constructed in Shakespearean sonnet form; see Figure 3.3 (Jonson 1616, 763).

Given that the second Parnassus play and Jonson's epigram were assembled around the same time, it might be worth noting the common allusion to 'sheep' in the last two lines of Jonson's verse and in the eventual employment of Philomusus and Studioso. Richard Dutton is in no doubt that "Poet-Ape is a preposterous poetaster, trying to forge a reputation by cobbling up ideas stolen from other people's works, and hoping it will not be noticed that they are not all of a piece" (1983, 86).

LVI.

ON POET-APE.

POore POET-APE, that would be thought our chiefe,
  Whoſe workes are eene the fripperie of wit,
From brocage is become ſo bold a thiefe,
  As we, the rob'd, leaue rage, and pittie it.
At firſt he made low ſhifts, would picke and gleane,
  Buy the reuerſion of old playes; now growne
To a little wealth, and credit in the *ſcene*,
  He takes vp all, makes each mans wit his owne.
And, told of this, he ſlights it. Tut, ſuch crimes
  The ſluggiſh gaping auditor deuoures;
He markes not whoſe 'twas firſt: and after-times
  May iudge it to be his, as well as ours.
Foole, as if halfe eyes will not know a fleece
  From locks of wooll, or ſhreds from the whole peece?

Figure 3.3 Ben Jonson's attack on a player who is also a broker (1616, 763). Key: 'frippery', second-hand clothing; 'brocage', buying plays; 'scene', possible allusion to the *Groats-worth*'s 'Shake-scene'.

Sabrina Feldman summarizes the theatre scene when this was composed.

> There were only about twenty-two professional playwrights during Shakespeare's time, and no more than a few of these were also actors. Among this small group, William surely saw himself as chief playwright — and so did Francis Meres, who praised him far above any other contemporary playwright in his 1598 commonplace book *Palladis Tamia*. Poet Ape must have been the Stratford actor. (Feldman 2011, 135)

Diana Price rules out Edward Alleyn as a contender, even though he was both an actor and play dealer. It seems his transactions, as recorded by theatre owner Phillip Henslowe, were not only "above-board", but he was held in such high esteem by Ben Jonson that in Epigram LXXXIX he is praised as such a "great Example" of acting that "as others speak, but only thou dost act" (Price 2012, 89).

When Ben Jonson's "Timber: or Discoveries made upon men and matter" was published posthumously as part of the second folio of his *Workes* (1640), we find his view that "the unskilful are naturally deceived" because they "think rude things greater than polished". There immediately follows his opinion of Shakspere:

> I remember, the Players have often mentioned it as an honour to *Shakespeare*, that in his writing, (whatsoever he penn'd) hee never blotted out line. My answer hath beene, would he had blotted a thousand. Which they thought a malevolent speech. I had not told posterity this, but for their ignorance, who choose that circumstance to commend their friend by, wherein he most faulted. (1640, 97–98)

Jonson continues:

> wherein he flow'd with that faculty, that sometimes it was necessary he should be stopp'd: *Sufflaminandus erat* [needs to apply the brake] as Augustus said of Haterius. His wit was in his owne power; would the rule of it had beene so too. Many times hee fell into those things, could not escape laughter: as when hee said in the person of *Casar*, one speaking to him; *Casar thou dost me wrong.* Hee replyed: *Casar did never wrong, but with just cause*; and such like; which were ridiculous. (1640, 97–98)[11]

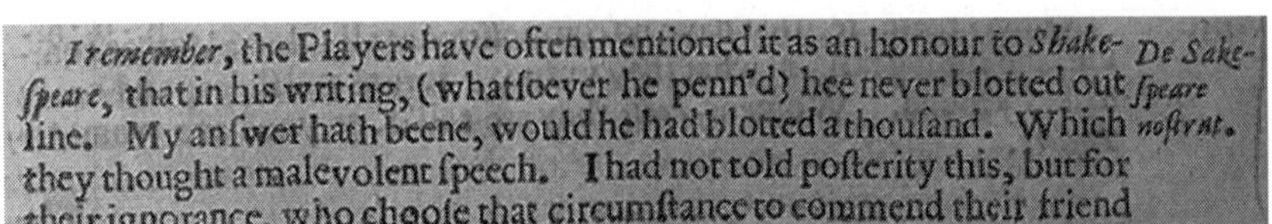

I remember, the Players have often mentioned it as an honour to *Shake-ſpeare*, that in his writing, (whatſoever he penn'd) hee never blotted out line. My anſwer hath beene, would he had blotted a thouſand. Which they thought a malevolent ſpeech. I had not told poſterity this, but for their ignorance, who chooſe that circumſtance to commend their friend

De Shake-ſpeare noſtrat.

Figure 3.4 Ben Jonson's criticism of Shakspere's literary talent (1641).

This is a telling reference to the Roman orator Haterius who had a reputation for confusing his words. The implication here is that Shakspere wrote lines of dialogue which Jonson did not appreciate. Can the accuracy of Jonson's testimony be undermined by arguing for professional jealousy? What should be taken into consideration is that in the *Timber* (1640) Jonson declares of Shakspere,

> I lov'd the man, and doe honour his memory (on this side Idolatry) as much as any [...] There was ever more in him to be praysed, then to be pardoned.

The question is, did Shakspere make any contribution at all to the plays under his name? We might imagine a school teacher who reprimands a student for making an error in his mathematics homework. If the student has submitted no homework then the admonishment is unnecessary. Likewise, if Shakspere has written no lines of dialogue then the accusation of having "faulted" in them seems illogical. So too would Jonson's wish that "hee had blotted a thousand" because why would the players take Jonson's words as a "malevolent speech" against Shakspere if the lines to be blotted were not composed by their fellow player? Jonson's qualifier "whatsoever he penned" invites caution in judging the extent of Shakspere's contribution, yet the implication is that something *was* contributed. So, the most credible interpretation is that Jonson is testifying that Shakspere had a hand in certain plays but is indicating that he does not appreciate the results. Shakspere could write but not very well.

The counter to all of this is the testimony of the *First Folio* (1623) where several eulogies are given in respect of Shakspere's sole authorship of the 36 plays therein. However, we shall now see why this evidence is unreliable.

Notes

1 This appears in a reprint of the 1640 edition, republished by Ginn and Company at Boston in 1892.
2 *Eastward Hoe* was played by the Blackfriars boys, while *Westward Hoe* was performed by Paul's boys.
3 The manuscript for the first two Parnassus plays can be found in a volume of the antiquarian Thomas Hearne's miscellaneous collections at the Bodleian Library, Oxford, as Rawlinson D 398. There are 20 folio leaves made by a copyist, and the outer leaf bears the name "Edmund Rishton, Lancastrensis"; see Macray (1886, vii).
4 For an argument that this refers to Jonson, see Bullen (1887, III 305n).
5 There is an alternative Weever epigram that Gullio might be referencing. "In obitum sepulcrum Gullionis" begins "Here lies fat *Gullio*, who caperd in a cord / To highest heau'n for all his huge great weight / His friends left at *Tiburne* in the yere of our Lord / 159 and 8" (Weeuer 1599, second week, Epigram 21). Since it is about a man hanged at Tyburn and bears no relation to drama, then it must be the Shakespeare epigram that Gullio intends.
6 "Sick-thoughted Venus makes amain unto him, / And like a bold-faced suitor 'gins to woo him." *Venus and Adonis* (1593), Stanza 1.

7 "Thrise fairer than myself [...]", *Venus and Adonis* (1593).
8 "so the sweete wittie soule of *Ouid* liues in mellifluous & hony-tongued *Shakespeare*" (Meres 1598, sig. Oo^{v}).
9 On 10 October 1601, an updated deed transferring ownership of the Globe and other Southwark properties mentions "Richard Burbage and William Shakspeare gentlemen" (NA, C 54/1722 membrane 7).
10 "since the cause why it [Poesie] is not esteemed in England, is the fault of Poet-apes, not Poets" (Sidney 1595; Jonson 1616, 783).
11 *Julius Caesar* was first printed in the *First Folio* (1623) where the following appears at the end of the following 14-line speech: "*Caesar.* Know, Caesar doth not wrong, nor without cause Will he be satisfied" (*Julius Caesar* 1599, 3.1.47–8).

Bibliography

Baker, Sir Richard. *A Chronicle of the Kings of England. From the Time of the Romans Government, unto the Death of King James.* London: Printed for Daniel Frere, 1643.

Bednarz, James P. "Marston's subversion of Shakespeare and Jonson: 'Histriomastix' and the War of the Theaters." *Medieval & Renaissance Drama in England* 6 (1993): 103–28.

Bullen, A. H., ed. *The Works of John Marston.* 3 vols. London: John Nimmo, 1887.

Crosse, Henry. *Vertue's Common-wealth or the Highway to Honour.* London: printed for Iohn Newbery, 1603. sig. P.

Davenport, Arnold, ed. "The Scourge of Villanie 1599, Satire III." *The Poems of John Marston.* Liverpool: Liverpool University Press, 1961.

Drummond, William. *Notes of Ben Jonson's Conversations with William Drummond of Hawthornden, January, M.DC.XIX.* London: Printed for the Shakespeare Society, 1842.

Dutton, Richard. *Ben Jonson: To the First Folio.* Cambridge: Cambridge University Press, 1983.

Feldman, Sabrina. *The Apocryphal William Shakespeare.* Indianapolis, IN: Dog Ear Publishing, 2011.

Greene, Robert. *The Myrrour of Modestie.* London: Imprinted by Roger Ward, 1584.

Greene, Robert. *Menaphon.* London: Printed by T. O. for Sampson Clarke, 1589.

Greene, Robert. *The Spanish Masquerado.* London: Printed by Roger Ward for Thomas Cadman, 1589.

Greene, Robert. *Farewell to Folly.* London: Imprinted by Thomas Scarlet for T. Gubbin and T. Newman, 1591.

Greene, Robert. *Groats-Worth of Witte, Bought with a Million of Repentance.* London: Imprinted for William Wright, 1592. STC: 12245.

Hirschfeld, Heather Anne. *Joint Enterprises: Collaborative Drama and the Institutionalization of the English Renaissance Theater.* Boston: University of Massachusetts Press, 2004.

Jonson, Ben. *The Workes of Benjamin Jonson.* London: William Stansby, 1616. STC 14751.

Jonson, Ben. "Timber: or discoveries made upon men and matter." In *The Workes of Benjamin Jonson*. London: Printed by Richard Bishop, 1641.
London Tax Commissioners, document E179/146/369.
Macray, W. D., ed. *The Pilgrimage to Parnassus with the Two Parts of The Return to Parnassus*. Oxford: Clarendon Press, 1886.
Marston, John. *The Scourge of Villanie*. London: I[ames] R[oberts], 1598. STC 17485.
Meres, Francis. *Palladis Tamia Wits Treasury being the Second Part of Wits Commonwealth*. London: Printed by P. Short, for Cuthbert Burbie, 1598. STC 17834.
National Archive (UK), C 54/1722 membrane 7.
Nelson, Alan H. "William Shakespeare of Stratford-upon-Avon and London." In William Leahy, ed. *My Shakespeare: The Authorship Controversy*. Brighton: Edward Everett Root Publishing, 2018.
Price, Diana. *Shakespeare's Unorthodox Biography*. Shakespeare-authorship.com, 2012.
Shakespeare, William. *Venus and Adonis*. London: Imprinted by Richard Field, 1593.
Shakespeare, William. *Lucrece*. London: Imprinted by Richard Field, 1594.
Shakespeare, William. *A Pleasant Conceited Comedie called Loue's Labour's Lost*. London: Imprinted by W. W. for Cuthers Burby, 1598.
Sidney, Philip. *The Defence of Poesie*. London: Printed for William Ponsonby, 1595.
Simons, Jay. *Jonson, the Poetomachia, and the Reformation of Renaissance Satire: Purging Satire*. New York: Routledge, 2018.
Smeaton, Oliphant, ed. *The Return from Parnassus, or the Scourge of Simony*. London: J. M. Dent and Co., 1905.
Weeuer, Iohn. *EPIGRAMMES in the Oldest Cut, and Newest Fashion*. London: printed by V.S. for Thomas Bushell, 1599.
The Works of Francis Bacon. 12 vols. London: Printed for M. Jones, 1815.

4 A Fraudulent *First Folio*

There are publications bearing Shakspere's name on work he had not composed, and works published in the *First Folio* (1623) containing other hands, and yet the Stratford man receives all the credit in the prefatory tributes. This raises serious doubts about the accuracy of the *First Folio* as a record of attribution.

4.1 Misattributions to Shakspere

The 1619 quarto of *The first part Of the true & honorable history, of the Life of Sir John Oldcastle, the good Lord Cobham* has "Written by William Shakespeare" on the title page,[1] a name that by this time had appeared on several quartos. For 16 October 1599, Henslowe's diary records a receipt of "ten pownd" by "Thomas downton of phillipp Henchlow to pay m^{r} Monday m^{r} drayton & m^{r} wilsson & haythway for the first pte of the lyfe of Sr Jhon Ouldcasstell & in earnest of the Second pte for the vse of the company" (Greg 1904, F.65 113). So this was certainly not Shakspere's. In 1608, *A Yorkshire Tragedy* appeared in quarto with "Written by W. Shakspeare" on the title page (Shakspeare [?] 1608). An entry in the *Stationers' Register* dated 2 May 1608 gives attribution to "Wylliam Shakespeare". However, his authorship has since been disputed by David Lake (1975, 163–74), MacDonald P. Jackson (1979, 43–53, 77–78, 86–87), and Roger Holdsworth (1994, 1–25), all of whom give the play to Thomas Middleton.

When the long poem *A Funerall Elegye* (1612) appeared, the printer George Eld had set the initials 'W.S.' on the title page. This almost certainly refers to 'William Shakspere' for the following reasons. The Stratford man's attribution was first suggested by Donald Foster whose study drew such approbation that the Norton, Riverside, and Longman Shakespeare collections ushered the poem into the Shakespeare canon (Foster 1989). The poem consists of a eulogy to William Peter of Devonshire who had recently been murdered in 1612. This immediately provides a motive as to why the true author might wish to conceal his identity. The murderer's associates might offer violent objections to the author of a pamphlet that had attacked them. Foster's attribution was subsequently challenged by Gilles Monsarrat (2002), and Brian Vickers (2002) who, correctly in my estimation, attributed the *Elegye* to the dramatist John Ford. However, Foster's suspicions were not without foundation. In an RCP study of the poem, five strong rare collocation matches with the Shakespeare work were revealed that all preceded it (see Table 4.1). This circumstance only allows the conclusion that the *Elegye* borrowed from the Shakespeare canon. Table 4.2 shows some

Table 4.1 Rare locutions from *A Funerall Elegye* (1612) that appear in an earlier Shakespeare work

No.	*Locution in* Elegye	*EEBO search*	*Source*	*Rarity*
5	"[may] pattern out" (sig. A3)	{pattern out}	*Measure for Measure*	9/5471(0.165%)
19	"secured fools" (sig. A4)	{secure(d) fool(s)}	*The tragedie of King Richard the second* and *The Merry Wives of Windsor*	1/5471(0.018%)
23	"sick desires" (sig. A4)	{sick desire(s)}	*All's Well That Ends Well*	4/5471(0.073%)
47	"seruile breath" (sig. B2)	{servile breath}	*The tragedie of King Richard the second*	8/5471(0.146%)
92	"noble in the mind" (sig. C2)	{noble(er)(est) in the mind}	*The Tragicall Historie of Hamlet* (Q2)	1/5471(0.018%)

Table 4.2 A selection of rare locutions from *A Funerall Elegye* (1612) that appear in a later John Ford work

No.	*Locution in* Elegye	*EEBO search*	*John Ford work*	*Rarity*
11	"incompast in a mortall frame" (sig. A3^{v})	{encompassed fby.4 frame}	*Christs bloodie sweat* (1613)	0/5471(unique)
21	"insnaring vice" (sig. A4)	{ensnaring vice(s)}	*Christs bloodie sweat* (1613)	0/5471(unique)
34	"[Cleane-]temper'd Moderation" (sig. A4^{v})	{tempered moderation}	*The golden meane* (1613)	0/5471(unique)
87	"dye, dye all" (sig. C^{v})	{die die all}	*Christ's Bloodie Sweat* (1613)	1/5471(0.018%)
91	"like a seeled dove" (sig. C2)	{seeled dove}	*The broken heart* (1633)	1/5471(0.018%)

of the rare correspondences after 1612 between Ford's work and the *Elegye*. The first column in Tables 4.1 and 4.2 gives the collocation number from the full RCP search results.[2] The final columns indicate the rarity of usage in documents located before the date of the *Elegye*. This is calculated from the number of documents returned by the search prior to 1612 divided by the 5,471 documents that are searchable before that date.[3]

Even though John Ford has only nine works in the EEBO database his work registers a total of 16 different rare matches (Clarke 2014, Table 4.4). There is only one John Ford example that precedes the *Elegye*, and that is "And set thee as a President to Men" (W. S. 1612, sig. B2^{v}), the entirety of which Ford had already used in *Fames memoriall* (1606). This provides a very strong unique prior match.[4] Taken together with the 15 matches that follow the *Elegye*, a conclusion of mutual borrowing can be reached, and the declaration that Ford originated the poem can be asserted with reasonable confidence.[5] The facts that both John Ford and William Peter had attended Exeter College from 1601 to 1602, that they had shared the same tutor there, and that memorial poems were Ford's province reinforce the association. It appears that the initials 'W.S.' had been used and identifiable locutions had been lifted from the Shakespeare canon with the sole purpose of concealing John Ford's identity and suggesting Shakspere's. So, there are several cases where Shakspere has unjustifiably been given the writing credit.

4.2 William Jaggard's Integrity

For the third edition of *The Passionate Pilgrime* (1612), the printer William Jaggard added work from Thomas Heywood's *Troia Britanica* (1609), which was one of his earlier printings. In *An Apology for Actors* (1612), Heywood protests of

> a manifest iniury done me in that worke, by taking the two Epistles of *Paris* to *Helen*, and *Helen* to *Paris*, and printing them in a lesse volume, vnder the name of another ['W. Shakespere'], which may put the world in opinion I might steale them from him; and hee [Heywood] to doe himself right, hath since published them in his owne name: but as I must acknowledge my lines not worthy his [Shakspere's] patronage, vnder whom he hath publish them, so the Author [Shakspere] I know much offended with M. Iaggard (that altogether vnknowne to him) presumed to make so bold with his name [Shakspere]. (Heywood 1612, sigs G4^{v} & G4$^{r)}$

In fact, the title page of the third edition of *The Passionate Pilgrime* (1612) clearly declares, "Where-unto is newly added two Loue-Epistles, the first from Paris to Hellen, and Hellens answere backe againe to

Paris". The result was that in later impressions of the book, the name 'W. Shakespere' on the title page was cancelled. Curiously, the Bodleian Library has a copy containing two title pages, the first without the name 'W. Shakespeare' and the second with it.[6] Diana Price, noting the confusing use of pronouns, concludes that "Heywood is the much offended 'Author' not 'Shakespeare'" (2012, 139).[7] However, if the 'hee' in the line "hee to doe himself right, hath since published them in his owne name" is Heywood (and we know he *had* since published them under his own name), then the passage makes sense. So I suggest that it was Shakspere who objected to his name being used—and the fact should be acknowledged that Heywood thought Shakspere *was* the 'author' of works in that publication—and so the point here is that Shakspere's name had again been used on work that was not his. Sidney Lee informs us that

> Jaggard's fraudulent methods of work as an anthologist are capable of almost endless illustration. A venture of the year in which Jaggard became a freeman of the Stationers' Company [1591] precisely anticipates Jaggard's conduct in printing in a single volume 'small poems' by various pens [... and] attributing them all on the title-page to one author who was only responsible for a few of them. (1905, 16)

4.3 The *First Folio*

After years of corrupt Shakespeare manuscripts finding their way into print as 'bad' quartos—usually derived from memorial reconstructions by actors who knew only their own part—improved versions of Shakespeare work appeared in *Mr. William Shake-speare's Comedies, Histories, & Tragedies* (1623), otherwise known as the *First Folio*. The printer was William Jaggard. The collection of 36 plays appeared on 1 November 1623, seven years after Shakspere's death, and apart from *Pericles* and *The Two Noble Kinsmen* it contains all the extant plays that are usually attributed to Shakspere. It originally sold at 15 shillings for an unbound copy and £1 bound in calfskin (Dutton 2016, 10).[8]

The only 'author' mentioned in the *First Folio* is the Stratford man. John Heminge and Henry Condell were fellow players in Shakspere's King's Men, and their *First Folio* opening address to the Earl of Pembroke and the Earl of Montgomery refers to the plays "out-liuing him [their author]" and lamenting that "he not hauing the fate, common with some, to be exequutor [sic] to his owne writings". Their motive in publishing, they say, is to "keepe the memory of so worthy a Friend, & Fellow aliue, as was our SHAKESPEARE, by humble offer of his playes". In their following address "To the great Variety of Readers" they maintain that "It had bene a thing, we confesse, worthie to haue bene wished, that the Author himself had liu'd to haue set forth, and ouerseen his owne writings". In other eulogies, Leonard Digges in "To the Memorie of the deceased author Maister W. Shakespeare" refers to "thy Workes", and Hugh Holland's "Vpon the Lines and Life of the Famous Scenicke Poet, Master William Shakespeare" informs us that "His dayes are done, that made the dainty Playes". These are clear statements that Shakspere was the sole author of the collection.

Ben Jonson also produced a tribute to "The Author Mr William Shakespeare" in the *First Folio* (1623) referring to the "Sweet Swan of Avon", an apparent reference to Stratford upon Avon:

> Sweet Swan of Auon! What a sight it were
> To see thee in our waters yet appeare,
> And make those flights upon the bankes of Thames,
> That so did take Eliza, and our Iames!

However, according to Edmund Malone "Neither Queen Elizabeth, nor King James the First, nor Charles the First, I believe, ever went to the publick theatre" (Malone 1800, 183), so wherever "Eliza and Iames" saw the "Swan of Auon" it was not on the banks of the Thames at Southwark. It would be natural to assume that "Avon" referred to Stratford. However, Alexander Waugh has pointed out that Hampton Court, which is near the Thames, was also known as 'Avon' (2014, 97–103) and refers to Camden's Latin quotation from John Leland's *Genethliacon* (1543):

> Est locus insolito rerum splendore superbus,
> Alluiturque uaga Tamisini fluminis unda,
> Nomine ab antique iam tempore dictus Auona.[9]

Camden renders this into English as

> A place, which Nature's choicest gifts adorn,
> Where Thame's kind streams in gentle currents turn,
> The name of Hampton hath for ages born (1695, 309–10).

This example alone suggests that Jonson is deliberately being cryptic in his preface and that his tribute to Shakspere should not be taken literally. He continues

> For a good Poet's made, as well as borne.
> And such wert though.
> Or, when thy sockes were on
> Leave thee alone, for the comparison
> Of all, that insolent Greece, or haughtie Rome
> Sent forth, or since from their ashes come.

The third line invites interpretation, and the temptation will be resisted here. Jonson now cites a well-known dichotomy of the Elizabethan age, the division of things into Nature and Art. This view located anything that did not originate from the reality of Nature (and so was "not of Nature's family") in the inventive sphere of Art:

> The merry Greeke, tart Aristophanes,
> Neat Terence, witty Plautus now not please;
> But antiquated, and deserted lye
> As they were not of Nature's family.
> Yet must I not give Nature all: Thy Art
> My gentle Shakespeare, must enjoy a part.

This is an ambiguous passage. The claim that "they were not of Nature's family" could mean that the work of these three classical dramatists was in some way unreal. Titus Maccius Plautus (251–184 BC) was born in the small Umbrian mountain village of Sarsina and rose to become ancient Rome's best-known comedy playwright. The English academic and poet, Nicholas Grimald (1519–62), commenting on his own translation of Cicero's *De Officiis* (1556), claimed that both Plautus and Terence assumed the ownership of work they had translated from Greek, and so "I call it mine as Plautus and Terence called the comedies theirs which they made out of Greek" (Ward and Waller 1964, IV 24–25). Grimald probably had the Greek writer Menander in mind whose comedies Plautus adapted.

Terence (190–159BC), or Publius Terentius Afer, was born at Cathage and was an African enslaved to the Roman senator Terentius Lucanus who had him educated before liberating him. Terence went on to write celebrated drama, or at least, that was how it appeared. In 1570, Roger Ascham, tutor to Elizabeth I, proposed Scipio as the real author of the Terence plays in his book *The Scholemaster* (1570):

> Bicause it is well known, by good recorde of learning and that by *Ciceroes* owne witnes, that some Comedies bearyng *Terence* name were written by worthy *Scipio*, and wise *Lælius*, and namely *Heauton*: and *Adelphi*. (Ascham 1570, 288)

Whether or not Terence really did act as a mask for Scipio is irrelevant. The point is that it was an Elizabethan point of view. Aristophanes (c.448–385 BC) was a Greek comedy writer whose first three plays, *The Banqueters*, *The Babylonians*, and *Acharnians*, were produced under the name of an older friend Callistratus. In fact, to disguise his youth, he had once entered *Acharnians* in a competition using the pseudonym Detalis. So it is feasible that Jonson is alluding to a misrepresentation of the ownership of work and that the last three lines associate these three writers with Shakspere.

This was not the only time that Terence was compared to Shakespeare. When John Davies of Hereford published the *Scourge of Folly*, a collection of epigrams, he presented Epigram 159 as a tribute "To our English Terence, Mr Will: Shake-speare" (Davies c.1611, 76). As for Jonson, one of his biographers, David Riggs, believes his contribution to Shakespeare's *First Folio* ran deeper than a couple of commendatory verses:

> the men who prepared the folio for the press (and Jonson may well have been one of them) remade Shakespeare in Jonson's image. Heminge's and Condell's prefatory letter "To the Great Variety of Readers" echoes Jonson's Induction to *Bartholomew Fair* [...] The prefatory poems by Jonson, Hugh Holland, James Mabbe, and Leonard Digges transform Shakespeare into a specifically literary figure whose works have achieved the status of modern classics; the closest analogue to these tributes are the poems prefixed to Jonson's 1616 folio. The scribes who prepared the copy for the Shakespeare folio abandoned the "light pointing" or "playhouse punctuation" of the Shakespeare quartos and adopted the so-called logical pointing that Jonson had employed in his *Works* (1616). The extensive use of parentheses, semicolons and end-stopped lines in the 1623 folio owes more to Jonson's example than to Shakespeare's habits of composition. (Riggs 1989, 276)

The "echo" that Riggs refers to in the Induction from *Bartholomew Fair* concerns Jonson's address to his audience:

> and it shall be lawful for any man to judge his six-pen'orth, his twelve-pen'orth, so to his eighteen pence, two shillings, half a crown, to the value of his place, provided his place get not above his wit. (Lines 89–93)

In Shakespeare's *First Folio* dedication "To the Great Variety of Readers", which is attributed at the end to John Heminges and Henry Condell, we find something similar:

> Judge your six-pen'orth, your shilling's worth, your five shillings' worth at a time, or higher, so you rise to the just rates, and welcome.

Also, in this same piece, it states that it would have been preferable if the author could have overseen his own writings, but "he by death departed from that right". Ian Donaldson points out that "The notion of an author departing with his rights recurs frequently in Jonson" (2011, 373). So was Heminge and Condell's *First Folio* commendation actually written by Ben Jonson? Did Jonson have a greater hand in the production of the *First Folio* than has previously been thought? We know that the *First Folio* had been edited (unless it was a sales trick) because in the "To the Great Variety of Readers" we find

> As where (before) you were abus'd with diuerse stolne, and surreptitious copies, maimed, and deformed by the frauds and stealthes of iniurious imposters, that expos'd them: euen those, are now offer'd to your view cur'd, and perfect of their limbes.

So one has to ask: Who edited them? Who had the breadth of knowledge of English history to take on such a task? Francis Bacon would be an outstanding candidate, and it might be worth noting that according to Archbishop Tenison, Ben Jonson later worked for Francis Bacon, translating his *Essays* (1625) into Latin:

> The Latin translation of them was a work performed by divers hands; by those of Dr Hackett (late Bishop of Lichfield), Mr. Benjamin Jonson (the learned and judicious poet) and some others whose names I once heard from Dr Rawley; but I cannot recall them now. (Tenison 1679, 60)

The theme that emerges here is that as a record of contribution to the plays, the *First Folio* (1623) is an unreliable document. Stories emerged several years later of Shakspere's theatrical activities. The Reverend John Ward, whose diary or commonplace book covers the period 1648–79, recorded, "I have heard that Mr. Shakespeare was a natural wit, without any art at all" (Severn 1839, 183). In 1687, the dramatist Edward Ravenscroft published his updated version of *Titus Andronicus*, where in "To the Reader" he states:

> I have been told by some anciently conversant with the Stage that it was Originally not his but brought by a private Author to be Acted, and he only gave some Master-touches to one or two of the Principal Parts or Characters. (Ravenscroft 1687)

We do not learn who this "private author" was, but mere "touches" are insufficient to award Shakspere authorship priority. The testimony of Ward and Ravenscroft might easily be dismissed as 'hearsay', but even so, modern stylistic methods have strongly suggested other hands in the plays (Vickers 2002): for example, Thomas Middleton in *All's Well That Ends Well* (Maguire and Smith 2012, 13),[10] Thomas Nashe in *1 Henry VI* (Taylor 1995, 145–205; Vickers 2007, 328–338), Christopher Marlowe in *3 Henry VI* (Burrows and Craig 2017), John Fletcher in *Henry VIII* (Spedding 1850, 115),[11] Thomas Middleton in *Macbeth* (Vickers 2010), Thomas Middleton in *Timon of Athens* (Wells and Taylor 2005, 943), and George Peele in *Titus Andronicus* (Wells and Taylor 2005, 155). As for two plays not in the *First Folio*, the first two acts of *Pericles* have been attributed to the minor dramatist George Wilkins (Jackson 2008), and *The Two Noble Kinsmen* was attributed in the 1634 quarto to "Mr John Fletcher and Mr. William Shakespeare" (Fletcher and Shakespeare 1634), although the latter attribution might have been to enhance sales.

4.4 RCP Results

RCP is a method that the present author developed in the years 2012–13. Here, a target play is painstakingly examined phrase by phrase, collocation by collocation, in order to identify the locutions from that work that were in rare usage at the time. For this, Chadwyck–Healey's EEBO database containing sixteenth- and seventeenth-century works is eminently suitable for the task. If a phrase is rare, which is arbitrarily defined as being in use by less than 0.17% of the searchable works in EEBO before the assumed date of the target play, a record is made of the authors who employed it both before and after this date.[12] When the target play searches have been completed, a contribution is assigned to a particular author only if rare phrases are shared with the unattributed play as mutual borrowing, that is, the author has rare matches both before and after the target date of the play. In this way, both *The Comedy of Errors* and *Love's Labour's Lost* have been found to contain contributions from Thomas Nashe and Francis Bacon, with Thomas Dekker and Thomas Heywood implicated as possible later contributors. *The Tempest* has strong contributions from Bacon, and in a more recent study *3 Henry VI* (both the *Octavo* and *Folio* versions) registers contributions from Christopher Marlowe, Robert Greene, and Anthony Munday. So, the notion that William Shakspere of Stratford was the single author of every single play in the *First Folio* is unsustainable. Yet no one else in the *First Folio* receives any credit. The testimony and indeed the integrity of those who provided eulogies in the preface must therefore be brought into question. It appears that Ben Jonson, being as forthright as he was, found a way of maintaining an uncorrupted conscience. He left an ambiguous tribute.

So far, a case has been presented that Shakspere was an opportunist businessman, that several publications appeared under his name that were either not his or contained other uncredited contributions, and that he bought plays from other dramatists which he passed off as his own. If he added any dialogue at all to these plays it seems not to have been well regarded. We now turn to his contemporary Francis Bacon and examine his interest in drama. Later we shall examine a selection of Shakespeare plays and use the RCP method to suggest their contributors.

Notes

1 The title page bears the year 1600. An earlier 1600 quarto has no attribution.
2 See Clarke (2014, Table 4.3).
3 Here the limit of 'rarity' below which a return is recorded is set at less than 0.17% of the documents dated to before 1612.

4 There is also "One example or president to both Noble and understanding men" in Ford (1613).
5 More accurately, the argument is for Ford's contribution, but the reasonable assumption has been made that being personal in character, a poem would not be revised from the work of some unknown originator.
6 Malone 328, Bodleian Library, Oxford. See also Sidney Lee (1905, 56).
7 There is also the illogical argument that since the title page without attribution is less worn than the one with, then the latter was the last of the two that was added. Surely, it must be the former that was last if it was less worn.
8 Twenty shillings was equivalent to £1, and £1 in 1623 had the spending power of £110 in 2006.
9 This appears under the heading 'AVONDVNVM' in Leland (1543).
10 This has been disputed by Brian Vickers and Marcus Dahl at www.ies.sas.ac.uk/about-us/news/middleton-and-shakespeare, accessed online 16 December 2017.
11 This followed an investigation of *Henry VIII* by Charles Knight in *Studies of Shakspere* (1849). Fletcher is given as a part contributor in Wells and Taylor (2005, 1245).
12 The level of rarity is defined as the maximum number of allowed EEBO returns from records prior to the assumed date of the play. It can be arbitrarily set, and there is no doubt that by allowing more returns and increasing the percentage rarity, more information will accrue. However, the advantage of producing additional data must be balanced against the disadvantage of the extra logging (see Appendix G).

Bibliography

Ascham, Roger. *The Scolemaster*. London: Printed by Iohn Daye, 1570.

Burrows, John, and Hugh Craig. "The joker in the pack? Marlowe, Kyd, and the co-authorship of *Henry VI, Part 3*." In Gary Taylor and Gabriel Egan, eds. *The New Oxford Shakespeare Authorship Companion*. Oxford: Oxford University Press, 2017.

Camden, William. *Camden's Britannia Newly Translated into English*. London: Printed by A. Swall and T. Child for A. and J. Churchil, 1695.

Clarke, Barry R. "A linguistic analysis of Francis Bacon's contribution to three Shakespeare plays: *A Comedy of Errors*, *Love's Labour's Lost*, and *The Tempest*." PhD thesis. Brunel University, UK, 2014.

Davies, John [of Hereford]. *Scourge of Folly*. London: Printed by E. A. for Richard Redmer, 1611.

Donaldson, Ian. *Ben Jonson: A Life*. Oxford: Oxford University Press, 2011.

Dutton, Richard. *Shakespeare, Court Dramatist*. Oxford: Oxford University Press, 2016.

Fletcher, John, and William Shakespeare [?]. *The Two Noble Kinsmen*. London: Printed at London by Tho. Cotes for Iohn Waterson, 1634. STC: 11075.

Ford, John. *Fames Memoriall, or the Earle of Deuonshire Deceased*. London: Printed [by R. Bradock] for Christopher Purset, 1606. STC: 11158.

Ford, John. *The Golden Meane*. London: Printed [by H. Lownes] for Jeffrey Chorlton, 1613. STC: 17757.

Foster, Donald W. *Elegy by W. S.: A Study in Attribution*. Newark: University of Delaware Press, 1989.

Greg, Walter, ed. *Henslowe's Diary*. London, A. H. Bullen, 1904.

Heywood, Thomas. *An Apology for Actors*. London: Printed by Nicholas Okes, 1612.

Holdsworth, R. V. "Middleton's authorship of *A Yorkshire Tragedy*." *Review of English Studies* 45 (1994): 1–25.

Jackson, MacDonald P. *Studies in Attribution: Middleton and Shakespeare*. Austria: University of Salzburg, 1979.

Jackson, MacDonald P. *Defining Shakespeare, Pericles as Test Case*. Oxford: Oxford University Press, 2008.

Lake, David. *The Canon of Thomas Middleton's Plays*. Cambridge: Cambridge University Press, 1975.

Lee, Sidney, ed. *The Passionate Pilgrim: Being a Reproduction in Facsimile of the First Edition 1599*. Oxford: Clarendon Press, 1905.

Leland, John. *Genethliacon*. London: R. Wolfe, 1543.

Macguire, Laurie, and Emma Smith. "Many hands – A new Shakespeare collaboration?" *Times Literary Supplement* (19 April 2012).

Malone, Edmund. *Historical Account of the Rise and Progress of the English Stage*. Basil: J. J. Tourneisen, 1800.

Monsarrat, Gilles D. "A Funeral Elegy: Ford, W.S., and Shakespeare." *Review of English Studies* 53 (2002): 186–203.

Price, Diana. *Shakespeare's Unorthodox Biography: New Evidence of an Authorship Problem*. Shakespeare-authorship.com, 2012.

Ravenscroft, Edward. *Titus Andronicus, OR THE Rape of Lavina*. London: Printed by J. B. for J. Hindmarsh, 1687.

Riggs, David. *Ben Jonson: A Life*. Cambridge, MA: Harvard University Press, 1989.

Severn, Charles, ed. *Diary of the Rev. John Ward*. London: Henry Colburn, 1839.

Shakspeare [?], W. *A Yorkshire Tragedy*. London: Printed by R. E. for Thomas Pauier, 1608.

Spedding, James. *Gentleman's Magazine* 178 (Aug–Oct 1850).

Taylor, Gary. "Shakespeare and others: The authorship of Henry the Sixth, Part One." *Medieval and Renaissance Drama* 7 (1995): 145–205.

Tenison, Archbishop. *Baconiana* or *Certain Genuine Remains of Sr. Francis Bacon*. London: J. D. for Richard Chiswell, 1679.

Vickers, Brian. *'Counterfeiting' Shakespeare*. Cambridge: Cambridge University Press, 2002.

Vickers, Brian. "Incomplete Shakespeare: or, denying coauthorship in '1 Henry VI'." *Shakespeare Quarterly* 58, No. 3. Special Issue, The Complete Shakespeare (Autumn 2007): 311–52.

Vickers, Brian. "Disintegrated: Did Middleton adapt Macbeth?" *Times Literary Supplement* 28 (May 2010).

Ward, A. W., and A. R. Waller, eds. *The Cambridge History of English Literature*. 15 vols. Cambridge: Cambridge University Press, 1964.

Waugh, Alexander. "The true meaning of Ben Jonson's phrase 'Sweet Swan of Avon'." *The Oxfordian* 16 (September 2014): 97–103.

Wells, Stanley, and Gary Taylor, eds. *The Oxford Shakespeare*. Second edition. Oxford: Oxford University Press, 2005.

W. S. *A Funerall Elegye In memory of the late Vertous Maister William Peter of Whipton neere Excester*. London: G. Eld for Thomas Thorpe, 1612. sig. B2^{v}.

5 Bacon's Dramatic Entrance

Francis Bacon's place in the politics of Jacobethan England is examined. Traditional academic biographies of Francis Bacon pay little attention to his composition of fictional entertainments. However, he appears to have been an active organizer and writer of Inns of Court masques and revels, as well as an author of devices for Queen's Day celebrations.

5.1 Contemporary Opinion of Bacon

Sir Francis Bacon was a philosopher, statesman, essayist, and lawyer, who, during the reign of King James, gained promotion to the office of Lord Chancellor. His academic gifts were held in such high esteem, that Dr Thomas Tenison, Archbishop of Canterbury, was brought to exclaim

> Such great Wits, are not the common Births of Time: And they, surely, intended to signifie so much who said of the Phoenix (though in Hyperbole as well as Metaphor) that Nature gives the World that *Individual Species*, but once in five hundred Years. (Tenison 1679, 5)

Ben Jonson, who did not distribute his encomiums liberally, enthused

> Yet there happened in my time one noble speaker, who was full of gravity in his speaking; his language, where he could spare or pass a jest, was nobly censorious. No man ever spake more neatly, more presly, more weightily, or suffered less emptiness, less idleness, in what he uttered. No member of his speech, but consisted of his own graces. His hearers could not cough, or look aside from him, without loss. He commanded where he spoke, and had his judges angry and pleased at his devotion. No man had their affections more in his power. The fear of every man that heard him was, lest he should make an end [...] I have and do reverence him, for the greatness that was only proper to himself, in that he seemed to me ever, by his work, one of the greatest men, and most worthy of admiration, that had been in many ages. (Jonson 1892, 30–31)[1]

Such was Bacon's command of his native tongue that Samuel Johnson, the author of one of the first English dictionaries, thought that "a Dictionary of the English Language might be compiled from Bacon's writings alone" (Boswell 1826, III 174). His mind might have been diverted by the glacial logic of the law courts, but, nevertheless, Percy Bysshe Shelley was led to remark,

> Lord Bacon was a poet. His language has a sweet and majestic rhythm, which satisfies the sense, no less than the almost superhuman wisdom of his philosophy satisfies the intellect. (Shelley 1840, I 32)

It seems that Francis Bacon also regarded himself as such. The barrister and poet, John Davies, was a friend of Bacon's and took a journey north to meet King James who was about to take up the English throne. Keen for advancement, Bacon wanted Davies to recommend him to the new king. So, in a letter to Davies dated 28 March 1603, Bacon revealed his activities in poetry (see Figure 5.1).[2]

It appears that others shared Shelley's view. Eulogy IV by the unidentified R. P. in *Manes Verulamiani*, a book of tributes to Lord Bacon published shortly after his death, alludes to his dressing of philosophy in the guise of comedy:

> As Eurydice wandering through the shades of Dis longed to caress Orpheus, so did Philosophy entangled in the subtleties of Schoolmen seek Bacon as a deliverer, with such winged hand as Orpheus lightly touched the lyre's strings, the Styx before scarce ruffled now at last bounding, with like hand stroked Philosophy raised high her crest; nor did he with workmanship of fussy meddlers patch, but he renovated her walking lowly in the shoes of Comedy. (*Manes Verulamiani* 1626, Eulogy IV)

Biographies on Bacon traditionally pass over his interest in drama; however, there is ample evidence of his commitment, and this will be presented here.[3]

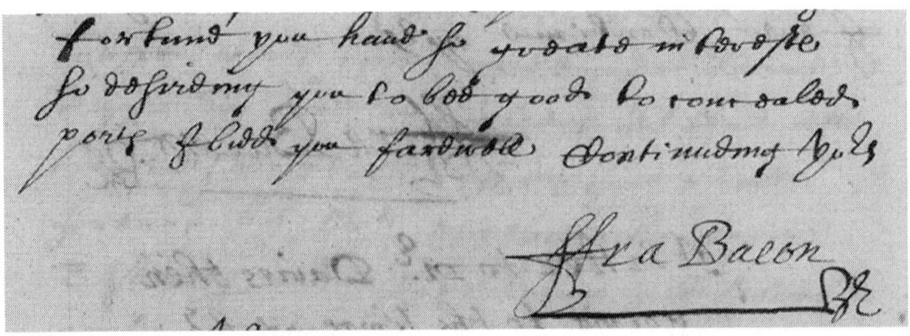

Figure 5.1 Copy of a letter from Francis Bacon to John Davies (1603). The second line is "so desiring you to be good to concealed poets".

5.2 Early Years

Francis Bacon took his first breath on 22 January 1561 at York House on the Strand. His parents had the genetic credentials that young Francis would later use to great advantage. His father Sir Nicholas Bacon had a sharp legal mind, having been appointed Lord Keeper of the Seal, while his mother, Lady Anne Bacon, was an expert in the classics. Anne could not only claim fluency in Latin, Greek, Italian, and French but could also boast a scholarly translation of the Anglican Bishop John Jewel's *Defence of the Church of England* from Latin into English. She was certainly well connected. Her father, Sir Anthony Coke, had tutored the young Edward VI, and her sister Mildred had married Sir William Cecil, Lord Burghley, the most powerful man in Queen Elizabeth's government.

There were five children in all, three from Sir Nicholas's first marriage, and two from his second with Anne. Of these last two, Francis was the younger, with Anthony three years his senior. The family's youngest undoubtedly enjoyed a privileged childhood at York House. Surrounded by walls and turrets, it was a substantial property, with four stables, ten cottages, and seven gardens, some of which stretched down to the Thames, where young Francis could watch the queen pass by on the colourful royal barge. The Lord Keeper was a major beneficiary from Henry VIII's break with Rome, accumulating wealth from confiscated monastic property and owning land in six counties. The aristocracy also grew rich on dissolved Catholicism, and the Protestant Elizabeth preferred to rely on them for her Privy Councillors, men whose favour had already been purchased.

In 1568, Sir Nicholas completed the building of Gorhambury House, two miles from St. Albans and 18 miles north-west of London in the Hertfordshire countryside. As well as a mill-house, a bakehouse, and a brewhouse, there was also a chapel, orchard, stables, excellent gardens, and water pipes that ran into each chamber from the ponds a mile away. The queen and her entourage visited four times, and with the rooms being low, Elizabeth once enquired why the house was so small. "Madam," replied Sir Nicholas, "my house is well, but it is you that have made me too great for my house" (Spedding *et al.*, 1857–74, XIII.357).

In April 1573, at the age of 12 years 3 months, Francis went with his brother Anthony to Trinity College, Cambridge, where they shared a chamber. His tutor was Dr John Whitgift, later Archbishop of Canterbury, and it was there that his objections to the Aristotelian system fell into place, which, according to Bacon's chaplain Dr William Rawley, came about

> not for the worthlessness of the author, to whom he [Bacon] would ever ascribe all high attributes, but for the unfruitfulness of the way; being a philosophy [...] only strong for disputations and contentions, but barren of the production of works for the benefit of the life of man; in which mind he continued to his dying day. (Rawley 1657, b2^{v})

They left Cambridge in March 1576 without qualifications, and six months later, during an apprenticeship in diplomacy, Francis set foot on French soil at Calais with Sir Amias Paulet, the Ambassador in France. There he followed the Court of Henry III, to Blois, Tours, and Poitiers. However, in mid-February 1579, his father died of a chill while sleeping under an open window. In the process, Lady Anne inherited Gorhambury House, and Anthony was heir to properties in Hertfordshire and Middlesex, but Francis was left with only some dubious properties and leases that raised a modest £300 per year. With no other means of income he quickly took on debt.

In 1579, in need of a profession, he enrolled at Gray's Inn law school and moved into his father's old chambers at Coney's Court just north of Holborn. There he studied the common law from manuscript case reports, from statute law as written in the Parliament rolls, and from treatises penned by former judges. According to Stow's *Annales*, the lawyer's journey to the top was tortuous:

> after some years well imployed in the Studies of their professions they obtain the degree and stile of Inner Barresters, and at the seven yeares end, they proceed or become Outer Barresters, and are then said to be called to the Barre, and shortly after that they are allowed to make publike profession and practise of the Law in all Courts and to give Councell unto all Clients and hereupon they are also called Councellors of the Law, and Learned Councell. (Stow 1631, 1073)

After several more years, they were allowed to read law publicly in their halls after which they could be called Reader, followed by Double Reader, Apprentice at Law, Bencher, and finally Ancient. While it usually took seven years to be qualified to plead as a barrister in Westminster Hall ("called to the Barre"), Francis Bacon achieved it in three, reporting that the queen "hath pulled me over the bar" (Spedding 1861–74, I.348). With his cousin Robert Cecil, Lord Burghley's son, intent on having no rivals in his quest for high office, the queen's opinion of Bacon became corrupted and he was overlooked for several executive positions.

On 27 June 1583, Bacon was declared an utter (or outer) barrister, and on 10 February 1586 he was allowed the privilege of attending Gray's Inn Pensions [committee meetings] with the proviso that "Mr. Francis Bacon maie have place with the Readers att the Reders table but not to have any voyce in pencon" (Fletcher 1901, 72). However, in the Lent term of 1587 he was promoted to Reader (Stewart and Knight 2012, 1.xxiii), a move that would have allowed him to contribute to Pensions and influence the affairs of Gray's Inn. He was a regular attendee at these meetings from 20 May 1586 throughout the 1590s, being privy to discussions regarding such business as the expulsion of undesirable students from the Inn, charitable donations, building alterations, the assignment of members to important posts, and the allocation of funds to Christmas revels and court masques.

In 1584, Bacon's plan for a new system of philosophy began to crystallize, a scheme he called his Great Instauration or Renewal of Learning. Observation and experiment would play a greater part than they had hitherto and would put an end to unproductive philosophical disputes that had disabled scientific progress. There would be new colleges that abandoned the Aristotelian approach and instead devoted their resources to the new mechanical methods. Realizing that he needed an influential position in government to implement his grand scheme, in 1584 he took his first step on the political ladder, entering Parliament to represent Melcombe in Dorset.

From 1584 to 1597, five Parliaments were summoned, and Bacon sat in each. In the Parliament of 1586 he sat for Taunton, in 1588 he sat for Liverpool, in 1592–3 he sat for Middlesex, and in 1597 he sat for Ipswich. However, from 1584 to 1597 Parliament sat only five times, and from 1607 to 1613 it sat for a total of only six months. The speeches which Bacon delivered and the committees he sat on absorbed only a small portion of his time. He was certainly underemployed in the years when the early Shakespeare work appeared, and he had ample time to prosecute substantial projects. Indeed, in his *Lives of the Lord Chancellors*, Lord John Campbell claimed that around 1593–94 Francis Bacon was not only impoverished but also had "abundant leisure" (Campbell 1851, II.247).[4]

It was around 1589 that Francis Bacon began to employ a team of scriveners to copy out work that was in progress, with his brother Anthony providing the finance. On 25 January 1595, Francis wrote to his brother from Twickenham

> I have here an idle pen or two, specially one that was cozened [cheated], thinking to have gotten some money this term; I pray send me somewhat else for them to write out besides your Irish collection which is almost done. There is a collection of Dr. James of foreign states, largeliest [sic] of Flanders, which, though it be no great matter, yet I would be glad to have it. (Spedding 1861–74, I.349)

One wonders why Francis Bacon kept scriveners in regular employment for his first recognized publication, a slim volume of ten essays bound up with his *Colours of Good and Evil* and *Religious Meditations*, did not appear until 1597.

5.3 Debt, Drama, and Design

The first record of Bacon's involvement in a dramatic production occurs in the credits at the end of the printed quarto of *The Misfortunes of Arthur*, an Inns of Court play that was performed at Greenwich before the queen on 28 February 1587–8 (see Figure 5.2).[5] By citing the records of the Audit Office, which show that the "gentlemen of grayes In" performed "betwixte Christmas & Shrouetid", Alan Stewart and Harriet Knight have queried the date of the enactment, pointing out that 28 February

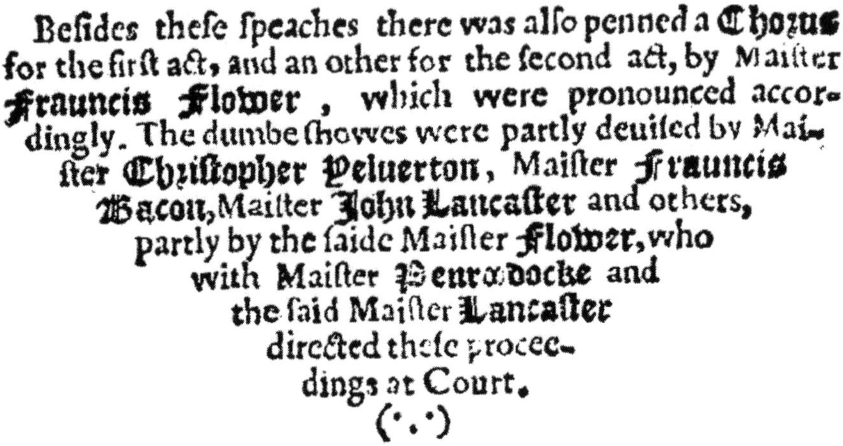

Beſides theſe ſpeaches there was alſo penned a Chorus for the firſt act, and an other for the ſecond act, by Maiſter Frauncis Flower, which were pronounced accordingly. The dumbe ſhowes were partly deuiſed by Maiſter Chriſtopher Yeluerton, Maiſter Frauncis Bacon, Maiſter John Lancaſter and others, partly by the ſaide Maiſter Flower, who with Maiſter Penroddocke and the ſaid Maiſter Lancaſter directed theſe proceedings at Court.

(·.·)

Figure 5.2 Francis Bacon credited with writing dumb shows in the play *The Misfortunes of Arthur* (1587–8). Thomas Hughes, *Certaine deu[is]es and shewes* (1587).

was "a full week *after* Shrovetide" (Stewart and Knight 2012, I.63–64). Although eight men were involved in the writing, the main credit went to Thomas Hughes (Foster 1889).[6] The play was published in 1588 and records that "The dumbe shows were partly devised by Maister Christopher Yelverton, Maister Frauncis Bacon, Maister John Lancaster and others, partly by the saide Maister flower"; see Figure 5.2 (Hughes 1557, sig. G2).[7] There are five dumb shows in *Misfortunes*, one before each act, but the precise allocation of credit is unknown. Nicholas Trotte, who wrote the Introduction to *Misfortunes*, featured prominently in Francis Bacon's financial life in the last years of Elizabeth's reign. Due to a series of loans from Trotte throughout the 1590s, by 1601 Bacon was indebted to him for £2,650 plus £1,479 interest (Jardine and Stewart 1999, 207–8).

The government lay in the hands of the queen, Lord Burghley, and about 20 Privy Councillors, so two years later Bacon was honoured to be elected to a committee which included all the Privy Councillors of the House. Meanwhile, his brother Anthony was in France visiting King Henry of Navarre, while sending intelligence reports at his own expense back from Europe to Lord Burghley who took all the credit. Characters from the court of Navarre would later appear in Shakespeare's *Love's Labour's Lost*. In 1592, Anthony returned to England, exhausted and burdened with gout. Francis introduced him to the queen's favourite, Robert Devereux, the second Earl of Essex, and together they moved in a circle that included the Earl of Southampton, the nobleman who, in the next two years, would patronize Shakespeare's long poems *Venus and Adonis* and *The Rape of Lucrece*.[8]

The manoeuvring for position in the royal court created factions. On the one side was the Earl of Essex, to whom Anthony attached himself, and on the other was Robert Cecil, whose father, Lord Burghley, was the most powerful man in England. At the age of 31, realizing that he needed his uncle's assistance, Francis Bacon revealed his life plan to his uncle, one which declared his commitment to philosophy. For a man as wise as Bacon, one wonders how he thought the revelation could advance his prospects in government:

> I confess that I have as vast contemplative ends as I have moderate civil ends, for I have taken all knowledge to be my province; and if I could purge it of two sorts of rovers, whereof the one with frivolous disputations, confutations, and verbosities, the other with blind experiments and auricular traditions and impostures, hath committed so many spoils, I hope I should bring in industrious observations, grounded conclusions, and profitable inventions and discoveries; the best state of that province.[9]

Bacon's intention was for a new kind of university founded on practical science, one equipped with mechanical devices; stones, plants, and animals for dissection; and facilities for studying medicine—in short, a departure from Aristotle's fruitless formal logic and a celebration of a new experimental method. From Lord Burghley, Bacon needed finance and, above all, the influence to set the project in motion. It was a clear statement of Francis Bacon's main purpose in life, the initiation of new institutions for investigative practical learning for which he needed the assistance of government. Unfortunately, Bacon's grand scheme found little sympathy with Burghley. For him it was a confession of Bacon's misplaced priorities, ones that did nothing to address the queen's real concerns: consolidation of the Protestant faith and the defence of England. Bacon soon realized that there was only one route to the queen's favour, so he aligned himself with Essex, the queen's darling, writing letters on his behalf and advising his family on their education.

On 17 November 1592, Queen's Day, the Earl of Essex presented a device before Elizabeth that Francis Bacon had devised. James Spedding, the Victorian editor of Bacon's *Works*, remarks that in 1734 Robert Stephens published "Mr. Bacon's discourse in prayse of his Soveraigne" and "Mr. Bacon in prayse of knowledge" from manuscripts written in a fair hand, which were given to him by Robert Harley, the first Earl of Oxford. Stephens thought they had originally been in the possession of Bacon's chaplain, Dr William Rawley, and that "both formed part of some fanciful device presented at the Court of Elizabeth in 1592" (Spedding 1870, v–vi).[10] Copies of both speeches entitled "Of Tribute, or giving what is dew" also appear in the Northumberland Manuscripts collection under the name of "M^{r}. ffrauncis Bacon" (Burgoyne 1902).[11]

The device consists of four parts: "The Praise of the worthiest virtue, Fortitude", "The Praise of the worthiest affection, Love", "The Praise of the worthiest power, Knowledge", and "The Praise of the worthiest person, Queen Elizabeth", the last two corresponding with the two speeches published by Stephens.[12]

In 1593, Bacon entered Parliament representing Middlesex, which included Westminster and the law courts, but naively made a speech in opposition to the queen's tax plans. He argued that the poor man could not afford the queen's triple subsidy, especially with such a short collection period. Parliament largely agreed, but the queen was incensed and denied him access to court. Although perturbed, he was not discouraged, and several times in 1594, beginning on 25 January, he argued cases for the King's Bench, hoping to demonstrate his suitability for the post of Attorney General, while Essex, who was now a Privy Counsellor, vigorously solicited the queen on his behalf. A barrister at Gray's Inn witnessed one of Francis Bacon's speeches and wrote to Anthony Bacon that he had "spangled his speech with unusual words" and that the reason his arguments were so hard to dispute was that one had first to overcome the obstacle of understanding them (Drinker–Bowen 1963, 57). On one occasion, his puritanical mother sent one of his letters to Anthony with the entreaty "Construe the interpretation. I do not understand this enigmatical folded writing" (Drinker–Bowen 1963, 66). Despite the attempt to impress, the post of Attorney General went to the Solicitor General, Edward Coke. Bacon fell ill with dyspepsia, as was usual when confronted with a setback, but by the Easter term of 1594, he had recovered sufficiently to argue alongside Coke in the celebrated *Chudleigh's Case*, involving the law of inheritance and the *Statute of Uses*.

For the legal year 1594, *The Pension Book of Gray's Inn 1569–1669* records that Francis Bacon was elected one of the two Treasurers (Fletcher 1901),[13] a post which he held until 26 November 1594, just before that year's Christmas revels:

> Mr Pooley paid to Mr Bacon one of the treasurers of this house by the hands of Mr Lany the some of xxix^{li} xvii^{s} xi^{d} in full discharge of his accompt of his office of Treasurershippe. (Fletcher 1901, 101)

This would have allowed him to oversee preparations for the 1594–5 Christmas revels. In 1688, details of the revels and the Shrovetide masque at Whitehall were printed by William Canning as the *Gesta Grayorum* (1688), although the depth of detail suggests that it was written shortly after the revels while events were still alive in the author's memory.[14] The *Gesta Grayorum* reports that On Innocents Day, 28 December 1594, "a Comedy of Errors (like to Plautus his Menechmus) was played by the Players"; see Chapter 8 (*Gesta Grayorum* 1688, 22). This is the first known performance of the play that was later identified as Shakespeare's. There are also connections of the revels proceedings with *Love's Labour's Lost*, which seems to have been planned but cancelled (see Chapter 9). It is fairly certain that Bacon wrote the six Counsellors's speeches for these festivities, and in the Inner Temple's Petyt Manuscript collection, there is an incomplete version of Bacon's Counsellors' speeches, written alongside miscellaneous verse by other authors in a single italic hand. The first two of the six Counsellors's speeches are given in full, with some of the third and the last part of the fourth but without the fifth and sixth. According to Alan Stewart and Harriet Knight, the differences between this manuscript version and Canning's text are evidence that the latter has errors (Stewart and Knight 2012, I.599–594).

For Queen's Day, Monday 17 November 1595, Francis Bacon composed another device for presentation by the Earl of Essex to Elizabeth. In a letter from Rowland Whyte to Sir Robert Sydney, dated Saturday 22 November 1595, we learn that there was a "dumb shew" and lines for an old Hermit [philosopher], a Secretary of State, a Soldier, and an Esquire who was played by Bacon's close friend Toby Matthew (Nichols 1823, III.371).[15] According to Brian Vickers "The ostensible plot, in which Philautia tries to persuade Erophilus not to love the queen, obviously represents Essex's own wooing of Elizabeth" (Vickers 2002, xxvii), and the intention of Philautia's orators—the Hermit, Soldier, and Statesman—is to deliver their case to Erophilus's Squire. Francis Bacon is not credited, but there is evidence that this was his work. In Lambeth Palace Library, there exists an unfinished rough draft of a similar device made in Bacon's hand, which informs us of its structure:

> The persons [are] to be three: one dressed like an Heremite or Philosopher, representing Contemplation; the second like a Capitain [sic], representing Fame; and the third like a Counsellor of Estate, representing Experience: the third to begin to the Squire, as being the master of the best behaviour or compliment, though he speak last. (Spedding 1861–74, I.376)[16]

Accompanying the design is a draft of the Hermit's speech. The actual speeches appear in another volume of the same collection, fairly copied with no heading, date, or docket. The pre-supper speeches consist of the Squire's brief introduction, followed by the Hermit's speech in the tilt yard. The after-supper entertainment features the Hermit again, then the Soldier, the Statesman, and finally the Squire's summation (Stewart and Knight 2012, I.678). These characters correspond substantially to Rowland Whyte's description. The Northumberland Manuscripts collection omits "The Squire's Speech in the tilt-yard" which is a brief introduction, but includes "the Hermitt's fyrst speech" which is a response to it and is an oration that does not appear in the Lambeth Palace manuscript. It is followed by "The Hermitt's second speech", "The soldier's speech", "The secretarie's speech", and "The Squyre's speech". Alan Stewart and Harriet Knight have pointed out correspondences between the Hermit's speech and Bacon's *Advancement of Learning* (Stewart and Knight 2012, I.686–87). In the former we find

> The monumentes of witt survive the monumentes of power. The verses of a Poet endure without a sillable lost, whiles States & Empires passe many periods.

The latter has

> wee see then howe farre the monuments of wit and learning, are more durable, than the monuments of power, or of the hands. For haue not the verses of *Homer* continued 25. hundred yeares, or more, without the losse of a sillable, or letter: during which time, infinite Pallaces, Temples, Castles, Cities haue been decayed, and demolished? (Bacon 1605, sig. M^v)

This shows that Bacon returned to his own themes while developing his philosophy.

There is a further piece connected with this device that was left unperformed. According to Dixon (1861, 62–63), Bacon wished to keep Essex and Raleigh on good terms, and since Raleigh had just returned from the Amazon, Bacon composed "a scene in happy allusion to the regions of the Amazon and to Raleigh's voyage". However, clearly affronted by the suggestion, Essex "strikes his pen through Bacon's lines, which drop from the acted scene and from the printed masque". There is a manuscript in the State Paper Office that is referred to in the original docket as "A Device made by the Earl of Essex for the Entertainment of her Majesty" (Bourchier 1853, II.501). It is written in a fair hand with no date attached and consists of two speeches: "The Squire's Speech" and "The Attendant or Conductor to the Indian Prince". An Amazonian king makes sacrifices in his temples in an attempt to cure his son, the Indian Prince, of his blindness. Consequently, the king receives an oracle which sends the Prince to England to be remedied by Queen Elizabeth. This piece appears to be the ill-fated invention by Francis Bacon.[17]

Meanwhile, Bacon's debt continued to accumulate, and soon his creditors circled, only keeping a distance on expectation of his promotion. Indeed, certain signals from court gave Bacon confidence that the queen had him in mind for Coke's vacated position of Solicitor General. So, Essex began to importune Elizabeth, and such was his persistence that the queen took offence. In October 1595, Serjeant Fleming was made Solicitor General, and Bacon blamed Coke. He was now desperate to improve his financial position. Francis persuaded Essex to ask for Lady Hatton's hand in marriage. Twenty years old, wealthy, and much admired, she was Lord Burghley's granddaughter and Sir Robert Cecil's niece, so she certainly had good connections. Somehow, the 46-year-old Edward Coke managed to get there first, with a marriage so hastily arranged that even the Archbishop asked questions. From now on, Bacon and Coke would stand as bitter rivals.

There is evidence that Bacon was also a producer of Inns of Court masques. In an undated letter discovered in the papers of the first Lord Burghley, Bacon writes,

> Yt may please your good Lordship I am sory the joynt maske from the fowr Innes of Cowrt faileth. Wherin I conceyue thear is no other grownd of that euent but impossibility. Neuerthelesse bycause it falleth owt that at this tyme Graies Inne is well furnyshed, of gallant yowng gentlemen, your lordship may be pleased to know, that rather then this occasion shall passe withowt some demonstration of affection from the Innes of Cowrt, Thear are a dozen gentlemen of Graies Inne that owt of the honour which they bear to your lordship, and my lord Chamberlayne to whome at theyre last maske they were so much bownden, will be ready to furnysh a maske wyshing it were in their powers to performe it according to theyr myndes. And so for the present I humbly take my leaue resting.[18]

This refers to three masques: the "last maske", the "joynt maske" that was intended but failed, and another that Bacon proposed as compensation. Since Lord Burleigh died on 4 August 1598, Spedding notes that "it must have been written before the autumn of 1598, but it seems impossible to determine on what occasion". He further reports that "on 15th of October, 1596, Bacon wrote to the Earl of Shrewsbury from Gray's Inn 'to borrow a horse and armour for some public shew'" and conjectures that "this may possibly have reference to the same" (Spedding 1861–74, II.370).[19] Without stating their reasons, Nelson and Elliott assign the Bacon–Burleigh letter to 1595–6 (Nelson and Elliott 2010, 126–27).

5.4 The Fall of Essex

Essex now found himself in a position to realize one of his ambitions, to pursue the Irish rebel Hugh Tyrone, and so he crossed to Ireland, heading an army of 18,000.

> Were now the Generall of our gracious Empresse,
> As in good time he may, from Ireland coming,
> Bringing Rebellion broached on his sword. (*Henry V*, 5.1.30–32)

Six months later, he returned home unsuccessful, having negotiated a truce and having abandoned his army in the field. A furious Elizabeth sought the advice of her Counsel Learned Extraordinary, Francis Bacon. She gave him the reversion of an office in Star Chamber worth £2,000 per annum and dined with him at his lodge at Twickenham Park. It would have been a great stride forward for Bacon if the queen's offer of an office had been realistically attainable, because the Star Chamber boasted the members of the Privy Council as well as the two Chief Justices of the King's Bench and Common Pleas. As it turned out, Bacon received neither the office nor the money for another 12 years. As for Essex, Bacon counselled Elizabeth to "turn the light of her favour towards my Lord". However, in 1601 a performance of Shakespeare's *Richard II* and a publication by John Hayward, a doctor of civil law, based on the play and dedicated to the Earl of Essex, were used by Essex to raise an army and incite an uprising against the queen. First the book appeared. The Queen's Counsel, Francis Bacon, takes up the story:

> For her Majestie, being mightily incensed with that booke [by John Haywood] which was dedicated to my Lord of Essex, being a story of the first yeare of King *Henry* the fourth, thinking it a seditious prelude to put into the people's heads boldnesse and faction, said, she had good opinion, that there was treason in it, and asked me if I could not find any places in it that might be drawn within case of treason: whereto I answered; for treason surely I found none, but for fellony very many. And when her Majesty hastily asked me wherein; I told her the Author had committed very apparent theft, for he had taken most of the sentences of *Cornelius Tacitus*, and translated them into English, and put them into his text. And another time, when the Queene would not be perswaded, that it was his writing whose name was to it, but that it had some more mischievous Author, and said with great indignation that shee would have him racked to produce his Author, I replied, Nay, Madam, he is a Doctor, never racke his person, but racke his stile; let him have pen, inke and paper, and help of books, and be enjoyned to continue the story wherein it breaketh off, and I will undertake by collecting [collating] the stiles, to judge whether he were the Author or no. (Bacon 1642, 10)

The Earl of Essex was brought before a hearing at York House, and after a reprimand from Bacon, the embattled earl took the view that both Bacon and Robert Cecil were conspirators in a plot to undo him. The queen set Essex free but banished him from her presence, while Bacon received threatening letters from Essex's followers.

Then, one Saturday afternoon in early February 1601, Shake-speare's *Richard II* was performed at the Globe Theatre. The performance of the play, in which the king resigns his crown to Henry Bolingbroke, was sponsored by Sir Gelly Merrick, a friend of Essex, who paid a reluctant

Lord Chamberlain's Men 40 shillings above their usual fee to perform it. Believing that it would incite the audience to join him, the next day Essex pulled together a small band of armed followers, staged a rebellion, and attempted to force his way into the royal presence. The coup failed. On 19 February 1601, Essex went to trial at Westminster Hall, where both Bacon and Coke spoke against him. Bacon urged Essex to confess, but the earl simply passed off his insurrection as an attack "against private enemies" who were barring his access to the queen. It would not save him. Six days later, on Ash Wednesday at eight in the morning, Essex was executed at Tower Hill. His partner in crime, the Earl of Southampton, went to the Tower, as did Hayward, the advertised author of the offending book, but Merrick, who had organized the performance of *Richard II*, went to the executioner. A representative of the acting company, Augustine Phillips was questioned, but no one associated with the play was prosecuted. In fact, the evening before Essex's execution, the Lord Chamberlain's Men were entertaining the queen at court. From this we can conclude that Bacon must have been aware of all the members of The Lord Chamberlain's Men, including William Shakspere.

By the time Queen Elizabeth died on 24 March 1603, the world had already lost Lord Burghley and Anthony Bacon. Petitioning began in earnest to win the favour of King James I, who had already reigned 35 years in Scotland. Unknown to Bacon, Robert Cecil had already been courting James's favour. Nevertheless, James had been an admirer of Essex and the fact that Anthony Bacon had assisted in the correspondence between Essex and James worked in his younger brother's favour, despite opposing Essex at his trial. On 23 July 1603, Francis Bacon received a knighthood at the Palace of Whitehall, with about 300 others. With it came a pension of 60 pounds per annum and a patent as King's Counsel Extraordinaire, a position only slightly higher than Barrister. However, with Edward Coke as Attorney General, he saw no immediate prospect of advancement. Instead he began work on a different kind of advancement, a method for attaining knowledge.

5.5 Bacon's Rise to High Office

The *Advancement of Learning* (1605), dedicated to King James, opens by defending the importance of learning in all aspects of life, while the second part divides knowledge into History, Poesy, and Philosophy, providing a detailed critique and suggestions for improvement. Bacon sent a copy to Sir Thomas Bodley, founder of the Bodleian Library in Oxford, with an enclosed letter that revealed the same motivation that he had earlier confessed to Lord Burghley:

> knowing myself by inward calling to be fitter to hold a book than to play a part, I have led my life in civil causes; for which I was not very fit by nature, and more unfit by the preoccupation of my mind. (Spedding 1861–74, III.253)

Around this time, Bacon was working on "Of the Interpretation of Nature". There exists a manuscript fragment from around 1603 that shows that Francis Bacon was intending to publish a draft of this work under two pseudonyms: Valerius Terminus and Hermes Stella.[20] It was eventually published in 1734 in Stephen's *Letters and Remains*, and the title page exhibits a list of contents in Bacon's newly adopted Italian-style handwriting.[21] The first ten chapters, although incomplete, correspond to the *Advancement of Learning* (1605), which was subsequently expanded into *De Augmentis Scientiarum*.

On 10 May 1606, Sir Francis Bacon married 14-year-old Alice Barnham, one of the daughters and coheirs of Benedict Barnham, Esquire and Alderman of London. It was an arranged marriage, in keeping with the times, and was proposed by Bacon to her parents when she was 11 years old. Her late father had been a rich draper to the queen, so it undoubtedly solved his financial problems. A letter, written a day later, describes Bacon the bridegroom as "clad from top to toe in purple". They had no children, there was no hint of romance, and Bacon left her nothing in his will. In his essay "Of marriage and single life" (1612) his attitude to the idea of a family is clear: "He that hath wife and children hath given hostages to fortune, for they are impediments to great enterprises" (Spedding *et al.* 1857–74, XII.101).

When the Chief Justice of the Common Pleas died in June 1606, Sir Edward Coke took his position, making way for Sir Henry Hobart to take his title of Attorney General. Sir Robert Cecil, now Lord Treasurer, had promised Bacon the position of Solicitor General, but nothing transpired. Bacon was aggrieved. However, a year later, his fortune turned. Not only was he made Solicitor General with the attendant salary of 100 pounds per annum and 1,000 pounds per annum in fees and perquisites, but he also acquired the office of Registrar of the Star Chamber promised by Elizabeth 12 years earlier with a pension of 2,000 pounds per annum. Among Bacon's duties was advising King James on his plantations in Virginia and Ireland, indicating the most suitable crops to grow there and the most appropriate craftsmen to select as settlers.

When in 1612, Sir Robert Cecil died Bacon felt that an obstacle had been removed. In a draft of a letter to King James dated 8 September 1612 he wrote "let me not live if I thought not of the taking away of that man" (Spedding 1861–74, IV.313n).[22] According to Bacon's chaplain Dr Rawley, Bacon certainly felt he had been thwarted:

> which might be imputed, not so much to Her Majesty's averseness and disaffection towards him, as to the arts and policy of a great statesman then, who laboured by all industrious and secret means to suppress and keep him down; lest, if he had risen, he might have obscured his glory. (Rawley 1657, b4^{r})[23]

Sir Francis Bacon now had the influence he had set out to achieve.

On Saturday 20 February 1612–13, a procession and masque organized jointly by Gray's Inn and the Inner Temple was presented to King James to celebrate the wedding of Frederick Count Palatine and Lady Elizabeth. The masque is credited to Inner Temple member and playwright Francis Beaumont, and the printed version has the following dedication to Sir Francis Bacon:

> Yee that spared no time nor trauell, in the setting forth, ordering, & furnishing of this Masque [...] as you did then by your countenance, and louing affection aduance it. (Beaumont 1613, sig. B)

Unfortunately, after a magnificently lit procession on the Thames involving the king's royal barge, James declared that he was too tired to concentrate, so Bacon postponed the performance of the masque, intended for the banqueting house at Whitehall, until the following Saturday.[24]

A year later, Sir Francis Bacon was the producer of another theatrical event. On 9 December 1613, the epistolarian John Chamberlain wrote to Sir Dudley Carleton:

> Sir Francis Bacon prepares a mask which will stand him in above £2000, and although he has been offered some help by the House [Gray's Inn], and specially by Mr. Solicitor, Sir Henry Yelverton, who would have sent him £500, yet he would not accept it, but offers them the whole charge with the honour. (Nichols 1828, II.705)

So on Twelfth Night, Thursday 6 January 1613–14, the gentlemen of Gray's Inn presented 'The Maske of Flowers' at Whitehall, on the occasion of the marriage between Robert Carr, the Earl of Somerset, and Lady Frances Howard, daughter of the Earl of Suffolk, the Lord Chamberlain. It was published in 1614 and sold at Robert Wilson's shop at "Graies-Inne new gate", with Bacon receiving the following credit (see Figure 5.3):

> To the verie Honorable Knight, Sir Francis Bacon [...] hauing beene the Principall, and in effect the onely person that did both incourage and warrant the Gentlemen, to shew their good affection towards so noble a Coniunction in a time of such Magnificence. (Coperario 1614, sig. A3)

Christine Adams has argued that Bacon not only financed but also wrote *The maske of flowers* (Adams 2008, 36–58). The device opens with the season of winter being represented by a gowned old man with white hair and a beard, and spring being attired like a nymph dressed in pearls and flowers. The sun sends instruction to them through his messenger Gallus. Winter must present two anti-maskes, one in song and the other in dance, on the theme that "Wine is more woorthie then Tobacco, and

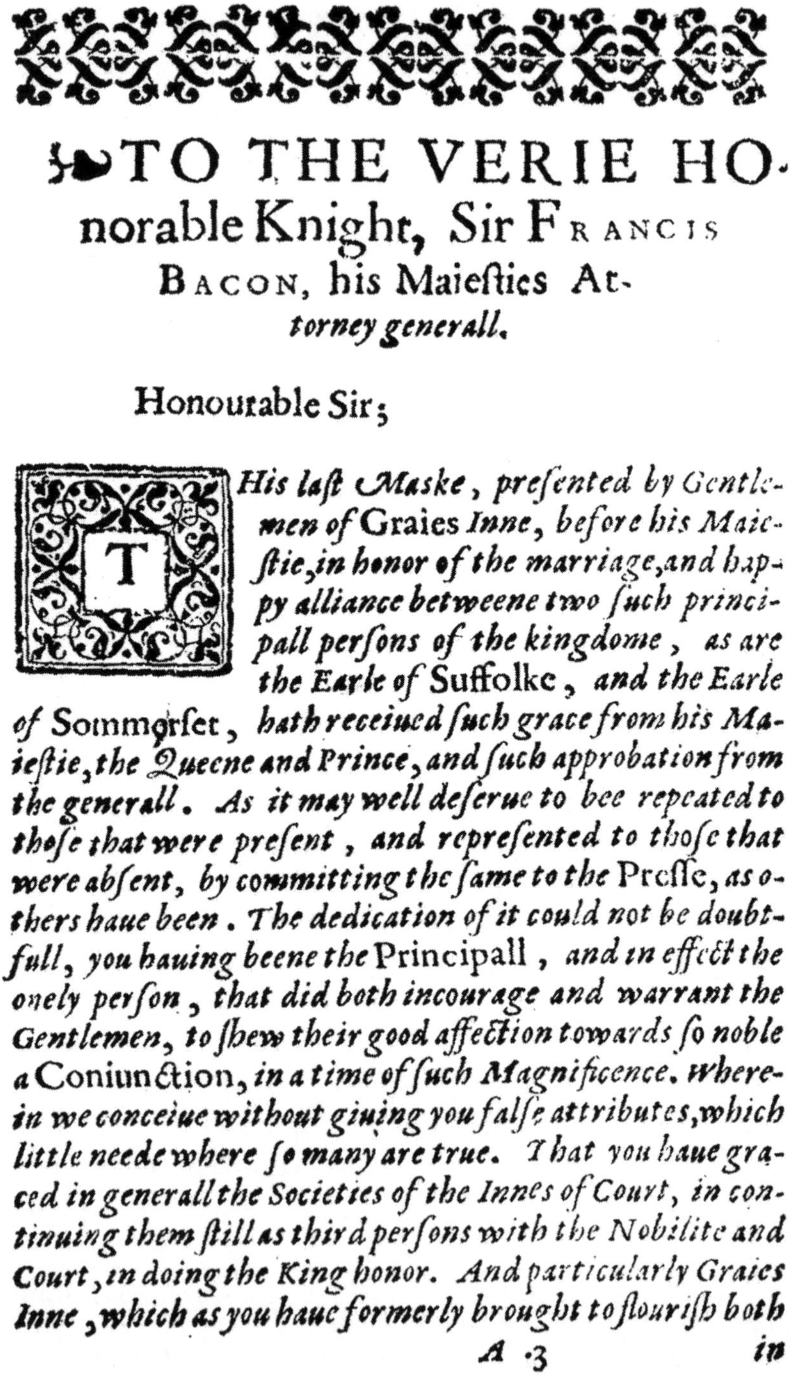

TO THE VERIE HONORABLE KNIGHT, SIR FRANCIS BACON, his Maieſties Attorney generall.

Honourable Sir;

THis laſt Maske, preſented by Gentlemen of Graies Inne, before his Maieſtie, in honor of the marriage, and happy alliance betweene two ſuch principall perſons of the kingdome, as are the Earle of Suffolke, and the Earle of Somnmorſet, hath receiued ſuch grace from his Maieſtie, the Queene and Prince, and ſuch approbation from the generall. As it may well deſerue to bee repeated to thoſe that were preſent, and repreſented to thoſe that were abſent, by committing the ſame to the Preſſe, as others haue been. The dedication of it could not be doubtfull, you hauing beene the Principall, and in effect the onely perſon, that did both incourage and warrant the Gentlemen, to ſhew their good affection towards ſo noble a Coniunction, in a time of ſuch Magnificence. Wherein we conceiue without giuing you falſe attributes, which little neede where ſo many are true. That you haue graced in generall the Societies of the Innes of Court, in continuing them ſtill as third perſons with the Nobilite and Court, in doing the King honor. And particularly Graies Inne, which as you haue formerly brought to flouriſh both

A 3 in

Figure 5.3 Francis Bacon credited as producer of the event. John Coperario, *The maske of flowers* (1614).

cheereth mans spirit more". Spring has a far more elaborate task: "That whereas of auncient time there were certain faire Youths turned into Flowers [...] That they be now returned to Men, and present a Dance" (Coperario 1614, sig. B2^{v}).

To this end, Spring presents four songs in the setting of a quartered flowered garden, a commendable construction built on a 40×40 sq.ft platform, six feet high at the front, rising to eight feet high at the back, with assorted flowers and trees.

At the centre of the garden, in the middle of a 24 ft circumference bowl raised 9 ft from the ground, Neptune holds a trident astride a dolphin that was "So cunningly framed, that a Riuer seemed to streame out of his mouth" (Coperario 1614, sig. C). Christine Adams (2008, 47) finds parallels in *The maske of flowers* between the presentation of the action and garden's construction, and the advice Bacon gives in his essays 'Of Masques and Triumphs' (1625)[25] and 'Of Gardens', concluding that

> Bacon's writing style, his garden preferences, and his knowledge of flowers, visible in his two garden descriptions and *The maske of flowers* support other evidence presented here that he [...] was equipped to script and produce one [a masque] with a garden of flowers as its defining theme and visual focus. (Adams 2008, 53)

At the very least, it can be claimed with confidence that Francis Bacon had an active interest in staging drama.

The law courts in Westminster Palace were divided into two factions. The king was represented in Chancery by the Lord Chancellor, the Attorney General, and the courts of Star Chamber, while the common-law courts of Kings Bench, Common Pleas, and Exchequer were supported by Parliament. The king, through his Lord Chancellor, wished to keep the judges under his rule by consultation, but Parliament was intent on maintaining independence. Coke supported Parliament, and from his position as Chief Justice of the Common Pleas he succeeded in causing obstructions by sending praemunires to Lord Chancellor Ellesmere whenever he attempted to overrule the judges, writs that effectively accused Lord Ellesmere of recognizing the power of the Pope above the king.

In the spring of 1613, the Chief Justice of the King's Bench died, a post higher than Chief Justice of the Common Pleas but with less financial reward and autonomy. Being under greater supervision from the king, Bacon wrote to James with a plan. Coke was to be brought under control by being assigned the vacant position, the malleable Hobart was to take Coke's place, and Bacon would accept the post of Attorney General. The king would then be strengthened when acting on constitutional questions. In October of that year, Bacon's Machiavellian scheme was set in motion: the post of Attorney General became his, and a furious Sir Edward Coke was shifted to a post he had not wanted.

June 1616 saw Bacon elevated to the Privy Council, and, following Coke's "deceit, contempt and slander of the government" and "his raising of troubles or new questions", which had offended the king, proceedings began to have him removed from the bench and from the Privy Council. On 13 November, the new Attorney General, Sir Francis Bacon, dispatched the discharge form for the king to sign, finally sealing Coke's fate.

When Lord Chancellor Ellesmere passed away in March 1617, Sir Francis Bacon reported that he wept "which I do not often". He took over as Lord Keeper of the Seal, at last being able to sit in the elevated marble chair at Westminster Hall where his father had once sat. In addition to hearing suits, the position came with the right to appoint justices of the peace and to act as speaker in the House of Lords. The new Lord Keeper was held in such high esteem that when King James visited Scotland he declared Bacon to be temporary Regent of England. As for Coke, he quietly manoeuvred for position. Opposed by his wife, he suggested the marriage of his 14-year-old daughter Frances to George Villiers, Earl of Buckingham, the king's new favourite, accompanied by a substantial dowry. Bacon, realizing the peril, opposed the plan but only succeeded in annoying both the king and Buckingham. The marriage went ahead, and Bacon was left to fall on bended knee with letters to the king imploring forgiveness. The following year, with Buckingham's influence, Bacon became Lord Chancellor and subsequently Lord Verulam. Such was his wealth, he could now afford to issue his servants with livery embroidered with his crest, a boar.

In October 1618, Lord Chancellor Francis Bacon was one of six commissioners appointed to examine Sir Walter Raleigh (Coke being another), who, on being released from a 15-year sentence in the Tower in order to seek gold in Guiana, had attacked the Spanish settlement at St. Thomas. It had been against the wishes of King James who was attempting to arrange the marriage of his son Prince Charles to the Infanta of Spain. Realizing how skilfully Raleigh could play on the affections of an audience, he was given a private hearing where it was decided that an old charge of treason should be consummated. On 29 October 1618, he went to his execution with such extraordinary calm that it became a notable event in history.[26]

When Sir Francis Bacon published his *Novum Organon* (1620) in Latin, setting out his plan for a new method of learning, he sent a copy to the King. Provocatively, he also sent one bound in vellum to his nemesis Sir Edward Coke, who, far from being grateful, scribbled the following on the title page:

> It deserveth not to be read in Schooles
> But to be freighted in the ship of Fooles.

This perhaps alluded to Barclay's rendering of Sebastian Brandt's verse *Ship of Fools*. Shortly after his 60th birthday, King James awarded his Lord Chancellor the title Viscount St Albans.

5.6 Bacon's Fall to Low Office

Bacon had been held back under Elizabeth, with Coke and Cecil managing to thwart every attempt to gain advancement. However, under James he had enjoyed great privilege. It was not to last. On 30 January 1621, in need of finance, King James called Parliament, the first for seven years. Lord Coke, now 69 years old, took his place amongst the elected common lawyers on the benches. Dissatisfied with the abuse of monopolies, the proposed marriage of Prince Charles to a Catholic, and the king's stranglehold on the judiciary, Parliament was looking for a way to disempower the monarch. First they turned their attention to his right-hand man, George Villiers, Marquis of Buckingham, accusing him of illegal earnings from patents. The right to manufacture certain commodities, such as gold lace, could be granted by whosoever the king cared to choose, usually a court favourite, who was pleased to make a profit. Anyone else who manufactured the products paid a fine from which Buckingham made a profit. At first, the House of Commons held their fire. Then two profiteers, the politician Sir Giles Mompesson and one of his agents Sir Francis Michael, were brought down. Sir Giles climbed out of a window and escaped to France. Sir Francis was less fortunate, finding himself in Finsbury Gaol with no prospect of release.

Next, the referees of monopolies—those who received payment for assessing the legal status of patents—were to be investigated, a committee being ready to sit on 8 March. Buckingham's brothers had been referees and so had Sir Francis Bacon. Buckingham decided to head off an attack by apologizing before the House of Lords for his brothers' conduct. However, it soon became apparent that a Committee for Inquiring into Abuses in the Courts of Justice, initiated by Privy Counsellor Sir Lionel Cranfield, whom Bacon had once offended, was investigating the Lord Chancellor's affairs. Bacon was accused of taking bribes in judging legal cases, with Sir Edward Coke heading a committee of four to hear the case. More witnesses came forward against the Lord Chancellor, all provided with immunity from prosecution. James sympathized, even confiding to the Venetian Ambassador that:

> If I were to imitate the conduct of your republic and begin to punish those who take bribes, I should not have a single subject left. (Perkins 2013, 31)

The list of 28 separate charges gave Bacon no hope of reprieve:

1 In the cause between Sir Rowland Egerton and Edward Egerton, the Lord Chancellor received 500 pounds on the part of Sir Rowland Egerton before he decreed the cause.
2 He received from Edward Egerton 400 pounds.

3 In the cause between Hodie and Hodye, he received a dozen of buttons of the value of 50 pounds about a fortnight after the cause was ended.
4 In the cause between Lady Wharton and the coheirs of Sir Francis Willoughby, he received of Lady Wharton 310 pounds. (Spedding 1861–74, VII.252–61)

And the list went on. Most of the gifts had been accepted after the judgement had been passed, some were loans that Bacon was pleased to take advantage of, and in one or two cases Bacon was unclear about the time of acceptance. Anyway, argued Bacon, his servants had been present most of the time. The impression Bacon creates is not so much one of wanton greed as naïve disinterest.

On 1 May, a committee of four was sent by the king to recover the Great Seal from Bacon. The next day he was summoned to appear in Parliament but failed to turn up due to ill health. Two days later, the Earl of Southampton and the Earl of Suffolk, two Lords whom Bacon had helped prosecute in the course of his profession, gleefully assisted in passing judgement. Southampton, who had spent two years in the Tower, argued for an additional loss of titles realizing that the forfeiture of Viscount St Albans and Baron Verulam would be a major humiliation. In the end, Southampton was defeated by two votes. Later that day the Commons assembled in the Lord's Chamber at Westminster Palace to hear the sentence:

1 That the Lord Viscount St. Alban, Lord Chancellor of England, shall undergo fine and ransom of 40,000 pounds.
2 That he shall be imprisoned in the Tower during the King's pleasure.
3 That he shall be forever incapable of holding any office, place, or employment in the State or Commonwealth.
4 That he shall never sit in Parliament nor come within the verge of the Court. (Spedding 1861–74, VII.270)

In fact, this was less severe than it appeared. In such situations, the king frequently revoked fines and released the defendant, often in no more than a month. Nevertheless, Southampton and Coke had exacted their revenge. Coke did not have the last word. He was later to spend time in the Tower himself for defiance of the king.

On the last day of May, Bacon was taken by barge to the Tower. Three days later he was free, largely through the influence of Prince Charles, and stayed at the house of Sir John Vaughan, one of Charles's servants.

Several years later, in fact two years after Bacon died, Thomas Bushell, one of his servants, gave his impression of events:

> [...it] grieues my soule, that so matchlesse a Peere should bee lost by such insinuating caterpillars, who in his owne nature scorn'd the least

> thought of any base, vnworthy, or ignoble act, though suiect to infirmities, as ordain'd to the wisest: for so much I must assure you was his hatred to bribery, corruption, or symmonie. (Bushel 1628, 128)

Dr Thomas Tenison, who inherited Bacon's literary estate, also thought Bacon was innocent:

> The great cause of his Suffering, is to some, a secret. I leave them to find it out, by his words to King James, *I wish (said he) that as I am the first, so I shall be the last of Sacrifices in your Times.* (Tenison 1679, 16)

By the autumn, King James had allowed Bacon to name recipients for his fine of £40,000, a move intended to satisfy creditors.

Fortunately for posterity, the impeachment unlocked the golden handcuffs that had seduced Bacon into the security of power and influence and had diverted him from his unfinished philosophical projects. For the first time since 1613, he had the leisure to resume his work, and by October 1621 he had finished a *History of the Reign of Henry VII*. In November 1622, his *History of the Winds* appeared, followed by the *History of Life and Death*. Bacon had compiled a list of 100 history titles, the third part of his Great Instauration, and had decided to write up these two examples himself. It was in this period that Shakespeare's *First Folio* (1623) collection of 36 plays was published, with its many amendments to the earlier published quartos (e.g. *Othello* was first published in quarto in 1622 but a year later appeared amended for the *First Folio*). In 1625, the third edition of Bacon's *Essays* appeared in Latin with 20 new additions. He also published *De Augmentis Scientiarum* in Latin, an extended version of *The Advancement of Learning*. In Book II, Chapter XIII, he addresses "the second principal branch of Learning, namely, Poesy". For Bacon, a play presented on the stage should be no idle entertainment, but should be exploited as an educational tool:

> And though in modern states play-acting is esteemed but as a toy, except when it is too satirical and biting; yet among ancients it was used as a means of educating men's minds to virtue. Nay, it has been regarded by learned men and great philosophers as a kind of musician's bow by which men's minds be played upon. And certainly it is most true, and one of the great secrets of nature, that the minds of men are more open to impressions and affections when many are gathered together than when they are alone. (Spedding *et al.* 1857–74, VIII.441–442)

His elder years were spent in his small house at Gray's Inn. He died on 9 April 1626 after falling ill between London and Highgate. Unable to return home, he sought rest at the Earl of Arundel's house at Highgate, who was away. There, in the last letter he wrote, he informs the earl that

> I was likely to have had the fortune of Caius Plinius the elder, who lost his life trying an experiment about the burning of the mountain Vesuvius. For I was also desirous to try an experiment or two, touching the conservation and induration of bodies. (Spedding 1861–74, VII.549–50)

According to Dr William Rawley, his literary executor, "the Defluxion of Rheume, fell so plentifull upon his Breast, that he died by Suffocation" (Rawley 1657, c4^{v}). In St. Michael's Church, St. Albans, there is a life-size statue of him in white alabaster that was erected by his secretary Sir Thomas Meautys after his death. It shows him reclined in a chair, hat on head, head in hand, deep in contemplation.

Notes

1 Taken from Felix Schelling's 1892 reprint. The original is in Jonson (1641).
2 The letter is a copy of the original in the hand of a state official, British Library, MS Harley 4761, f.174v. The original is Lambeth MS 976, folio 4, has the signature and docket in Bacon's hand while the body of the letter is by one of his scriveners.
3 For example, Spedding *et al.* (1857–9), Peltonen (1996), and Jardine and Stewart (1999) present almost nothing on their subject's dramatic interests.
4 "that he was no favourite with the attorneys is clear from his own statements of his progress, from the abundant leisure which he still enjoyed, and from the poverty in which (without any extravagance) he continued to be involved" (Campbell 1851, II.247).
5 The title page states that it was presented on "the twenty eighth day of Februarie".
6 There are two entries for Thomas Hughes in the Admissions Register: "Thomas Hughes (or Hayes), of Staple Inn" in 1580 (Foster 1889, 56), and "Thomas Hayes (Feb 9)" in 1580–1 (Foster 1889, 40 & 58). Doubt has been expressed about the extent of Hughes's contribution (Stewart and Knight 2012, I.75–6).
7 A dumb show is a pantomime enacted in silence, sometimes to music, and is usually intended to illustrate the theme of the play that incorporates it. These dumb shows are included in Stewart and Knight (2012, I).
8 Patronage need not necessarily mean that the author was acquainted with the patron.
9 Lambeth MS. 650.28. Written in Bacon's own hand.
10 The evidence for the dating of this is that the first speech was expanded as 'Certain Observations upon a Libel', which Bacon published in 1592.
11 The collection seems to have been damaged by fire at Northumberland House on 18 March 1780, and was discovered there in a large black box in August 1867 by the antiquarian John Bruce. James Spedding dates the collection to 1597 and asserts that "there is no trace of Bacon's own penmanship in any part of the volume" (Spedding 1870, xxiv–xxv).

12 The structure for 'Of Tribute' is as follows. Four friends, distinguished as A, B, C, and D, meet for intellectual amusement. Friend A sets out the direction of their proceedings, and proposes that each in turn shall make a speech in praise of whatever he holds most worthy. So B (after a word or two of protest in favour of satire, as better suited to the humour of that time than praise) begins with a speech in praise of the "worthiest virtue" namely, Fortitude. Friend C follows with a speech in praise of "the worthiest affection", namely, Love, while friend D has a speech in praise of "the worthiest power", namely, Knowledge. Friend A then returns to conclude with a speech in praise of "the worthiest person", namely, the queen (Spedding 1870, ix).

13 The Gray's Inn Pension Book shows that around this time, where a record exists, two Treasurers were elected, for example, in November 1586–8, 1590, 1594–96 (Fletcher 1901).

14 Nichols (1823, III.262n) thought that "The publisher was Mr. Henry Keepe, who published the 'Monuments of Westminster'".

15 Sydney Papers, i. 362.

16 Lambeth Palace Library, Gibson Papers, vol. viii.

17 For a more detailed overview of the 1595 events see Hammer (1998, 41–66).

18 British Library, Burghley Papers, Lansdowne MS 107, f.13; in Bacon's hand, no address, flyleaf missing, docketed "Mr Fra. Bacon".

19 The Northumberland Manuscripts collection has a speech listed on the Contents sheet "For the Earl of Sussex at ye tilt an: 96" (Burgoyne 1902, MS fols 53–54) which appears in the collection, and is "addressed to the Queen being meant apparently to convey an apology for the absence of the Earl of Essex" (Spedding 1870, xvii). The author is unknown, but this might also serve as a candidate for Bacon's "public shew".

20 Hermes Stella was the fictitious name of the annotator.

21 The MS resides in the British Library, Harley 6463. In the Lambeth Library, there is a copy of a letter from Bacon to Lord Kinlosse, dated 25 March 1603, written in the same scrivener's hand.

22 Bacon had deleted this passage before sending the letter.

23 William Rawley, 'The life of the honourable author', in Spedding *et al.*, Works, Vol. 1 (London: Longman and Co., 1858),7.

24 For the identity of the musicians at the masque see Stainer (1906, 21–24).

25 The maske of flowers avoids 'dancing in song' which Bacon abhorred but has 'acting in song' and 'dancing without song', the latter involving dancing the measures.

26 There is an argument that the Thane of Cawdor in *Macbeth* plays out Raleigh's alleged treason. In 1603, Raleigh had been sent to trial on the false charge that he had accepted Spanish money to assist in removing King James. (1) Raleigh admitted that "Lord Cobham offered me 10,000 crowns for the furthering of peace between England and Spain [...]". In *Macbeth*, the Thane of Cawdor is seen to be traitorously assisting the Norwegian invaders and Rosse, the king's messenger, reports that "Nor would we deigne him [the Norwegian king] burial of his men, / Till he disbursed, at Saint Colmes ynch, / Ten thousand Dollars to our general use." (1.3.68–72). Holinshed's *Chronicles* only describes an exchange of "a great summe of gold". (2) In Malcome's speech in the Palace at Forres, he remarks on the Thane of Cawdor's execution that "He dy'de / As one that had been studied in his death, / To throw away the dearest thing he ow'd, / As 'twere a carelesse trifle." (1.4.9–12) This echoes Raleigh's calmness in facing the axe in October 1618. If this indeed alludes to Raleigh, someone must have amended the play

after Shakspere's death in 1616. Observation (2) has previously been made by James Spedding (1861–74, VI.372), but (1) seems to be recorded here for the first time. Bacon was one of six Commissioners appointed to oversee the 1618 hearing.

Bibliography

Adams, Christine. "Francis Bacon's wedding gift of 'A garden of a glorious and a strange beauty' for the Earl and Countess of Somerset." *Garden History* 36, No. 1 (Spring 2008): 36–58.

Bacon, Francis. *The Twoo Bookes of Francis Bacon. Of the Proficience and Aduancement of Learning, Diuine and Humane*. London: Printed for Henrie Tomes, 1605.

Bacon, Francis. *His Apologie, in Certaine Imputations Concerning the Late Earle of Essex (1604)*. London, 1642.

Beaumont, Francis. *The Masqve of the Inner Temple and Grayes Inne*. London: Imprinted by F[elix] K[ingston] for George Norton, 1613. STC: 1664.

Boswell, James. *The Life of Samuel Johnson*. 4 vols. Oxford: Talboys and Wheeler, 1826.

Bourchier, Walter, ed. *Lives and Letters of the Devereux, Earls of Essex*. 2 vols. London: John Murray, 1853.

Burgoyne, Frank J., ed. *Northumberland Manuscripts. Collotype Facsimile and Type Transcript of an Elizabethan manuscript Preserved at Alnwick Castle, Northumberland*. London, New York, and Bombay: Longmans, Green & Co., 1902.

Bushel, Thomas. *The Firste Part of Youth's Errors*. London: [By T. Harper], 1628. STC: 4186.

Campbell, John. "The life of Bacon." *The Lives of the Lord Chancellors and Keepers of the Great Seal of England*. 7 vols. Philadelphia: Blanchard and Lea, 1851.

Coperario, John. *The Maske of Flowers. Presented by the Gentlemen of Graies-Inne, at the court of White-hall, in the Banquetting House, vpon Twelfe Night, 1613*. London, 1614. STC 17625.

Dixon, William Hepworth. *Personal History of Lord Bacon*. London: John Murray, 1861.

Drinker-Bowen, Catherine. *Francis Bacon: The Temper of a Man*. Hamish Hamilton, 1963.

Fletcher, Reginald J., ed. *The Pension Book of Gray's Inn 1569–1669*. London: Printed by N. O[kes] for R. Wilson, 1901.Foster, Joseph, ed. *The Register of Admissions to Gray's Inn, 1521–1889*. London: Hansard Publishing Union, 1889.

Gesta Grayorum: or the History of the High and mighty Prince, Henry. London: Printed for W. Canning, 1688.

Hammer, Paul E. J. "Upstaging the Queen: the Earl of Essex, Francis Bacon and the Accession Day celebrations of 1595." In David Bevington and Peter Holbrook, eds. *The Politics of the Stuart Court Masque*. Cambridge: Cambridge University Press, 1998.

Hughes, Thomas. *Certaine deu[is]es and shewes presented to her Maiestie by the gentlemen of Grayes-Inne at her Hignesse court in Greenewich*. London: Robert Robinson, 1587 [1588]. STC: 13921.

Jardine, Lisa, and Alan Stewart. *Hostage of Fortune: The Troubled Life of Francis Bacon*. New York: Hill and Wang, 1999.

Jonson, Ben. "Timber: or discoveries; made upon men and matter." *The Workes of Benjamin Jonson*. London: Printed by Richard Bishop, 1641.

Jonson, Ben. *Timber: or discoveries; made upon men and matter*. Felix E. Schelling, ed. Boston: Ginn & Co, 1892.

Manes Verulamiani. London: John Haviland, 1626.

Nelson, Alan H., and John R. Elliott Jr., eds. *Records of Early English Drama: Inns of Court*. 3 vols. Martlesham: D. S. Brewer, 2010.

Nichols, John. *The Progresses and Public processions of Queen Elizabeth*. 3 vols. London: J. Nichols and Son, 1823.

Nichols, John. *The Progresses, Processions, and Magnificent Festivities, of King James the First*. 4 vols. New York: AMS Press Inc., 1828.

Peltonen, Markku, ed. *The Cambridge Companion to Francis Bacon*. Cambridge: Cambridge University Press, 1996.

Perkins, Ivan. *Vanishing Coup: The Pattern of World History Since 1310*. Lanham: Rowman & Littlefield, 2013.

Rawley, William. "The life of the honourable author." In *Resuscitatio*. London: Printed by Sarah Griffin for William Lee, 1657.

Shelley, Percy Bysshe. "A defence of poetry." In Shelley, ed. *Essays, Letters from Abroad*. 2 vols. Philadelphia, PA: Lea and Blanchard, 1840.

Spedding, James. *The Letters and Life of Francis Bacon*. 7 vols. London: Longman, Green, Longman, and Roberts, 1861–74.

Spedding, James, ed. *A Conference of Pleasure, Composed for Some Festive Occasion About the Year 1592 by Francis Bacon*. London: Printed by Whittingham and Wilkins, 1870.

Spedding, James, Robert Leslie Ellis, and Douglas Denon Heath, eds. *The Works of Francis Bacon*. 14 vols. London: Brown and Taggard, 1857–74.

Stainer, J. F. R. "The middle temple masque." *The Musical Times* 47, No.755 (Jan 1 1906): 21–24.

Stewart, Alan, and Harriet Knight, eds. *The Oxford Francis Bacon*, 15 vols. Oxford: Clarendon Press, 2012.

Stow, John. *Annales, or Generall Chronicle of England*. London: [Printed by John Beale], 1631.

Tenison, Thomas. *Baconiana, Or Genuine Remains of S^R Francis Bacon*. London: Printed by J. D. for Richard Chiswell, 1679.

Vickers, Brian, ed. *Francis Bacon: The Major Works*. Oxford: Oxford University Press, 2002.

6 A Charge of Brokerage

The open letter to the three dramatists in Robert Greene's *Groats-worth of Witte (1592)*, which refers to Shakspere in relation to *3 Henry VI*, is analyzed in detail to discover what is being claimed. Opinion is divided as to whether or not Robert Greene contributed to this play but the method of RCP given here now suggests that he did. This means that rather than being jealous of Shakspere as a new dramatist as some have suggested, Greene was instead complaining that Shakspere had paid him only a hireling rate for his contribution and was now profiting from his work while Greene suffered in poverty.

6.1 The *Groats-worth* Letter

The first reference to Shakspere in print appears in a posthumous publication, originally discovered by the Shakespearean scholar Thomas Tyrwhitt who refers to

> a passage, which not only points at Shakespeare as the author of them [the three plays of Henry the Sixth], but also shews, that, however meanly we may now think of them in comparison with his later productions, they had, at the time of their appearance, a sufficient degree of excellency to alarm the jealousy of the older playwrights. The passage, to which I refer, is in a pamphlet, entitled, *Greene's Groatsworth of Witte*, supposed to have been written by that voluminous author, Robert Greene. (Tyrwitt 1778, VI.565–66)

A counterargument will now be raised against the claim that Greene was expressing his 'jealousy' of Shakspere.

Seventeen days after the dramatist and pamphleteer Robert Greene died at the age of 32 on 3 September 1592, fellow penman Henry Chettle oversaw the publication of the *Groats-worth*. It contains a letter "To those Gentlemen his Quondam acquaintance, that spend their wits in making plaies, [to whom] R. G. wisheth a better exercise, and wisdome to preuent his extremities", which was intended for three of his fellow dramatists. Although they are not explicitly identified, there are sufficient clues to fill in the gaps. The first was drawn as

> thou famous gracer of Tragedians, that Greene, who hath said with thee (like the foole in his heart) There is no God. (Greene 1592)

This is generally agreed to be Christopher Marlowe, whose atheism Greene had shared up until his last days. Thomas Nashe seems to be "yong Iuvenall, that byting Satyrist, that lastly with mee together writ a Comedie", and George Peele is a good candidate for "sweete St. George". In fact, in Nashe's introduction to Greene's *Menaphon* (1589), after characterizing Peele as the "Atlas of Poetry", he goes on to discuss "Sundry other sweete Gentlemen I doe know" (Nashe 1589, sigs B3r–B3v).

The main body of the *Groats-worth* letter cautions them to beware of a particular player, referred to as "Shake-scene" (see Figure 6.1):

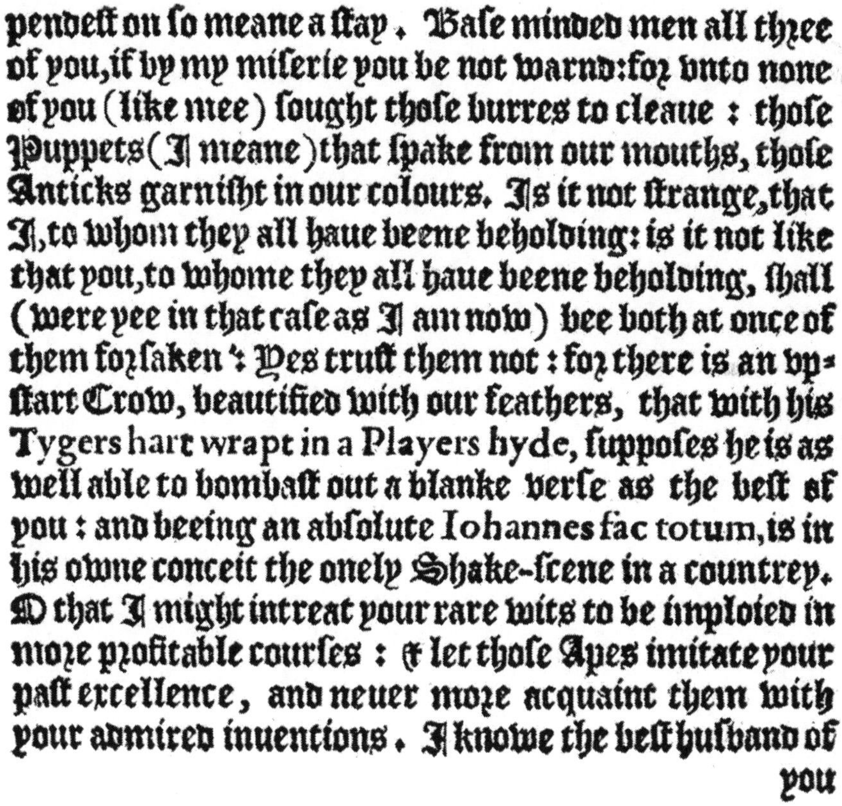

pendeſt on ſo meane a ſtay. Baſe minded men all three
of you, if by my miſerie you be not warnd: for vnto none
of you (like mee) ſought thoſe burres to cleaue: thoſe
Puppets (I meane) that ſpake from our mouths, thoſe
Anticks garniſht in our colours. Is it not ſtrange, that
I, to whom they all haue beene beholding: is it not like
that you, to whome they all haue beene beholding, ſhall
(were yee in that caſe as I am now) bee both at once of
them forſaken? Yes truſt them not: for there is an vp-
ſtart Crow, beautified with our feathers, that with his
Tygers hart wrapt in a Players hyde, ſuppoſes he is as
well able to bombaſt out a blanke verſe as the beſt of
you: and beeing an abſolute Iohannes fac totum, is in
his owne conceit the onely Shake-ſcene in a countrey.
O that I might intreat your rare wits to be imploied in
more profitable courſes: & let thoſe Apes imitate your
paſt excellence, and neuer more acquaint them with
your admired inuentions. I knowe the beſt huſband of
you

Figure 6.1 Warning letter to the three dramatists about Shakspere. Robert Greene, *Greenes Groats-worth of Witte* (1592, sig. Fv).

> Base-minded men all three of you, if by my miserie you be not warnd: for unto none of you (like mee) sought those burres to cleaue: those Puppets (I meane) that spake from our mouths, those Anticks garnisht in our colours. [...] Yes, trust them not: for there is

> an upstart Crow, beautified with our feathers, that with his *Tygers hart wrapped in a Players hyde*, supposes he is as well able to bombast out a blanke verse as the best of you: and beeing an absolute *Iohannes fac totum* [Jack-of-all-trades], is in his owne conceit the onely Shake-scene in a countrey. O that I might intreat your rare wits to be imploied in more profitable courses: & let those Apes imitate your past excellence, and neuer more acquaint them with your admired inuentions. (Greene 1592, sig. F^{v})

Here, in referring to “Puppets”, “Anticks”, “Players”, and “Apes”, the attack is on actors who recite the lines of scholarly playwrights. The “Tygers hart wrapped in a Players hyde” alludes to a line from *3 Henry VI* given to York who is about to be executed by the Lancastrian Queen Margaret:

> *Yorke*. […] Oh Tygres Heart, wrapt in a Woman’s Hide,
> How could’st though drayne the Life-blood of the Child,
> To bid the Father wipe his eyes withall,
> And yet be seene to beare a Woman’s face? (*3 Henry VI*, 1.4.137–40)

What follows in the letter next might suggest a motive for the *Groats-worth* complaint.

> I knowe the best husband of you will neuer proue an Usurer [moneylender] […] yet whilest you may, seeke you better Maisters; for it is pittie men of such rare wits, should be subiect to the pleasure of such rude groomes.

Perhaps he had gone to the actor ‘Shake-scene’, a man whom he regarded as lower class than himself, to obtain a loan. This theme reoccurs in other parts of the pamphlet. Greene tells the tale of Roberto who meets an actor and learns from him that “men of my profession gette by schollers [playwrights] their whole living” (Greene 1592, sig. $D4^{v}$). Greene later reveals that Roberto’s “life in most parts agreeing with mine” (Greene 1592, sig. $E3^{r}$). Roberto attempts to con his brother Luciano out of his inheritance, meets an actor, and makes his fortune as a playwright. Unfortunately, he wastes all his earnings and soon finds himself close to death, ruined and penniless. At the end of the pamphlet, we find Aesop’s fable of the ant and the grasshopper. While the former stores provisions for the winter, the latter makes no such preparation, and after an unsuccessful plea to the ant to help him, the grasshopper expires due to his own negligence. So, the whole theme running through the *Groats-worth* is about the lack of preparation for times of want, which was the state Greene had found himself in on his deathbed.

Citing the work of Thomas Nashe, Brian Vickers points out

> the increasing prosperity and social recognition that the actors were enjoying. Greene was not the first to express the resentment of the university-educated playwrights at the actors' social rise and professional success. (Vickers 2017, 244–67)

In fact, Robert Greene had a history of despising players whom he relied on to buy his work (Vickers 2017, 251).

6.2 The Letter's Meaning

Several researchers have taken the letter as evidence for Shakspere's burgeoning reputation as a dramatist. An early interpretation saw James Halliwell-Phillipps declare that it had been "composed under the influence of a profound jealousy of Shakespeare" (1883, 92). Edmund Chambers thought that the letter was "sufficient to show that by September 1592 Shakespeare was both a player and a maker of plays" (1930, I.59). In more recent times, Jonathan Bate takes Greene to be declaring that "as an upstart writer he [Shakspere] is now imitating their style", and that '*Johannes fac totum*', when "applied to Shakespeare, it means first actor, then dramatist" (2016, 15–16). Bate contends that in using the term 'upstart', Greene is declaring Shakspere to be "an important new voice in the theatre" and "thanks to the *Henry VI* plays, his new career as a writer was just taking off". To respond to this claim, our first course will be to clarify Greene's meaning in the letter. Returning to the *Groats-worth*'s "upstart Crow, beautified with our feathers", Robert Greene had previously used the 'crow and feathers' metaphor at least three times before. For example, in his dedication to the Countess of Derby in *The Myrrour of Modestie* (1584b) he attempts to excuse himself for making use of Homer's tale of *Ulysses* (see Figure 6.2):

> But your honour may thinke I play like Ezops Crowe, which dekt hir selfe with others feathers, or like the proud Poet Batyllus, which subscribed his name to Virgils verses, and yet presented them to Augustus.

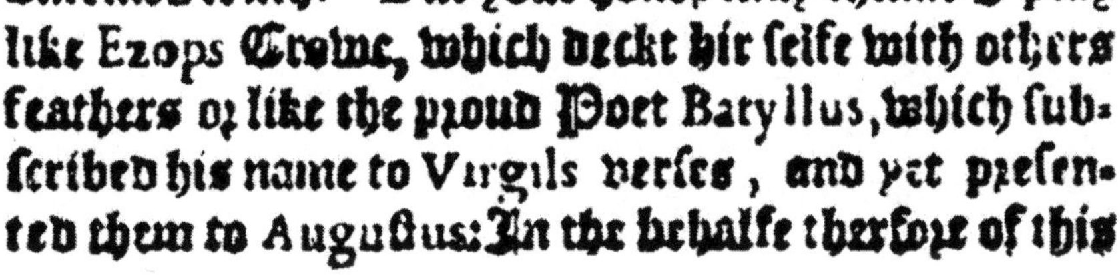
vnfeined truth. But your honor may thinke I play like Ezops Crowe, which deckt hir selfe with others feathers or like the proud Poet Batyllus, which subscribed his name to Virgils verses, and yet presented them to Augustus: In the behalfe therfore of this

Figure 6.2 Contextual use of 'Ezops's Crowe'. Robert Greene, *The Myrrour of Modestie* (1594, 'Dedication').

Aesop's fable, 'The Crow, the Eagle, and the Feathers' is directed against people who boast that they have something they do not. In seeming to have invented Homer's plot, this is also the sense in which Greene is using it. In his 'Orpheus's tale' in *Orpharion* (1599), he reveals more about the association he intends to be made with Aesop's Crow (1599, sig. D^{v}); see Figure 6.3:

The Thracian general Acestes addresses Princess Lydia whom she regards to be below her:

> if he [Lydia's father] knewe of thy daring presumtion, he would repay thy follie with such punishments, as thy aspiring thoughts doe merrit: hee would unplume thee of all thy feathers: and like Esops Crowe turne thee naked to the worlde: that they which grudged at thy hastie promotion, might laugh at thy sudaine fall

So, when Robert Greene wanted to claim that someone was acting above their station he used Aesop's Crow.[1]

However, when he wanted to allude to plagiarism he used Battilus, as the following extract from 'To the Reader' in *Farewell to follie* testifies:

> which for their calling and grauitie, being loth to haue anie prophane phamplets passe vnder their hand, get some other Batillus to set his name to their verses: Thus is the asse made proud by this vnder hande brokerie. (1591, sig. $A4^{r}$)

Also, from "To the Gentlemen Readers, health" in his *Menaphon* (1589) he introduces

> Batillus the ouer bold poet of Rome, that at euerie winke of Caesar would deliuer up an hundred verses, though neuer a one plausible, thinking the Emperours smile a priuiledge for his ignorance.

So, for Robert Greene it is Batillus who represents the plagiarist, stealing the work of another without compensation, but he does not produce him in the *Groats-worth* letter. Instead it is Aesop's Crow, which, for Greene, simply means assuming a higher rank than is justified.

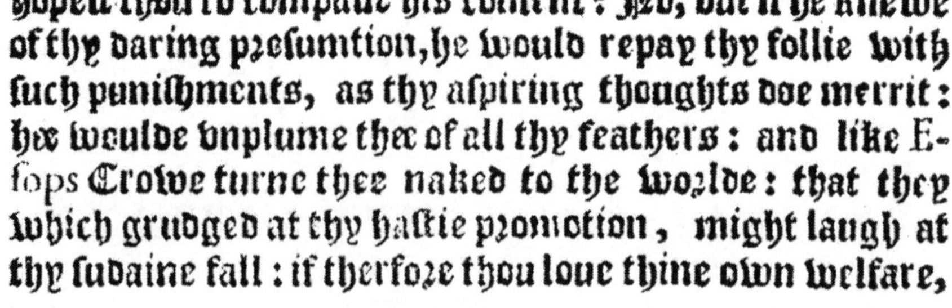
hopeſt thou to compaſſe his conſent ? No, but if he knewe
of thy daring preſumtion, he would repay thy follie with
ſuch puniſhments, as thy aſpiring thoughts doe merrit :
hee woulde vnplume thee of all thy feathers : and like E-
ſops Crowe turne thee naked to the worlde : that they
which grudged at thy haſtie promotion, might laugh at
thy ſudaine fall : if therfore thou loue thine own welfare,

Figure 6.3 Contextual use of 'Esops Crowe'. Robert Greene, *Orpharion* (1599, D^{v}).

6.3 *Groats-worth* and *Vertues Common-Wealth*

There is another item of evidence that is worth considering before reaching a judgement on "Shake-scene", and it appears in a puritanical pamphlet under the name of Henry Crosse. *Vertues Common-wealth or The Highway to Honor* (1603) was an attack on all those who led an undisciplined life, including those who were attracted to lewd and lascivious theatre plays. It is relevant to the present purpose in that it contains multiple references to the *Groats-worth* pamphlet. For example, it makes use of the fable of the ant and the grasshopper.[2] Greene's pamphlet has

> Now to all men I bid farewell in like sort, with this conceited fable of that olde Comedian Aesope. An Ant and a Grashopper walking together on a Greene, the one carelessly skipping, the other carefully prying what winters prouision was scattered in the way: the Grashopper scorning (as wantons will) this needless thrift (as hee tearmed it) reproved him thus. (1592, sig. F2^{v})

Vertues Common-wealth also uses 'conceited fable', 'walking together on a', 'carelessly skipping', 'prying', and 'what [...] provision was scattered in the way' as follows:

> Esope affoorded a pleasant conceited fable: The Ant & the Grassehopper (saith he) walking together on a sunnie banke, the one piping [singing] and carelesly skipping, looked after nothing; the other circumspect in prying about what prouision was scattered in the way. (Crosse 1603, sig. R4^{v})

Greene continues with

> The grasshopper was sent away and "foodlesse, helpless and strengthles [...] yielding to the wethers extremit, died comfortles without remedy". (1592, sigs F3^{r}–F3^{v})

Henry Crosse also uses 'foodlesse', 'weathers extremeties', and 'died [...] without remedie':

> With this the Grashopper yielding to the weathers extremeties, foodlesse, comfortlesse, and succourlesse, died without remedie. (1603, sig. R4^{v})

The term "base minded" in the *Groats-worth* letter also appears in *Vertues* as "in such base minded people" (Crosse 1603, sig. T2^{r}), and the letter concludes with "In this I might insert two more, that both haue writ against these buckram Gentlemen" (Greene 1592, sig. F2^{r}). The Reverend Alexander Grosart (1822–99), who republished Crosse's pamphlet, noted

To conclude,it were further to be wiſhed, that thoſe admired wittes of this age, Tragædians,and Comædians,that garniſh Theaters with their inuentions,would ſpend their wittes in more profitable ſtudies, and leaue off to maintaine thoſe Anticks,and Puppets,that ſpeake out of their mouthes : for it is pittie ſuch noble giftes, ſhould be ſo baſely imployed, as to proſtitute their ingenious labours to inrich ſuch buckorome gentlemen.

Figure 6.4 Repetition of the *Groats-worth's* "buckorome gentlemen". Henry Crosse, *Vertues Common-wealth* (1603, Q3^{v}).

that "buckorome gentlemen" also appears in *Vertues* (Crosse 1603, Q3^{v}), suggesting that the *Groats-worth* letter was "perhaps in Crosse's mind when he wrote this paragraph" (Grosart 1878, 122); see Figure 6.4.[3] So, both pamphlets mention 'Antics', 'Puppets', and 'buckram Gentlemen'.

Another striking phrase in Crosse's pamphlet is the *Groats-worth*'s "bombast out a blancke verse"; see Figure 6.1 for Greene (1592, sig. F^{v}), and Figure 6.5 for Crosse (1603, sig. P^{r}).

However, Crosse makes a further charge, see Figure 6.6 (1603, sig. P^{r}), which has echoes of Greene's mention of Batillus in *The Myrrour of Modestie* (1584). Since the *Groats-worth of Witte* aims the charge at Shakspere, and *Vertues Common-wealth* is parodying it, then the claim is now clear. Shakspere is "writing verse not worth the reading" and claiming as his own "the well deseruing labours of other ingenious spirits". Towards the end of the *Groats-worth* letter we have "whose loose life hath made religion loathsome to your eares" (1592, sig. F2^{r}). In fact, this whole line appears verbatim in *Vertues Common-wealth* (1603, T^{r}).[4]

In case any doubt remains that *Vertues Common-wealth* is taking aim at Shakspere, consider the following. In September 1601, Shakspere's father died, and he inherited his heraldic arms and the title of esquire. Eight months later, Shakspere purchased 107 acres of land near Stratford-on-Avon for £320. This fact led James Halliwell-Phillips to remark:

> It may be that this acquisition is referred to by Crosse in his Vertues Common-wealth, 1603, when he speaks thus ungenerously of the actor and dramatists of the period, — "as these copper-laced gentlemen growe rich, purchase lands by adulterous playes, and not few of them usurers and extortioners, which they exhaust out of the purses of their haunters, so are they puft up in such pride and selfe-love as they envie their equalles and scorne theyr inferiours". (Crosse 1603, sig. Q; Halliwell-Phillipps 1883, 172 & 326)

> Hee that can but bombaſt out a blancke verſe, and
> make both the endes iumpe together in a ryme, is forth-
> with a poet laureat, challẽging the garland of baies, and
> in one ſlauering diſcourſe or other, hang out the badge
> of his follie. O how weake and ſhallow much of theyr

Figure 6.5 Repetition of the *Groats-worth's* "bombast out a blancke verse". Henry Crosse, *Vertues Common-wealth* (1603, sig. P^{r}).

> bour : in ſo much that oftentimes they ſticke ſo faſt in
> mudde, they looſe their wittes ere they can get out, ei-
> ther like *Chirrillus*, writing verſe not worth the reading,
> or *Battillus*, arrogating to themſelues, the well deſeruing
> labours of other ingenious ſpirits. Farre from the deco-
> rum of *Chauſer*, *Gowers*, *Lidgate*, &c. or our honourable
> moderne Poets, who are no whit to be touched with
> this, but reuerently eſteemed, and liberally rewar-
> ded.

Figure 6.6 Mention of Chirrulus and Battillus. Henry Crosse, *Vertues Common-wealth* (1603, sig. P^{r}).

Here, he must have had in mind the *Return from Parnassus* comedies which were acted during the Christmas revels of 1601–2 by the students of St John's College, Cambridge. In the third *Return from Parnassus* there are several lines that appear to refer not only to actors in general but to Shakspere in particular (see Studioso's speech at the end of Section 3.3): "With mouthing words that better wits have framed, \ They purchase lands and now Esquires are named" (Anon 1606, sig. H^{r}). Again, the claim is being made that an actor is profiting from the work of scholars. The conclusion is inescapable that the author of *Vertues Common-wealth* had not only inspected the *Groats-worth* pamphlet but was reiterating its opinion of Shakspere as a man who wrote poor-quality blank verse, bought plays from scholars to make a profit, and pretended it was all his own work.

6.4 Chettle, Greene, or Nashe?

Robert Greene published over three dozen books in his 12-year career and tended to publish several pamphlets on one particular genre before moving on to the next. Steve Metz has produced a table breaking down the *Groats-worth* into 13 parts, relating each to one of the seven genres' that spanned Greene's prose career. For Metz, the pamphlet is a "complete and strategic summary of Greene's multifaceted career as prose author" (2008, Table 2, 126). However, doubts were expressed shortly after its publication as to whether or not Robert Greene had actually composed the *Groats-worth* letter. William Wright had entered it in the Stationers Register "upon the peril of Henrye Chettle", and Chettle the dramatist quickly came under suspicion as the letter's author. In 1969, Warren Austin presented a stylistic test that led him to suggest that Chettle had composed it. Diana Price has also adopted this position, entreating us to "recall that Henry Chettle passed off his attack on Shake-scene under a dead man's name to avoid retaliation" (2012, 100). However, Austin's work has now been rejected chiefly on the grounds that he studied only 5 of Greene's 32 prose works and excluded rare words that Greene used but Chettle did not (Westley 2006).

In "To the Gentlemen Readers", which prefaced *Kind Hart's Dream* (1592),[5] Chettle reveals that:

> About these three moneths since died M. Robert Greene […] his Groatsworth of Wit, in which a letter written to diuers play-makers, is offensiuely by one or two of them taken […] How I haue all the time of my conversing in printing hindred the bitter inueying against schollers, it hath been very well knowne.

The ones that took offence were amongst those three to whom the letter was written, and their identity is amplified by the fact that Chettle also defends himself against "the bitter inueying against schollers". Since Shakspere had no university education, he must be referring to any two of Marlowe (Corpus Christi, Cambridge), Nashe (St John's College, Cambridge), and Peele (Christ Church College, Oxford). He continues:

> With neither of them that take offence was I acquainted, and with one of them I care not if I neuer be.

The latter reference suggests the atheist Marlowe. The way Chettle uses 'neither' suggests that exactly two took offence and included in these two was the one "I care not about", rather than there being two who took offence and then there was an additional third one he cared not about. The reason for this interpretation is that Chettle goes on to inform us that:

> The other [of the three], whome at that time I did not so much spare […] myselfe have seen his demeanor no lesse ciuill than he exelent in the qualitie he professes: Besides, diuers of worship haue reported his vprightness of dealing, which argues his honesty, and his facetious grace in writting, that aprooues his art.

This third person is different from the two that 'neither' denotes, and different from than the one he cared not about, and so this dramatist must be Nashe or Peele. It turns out that the facts fit Thomas Nashe. There is evidence that Nashe had already been suspected of composing the letter before Chettle's apology was published. In "A priuate Epistle of the Author" in the second edition of his *Pierce Penilesse* (1592),[6] Nashe refers to the *Groats-worth* as a "scald lying trivial pamphlet [...] given out to be my doing". That Nashe was suspected is confirmed by Chettle's claim in *Kind Harts Dream* that the misdeed was "not mine nor Maister Nashes, as some vniustly haue affirmed". However, Nashe takes care to assure his readers that not "the least word or sillable in it proceeded from my pen".

So, can stylistic evidence decide between Chettle, Greene, and Nashe? The letter to the three dramatists contains the phrase "Sweet S. George", and in Nashe's introduction to Greene's *Menaphon* (1589) he refers to George Peele as the "Atlas of Poetrie" in the context of "Sundry other sweete Gentlemen I doe know" (Nashe 1589, sigs B3^{r}–B3^{v}). Of course, Robert Greene must have known about this and might have borrowed it for the *Groats-worth*. Table 6.1 shows the results of RCP searches carried out on the letter for EEBO texts dated before 1592. In fact, it is a low-grade RCP test as some of the locutions are not particularly rare, but they are included to allow a comparison between these three authors as contributors to the letter. Here, a return is logged in the table only when at least one of these three writers uses it. For example, for locution No. 1 "Quondam" has a rarity of 2.887%, which is not particularly impressive. However, of the three candidates, Robert Greene is the first to use it as an adjective to an English noun (as the *Groats-worth* does) in *Farewell to folly* (1591) with "quondam king Vadislaus". Thomas Nashe has prior use of "quondam", but he includes it in a Latin tag "Ille ego qui quondam" in *An almond for a parrat* (1589). Chettle does not register at all. It should be clear from an inspection of Table 6.1 that, of the three suspects, Greene has evidence of a far greater first use of unusual phrases and collocations (see Column 4, Table 6.1) that appear in the letter than either Nashe or Chettle. In fact, Henry Chettle explicitly states in his introduction to *Kind Hart's Dream* (1592) that "onely in the letter I put something out, but in the whole booke not a worde in, for I protest it was all Greene's [...]".

The *Groats-worth* clearly registers its disdain for players, and in the spring of 1592, a few months before its publication, Robert Greene did just that in *The Defence of Conny Catching* (1592), which he published under a pseudonym:

> Aske the Queens Players, if you sold them not Orlando Furioso for twenty Nobles, and when they were in the country, sold the same Play to the Lord Admirals men for as much more. Was not this plaine Conny-catching Maister R.G.? [...] But I heare when this was

Table 6.1 RCP results for *Groats-worth* letter from EEBO texts dated before 1592

No.	*Locution in letter*	*EEBO search*	*Work*	*Rarity*
1	"Quondam acquaintance"	{quondam} [context: adjective to English noun]	Greene *Farewell to folly* (1591).[a]	120/4156(2.887%)
2	"this Apostata perished"	{Apostata}	Greene *Gvvydonius* (1584)	305/4156(7.339%)
3	"base-minded men"	{base minded}	Greene *Gvvydonius* (1584)[b]	37/4156(0.890%)
4	"bombast out a blanke verse"	{bombast near.5 verse}	Nashe introduction to Greene's *Menaphon Cammillus alarum to slumbering Euphues* (1589)[c]	1/4156(0.024%)
5	"it skils not though they make a least at them"	{it skills not}	Greene *The third and last part of conny-catching* (1592)[d]	18/4156(0.433%)
6	"Flie lust, as the deathsman of the soule"	{deathsman}	Greene *Ciceronis amor* (1589)[e]	2/4156(0.048%)
7	"which I am forst to knit vp in some fewe lines of words"	{to knit up}	Greene *Gvvydonius The carde of fancie* (1584)[f]	103/4156(2.478%)

[a]Greene has "quondam king Vadislaus". Nashe in *An almond for a parrat* (1589) has the Latin "Ille ego qui quondam" as well as in other later publications but never uses it in as an adjective to an English noun.

[b]Greene has the 15th use of all returned authors in EEBO with "my father is not so base minded as to bestow me". In *Euphues his censure* (1587), Greene uses it as an adjective "base mynded cowarde" and again three times in *The second part of conny-catching* (1591) with "Base minded Cooseners/cutpurses/leachers". In *Greenes mourning garment* (1590) it appears as "A[?]thocles was base minded". Neither Nashe nor Chettle records a use.

[c]In 'To the Gentlemen students of both Uniuersities' Nashe writes "with the swelling bombast of a bragging blank verse". Henry Crosse has "Hee that can but bombast out a blancke verse" *Vertues Common-wealth* (1603).

[d]Greene has "it skilles not how they come by it [domestic ruin]". Nashe uses it later in *Pierce Penilesse* (1592).

[e]Greene has "but in loue delay is the vnhappie deathsman". He also has the other use before 1592 with "Well Democles commanded the deathsman to doo his deuoyre" in *Menaphon Camillus alarum* (1589), which is separate from the introductory part that Nashe wrote. It also appears in two plays given to William Shakespeare, *The First and Second Part of the Troublesome Raigne of Iohn King of England* (1611) and in *The Tragedie of King Lear* (1623).

[f]Greene has "if my Father were content to knitte vp the knotte", and he also uses it in *Planetomachia* (1585). Nashe's earliest use is "To knit vp this description" in *The Terrors of the Night* (1594), and he repeats it in *The vnfortunate traueller* (1594). Chettle has no recorded usage.

> objected, that you made this excuse: that there was no more faith to be held with Plaiers, than with them that valued faith at the price of a feather; for as they were Comoedians to act, so the actions of their liues were Cameleon like, that they were vncertaine, variable, time pleasers, men that measured honestie by profite, and that regarded their Authors not be desart, but by necessitie of time. (*Cuthbert Cunny-catcher* 1592, sigs C3–C3^{v})

Henry Chettle seems not to have had a clear motive for attacking Shakspere.[7] So, either the letter was written by Thomas Nashe who was expressing his own grievance, and cloaked his involvement by making himself one of the three addressees of the letter, or Robert Greene was "copying that ['bombast out a blanke verse'] by Nashe in his Preface to *Menaphon* three years earlier" (Vickers 2017, 37). Out of the three, the comparative stylistic evidence in Table 6.1 points emphatically to Robert Greene as the complainant against Shakspere, and this actually supports Henry Chettle's testimony.

6.5 The Malone–Alexander Debate

The following analysis of the *Groats-worth* letter supports Peter Alexander's argument for Shakspere actually writing lines of dialogue. However, it opposes his view that Shakspere would not have worked on the plays of others.

In 1734, Lewis Theobald suggested that the play *3 Henry VI* had "been brought to him [Shakspere] as a director of the stage" (Steevens and Rowe 1804, VI.i–ii). In his *Dissertation on the Three Parts of King Henry VI* (1787), the Irish Shakespearean scholar Edmund Malone asks of the letter

> what does the writer mean by calling him [Shakspere] "a crow beautified with our feathers?" My solution is, that GREENE and PEELE were the joint authors of the two quarto plays [Henry VI, Parts 2 and 3 …] or that Greene was the author of one, and Peele of the other. (1787, 19)

He continues

> [Shakspere] not long before the year 1592, when Greene wrote this dying exhortation to his friend […] new modelled and amplified these two pieces […] exhibiting two plays, formed upon old dramas written by them […] a proceeding which the authors of the original plays considered as an invasion both of their literary property and character. (1787, 20)

In response, Peter Alexander cites the fact that Robert Greene had previously used Aesop's Crow to characterize a player in ancient Rome who was merely reciting the lines of others, rather than asserting ownership of them (1929, 43). In *Francesco's Fortunes* (1590), Greene writes of the boastful actor Roscius who was invited to dinner as a guest of Archias the poet. There he met the famous orator Tully with whom he dared to compare his own skill. Tully lost no time in reducing him with

> Why Roscius, art thou proud with Esops Crow, being pranct with the glorie of others feathers? of thy selfe thou canst say nothing [...] what sentence thou utterest on the stage, flowes from the censure of our wittes. (Greene 1590a, sig. C^{v})

So the accusation against Shakspere as an actor could simply be that he was gaining an advantage from reciting the lines of others.

In reference to the *Groats-worth* line "with his *Tyger's hart wrapped in a Player's hyde*, supposes he is as well able to bombast out a blanke verse as the best of you" Peter Alexander provides a good argument for Shakspere being a contributor to the play:

> this use of *his* [Tyger's hart] indicates that the victim [Shakspere] is being condemned out of his own mouth. (1929, 48)

In other words, the employment of "his" must be evidence that Greene understood this line as having being composed by Shakspere. In fact, this might be the only line that we can be sure Shakspere ever wrote!

On the issue of Shakspere revising a play by Robert Greene, Alexander states:

> there is no clear example of a play written by one man being added to during the author's lifetime by another of respectable standing who was not his friend or collaborator. (1929, 45)

Henry Chichester Hart further suggests that

> In *The True Tragedy* I see a little of Marlowe, less of Greene, more of Peele and much more of Shakespeare. [...] Those [parallels] from Greene are not numerous or important enough to be made special reference to. (1925, xxii)

John Dover–Wilson thought the weight of evidence was elsewhere. He thought that Robert Greene took "the main scheme of *2* and *3 Henry VI* from Hall [*Chronicle*]" (1952, xix) so that

> Richard, 'the murderous Machiavel', from one standpoint, as saintly Henry from another, reflects the anarchy and the agony that reigned in England between the battles of St Albans and Tewkesbury. And it

> was this that Part III was specially designed to bring out, originally designed, I believe, by Robert Greene, but with new lines added and the whole strengthened and tightened up by the hand of the master dramatist. (1952, xxvii)

In more recent times, Randall Martin has claimed that "Past suggestions of possible co-authors, such as Robert Greene, lack any substantial basis of evidence" (2001, 96n).

So, Malone assigns *3 Henry VI* to Greene and/or Peele; Dover–Wilson gives it to Greene; and Hart attributes *The True Tragedy* (1595), the low-quality Octavo version of *3 Henry VI*, to Marlowe and Peele, but mostly to Shakspere, while ruling out Robert Greene. The trouble is, for the case of *3 Henry VI*, there is insufficient evidence to decide the matter, and so at this point we turn again to the new method of RCP.

6.6 RCP of the Octavo and Folio *3 Henry VI*

Stylometric methods are at their least effective when there is more than one contributor to the section of text (segment) that a word count is taken from. If the demand for a section of text to be uniform in one contributor is not met, then a reliable comparison with other known single-author plays cannot be made. The play *3 Henry VI* appears to have several contributors, and possibly later revisers who might have corrupted the uniformity of the segments. Samuel Schoenbaum suggests that *The true Tragedie of Richard duke of Yorke* (Octavo) is a "Bad Quarto" of *The third Part of Henry Sixt* and so "the authorities have analyzed the style of what [is], in effect, [a] non-existent [play]" (Schoenbaum 1966, 174). In fact, the latter contains nearly 1,000 lines that are not in the former.

In 2005, John Burrows developed the Zeta test, which divides a target text into 2,000-word segments, performs a count of prepared lexical words in each segment, and relies on the assumption that the play under test has a single author (Burrows 2002). This will be examined in more detail in Chapter 13. Burrows subsequently collaborated with Hugh Craig to apply it to the *First Folio* version of *3 Henry VI* entitled *The third Part of Henry Sixt with the death of the Duke of YORKE* (Burrows and Craig 2017, 201–02). In Figure 11.3 of their work (schematically reproduced in Figure 6.7), they show that when considering the lexical words that Greene commonly uses, and those he infrequently uses, the segment counts taken from *3 Henry VI* do not fall within those obtained from Greene's corpus. So they rule out Greene. However, as already stated, the dubious assumption is made that none of the segments in *3 Henry VI* has undergone a later revision.

In RCP, a systematic and exhaustive assessment of the rarity of each phrase and collocation in the play is carried out against contemporary texts in the EEBO database. This is set out in greater detail in

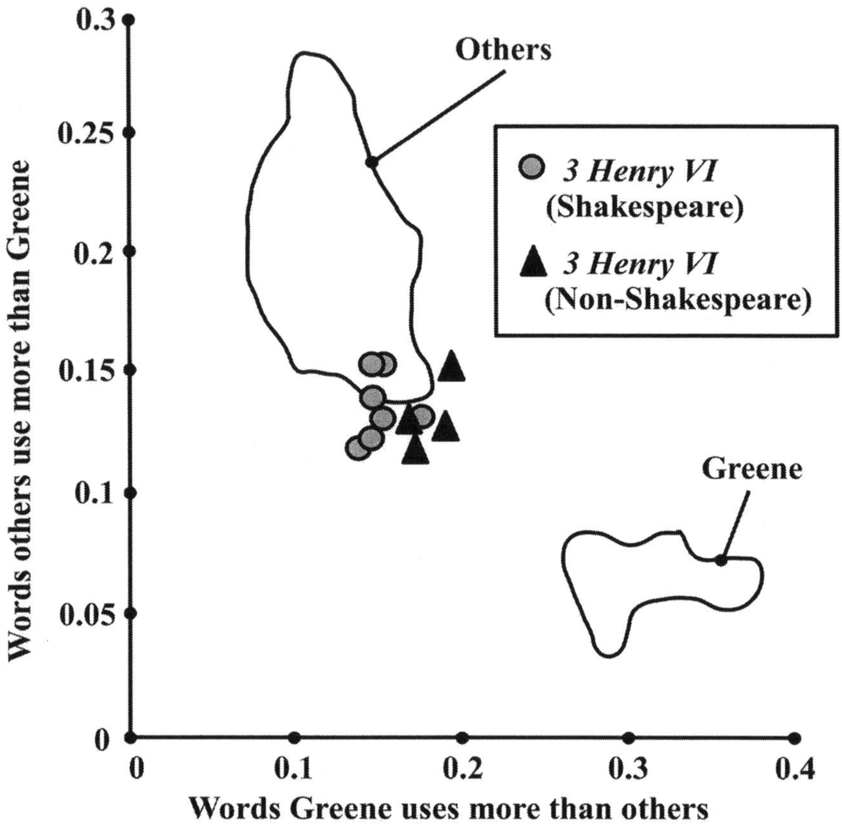

Figure 6.7 Result of Burrows and Craig (2017, Figure 11.3) Zeta test showing that words most commonly used by Greene do not correspond with those in *3 Henry VI*.

Chapter 14. The located authors who used these rare phrases, both before and after the assumed date of the target text, can then be recorded for assessment as contributors to the play. Only if a particular author identified by these rare correspondences appears to have borrowed from the play (his rare locutions are later than the target), and the play appears to have borrowed from this author (his rare locutions appear earlier than the target), can we make the claim for a contribution to the play. For *3 Henry VI*, the most RCP returns occur for Robert Greene, Christopher Marlowe, Anthony Munday, and Thomas Lodge, and these are presented in Tables A.1–A.4 in Appendix A for both the Octavo (1595) and *First Folio* (1623) versions. The results of RCP profiling suggest that Robert Greene contributed to Acts 2, 3, and 5; Christopher Marlowe to Acts 2 and 5; Anthony Munday to Acts 4 and 5; and Thomas Lodge to Act 3.

6.7 The Verdict

The argument presented here is that Robert Greene had more reason to complain about Shakspere than Nashe or Chettle. Here was an upstart actor who was not only appending lines to a Greene–Marlowe–Munday play but was also making a handsome profit from it, while Greene, who was one of its main contributors, remained poverty-stricken. Greene seems to have received the nominal financial reward for his part in the writing, but he evidently lost any credit that was due. Now, according to Brian Vickers, "the primary motive for Greene's attack on Shakespeare was his new status as both an actor and a dramatist, and the threat that he posed to the university-educated playwrights" (2017, 13). This notion of "threat" and the implication of Shakspere's skill are not what the evidence suggests. Greene's complaint is about a particular actor who recites lines from better pens, that is, scholars such as himself, and makes a considerable profit while Greene sinks inexorably into poverty. The *Groats-worth of Witte* letter simply reinforces the claim that Shakspere was a play broker who added lines to the plays of others then claimed it all as his own work.

Notes

1 Robert Greene also uses it again elsewhere in *Gwydonivs* to characterize folly, "he would unplume thee of all his feathers, that like Aesops Crowe thou mighst receiue the reward of thy rashnesse" (1584a, 35^{v}), and in *Greenes Neuer Too Late* (1590b, sig. C^{r}).
2 The fable of "the Ant and the Sygale" appears in *Aesop's fables* (1584).
3 An EEBO search reveals that 'buckram' or 'buckeram' is returned in one record out of a possible 4,339(0.023%) before 1603, so I suggest it is rare. The nineteenth-century Grosart edition has page numbers, while the original seventeenth-century copies have page signatures.
4 Crosse has "Father *Cato* was wont to say, it was lost labour to talke of *Vertue* to the belly, for that it hath no eares to heare, because their loose life maketh religion loathsome to their eares".
5 Registered 8 December 1592.
6 Registered 8 August 1592; 1st edition published 8 September 1592; 2nd edition almost immediately after.
7 Harold Jenkins declared that "it is difficult to conceive how Chettle could have been so bitter against men with whom he was totally unacquainted" (1935, 33).

Bibliography

Aesop. *Aesop's fables*. Westmynstre: Printed by William Caxton, 1584.
Alexander, Peter. *Shakespeare's Henry VI and Richard III*. Cambridge: Cambridge University Press, 1929.
Anon. *The Returne from Pernassus: or The Scourge of Simony*. London: Printed by G. Eld for Iohn Wright, 1606. STC: 19309.
Austin, Warren. *A Computer-Aided Technique for Stylistic Discrimination: The Authorship of Greene's Groatsworth of Wit*. Washington, DC: U.S. Department of Health, Education, and Welfare, 1969.

Bate, Jonathan. *The Genius of Shakespeare*. London: Picador, 2016.

Burrows, John. "'Delta' – A measure of stylistic difference and a guide to likely authorship." *Literary and Linguistic Computing* 17, No. 3 (2002): 131–47.

Burrows, John, and Hugh Craig. "The Joker in the Pack? Marlowe, Kyd, and the Co-authorship of *Henry VI, Part 3*." In Gary Taylor and Gabriel Egan, eds. *The New Oxford Shakespeare Authorship Companion*. Oxford: Oxford University Press, 2017.

Chambers, Edmund K. *William Shakespeare: A Study of the Facts and Problems*. 2 vols. Oxford: Clarendon Press, 1930.

Chettle, Henry. *Kind–harts Dreame*. London: Imprinted for William Wright, 1593. STC: 5123.

Crosse, Henry. *Vertue's Common-wealth or the Highway to Honour*. London: Printed for Iohn Newbery, 1603.

Cunny-catcher, Cuthbert. *The Defence of Conny Catching*. London: A. I[effes] for Thomas Gubbins, 1592.

Dover Wilson, John, ed. *The Third Part of King Henry VI*. Cambridge: Cambridge University Press, 1952.

Greene, Robert. *Gwydonivs. The Carde of Fancie*. London: Imprinted [by T. East] for William Posonby, 1584a.

Greene, Robert. *The Myrrour of Modestie*. London: Imprinted by Roger Ward, 1584b.

Greene, Robert. *Menaphon Camillas Alarum to Slumbering Euphues*. London: Printed by T[Thomas] O[Orwin] for Sampson Clarke, 1589.

Greene, Robert. *Franscesco's Fortunes, or the Second Parte of Greene's Neuer Too Late*. London: Imprinted for N. L. and Iohn Busby, 1590a.

Greene, Robert. *Greenes Neuer Too Late*. London: Printed by William Stansby for Iohn Smithwicke, 1590b.

Greene, Robert. *Farewell to Folly*. London: Imprinted by Thomas Scarlet for T. Gubbin and T. Newman, 1591.

Greene, Robert. *Groats-worth of Witte, Bought with a Million of Repentance*. London: Imprinted for William Wright, 1592.

Greene, Robert. *Orpharion*. London: Printed [by J. Roberts] for Edward White, 1599.

Grosart, Alexander B., ed. *Vertues Commonwealth by Henry Crosse (1603)*. Private publication, printed for the subscribers. Call No. 2704 d.26, Oxford: Bodleian Library, 1878.

Halliwell-Phillips, J. O. *Outlines of the Life of Shakespeare*. London: Longmans, Green, and Co, 1883.

Hart, H. C. *The Third Part of King Henry the Sixth*. London: Methuen and Co., 1925.

Jenkins, Harold. "On the authenticiy of Greene's Groatsworth of Wit and the Repentence of Robert Greene." *The Review of English Studies* 11, No. 41 (1935): 28–41.

Malone, Edmond. *A Dissertation on the Three Parts of King Henry VI*. London: Henry Baldwin, 1787.

Martin, Randall. *Henry VI, Part 3*. The Oxford Shakespeare. Oxford University Press, 2001.

Metz, Steve. "Forming Greene: Theorizing the early modern author in Groatsworth of Wit." In Kirk Melnikoff and Edward Gieskes, eds. *Writing Robert Greene: Essays on England's First Notorious Professional Writer.* New York: Routledge, 2008.

Nashe, Thomas. "To the gentlemen students." In Robert Greene, ed. *Menaphon Camillas Alarum to Slumbering Euphues.* London: Printed by T[Thomas] O[Orwin] for Sampson Clarke, 1589.

Nashe, Thomas. *Pierce Penilesse His Supplication to the Deuill.* London: Printed by Abell Ieffries, 1592. STC: 18373.

Price, Diana. *Shakespeare's Unorthodox Biography: New Evidence of an Authorship Problem.* Shakespeare-authorship.com, 2012.

Schoenbaum, S. *Internal Evidence and Elizabethan Dramatic Authorship.* Evanston, IL: Northwestern University Press, 1966.

Steevens, George, and Nicholas Rowe. *The Plays of William Shakespeare.* 10 vols. London: Printed by T. Bensley, for Wynne and Scholey, 1804.

Tyrwhitt, Thomas. *The Plays of William Shakespeare. In Ten Volumes. With the Corrections and Illustrations of Various Commentators: To Which are Added Notes by S. Johnson and G. Steevens.* 10 vols. Second edition. London: Printed for C. Bathurst, 1778.

Vickers, Brian. "Upstart Crow? The myth of Shakespeare's plagiarism." *The Review of English Studies* 68, No. 284 (April 2017): 244–67.

Westley, Richard. "Computing error: Reassessing Austin's study of Groatsworth of Wit." *Literary and Linguistic Computing* 21, No. 3 (September 2006): 363–78.

7 Bacon's *Vertues*?

Vertues Common-wealth (1603) by Henry Crosse contains strong echoes of the *Groats-worth* letter that accuses Shakspere of hiring scholars to write for him and taking all the credit. When the antiquarian Alexander Grosart tried to find a biography for Henry Crosse, *Vertues*' putative author, he sought in vain. It turns out that there are several unusual apophthegms and rare locutions shared by the pamphlet and Francis Bacon's work. These are presented together with an estimate of their rarity, which suggests, at the very least, that Bacon borrowed from *Vertues* and knew of the *Groats-worth* accusation against Shakspere.

7.1 History of *Vertues Common-Wealth*

In Chapter 6, evidence was given that a pamphlet published in 1603 under the name of Henry Crosse, *Vertues Common-wealth or The Highway to Honour*, contains multiple references to the *Groats-worth of Witte* letter in which "Shake-scene" is portrayed. In fact, locutions such as "Antics", "Puppets", "buckram gentlemen", "bombast out a blank verse", and "whose life hath made religion loathsome to your ears" appear in both. We shall now look at the messages conveyed in *Vertues* and investigate its 'author'.

In 1603, John Newbery published *Vertues Common-wealth: or The Highway to Honour* by Henry Crosse.[1] It is dedicated on Leaf A3 "To the right honourable the Lord Mayor [of London]", and a reprint in the same year modifies this "To the right honourable Robert Lee, Lord Maior". At this point, the error "indiuiam" on the title page is corrected to "inuidiam". Lee was knighted on 22 May 1603 after which time he would have been addressed as Sir Robert Lee. The queen, who died on 24 March 1603, is mentioned twice, in both the 1603 and the single extant 1605 edition, as the "Queenes high-way" (Crosse 1603, sigs. G^{v}) and the "Queene and Common-wealth" (Crosse 1603, sig. $L4^{v}$), which suggest that although Crosse wrote it before Lee's knighthood and the queen's death it was decided not to reset the type for later editions.

After a discussion of virtue, it proceeds to attack all those who are engaged in vice, including drunkards, spendthrifts, moneylenders, theatregoers, and women with painted faces. Two years later, the book was reissued as *The Schoole of Pollicie: or the araignement of State-abuses*, which was identical to *Vertues Common-wealth* except for a new title page printed by Valentine Sims and the cancelling of the dedication on Leaf A3.[2] In 1878, the Rev. Alexander Grosart (1827–99), a collector of Puritan theology, printed a limited edition of 50 copies of the Bodleian version, which he incorrectly thought to be the only extant copy (Hummel 1949, 196–99).[3] Crosse also refers to a "Treatise of Iustice, which I suppose shall succeed this work"; however, no such work has yet been identified.

Grosart's "Introduction" to his reprint of *Vertues* is revealing:

> Of Henry Crosse, — the author of *Vertue's Common-wealth*, — I have absolutely failed to recover anything biographical. Various CROSSES have turned up in the course of my utterly disproportionate researches — one, Thomas Crosse a Verse-writer and Verse-collector contemporary, of whom I should gladly learn more — but nothing whatever on this our Henry Crosse. Nor is there in his book those personal allusions that in not a few cases have guided to information.

Mark Eccles has speculated that

> He may have been the Henry Crosse of London, gent., "alias Sir Jeffrey Candlemas," who was accused on 3 April 1611 of beating and wounding a constable after midnight in a tavern at All Hallows Barking, along with Edward Pistor alias Pistoll and John Chillcott alias William Philpott and other persons of ill name, fame, and conversation. (1982, 27)

However, the fact is that nothing is known about Henry Crosse, and Diana Price who thought that Chettle composed the *Groats-worth* letter, incorrectly in my view, has noted the *Vertues* allusions to it and suggested that "the name Crosse (X?) may be a pseudonym (for Chettle?)" (2012, 53n).

7.2 Content of *Vertues Common-Wealth*

Michael Waltzer frames the publication as

> a dissertation on the dangers of wealth, the typical product of a moralist responding unhappily to the sudden affluence of his society. Money and greed for money, Crosse thought, set men in motion, drew them from their ancient homes and their fixed vocations, lured them to the corrupting cities. (1965, 207)

Crosse was anxious about the state of disorder in society.

> Thus he joined in the Puritan attack upon the theatre not so much because the plays were 'scandalous' and immoral, but because their showing was an occasion for riot and their audiences were 'for the most part the lewdest persons in the land [...] an unclean generation'. (Waltzer 1965, 207–8)

Whoever Crosse was, he evidently saw himself as part of the elite:

> the rude opinion lookes at nothing but the outward picture [...] for the rusticke & common sort, are as Apes, that will imitate in themselues, that which they see done by others [...] what true glory then can they [scholars] iustly merit, that they are praised by the witlesse and brain-sicke multitude. (Crosse 1603, sigs. L3^{r}, P4^{r}; Q^{r})

In his Squire's speech for Queen's Day November 1595, Bacon has the Squire describe his absent master Erophilus, who represents the Earl of Essex, as a "mutinous brain-sick soldier" (Spedding 1861–74, I.378).[4] As for Crosse, riches and wealth are a "means to do good" (1603, sig. F4^{r}), and his advice is:

> Let a man be content with his portion, and not seeke to aspire unto terrestrial honour, by tearing out the bowelles of his brethren, with usurie, extortion, and unconscionable brokerie. For it is better to be contentedly poor than miserably rich. (1603, sig. F4^{r})

There is also a hint of misogyny

> women [...] who because they want beautie, colour their faces with painting, to get that by art, that nature hath denied them. (1603, sig. F^{v})[5]

However, Crosse reserves his greatest misery for plays

> Some playes as they are now in vse, are scandalous and scurrilous, detract from *Vertue*, & add to Vice, and the very May-games of all sin and wickednesse [...] often sporting at that which should rather moue pittie and compunction [...] tales of carnall loue, adulterie, ribaldrie, lecherie, murther, rape [...] is not this the way to make men ripe in all kinde of villainie, and corrupt the manners of the whole world? [...] must the holy Prophets and Patriarkes be set vpon a Stage, to be derided, hist, and laught at. (1603, sig. P2^{v})

His proposed remedy is radical

> And therefore it were to bee wished, that all loue-books, Sonnets, and vile pamphlets, were burned. And no more suffered to be printed, nor filthy Playes rehearsed, which are the bellowes to blowe the coales of lust, soften the minde, and make it flexible to evil inclinations[6] [... and] giue order that it be not permitted to any man to publish any thing hee hath composed, except it be first perused and allowed by indifferent Iudges therevnto assigned. (Crosse 1603, sigs Q3^{r}-Q3^{v}, sig. V3^{r})

It was a sentiment shared by Francis Bacon

> the stage is capable of no small influence both of discipline and corruption. Now of corruption in this kind we have enough, but the discipline has in our times been plainly neglected. (Bacon 1623, Book II, Chapter XIII; Spedding *et al.* 1863, VIII.441)

In fact, there are several striking correspondences between ideas in Francis Bacon's corpus and *Vertues Common-wealth*, which will now be examined.

In providing us with a definition of honour, which it seems the reader is being advised to adopt, Henry Crosse informs us that

> Tully [...] defineth honour to be a vnion of praises of good men, which iudge of virtue without partialitie, and not by the opinion of the multitude, which looke more to a veluet Iacket, the outward brauerie, then to a mind how it is qualified. (Crosse 1603, sig. D^{r})

In his 1612 essay "Of Praise", Sir Francis Bacon also cautions us to beware of the source of approbation (see also No. 6, Table 7.1):

> Praise is the reflection of vertue [...] If it be from the common people, it is commonly false and naught; [...] of the highest *vertues* they haue no sense or perceiuing at all [...] But if persons of quality & judgment concur, then it is as the Scripture saith, *Nomen bonum instar unguenti fragrantis* [a good man is like a sweet smelling ointment]. (Bacon 1612, 204)

Both Crosse and Bacon also emphasize that poetry and drama can be used to raise minds to virtue. First, Crosse assures us that:

> I would not have any man think, that I inveigh against, or discommend poetry; for in all ages it hath been thought necessary [...] The true vse of Poetry standeth in two parts; the one in teaching the

> way to *Vertue*; the other to moue and delight therevnto: for honest delight stirreth vp men to take that goodnesse in hand [...] So that poetry in no other thing, but a lively presentation of things ingeniously disposed, where by virtue is painted out with such fresh colours, that the mind is inflamed with her excellent properties. (Crosse 1603, sig. O^{r})

In 1623, Bacon published *De Augmentis Scientiarum*, in which his view on the relationship between plays and moral philosophy seems to echo Crosse's:

> And though in modern states play-acting is esteemed but as a toy, except when it is too satirical and biting; yet among the ancients it was used as a means of educating men's minds to virtue. Nay, it has been regarded by learned men and great philosophers as a kind of musician's bow by which men's minds may be played upon. And certainly it is most true, and one of the great secrets of nature, that the minds of men are more open to impressions and affections when many are gathered together than when they are alone. (Spedding *et al.* 1863, 441–42)

Bacon also opposed the Copernican heliocentric theory, an objection that he expressed several times in print.[7] In *Vertues Common-wealth*, we also find a reaffirmation of the Aristotelian position "the Sunne like a ramping Lyon, runneth about the world with a swift reuolution" (Crosse 1603, sigs V^{r}–V^{v}). Surely, this is a matter that would mainly interest a philosopher.

7.3 Apophthegms: Crosse–Bacon

The most striking resemblances between the Crosse pamphlet and Bacon's corpus take the form of apophthegms, that is, short witty aphorisms. The aim here will be to show their relative rarity by interrogating the Chadwyck–Healey EEBO database. Bacon used them all later than *Vertues*, a circumstance that will serve as evidence of his borrowing from the pamphlet. Table 7.1 sets out several of these, two of which are illustrated by Figures 7.1–7.4.

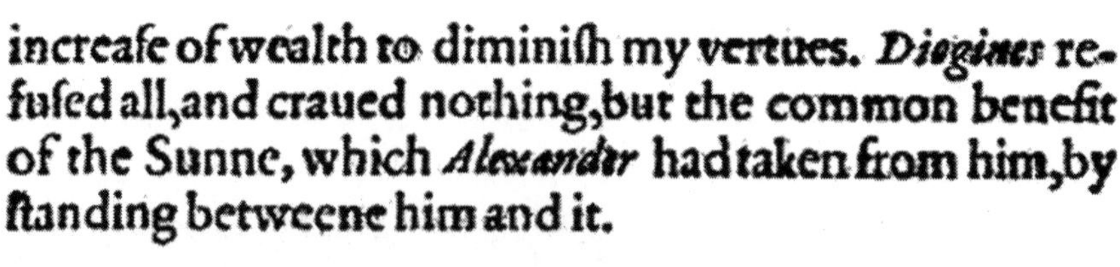
increaſe of wealth to diminiſh my vertues. *Diogines* refuſed all,and craued nothing,but the common benefit of the Sunne, which *Alexander* had taken from him,by ſtanding betweene him and it.

Figure 7.1 Diogines and the Sun, see Table 7.1, No. 4. Henry Crosse, *Vertues Common-wealth* (Crosse 1603, sig. E2^{v}).

Table 7.1 Comparison of apophthegms in *Vertues Common-wealth* with Bacon's work[a]

<table>
<tr><th>No.</th><th>Vertues</th><th>EEBO search</th><th>Bacon's work</th><th>Rarity</th></tr>
<tr><td>1</td><td>"The Poets faine, that Plutus the god of money is lame when he commeth, but hath wings swiftly to depart: signifying that as riches are long in getting, so they are suddenly lost" (sig. N[v]).</td><td>{Plutus near.20 riches} [context: riches slowly accumulating]
{Plutus near.20 money}</td><td>"The Poets faigne that when Plutus (which is Riches) is sent from Iupiter, he limps and goes slowly; But when he is sent from Pluto, he runnes, and is Swift of Foot; Meaning that Riches gotten by Good Meanes, and Iust Labour, pace slowly"[b].</td><td>2/4339(0.046%)
1/4339(0.023%)
Rarity based on texts before 1603</td></tr>
<tr><td>2</td><td>"Demosthenes beeing called to declaime against the rude multitude that had assembled themselues in the Forum of Athens, answered he was not yet readie, if he that had Facacia ingenij, the very soule of wit durst not speak in a serious manner without preparing himselfe before" (sig. O3[v]).</td><td>{Demosthenes near.20 [speak|speech]}
{Demosthenes near.10 multitude}
{Demosthenes near.20 [study|studying|studied]} [context: prepared speeches]</td><td>"We likewise see the exact diligence of Demosthenes, who in regard of the great force, that the entrance and accesse into causes hath to make a good impression; had readie framed a number of Prefaces for Orations and Speeches"[c].</td><td>3/4628(0.065%)
2/4628(0.043%)
3/4628(0.065%)
Texts before 1605</td></tr>
<tr><td>3</td><td>"Phocion,[d] in like manner, when the king had sent him a great beneuolence, hee asked him that brought it, what mooued his maister to send him so much mony, seeing the king did not know him? answered, it was in respect of the great fame he heard of his vertues: If that be the cause (quoth he) carry it backe to him againe, and let him leave me as I am, and not by increase of wealth to diminish my vertues" (sig. E2[v]).</td><td>{Phocion near.30 money} [context: full story being told]</td><td>"Alexander sent to Phocion a great present of money. Phocion said to the messenger; Why doth the king send to me and to none else? The messenger answered; Because he takes you to be the only good man in Athens. Phocion replied; If he think so, pray let him suffer me to be good still [to remain good]"[e].</td><td>5/4339(0.115%)
Texts before 1603
8/7389(0.108%)
Texts before 1625</td></tr>
</table>

No.	*Vertues*	*EEBO search*	*Bacon's work*	*Rarity*
4	"Diogines refused all, and craued nothing, but the common benefit of the Sunne, which *Alexander* had taken from him, by standing between him and it" (sig. E2^{v}).	{Diogenes near.30 sun} [context: blocking the sun]	"Alexander visited Diogenes in his tub. And when hee askt him; What hee would desire of him? Diogenes answered; That you would stand a little aside, that the sunne may come to me"[f].	7/4339(0.161%) Texts before 1603 9/7213(0.125%) Texts before 1624
5	"Solon compareth (not vnfitly) laws to copwebs, for that great flies can breake through at ease, when the lesser are intangled" (sig. E^{v}).	{law(s) near.5 cobweb(s)} [context: great flies breaking through]	"One of the seven [wise men of Greece] was wont to say That laws were like cobwebs; where the small flies were caught, and the great break through"[g].	8/4339(0.184%) Texts before 1603 12/7213(0.166%) Texts before 1624
6	"When Phosion had made an eloquent oration before the people, and seeing them clap their hands for joy, questioned such as were next to him, if he had vttered any foolish and vnseemly thing: teaching vs by this, that we ought always to suspect the rude multitude, for that their weake iudgements can hardly discerne betweene Vice and Vertue"[h].	{Phocion near.15 clap(ped)} 0/4339 {Phocion near.15 evil} {Phocion near.15 applaud(ed)} {Phocion near.10 oration} [Context: applauding crowd]	"Phocyon, the Athenian, (a Man of great severity, and no wayes flexible to the will of the People) one day, when hee spake to the People, in one part of his speech, was applauded: Whereupon, he turned to one of his Frends, and asked, *What haue I said amisse?*"[i].	0/4339(unique) 0/4339(unique) 0/4339(unique) 1/4339(0.023%) Texts before 1603

[a] EEBO searches conducted July 2012.
[b] Bacon (1625b, 206–7). On the issue of wealth, Crosse states, "a man should be rich in charity and poor in desire, and impart the benefit to the needments of and necessity of other" (Crosse, sig. N^{v}). In 1612, Bacon's view was that "of great riches there is no real use, except it be in distribution", see Bacon (1612, 125–6).
[c] Bacon (1605, sig. 52^{v}).
[d] EEBO gives '*Pho[...]n*'.
[e] Bacon (1625a, No. 205). Bacon seems to have taken his form of the story from Desiderius Erasmus of Rotterdam, see Udall (1542, sig. 294v).
[f] Bacon (1625a, No. 265).
[g] Bacon (1625a, No. 181).
[h] Crosse (1603, sig. P4^{v}). This version appears to have been taken from De L'Espine (1592, sig. G2^{r}) which has "having made an eloquent oration [...] if he had vttered any absurd or foolish thing [...] we ought always to suspect the applause of the people [...] for that they can hardly discerne between vice & virtue".
[i] Bacon (1625a, No. 30). This is contained in the original edition in Octavo but was omitted from later ones. Bacon's rendering seems to be closer to Plutarch (who was not returned by the searches) than De L'Espine (1592), see Plutarch (1597, 800). De L'Espine and Crosse record, respectively, that Phocian "demaunded of such as stood next to him" and "questioned such as were next to him", whereas Plutarch and Bacon have "he turned backe to his friendes, and asked them" and "he turned to one of his Frends, and asked", respectively. Also the latter pair actually provide Phocian with a speech, Plutarch giving it as "hath not some euill thing slipped my mouth vnawares?"

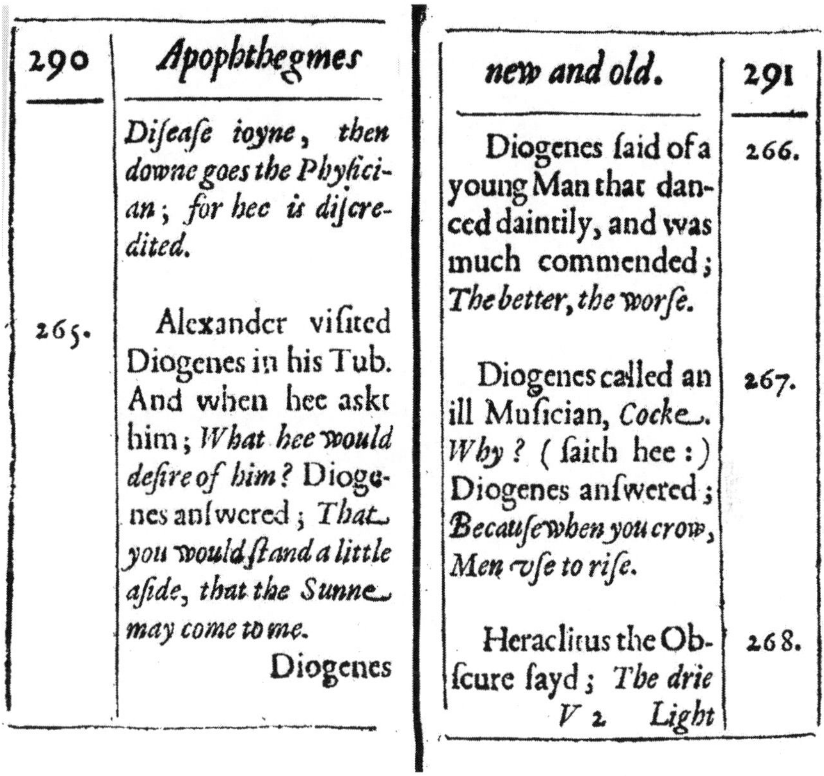
290 *Apophthegmes* *new and old.* 291

Diſeaſe ioyne, then downe goes the Phyſician; for hee is diſcredited.

265. Alexander viſited Diogenes in his Tub. And when hee askt him; *What hee would deſire of him?* Diogenes anſwered; *That you would ſtand a little aſide, that the Sunne may come to me.*

Diogenes

Diogenes ſaid of a young Man that danced daintily, and was much commended; *The better, the worſe.* 266.

Diogenes called an ill Muſician, *Cocke.* *Why?* (ſaith hee:) Diogenes anſwered; *Becauſe when you crow, Men vſe to riſe.* 267.

Heraclitus the Obſcure ſayd; *The drie* 268.

V 2 *Light*

Figure 7.2 Diogenes and the Sun, see Table 7.1, No. 4. Francis Bacon, *Apophthegmes new and old* (1625a).

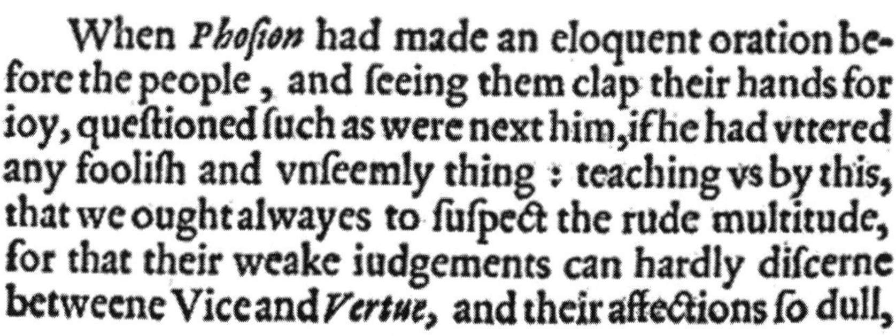
When *Phoſion* had made an eloquent oration before the people, and ſeeing them clap their hands for ioy, queſtioned ſuch as were next him, if he had vttered any fooliſh and vnſeemly thing: teaching vs by this, that we ought alwayes to ſuſpect the rude multitude, for that their weake iudgements can hardly diſcerne betweene Vice and *Vertue*, and their affections ſo dull,

Figure 7.3 Phocian's reaction to popular applause, see Table 7.1, No. 6. Henry Crosse, *Vertues Common-wealth* (Crosse 1603, sig. P4[v]).

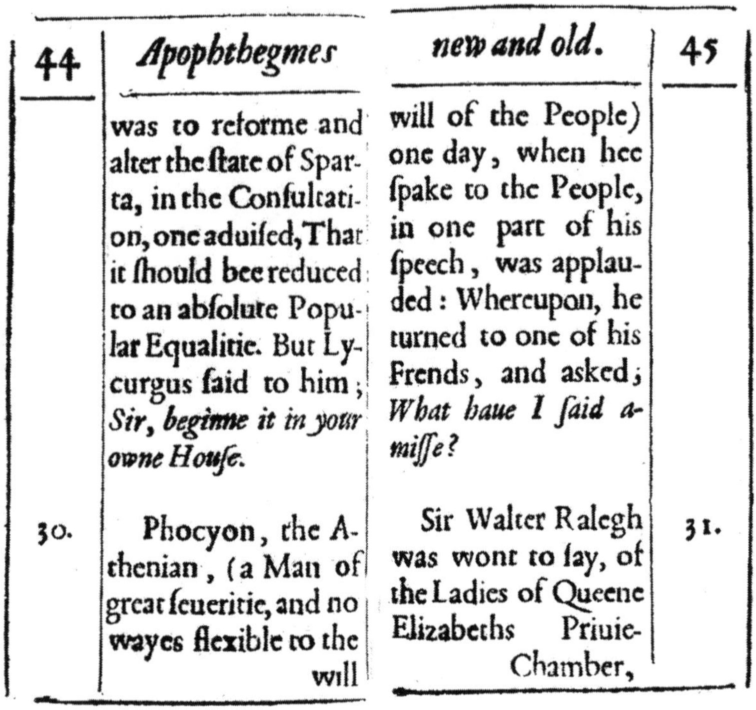

44 *Apophthegmes* *new and old.* 45

was to reforme and
alter the ſtate of Spar-
ta, in the Conſultati-
on, one aduiſed, That
it ſhould bee reduced
to an abſolute Popu-
lar Equalitie. But Ly-
curgus ſaid to him;
Sir, beginne it in your
owne Houſe.

30. Phocyon, the A-
thenian, (a Man of
great ſeueritie, and no
wayes flexible to the
will

will of the People)
one day, when hee
ſpake to the People,
in one part of his
ſpeech, was applau-
ded: Whereupon, he
turned to one of his
Frends, and asked;
What haue I ſaid a-
miſſe?

Sir Walter Ralegh
was wont to ſay, of
the Ladies of Queene
Elizabeths Priuie-
Chamber, 31.

Figure 7.4 Phocyon's reaction to popular applause, see Table 7.1, No. 6. Francis Bacon, *Apophthegmes new and old* (Bacon 1625a, No. 30, 44–45).

7.4 Rare Phrases: Crosse–Bacon–Shakespeare

There now follows a collection of rare phrases and collocations that *Vertues* and Bacon share. Again Bacon's use is later than the Crosse pamphlet, which suggests *Vertues* as a source. Table 7.2 shows four of these, one of which is given in Figures 7.5 and 7.6.

Unusual phrases that Henry Crosse and the Shakespeare canon share are presented in Table 7.3.

Table 7.2 Comparison of rare locutions in *Vertues Common-wealth* with Bacon's work[a]

No.	*Vertues Common-wealth*	*EEBO s earch*	*Bacon work*	*Rarity*
1	"Neither can the allegations imputed to this vice, excuse the dangerous effects which proceed from her monstrous deformitie" (sig. S4[r]).	{monstrous deformity}	"represented by the monstrous deformity of Typhon"[b].	2/5531(0.036%)

No.	*Vertues Common-wealth*	*EEBO s earch*	*Bacon work*	*Rarity*
2	"he is no otherwise, but as the print of honour set upon base bullion" (sig. I3^{v}).	{print of} [context: positive human virtue][c]	"but the face towards action hath the print of Good"[d].	4/5531(0.072%)
3	"for hee is as one dead, among the liuing" (sig. L2^{v}).	{dead fby.3 living} [entire string 'dead among the living']	"seeking for the dead among the living"[e].	4/5531(0.072%)
4	"the spurre of honour" (sig. C4^{v}).	{spur of honour}	"no spur of honour"[f].	5/5531(0.090%)

[a]Also, EEBO searches conducted for texts before 1603. Date searched 9 November 2017.

[b]Bacon (1619, sig. A4^{r}), a Latin translation supervised by Bacon. The other two returns are Harding (1558) and Munday (1602, sig. Z2^{r}). The latter is sometimes attributed to Francisco de Morais and Luis Hurtado.

[c]Those virtues that were admitted are "paternall loue", "his Truth", "*vertues* scale", and "goodnesse".

[d]Bacon (1605, sig. Mm3^{r}).

[e]Bacon (1605, sig. GGg^{v}).

[f]"Petition for leave to treat for tenures delivered in the House of Lords in 1610", British Library, Harleian MS 6797, f.136, copy corrected in Bacon's hand.

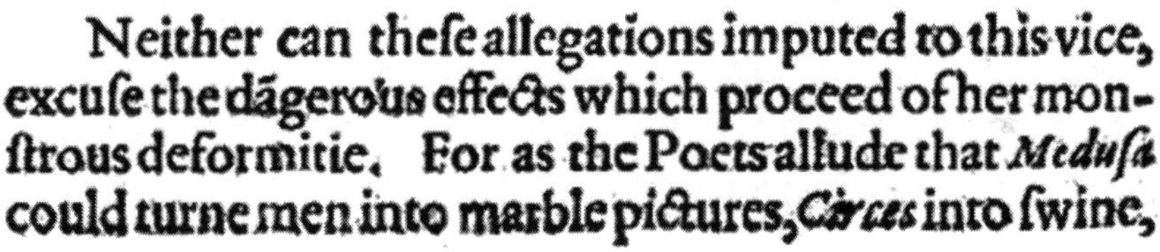
Neither can these allegations imputed to this vice, excuse the dãgerous effects which proceed of her monstrous deformitie. For as the Poets allude that *Medusa* could turne men into marble pictures, *Circes* into swine,

Figure 7.5 Use of "monstrous deformitie", see Table 7.2, No. 1. Henry Crosse, *Vertues Common-wealth* (Crosse 1603, sig. S4^{v}).

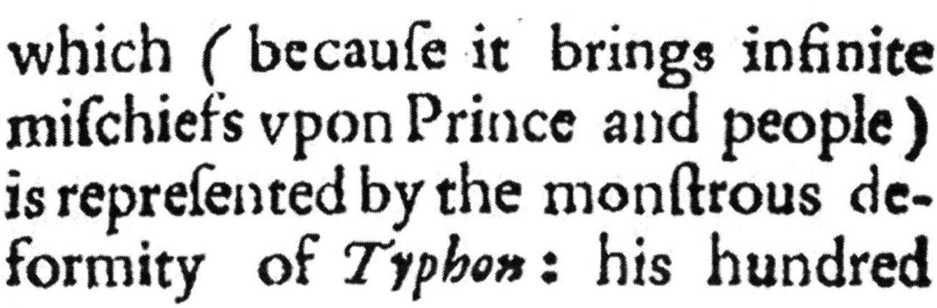
which (because it brings infinite mischiefs vpon Prince and people) is represented by the monstrous deformity of *Typhon*: his hundred

Figure 7.6 Use of "monstrous deformity", see Table 7.2, No. 1. Francis Bacon, *The wisedome of the ancients* (Bacon 1619, sig. A4^{r}).

Table 7.3 Comparison of rare phrases in *Vertues Common-wealth* with the Shakespeare work[a]

No.	*Vertues Common-wealth*	*EEBO search*	*Shakespeare's work*	*Rarity*
1	"and intrinsicate into the maior of the matter" (sig. L3^v).	{intrinsicate}	"With thy sharp teeth this knot intrinsicate / Of life at once untie" *Anthony and Cleopatra*, 5.2 (1623).	2/7077(0.036%) Texts before 1623
2	"the body by too much ease is like a pampered Iade vnseruiceable" (sig. Q4^v).	{pampered jade}	"and hollow pamperd iades of Asia" *2 Henry IV*, 2.4 (1596–9, publ. 1600)[b].	1/4339(0.023%) Texts before 1603
3	"dimme his glorie" (sig. E2^r).	{dim fby.2 glory} [entire string 'dim his glory']	"To dim his glory" *Richard III*, 3.3 (c.1592).	1/4339(0.023%) Texts before 1603
4	"To inrich such buckorome gentlemen" (sig. Q3^v).	{buckorome gentlemen}	"Eleven buckram men grown out of two" *1 Henry IV*, 2.4 (1597, publ. 1598)[c].	1/4339(0.023%) Texts before 1603
5	"thus do they proceed like cankers to eate off the tender buddes" (sig. O3^r).	{canker(ed)(ing)(s) near.10 bud(s)}	"But now will canker sorrow eat my bud" *King John*, 3.4 (1596–7, publ. 1623)[d].	3/4339(0.069%) Texts before 1603

[a]EEBO searches conducted in July 2012.

[b]The single return is "I at Ambitions strike, haue at his pampered Iade" in Wilson (1590). Due to the apostrophe in "pamper'd", EEBO missed the earliest example "Holla, ye pamper'd jades of Asia!" in Marlowe (1590, 4.3). Also missed is Shakespeare's *2 Henry IV* due to the spelling "pamperd" in the 1600 quarto edition.

[c]Apart from Robert Greene's *Groats-worth*, the only other example is "The terror of whose Name can out of seven / (Like Falstsff's Buckram men) make flie eleven" in the anonymous *The most renowned Prince Rupert*, a single folio sheet printed from the author's manuscript sometime between 1600 and 1699.

[d]The Shakespeare work also had different versions: "And loathsome canker lives in sweetest bud" in Sonnet 35 and "Some to kill cankers in the musk-rose buds" in *A Midsummer Night's Dream* (1600, sig. C3^r).

7.5 Further Research

With textual parallels supported by EEBO searches to establish rarity, the case is strong that *Vertues Common-wealth* (1603) acted at least as a source for Francis Bacon. This means that he knew about the *Groats-worth* letter and its claims against Shakspere. As pointed out in Section 7.2, Bacon has a rare correspondence with *Vertues* from 1595, before the date of Crosse's pamphlet. This is "brain-sicke" which was located without EEBO using a Google search. So there is also a hint of *Vertues* borrowing from Bacon. However, this is not quite enough to assert a state of mutual borrowing, which is essential for arguing his contribution. For the present purpose, the aim is merely to present stylistic evidence that Bacon knew about the *Groats-worth* charge against Shakspere.

The tables presented contain parallels that have been recognized by restricting attention to Bacon's corpus and *Vertues Common-wealth*, rarity-testing fortuitously observed correspondences using EEBO, and thereby identifying earlier sources. This is not the same as a full systematic RCP analysis of the pamphlet in which *every* seemingly unusual phrase and collocation in Crosse's pamphlet would be checked and rare returns logged. Not only might this suggest other contributors, but it could yet establish mutual borrowing for Bacon, which would then mean that he had a hand in the pamphlet. In that case, he would then seem to be making the same charge against Shakspere that Greene had made, a complaint that his work had been acquired by the Stratford man and that full credit had been appropriated. However, without a full investigation, this must rest for the present as a promising but uncorroborated conjecture.

Notes

1 Newbery had entered the book in the *Stationers' Register* on 15 November 1602.

2 There is a copy of the first 1603 edition in the Folger Shakespeare Library and two copies of the second edition—one in the Henry E. Huntingdon Library and the other in the Bodleian Library. The Bodleian copy has no A4 leaf "To the courteous Reader". The Folger 1603 edition of *Vertues* has a handwritten verse on Leaf A3^{v} which begins "A thief condemned for a heinous crime [...]". Its thrust is that a convicted criminal persuades the judge to agree to the penalty of the loss of his ears rather than his tongue. When it is found he has no ears, the criminal declares "[...] Where there is naught, the king must lose his right". The earliest return from EEBO of this verse appears in Herbert (1640, No. 396). The Folger has a copy of *The Schoole of Pollicie* (1605).

3 One of the subscribers is listed as "H. H. FURNESS, Esq., Philadelphia, U.S.A.".

4 Lambeth Palace Library, Gibson Papers, vol. v. No. 118. The phrase 'brain-sicke' has 28/4464 returns in documents dated before 1595, but only 10/4464(0.224%) are in the context of it being an adjective for a person or persons, for example, "brain-sick youth" (Melbancke 1583).

5 Also "when many female serpents lie in wait to deceive young wits with trains of love and set out their gay bodies to sight, as pleasing objects to intrap the soul, that tender youth may make anatomy of misery by their own woes [...] they are [...] the cabanet of evil [...] scorpions" (Crosse 1603, sig. L^{v}).

6 Possible sources are "And kindling coals of lust" Edmund Spenser, *The Faery Queen* (1590–96, Book I, Canto VI, XXII); and "absence is rather a bellows to renewe the coals of affection", Etienne Pasquier, *Monophylo* (1572, 24)

7 For example, in the *Novum Organon* we find "But this [theory of the tides] he [Galileo] devised upon an assumption which cannot be allowed, viz. that the earth moves" (Spedding *et al.* 1858, IV. 212). Objections to the heliocentric theory were also twice scripted into the 1597–8 Middle Temple revels as described in *Le Prince d'Amour* (1660).

Bibliography

Bacon, Francis. *The Tvvo Books of Francis Bacon. Of the Proficience and Aduancement of Learning, Diuine and Humane.* London: Printed for Henrie Tomes, 1605.

Bacon, Francis. *The Essaies of Sr Francis Bacon Knight.* Imprinted in London by Iohn Beale, 1612.

Bacon, Francis. *The Wisedome of the Ancients. Written in Latine. Done into English by Sir Arthur George Knight.* London: Imprinted by Iohn Bill, 1619.

Bacon, Francis. *De Dignitate et Augmentis Scientiarum.* London: Ioannis Haviland, 1623.

Bacon, Francis. *Apophthegmes New and Olde.* London: Printed for Hanna Barret, and Richard Whittaker, 1625a.

Bacon, Francis. *The Essayes or Covnsels Civill and Morall.* London: Printed by Iohn Haviland, 1625b.

Crosse, Henry. *Vertues Common-Wealth: Or the Highway to Honour.* London: Printed for Iohn Newbery, 1603. [Huntingdon Library].

Crosse, Henry. *The Schoole of Pollicie, or the Araignement of State-Abuses.* London: Printed by Valentine Sims for Nathanael Butler, 1605.

De L'Espine, M. I. *A Very Excellent and Learned Discourse Touching the Tranquilitie and Contentation of the Minde.* Cambridge, 1592.

Eccles, Mark. "Brief lives: Tudor and Stuart authors." *Studies in Philology* 79, No. 4 (Autumn 1982). University of North Carolina Press: 1–135.

Grosart, Alexander B., ed. *Vertues Commonwealth by Henry Crosse (1603).* Private publication, printed for the subscribers, 1878. Call No. 2704 d.26, Bodleian Library, Oxford.

Harding, Thomas. *A Detection of Sundrie Foule Errours.* Lovanii: Apud Ioannem Foulerum, 1568.

Herbert, George, ed. *Witts Recreations.* London: Printed by R[ichard] H[odgkinson and Thomas Paine] for Humphrey Blunden, 1640.

Hummel, Ray O. "Henry Crosse's '*Vertues* common-wealth'." *Bibliographical Society of America* Papers 43 (1949): 196–99.

Le Prince d'Amour, or the Prince of Love. With a Collection of Several Ingenious Poems and Songs. By the Wits of the Age. London: Printed for William Leake, 1660.

Marlowe, Christopher. *Tamberlaine the Great.* London: Printed by Richard Ihones, 1590.

Melbancke, Brian. *Philotimus. The Warre Betwixt Nature and Fortune.* Imprinted at London by Roger Warde, 1583. STC: 17801.

Munday, Anthony, transl. *The Third and Last Part of Palmerin of England.* London: Printed by I[ames] R[oberts] for William Leake, 1602.

Plutarch. *The Lives of the Noble Grecians and Romaines.* London: Printed by Richard Field, 1579.

Price, Diana. *Shakespeare's Unorthodox Biography: New Evidence of an Authorship Problem.* Shakespeare-authorship.com, 2012.

Shakespeare, William. *A Midsommer Night's Dreame.* London: Imprinted for Thomas Fisher, 1600.

Spedding, James. *The Letters and Life of Francis Bacon.* 7 vols. London: Longman, Green, Longman, and Roberts, 1861–74.

Spedding, James, Robert Leslie Ellis, and Douglas Denon Heath. *The Works of Francis Bacon*. Translations of the Philosophical Works. London: Longman & Co, 1858.

Spedding, James, Robert Leslie Ellis, and Douglas Denon Heath. *The Works of Francis Bacon*. Translations of the Philosophical Works. Boston: Taggard and Thompson, 1863.

Udall, Nicholas. transl. *Apophthegmes*. London: Imprinted by Jhon [sic] Kingston, 1542.

Walzer, Michael. *The Revolution of the Saints: A Study on the Origins of Radical Politics*. Cambridge, MA: Harvard University Press, 1965.

Wilson, Robert. *The Pleasant and Stately Morall*. London: Printed by R. Ihones, 1590.

Part II

Bacon's Influence on Selected Plays

8 *The Comedy of Errors*

The first known performance of *The Comedy of Errors* (CE) took place at the 1594–5 Gray's Inn Christmas revels, an account of which appears in the *Gesta Grayorum* (GG) published in 1688. Several correspondences between the GG and two Shakespeare plays, CE and *Love's Labour's Lost* (LLL), have already been noted in the academic literature, but new parallels are exhibited here, reinforcing the notion that the revels were designed with these plays in mind. This chapter focusses on CE and the evidence that it was written specifically for these festivities. Edmund Chambers claims that it was the Lord Chamberlain's Men who performed the play on Innocents Day 1594 at Gray's Inn. However, the evidence suggests that they were not present, that the Inns of Court used their own players, and that Shakspere received no remuneration.

8.1 The 1594–5 Gray's Inn Revels

In the early 1590s, the theatres and other places of congregation in London had been closed by the plague, so the 1594–5 Christmas revels at Gray's Inn law school at High Holborn were the first for "three or four yeares" (*Gesta* 1914, 1). A detailed contemporary account of the proceedings has come down to us in the *Gesta Grayorum* [*Affairs of Gray's Inn*], a 68-page pamphlet that was first published in 1688 by William Canning in London, see Section 9.1. The document is of particular interest because it reveals that on the evening of Innocents Day, 28 December 1594, "a Comedy of Errors (like to Plautus his Menechmus) was played by the Players" (*Gesta* 1914, 22), which was its first known performance.

The revels of 1594–5 were centred round the affairs of a mock government to be "performed by witty Inventions" (*Gesta* 1914, 2) before members of Gray's Inn, their guests from the Inner Temple, and the invited nobility. Desmond Bland informs us that they were assembled specifically for the law students, being:

> intended as a training ground in 'all the manners that are learned by nobility' [...] Dancing, music, declamation, acting, the etiquette of a formal precession, on foot or on horseback, the proper ordering of a banquet, the exchange of courtesies in speech or in writing, all these are part of the elaborate make believe. (1968, xxiv–xxv)

Allusions to *CE* in the *GG* have previously been noted (Whitworth 2002, 1–2), and it is maintained here that the revels were written with this play in mind, echoing a content that was designed for a legal-academic audience. The evidence does not support the contention that "the company that gave it was the Lord Chamberlain's Men" (Whitworth 2002, 2), since there is a stronger case for Inns of Court players. The facts further suggest that Shakspere not only received no fee, but he did not even attend.

8.2 Gray's Inn Connections

Based mainly on two plays—the *Menaechmus* and *Amphitruo*—by the third-century Roman dramatist Plautus, *CE* is a classical five-act structure farce that lacks the lyricism and romantic intrigue that would have appealed to a popular Elizabethan audience. As we shall see, it does not appear to have been conceived for the public theatre, and there is no record of it having been played in one prior to its first publication in Shakespeare's *First Folio* (1623). However, it was played at court, with the Council Register for 1604 recording that "On Inosents Night the Plaie of Errors" was performed before the king by the King's Men, with an attribution to "Shaxberd" (Dasent *et al.* 1890–1964, 204).

The *GG* reveals that at 9 pm on the night of 28 December 1594, Innocents Day, the invited 'Ambassador' of the Inner Temple and his retinue, together with "a great Presence of Lords, ladies and worshipful Personages", took their places, ready to enjoy the entertainment of the revels. However, the crowds were so great that "there was no convenient room for those that were actors" and "no Opportunity to effect that which was intended". The Ambassador left disappointed. Nevertheless, after some dancing, "a Comedy of Errors (like to Plautus his Menechmus) was played by the Players", and because of these events the evening was subsequently referred to as the "Night of Errors" (Gesta 1914, 22).

Reginald Fletcher claims that the author of the *GG* demonstrates "the naïve expression of a low esteem for the 'Comedy of Errors' and its author" (Fletcher 1901, 108n). The passage to which he refers runs as follows (see Figure 8.1):

> In regard whereof [the disorder in the crowd], as also for that the Sports intended were especially for the gracing of the Templarians, it was thought good not to offer any thing of Account, saving Dancing and reveling with Gentlewomen; after such Sports, a Comedy of Errors (like to *Plautus* his *Menechmus*) was played by the Players. (*Gesta* 1914, 22)

One can be forgiven for interpreting "not to offer any thing of account" as referring not only to the "Dancing and reveling with Gentlewomen" but also to the "Comedy of Errors". The compiler of the *GG* has taken no care to eliminate this reading. Let us consider the case that the compiler

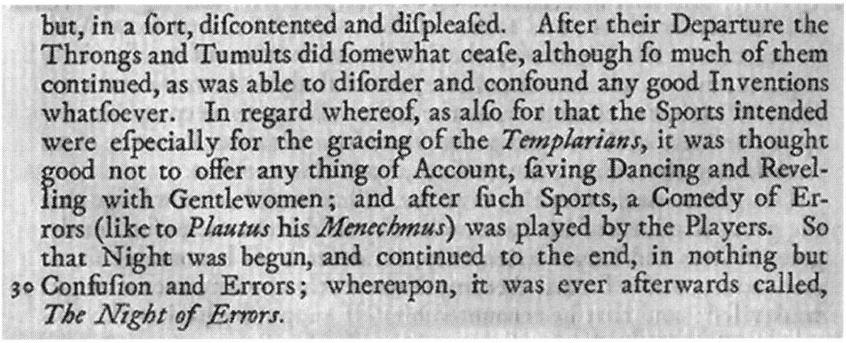
but, in a ſort, diſcontented and diſpleaſed. After their Departure the Throngs and Tumults did ſomewhat ceaſe, although ſo much of them continued, as was able to diſorder and confound any good Inventions whatſoever. In regard whereof, as alſo for that the Sports intended were eſpecially for the gracing of the *Templarians*, it was thought good not to offer any thing of Account, ſaving Dancing and Revelling with Gentlewomen; and after ſuch Sports, a Comedy of Errors (like to *Plautus* his *Menechmus*) was played by the Players. So that Night was begun, and continued to the end, in nothing but Confuſion and Errors; whereupon, it was ever afterwards called, *The Night of Errors.*

Figure 8.1 Reference to "a Comedy of Errors". *Gesta Grayorum* (1688, 22).

had no involvement in the writing of this play; then, it could easily be taken as an inappropriate attack on another author's work.

Although the Ambassador from the Inner Temple left disappointed on Innocents Day, he was insufficiently offended to avoid returning on 3 January when members of Gray's Inn performed a Masque of Amity:

> which was devised to that end, that those that were present might understand, that the unkindness which was growing betwixt the Templarians and us, by reason of the former Night of Errors [...] was now clean rooted out and forgotten, and that we now were more firm friends. (*Gesta* 1914, 25–26)

John Hotson argues that it was a contrived disorder to follow a theme of 'conflict and reconciliation' (1964, 50),[1] while Evelyn May Albright too was "not altogether convinced the quarrel was real" (1926, 505). Andrew Zurcher concurs suggesting that that the errors were "scripted in order to make way for the elaborate restitutions that followed" (2008, 33), in particular, the mock trial of the sorcerer who was held to be responsible for the chaos, and the restorative Masque of Amity on 3 January. In fact, the coincidence of terms between the account of the mock trial in the *GG* and *CE* is striking, with "conjuror", "sorcerer", "witchcraft", "juggling", and "wretch" being common to both. There is also the reference to an "Abbess" (*Gesta* 1914, 12; *CE* 5.1.49–54) and various euphemisms relating to prostitution and venereal disease such as "nuns", "lamp", and "burning" (*Gesta* 1914, 12; *CE* 4.3.51–52); see also Crystal and Crystal (2002). As Ros King notes:

> There is considerable correspondence between the language and themes of the *Gesta* and those of Shakespeare's play [*CE*]. This indicates that far from being a last-minute substitution, the play was chosen, and the words of the *Gesta* devised, to complement each other. (2004, 33)

However, it is possible to reach even further and show that the *CE* was not only chosen but also *designed* for an Inns of Court audience. The evidence is as follows.

Argument 1

The staging of the play is unique for a Shakespeare play, requiring three fixed locations at the back of the stage, which, from left to right facing the stage, are the Priory, the courtesan's house (the Porpentine), and the house of Antipholus. Medieval productions of Roman plays used an arcade setting, consisting of a screen with entrances into houses or *domus*, and the

> traditional architectural screen of arches and curtains was still the type of background for academic productions in 1605 when Inigo Jones devised a scheme (following Vitruvius) of turning sections of it around for scene changes [at Christ's Church College, Oxford]. (Kernodle 1944, 164).[2]

More significantly, the three locations were a common stage plan for an Inns of Court play.[3] Thomas Norton and Thomas Sackville's *Gorboduc*, produced at the Inner Temple in 1561, required two entrance ways and a throne; in 1566, George Gascoigne and Francis Kinwelmarsh's *Jocasta* was played at Gray's Inn with a central palace doorway flanked by two side doors; and Thomas Hughes's *The Misfortunes of Arthur* at Gray's Inn in 1588 had the houses of Mordred and Arthur, with a third entrance for the cloister of nuns (Foakes 1962, xxxv–xxxvi). David Bevington reveals that "I have never seen a production of the *Comedy of Errors* without a stage door of some sort visible throughout. That is the way it would have been done on the ancient Roman stage" (Bevington 2003, 23).

Argument 2

CE was based mainly on two plays, the *Menaechmi* and *Amphitruo*, by the third-century Roman dramatist Plautus. The William Warner (1558–1609) translation of the *Menaechmi* was registered on 10 June 1594 and published in 1595. Thomas Creede, the printer, reveals the following about Warner in "The Printer to the Readers":

> The writer hereof (louing Readers) hauing diuerse of this Poettes [Plautus] Comedies Englished, for the use and delight of his priuate friends, who in Plautus owne words are not able to understand them: I haue prevailed so far with him as to let this one go farther abroad, for a publicke recreation. (Plautus 1595, sig. A3)

So, Warner kept various translations of works in a manuscript copy shared them with his friends, and this particular one went to publication. The printed version being too late, *CE* might well have been composed following the acquisition of a manuscript copy from Warner; in fact, Edmund Chambers has noted similarities between the play and the Warner translation (Chambers 1945, I.311), although Reginald Foakes does not see sufficient evidence that *CE* borrowed from it (1962, xxii). Although there is no record of Warner being a member of Gray's Inn (Foster 1889), he is known to have served as an attorney in London.[4]

CE is based on translations of classical works in line with previous Inns of Court plays, such as the Senecan *Gorboduc*. Charles Whitworth, realizing that the law students would have been familiar with Plautus, suggests that "if Shakespeare was composing with such an audience particularly in mind [...] the tight, classical structure as well as the Plautine plot material must have virtually suggested themselves" (2002, 6). Since "the institutions of learning produced the classical drama, the private theaters the courtly drama, and the public theaters the sensational drama" (Lawrence 1927, 28–29), then in this respect, *CE* has the hallmarks of a play conceived for an academic audience.

Argument 3

Several researchers have argued that in the dialogue involving the gold chain, an item that does not appear in the Plautine version, *CE* provides a test case for the developing law of contract,[5] which consisted of the tension between the traditional action of debt and the then recently introduced action of *assumpsit* (Zurcher 2008; Raffield 2009; Kreps 2010, 262–72). This culminated in the settlement of the landmark *Slade's case* in 1602. The theory is now presented in detail to show that the complexity of the argument was more suitable for an audience of lawyers than for the general public (Zurcher 2008, 19–37).

Modern contract law awards compensation for a breach of contract, but medieval law focussed entirely on enforcing a contract's execution. The difficulties occurred when the litigant had no written agreement (deed) to furnish as proof. The Court of Common Pleas would allow an action of debt based on an oral agreement (parol undertaking) providing that the plaintiff could demonstrate *quid pro quo*, that is, the contract had been activated. An example of this was a down payment or a supply of goods, for which the plaintiff might reasonably expect a return.[6]

To provide an alternative remedy in law, as early as 1510, the King's Bench began to hear an action of *assumpsit*, a writ to settle debt claims proceeding from the plaintiff's injury or loss (law of tort) resulting from his belief that the promise would be kept.[7]

In 1530, the more conservative Court of Common Pleas refused to entertain an action on *assumpsit* unless a genuine 'consideration' was included, that is, a present or future concession by the plaintiff to the defendant that demonstrated an intent to act on the contract and for which a return might reasonably be expected.[8] Without it the agreement was reduced to a 'naked bargain' (*nudum pactum*), and then the court frequently rejected the action.[9] In 1585, the Exchequer Chamber was established to deal with disputes arising from *assumpsit* cases, and by 1596 these often resulted in a reversal of King's Bench judgements. This culminated in the landmark *Slade v Morley* (1597–1602) case, where out of the conflict between the judges of the King's Bench and Common Pleas, the details of modern contract law were refined.

Referring to incidents in *CE* (3.1, 3.2), Andrew Zurcher concludes that

> Angelo [the goldsmith who has given out the chain] ought to have action of debt against Antipholus of Ephesus [who orders the chain, does not receive it since it is mistakenly given to his twin Antipholus of Ephesus, and so refuses to pay] (for the original contract) but with the consideration of forbearance [Angelo delaying acceptance of payment from Antipholus of Syracuse, who is mistakenly given the chain] and his financial injury he would have an *assumpsit* [in the King's Bench court] against his brother [Antipholus of Syracuse who although perplexed to receive the chain offers payment, but Angelo delays collecting the debt].

Shakespeare's play demonstrates the unreliability of the law of contract as it stood in 1594, showing that an action of debt and an action of *assumpsit* were not mutually exclusive but could be brought at the same time by the same party [Angelo] for the same issue. Andrew Zurcher remarks that Shakespeare "seems to jeer at the epistemological smugness of the doctrine of consideration" (Zurcher 2008, 26).

There is a difference of opinion as to what kind of audience would have been suitable to appreciate these issues. Andrew Zurcher believes that "Shakespeare's awareness of debates over *assumpsit* would probably have gone down as well with termers on the public stage, as with lawyers in their hall" (Zurcher 2008, 35). However, Barbara Kreps (2010, 271) and Paul Raffield (2009, 207) suggest otherwise, noting that these matters were especially meaningful to an audience of lawyers. While it is true that plays on the public stage often made use of legal terminology,[10] which an audience need not have understood to follow the action, it is rather a different matter to expect a public audience to grasp a subplot that amounts to an intricate exposition of legal theory. So, this issue seems not to have been intended for the public theatre but was aimed at legally trained ears such as those students of law who witnessed the 1594–5 revels.

The Rt. Hon. Sir Dunbar Plunket Barton, a Judge of the High Court of Justice in Ireland and a Bencher at Gray's Inn, reveals an incident that might have inspired the events surrounding the gold chain in *CE*. It turns out that Sir Roger Manwood (1525–92), who was Lord Chief Baron of the Exchequer and a member of the Inner Temple,

> was the central figure of a sensational proceeding which occupied the attention of the Star Chamber in the years 1591 and 1592. Hearing that his son had disposed of a certain gold chain to a goldsmith named Underwood, he sent for the goldsmith and terrified him into handing over the chain, which he put into his pocket and refused to give back. The goldsmith complained to the Star Chamber, with the result that the episode made a noise in Westminster Hall, of which the *Comedy of Errors* is supposed to have contained an echo. (Barton 1927, 493; Barton 1929)[11]

Adwin Wigfall Green suggests that it was the kind of allusion that would have appealed to an Inns of Court audience:

> Much of the diversion of members of the Inns of Court, and particularly of the students during the sixteenth and seventeenth centuries, consisted in satirizing legal forms, procedure and personages. (Green 1931, 1)

8.3 The Identity of the Players

We now address the question as to the identity of the players that enacted *CE* at the revels. Despite the absence of clear evidence, Alan Nelson and John Elliott state that:

> All Inns of Court plays subsequent to 1587/8 seem indeed to have been performed by professionals, including Shakespeare's *Comedy of Errors*, given at Gray's Inn on 28 December 1594; unnamed comedies at the Middle Temple on 28 December 1597 and 2 January 1597/8; and Shakespeare's *Twelfth Night*, given at the *Middle Temple* on 2 February 1601/2 [Candlemas]. (Nelson and Elliott 2010, I.xxii)[12]

However, this is an extrapolation from two premises: (i) both plays are attributed to Shakespeare in the *First Folio* (1623), and (ii) the company that played Shakespeare's plays from 1594 was necessarily the Lord Chamberlain's Men (later known as the King's Men). As for the first premise, we have already examined in Chapter 4 the unreliability of the *First Folio* as an accurate record of attribution. However, as we shall see, the second of these premises is also highly dubious. So it is not possible to justify the assertion that the Lord Chamberlain's Men must have been present.[13]

Table 8.1 Plays that Nelson and Elliott claim were performed by visiting players (1416–1602), where FI: Furnival's Inn, LI: Lincoln's Inn, MT: Middle Temple, GI: Gray's Inn[a]

Season	*Date*	*Item*	*Inn*	*Nelson and Elliot's view*	*Evidence?*
1416–17	Christmas	Play	FI	Visiting players	*no*
1417–18	Christmas	?	FI	Visiting players	*no*
1491–2	Christmas	?	FI	Visiting players (?)	*no*
1494–5	?	?	LI	Visiting players	*no*
1509–10	Christmas	?	MT	Visiting players	*no*
1564–5	2 Feb	Play	LI	Children of the Chapel, Edwards	*yes*
1565–6	2 Feb	Play	LI	Children of the Chapel, Edwards	*yes*
1569–70	2 Feb	?	LI	Lord Rich's players	*yes*
1579–80	9 Feb	Comedy	LI	Children of the Chapel, Farrant	*yes*
1594–5	28 Dec	Comedy	GI	Visiting players	*no*
1601–2	2 Feb	Comedy	MT	Probably Lord Chamberlain's Men	*no*

[a]Nelson and Elliott (2010, xxii, 757–9).

A record of the Inns of Court plays that are claimed to have been performed by visiting players is shown in Table 8.1 (Clarke 2014, Section 2.4).

In order to identify the players that performed *CE* at the 1594–5 Gray's Inn revels, the records of the Inns of Court are now examined to determine whether the evidence is for, against, or unavailable for each of the following: (a) the Lord Chamberlain's Men, (b) A professional company, or (c) Inns of Court players.

(a) The Lord Chamberlain's Men

In 1913, Henry Chichester Hart suggested that "Shakespeare himself was perhaps not present [at the 1594–5 revels] since he was acting on the same day before the Queen at Greenwich" (Hart 1930, xxviii). This is in direct contradiction to Edmund Chambers's earlier assertion that the Accounts of the Treasurer of the Chamber (see Figure 8.2) for the Greenwich performance is in error and that the date Shakespeare was at Greenwich was 27 December, instead of "Innocent's Day", 28 December, as recorded on the warrant. This dismissal of the evidence as Chambers recommends would then release Shakspere to perform at Gray's Inn on the 28 December (Chambers 1906, 10–11).[14]

There were two kinds of accounts that recorded royal performances: the Accounts of the Revels Office, which was concerned with

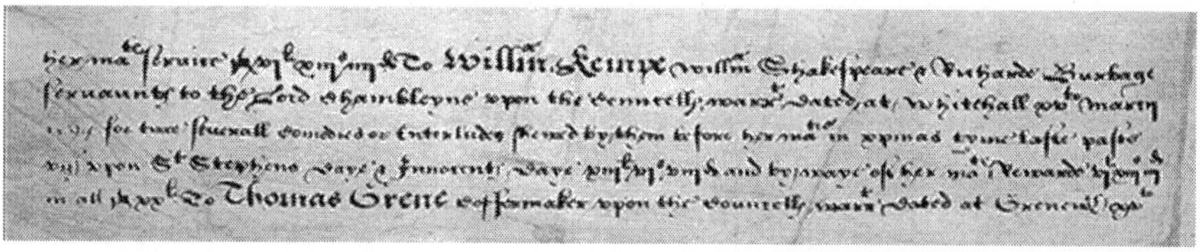

Figure 8.2 William Shakespeare and the Lord Chamberlain's Men recorded as being at Greenwich on Innocents Day, 28 December 1594. Public Record Office, Exchequer, Pipe Office, Declared Accounts, E.351/542, f.104v.

expenditure relating to the material or logistical staging of entertainments in the royal household, and the 'rewards' paid to performers by the Treasurer of the Chamber. For the latter, which is the sole concern here, a warrant for payment had to be delivered by the performer to the Privy Council for approval by the Treasurer of the Chamber. There are two independent records of these payments: the [Privy] Council Register (Dasent *et al.* 1890–1964) and a more detailed version in the Accounts of the Treasurer of the Chamber, which, unlike the former, usually give the performance dates. There are also two versions of the latter: Original Accounts for declaration in the Exchequer and Declared Accounts, which are abstracts of the Original Accounts prepared by the auditors, one copy of which went to the Pipe Office (Chambers 1906, 1–13).

Of particular interest is a Pipe Office document (see Figure 8.2), recording a payment made

> To Willm Kempe Willm Shakespeare Richarde Burbage servants to the Lord Chamberlayne [...] dated at Whitehall xv^{to} [15th] Martij [March] 1594 [1595] for twoe severall comedies or Interludes shewed by them before her ma^{tie} [majestie] in xpmas tyme laste paste viz upon St Stephens daye & Innocents daye.

However, on Innocents Day, the Lord Chamberlain's Men could not perform both at Gray's Inn after 9 pm (*Gesta* 1914, 22) *and* for the queen at Greenwich since "the Court performances were always at night, beginning about 10pm and ending at about 1am" (Chambers 1945, I.225). Their appearance at Greenwich on 28 December 1594 (Innocents Day) was on the same day as a performance by "Edwarde Allen, Richarde Jones & John Synger, seruaunts to the Lord Admiral" (Chambers 1945, I.165). So, Chambers, believing that having two companies simultaneously at Greenwich was less likely than the absence of the Lord Chamberlain's Men from Gray's Inn, suggested that the "Innocents daye" recorded on the warrant really meant 27 December, a day earlier, freeing Shakespeare to appear at Gray's Inn on 28 December. However, any error in this document could not have arisen from a careless slip of the pen, a distracted writing of a "xxviij" [28th] instead of a "xxvij" [27th], because we can see from Figure 8.2 that the administrator explicitly wrote "Innocents daye" [28th]. Also, as Edmund Chambers confessed with regard to a double-booking at Greenwich, "Two plays on one day would not be unprecedented" (Chambers 1906, 11) or indeed unusual because in the following 1595–6 season, both "John Hemynge and George Bryan servuantes to the late Lorde Chamblayne and now servuantes to the Lorde Hunsdon" and "Edwarde Allen and Martyn Slater servuauntes to the Lorde Admyrall" were engaged for performance on 22 February (Chambers 1945, IV.164–65).

In favour of a dating error, he goes on to argue that in the *GG* we find that "a company of base and common fellows" performed on the "Night of Errors", which typically means a professional acting company, such as the Lord Chamberlain's Men. However, this remark has been presented out of context because it appears as a comic charge read by the Clerk of the Crown who referred to "a great Witchcraft used the Night before" at which time "a Sorceror or Conjuror" was accused of "foisting a Company of base and common Fellows, to make up our disorders with a Play of Errors or Confusions" (*Gesta* 1914, 23).

If the Lord Chamberlain's Men had been the target of this jibe then Lord Hunsdon, the Lord Chamberlain, might well have taken offence when he heard of the intentional ridicule of his servants' humble origins.[15] However, the court scene was intended as a comedy sketch rather than a platform for invective, and so taking the context into consideration, the company would have needed not to be "base and common fellows" both to avoid offence and for the jest to work. In other words, it was aimed at the gentlemen Gray's Inn players who were certainly not "base and common Fellows".

So, there is no reason connected with the procedure of the court revels that justifies the Accounts of the Treasurer of the Chamber being in error, and this document should be given the respect it deserves and taken as reliable evidence against the Lord Chamberlain's Men playing *CE* at the 1594–5 Gray's Inn revels.

(b) A Professional Company

There is no evidence that Shakspere's company had possession of this play in 1594. The first known association of Shakspere with the play occurs when Francis Meres mentions Shakespeare and "his *Errors*" in *Palladis tamia* (1598, 282). Presumably, it was then in public performance, and it was next recorded on 28 December 1604 for enactment at court (Dasent *et al.*, 1890–1964, 10). For the 1594–5 revels, there is no record in the Pension Book of Gray's Inn of anyone being paid for a performance on Innocents Day 1594–5, dramatist or company. Neither is there a record in the Gray's Inn Ledger Book (Nelson and Elliott 2010,

I.121–24), which only records a payment to William Johnson of Gray's Inn who had been assigned to distribute money to the gentlemen of the Inn for their show before the queen at Shrovetide:

> Mr Iohnson by order of the pencion in full discharge of all his disbursementes for the Christmas sportes iij li. xvij s. & x d. [£30.89]. (Nelson and Elliot 2010, 124)

So without evidence in the Gray's Inn records for 1594–5—and the Pension Book was including records of payments to outsiders around that time[16]—the claim that a professional company played *CE* has no basis in fact. Ros King summarizes the Inns of Court records as follows:

> Theatre performances will not appear in financial records unless an exceptional effort is being made to impress guests, a visiting company (professional or amateur) is being rewarded, or damage has been done to the fabric of the household. (King 2004, 31)

In the present case, there is no hint in the records of a "visiting company", despite there being "a great Presence of Lords, Ladies and Worshipful Personages" (*Gesta* 1914, 20) on the night *CE* was given.

Gray Inn's policy on expenditure during the revels is made clear in the *GG*, which notes that "about 12th of December [...] it was determined that there should be elected a Prince of Purpoole [...] which was intended to be for the Credit of Gray's Inn, and rather to be performed by witty inventions rather than chargeable Expences [sic]" (*Gesta* 1914, 2). This suggests that no payment was made to a non-member of the Inns of Court, either for writing or performing, which therefore excludes the booking of a professional company who, in contrast to Inns of Court players, would certainly have demanded a fee.

During the period 1587–1604, professional players were unwelcome at both Oxford and Cambridge Universities. In fact, the authorities were so determined to defend the University stage from professional companies that on 29 June 1593, the Privy Council sent a letter to the Vice Chancellor of Cambridge University, complaining that "common Plaiers do ordinarily resorte to the Vniuersytie of Cambridge there to recite Interludes and Plaies some of them being full of lewde example" proclaiming that "no Plaies or Interludes of common Plaiers be vsed or sette forth either in the vniuersity or in any place within the compasse of ffiue miles" of the town. It also mentions "The like lettre to Vicechancellor [sic] and Heades of the houses and seuerall colledges of Oxenforde" (Nelson 1989, 348–49), but there the companies were protected by the city authorities. In the end Oxford University resorted to bribes. The Vice Chancellor's account records that companies patronized by the Earl of Leicester, the queen, Lord Morley, and the Lord Admiral were actually paid by the University Vice Chancellor to stay away, and any Master, Bachelor, or Scholar above the age of 18 found attending any such performance was incarcerated (Boas 1923, 17–18). One of the functions of Inns of Court revels was to give the students experience and instruction in royal court etiquette and legal court rhetoric, so it is feasible that this attitude of scholars to professional companies also extended to the Third University, the Inns of Court.[17]

The only professional companies that were known to have acted at the Inns of Court appeared at Lincoln's Inn from 1565–80; see Table 8.1 (Nelson and Elliott 2010, I.108–37, III.880–92). As for Gray's Inn in particular, of the six known plays involving it in the 50 years leading up to the 1594–5 Gray's Inn revels, three were written by members, at least two were acted by members—three, if Chambers's claim for *Jocasta* is accepted (see Inns of Court Players)—and all six were played at Gray's Inn (see Table 8.2). None of these are known to have involved an outside writer or playing company. So, precedent favours Inns of Court players.

(c) Inns of Court Players

Summarizing the information in Table 8.2, *Gorboduc*, a play penned by two Inner Temple members, Thomas Norton and Thomas Sackville, was performed before the queen on 18 January at Whitehall by members of the Inner Temple, although it is unknown who performed it at the Inner

Table 8.2 Plays written and performed by Inns of Court members (1526–88) where GI: Gray's Inn, IT: Inner Temple

Season	*Date*	*Title*	*Attribution*	*Players*	*Venue*
1526–7	Unknown	Unknown	John Roo (GI)	GI	GI
1561–2	Unknown	*Gorboduc*	Norton and Sackville (IT)	Unknown	IT
	18 Jan	*Gorboduc*	Norton and Sackville (IT)	IT	Whitehall
1566–7	Unknown	*Jocasta*	Gascoigne & Kinwelmarsh (GI)	Unknown	GI
		Supposes	Gascoigne (GI)	Unknown	GI
1567–9	Unknown	*Gismond of Salerne*	Wilmot *et al.* (IT)	IT	Probably Greenwich
1579–80	2 Feb	Unknown	Unknown	Unknown	GI
1580–1	Unknown	Unknown	Unknown	Unknown	GI
1587–8	Unknown	*Sylla Dictator*	Unknown	GI	GI
	28 Feb	*Misfortunes of Arthur*	Hughes *et al.* (GI)	GI	Greenwich

Temple earlier that Christmas season. Both *Jocasta* and *Supposes* were written by Gray's Inn members in 1566, but the players who performed at Gray's Inn remain unidentified although Edmund Chambers takes *Jocasta* to have been performed by Gray's Inn players (1945, III.320–21).[18] Two years later, *Gismund and Salerne* was "compiled by the gentlemen of the Inner Temple and by them presented before her Maiestie", in which case Greenwich rather than Inner Temple Hall was the likely location (Chambers 1945, III.514; Bellot 2007, 194).

For the 1587–8 Gray's Inn revels season, the Gray's Inn Christmas prince or "Dominus [Lord] de purpoole" was named as "[William] Hatclyff" who in Michaelmas term saw the performance of a Roman comedy, often referred to as *Catelyne* or *Sylla Dictator*, given by Gray's Inn players (Nelson and Elliott 2010, I.112–13, II.746, III.926–27; Boas 1923, 17–18). On 16 January 1587 [1588], a cast of 26 presented it before Lord Burghley. This is referred to in *The Pension Book of Gray's Inn 1559–1669*, which informs us that on 23 January 1588 "there was allowed out of the stocke of the house towards the charge of the comedy or shew set forth by the gentlemen of this house this last Christmas xx marks" [£13.33 in modern currency] (Fletcher 1901, I.78).

The Misfortunes of Arthur was written by several Inn members, most notably Thomas Hughes of Gray's Inn, and was acted by the Gray's Inn players at Greenwich before the queen on 28 February 1588. Taking *Sylla Dictator* and *The Misfortunes of Arthur* from 1588, these examples provide the best indication of Gray's Inn policy with respect to the writing and acting of plays as the 1594–5 Christmas revels approached. As far as the use of actors was concerned, the choice of Gray's Inn players was the immediate precedent for the 1594–5 revels. In fact, an entry in the Gray's Inn Pension Book dated 11 February [1595] states that:

> One hvndryd markes to be layd out & bestowyd vppon the Gentlemen for ther sportes & shewes this Shrovetyde at the Court before the Queenes Maiestie. (Nelson and Elliott 2010, I.121–22)

This demonstrates that Gray's Inn had an active playing company during the revels and was proficient enough to entertain the queen, so the enactment of *CE* at Gray's Inn would have posed no difficulties. So, there is significant circumstantial evidence that Inns of Court players appeared in this play. Adwin Wigfall Green concludes that "the feeling, which was somewhat general during the sixteenth and seventeenth centuries, that the professional actor was tainted because he followed his art for profit was rather strong at the Inns, where the gentlemen acted for amusement only" (1931, 17n & 157). This concludes the examination of the evidence to decide which company played at the 1594–5 Christmas revels at Grays Inn.

As for the writing of plays, in the period 1522–88, there is only one known precedent for an outsider writing for the Inns of Court. As alluded to in Gerard Legh's *Accedens of Armory* (1562), Arthur Brooke's *Masque of Beauty and Desire* was performed at the Inner Temple Hall in the 1561–2 Christmas season.[19] Brooke was not an Inn member, and a Latin entry in the Inner Temple Admissions Register can be translated as "Arthur Brooke of London specially (admitted) on 18 December, the pledges being Thomas Sackville (and) Thomas Norton" (Nelson and Elliott 2010, III.865). The Inner Temple evidently had a capable company of players at the time who performed *Gorboduc* for the queen, so, presenting this masque would have been within their range. This is the only known occasion prior to the 1594–5 Gray's Inn revels when an outside dramatist wrote for one of the Inns of Court, and in order to do so, it was necessary for him to obtain special admission. It was also placed on record. In an Inner Temple Parliament held on 4 February 1561–2, the following was recorded: "Order that Arthur Broke shall have special admission, without payment, in consideration of certain plays and shows at Christmas last set forth by him" (Inderwick 1896, I.220; Nelson and Elliott 2010, I.85, I.85n).

The *GG* also records that Gray's Inn took a 'Masque of Proteus' to court at Shrovetide on 3 or 4 March 1594–5 (*Gesta* 1914, vi). The writers of the two short pieces that preceded the masque were both Gray's Inn members. Thomas Campion, who was admitted in 1596 (Foster 1989, 516), wrote 'A Hymn in Praise of Neptune' (*Gesta* 1914, 58), which was sung prior to the masque's speeches and was later credited to him in Francis Davison's *A poetical rapsody* (1602, sig. K8). Davison, who was admitted in 1593 (Foster 1889, 523), wrote Sonnet IIII, which also appeared later in *A poetical rapsody* and was recited before the hymn was sung (*Gesta* 1914, x; Davison 1602, sig. D3^{v}). There is also some evidence that Davison wrote the masque himself,[20] although with one of its characters framed as a Squire it is reminiscent of a device that Bacon later wrote for Queen's Day November 1595 (see Section 5.3). The point is that all the writers at these revels, at least the ones who are identifiable—Bacon, Campion, and Davison—were Gray's Inn members.

We have already seen that Arthur Brooke, a non-member of the Inns of Court, was granted special permission when he submitted a manuscript for performance. Several people were granted special admission to Gray's Inn for the 1594–5 Christmas revels. On 25 December there was John Cooke and Edward Cooke; John Spencer, mayor of London; Anthony Fletcher of Cockermouth; Thomas Thomkins of the city of London; John Lyly of the City of London; and Thomas Smyth of Framingham; while on 6 February we find Edward Devereux of Bromwich Castle; Francis Dethicke of New Hall in Derbyshire; William Pope of Roxton in the county of Oxford; and Francis East of Cambridge (Nelson and Elliott 2010, I.124–25, III.886). They were all signed in by the mock Prince of Purpoole, Henry Helmes. However, there is no record that William Shakspere was granted such a privilege to allow him to submit *CE* for performance on 28 December 1594, paid or otherwise.

We might also consider the difficulty that another outsider had in getting his work performed at the Inns of Court. Ben Jonson's *Workes* (1616, 73) records that his play *Every Man Out of His Humour* was performed by "the then Lord Chamberlaine his servants" in 1599. Jonson was not an Inns of Court member, but it is clear that he wanted to write for their revels because his *Workes* (1616) is dedicated "To the Noblest Novrceries of Hvmanity, and Liberty, in the Kingdome: The Innes of Court". However, there is no evidence that his play appeared in one and some evidence that it did not. Jonson writes:

> I command, it lye not in the way of your more noble, and vse-full studies to the publike. For soe I shall suffer for it: But, when the gowne and cap is off, and the Lord of liberty raignes; then, to take it in your hands, perhaps may make some Bencher, tincted with humanity, reade: and not repent him. (Jonson 1616, 75)

The "Lord of liberty" seems to be a reference both to the Christmas Lord of Misrule that reigned at Inns of Court revels and the recreation time of the Inn members.[21] Jonson seems particularly keen to impress the Benchers because it was they who decided what would be played at the revels.[22] The dedication appears to confirm that a Bencher had not yet taken it in his hands, despite Jonson's claim that "I had friendship with diuers in your societies". This suggests that being an outsider as Jonson was, Shakspere would also have found it difficult to get his work enacted at the Gray's Inn revels.

So, neither Gray's Inn for *The Comedy of Errors* (1594) nor the Middle Temple for *Twelfth Night* (1602) can be shown to have employed a professional company prior to these productions (see Table 8.1). For the 1587–8 Gray's Inn revels, which took place only seven years before *CE* was presented at Gray's Inn, both *Sylla Dictator* and *The Misfortunes of Arthur* were enacted by Gray's Inn players. The latter is known to have been written by a team of writers from Gray's Inn. There is no known precedent for an external author having written a Gray's Inn play. In contrast, Roo, Gascoigne and Kinwelmarsh, and Hughes (in collaboration with seven others) provide examples of previous Gray's Inn authorship (see Table 8.2). So, not only was Shakspere absent when *CE* was enacted at Gray's Inn, but no one appears to have been paid for either its performance or its design. From all appearances, this was a play that came out of the Inns of Court.

8.4 RCP Analysis of *The Comedy of Errors*

Appendix B shows the results of an RCP investigation into the play together with a list of Francis Bacon's works in the EEBO database. The authors who register the greatest number of rare matches (with reference to the number of correspondences before and after 1595) are as follows: Thomas Heywood (9 after), Francis Bacon (1 before, 7 after), Thomas Nashe (3 before, 1 after), Thomas Dekker (4 after), and Thomas Middleton (4 after). Tables B.1–B.4 give the locution in the play, EEBO search string, work it appears in, and an estimate of the locution's rarity for the first three authors. A claim can be made for an author borrowing from the play if several such matches occur after the assumed play date. If several occur before this date, this play can be said to have borrowed from this author. If both occur together, a state of mutual borrowing is suggested, and this renders an author a good candidate for contributing to the play. Unfortunately, for a 1595 date of conception, the results are inconclusive, with Francis Bacon raising only a suggestion of a contribution. For Thomas Heywood, whose locutions correspond to Acts 1, 4, and 5, his contribution would be secure if there had been a revision any time from 1607–23. An interesting problem is how to interpret the three rare locutions that Thomas Nashe shares with the play before 1595. Was it originally a Nashe manuscript? This is also inconclusive.

At all events, the best estimate of the history of contribution to *CE* must be that both Bacon and Nashe display a hint of a hand, after which the play appears to have undergone revision, especially to Acts 1, 4, and 5. The best candidate for carrying this out appears to be Thomas Heywood.

Notes

1 Three years later [1597–8] this identical programme of disorder and lovers' quarrel with the indignant departure of invited allies [Lincoln's Inn] is reported [by Sir Benjamin Rudyerd] from the Kingdom of Love at the Middle Temple under Richard, Prince d'Amour [prince elected over Christmas]; see *Le Prince d'Amour* (1660, 88–89).

2 The arcade façade was already being used in European street theatres in the fifteenth century and consisted of entrances in a background screen to compartments. It was copied by fifteenth-century theatre directors in Rome to accommodate the entrance ways to houses in their stagings of Terence (Kernodle 1944, 160–64).

3 For a reconstruction of the staging of a typical play in Gray's Inn Hall during the 1594–5 revels, see Knapp and Kobialka (2001, 431–45).

4 There is an entry from 1609 in Thomas Hassall's Parish Register of Amwell in Hertfordshire: "Mr. William Warner, a man of good teares and of honest reputation, by his profession an atturnye at the Common Plese, author of *Albion's England*, who dijinge suddanly in the night in his bedde without any former complaynt or sicknesse on Thursday night, beeing the 9th daye of

March" located at http://www.hertsmemories.org.uk/content/herts-history/people/local-folk/a-selection-of-burial-records-1600-1657, accessed online 23 December 2017.

5 "[A contract once] denoted a transaction, such as a sale or a loan, which transferred property or generated a debt" (Baker 1979, 263).

6 The defendant was permitted to exercise the right to present 11 assistants to ratify his oath (wager of law), a process that weighed against the plaintiff, for the assistants were sometimes hired to secure a dishonest advantage.

7 For example, a carpenter who had neglected his undertaking to build a house might cause the plaintiff loss in having to rent temporary accommodation, or if the carpenter had built a roof that leaked, this might cause damage to the plaintiff's furnishings.

8 For example, agreeing to delay the collection of a payment.

9 Apart from its departure from the traditional action of debt, the Court of Common Pleas also objected to the fact that, in *assumpsit* cases before the King's Bench, the defendant had no prior knowledge of the case against them and no contract details were presented in court.

10 For example, in *The Staple of Newes*, Ben Jonson's Picklock speaks "In all the languages of Westminster-Hall, Fleas, Bench, or Chancery. Fee Farme, Fee-Tayle […]" (Jonson 1631, 60).

11 The book originally appeared in serial form in the Law Journal.

12 The view apparently originates from Finkelpearl (1966, 223–34). John Manningham's diary which mentions a performance of "Twelue night, or What you Will" on 2 February 1601–2 casts no light on the matter (Bruce 1868, 18).

13 In fact, in an email correspondence dated October 2014, Professor Nelson informed me that the *REED* editors "insisted that I soften my claim about that performance and would not allow me to state positively that the play was *Comedy of Errors* or that Shakespeare was involved".

14 This notion was lent support in 1923 by Adams (1923, 208n) and Sullivan (1926, 108).

15 On 3 January, the Lord Keeper, Lord Burghley, and Sir Robert Cecil were among those present at which time they would have learned of this slight.

16 For example, on 11 February 1595–6 we find "It is ordered that there shall bee payed out of thadmittance money to Somersett the Herold reasidue of a debt due xl^{s} iii^{d}", this being William Segar, who supplied "nyne shields & their emprisses" and who did not become a Gray's Inn member until 1617 Fletcher (1901, 111n & 113).

17 The type of academic mind that attended the Inns of Court was similar to that at Oxford or Cambridge. Finkelpearl (1969, 6) notes that "[from] 1587 to 1603, the records of the Middle Temple mention 1,070 names, of whom forty-three percent definitely spent some time at Oxford or Cambridge".

18 *Jocasta* is recorded as "A Tragedie written in Greke by Euripedes, translated and digested into Acte by George Gascoyne and Francis Kinwelmershe of Grayes Inne, and there by them presented". *Supposes* is described as "A Comedie written in the Italian tongue by Ariosto, and Englished by George Gascoyne of Grayes Inne Esquire, and there presented".

19 For a reconstruction of the 1561–2 Inner Temple revels, see Axton (1970, 356–78).

20 See *Gesta* (1914, xii–xxi). The masque does not appear in *A poetical rapsody*, but see *Gesta* (1914, vii) and also British Library, MS Harley 541, art 9, fol. 138.

21 For the relation of the play to the Inns of Court revels tradition see Jonson (2001, 28–38).

22 At Gray's Inn the equivalent was a Reader.

Bibliography

Adams, Joseph Quincy. *A Life of William Shakespeare.* Boston and New York: Houghton Mifflin Company, 1923.

Alright, Evelyn May. "The Faerie Queene in Masque at the Gray's Inn Revels." *Journal of the Modern Language Association of America* 41, No. 3 (September 1926): 497–516.

Axton, Marie. "Robert Dudley and the Inner Temple Revels." *The Historical Journal* 13, No.3 (September 1970): 365–78.

Baker, John Hamilton. *An Introduction to English Legal History.* Second edition. London: Butterworth & Co., 1979.

Barton, Dunbar Plunket. "Links between Shakespeare and the law." *The Law Journal* 63 (1927): 493.

Barton, Dunbar Plunket. *Links between Shakespeare and the Law.* Boston and New York: Houghton Mifflin Company, 1929.

Bellot, Hugh. *The Inner and Middle Temple: Legal, Literary and Historic Associations.* Whitefish, MT: Kessinger Publishing Company, 2007.

Bevington, David. "The Comedy of Errors as early experimental Shakespeare." *Bulletin of the American Academy of Arts and Sciences* 56, No. 3 (Spring 2003): 13–25.

Bland, Desmond, ed. *Gesta Grayorum.* Liverpool: Liverpool University Press, 1968.

Boas, Frederick S. *Shakespeare & the Universities.* Oxford: Blackwell, 1923.

Bruce, John, ed. *Diary of John Manningham.* Printed for the Camden Society. London: J. B. Nichols and Sons, 1868.

Chambers, Edmund K. "Court performances before Queen Elizabeth." *Modern Language Review* 2 (1906): 1–13.

Chambers, Edmund K. *The Elizabethan Stage.* 4 vols. Oxford: Clarendon Press, 1945.

Clarke, Barry R. "A linguistic analysis of Francis Bacon's contribution to three Shakespeare plays: *The Comedy of Errors*, *Love's Labour's Lost*, and *The Tempest*." PhD thesis, Brunel University, UK. 2014. Accessed online at http://barryispuzzled.com/PhDThesis.pdf on 13 September 2018.

Crystal, David, and Ben Crystal. *Shakespeare's Words.* London: Penguin, 2002.

Dasent, J. R., E. G. Atkinson, J. V. Lyle, R. F. Monger, and P. A. Penfold, eds. *Acts of the Privy Council of England (1542–1631).* 45 vols. London, 1890–1964.

Davison, Francis. *A Poetical Rhapsody.* London: Printed by V. S[immes] for Iohn Baily, 1602. STC: 6373.

Finkelpearl, Philip J. "John Marston's Histrio-Mastix as an Inns of Court play." *Huntingdon Library Quarterly* 29, No. 3 (May 1966): 223–34.

Finkelpearl, Philip J. *John Marston of the Middle Temple.* Cambridge: Harvard University Press, 1969.

Fletcher, Reginald J., ed. *The Pension Book of Gray's Inn 1569–1669.* London: Chiswick Press, 1901.

Foakes, Reginald A., ed. *The Comedy of Errors.* Arden Shakespeare. London: Methuen, 1962.

Foster, Joseph, ed. *The Register of Admissions to Gray's Inn, 1521–1889.* London: Hansard Publishing Union, 1889.

Gesta Grayorum, The History of the High and Mighty Prince Henry. London: W. Canning, 1688. Reprinted by the Malone Society, Oxford: Oxford University Press, 1914.

Green, A. Wigfall. *The Inns of Court and Early English Drama*. New Haven: Yale University Press, 1931.

Hart, H. C., ed. *Love's Labour's Lost*. Second edition. 1913; Reprinted, London: Methuen, 1930.

Hotson, John Leslie. *Mr. W.H.* London: Rupert Hart-Davis, 1964.

Inderwick, Frederick A., ed. *A Calendar of the Inner Temple Records*. London: Inner Temple, 1896.

Jonson, Ben. *The Workes of Beniamin Jonson*. London: Imprinted by W. Stansby, 1616.

Jonson, Ben. "The staple of newes." *Bartholmew fayre*. London: Printed by I. B. for Robert Allot, 1631. STC: 14753.5.

Jonson, Ben. *Every Man Out of His Humour*. Edited by Helen Ostovich. Manchester: Manchester University Press, 2001.

Kernodle, George R. *From Art to Theatre*. Chicago, IL: University of Chicago Press, 1944.

King, Ros. "Introduction." In T. S. Dorsch, ed. *The Comedy of Errors*. Cambridge: Cambridge University Press, 2004.

Knapp, Margaret, and Michal Kobialka. "Shakespeare and the Prince of Purpoole: The 1594 production of *The Comedy of Errors* at Gray's Inn Hall." In Robert S. Miola, ed. *The Comedy of Errors: Critical Essays*. New York: Routledge, 2001.

Kreps, Barbara. "Playing the law for lawyers: Witnessing, Evidence, and the law of contract in *The Comedy of Errors*." In Peter Holland, ed. *Shakespeare Survey Volume 63: Shakespeare's English Histories and their Afterlives*. Cambridge University Press, 2010.

Lawrence, William J. *Pre-Restoration Stage Studies*. Cambridge, 1927.

Meres, Frances. *Palladis Tamia. Wits Treasury Being the Second part of Wits Commonwealth*. London: Printed by P. Short, for Cuthbert Burbie, 1598.

Nelson, Alan H., ed. *Records of Early English Drama: Cambridge*. 2 vols. Toronto: University of Toronto Press, 1989.

Nelson, Alan H., and John R. Elliott Jr, eds. *Records of Early English Drama: Inns of Court*, 3 vols. Woodbridge: D. S. Brewer, 2010.

Plautus, Titus Maccius. *Menaecmi*. London, 1595. STC: 20002.

Raffield, Paul. "*The Comedy of Errors* and the Meaning of Contract." *Law and Humanities* 3, No. 2 (2009): 207–29.

Rudyerd, Benjamin. *Le Prince d'Amour, or the Prince of Love. With a collection of several ingenious Poems and Songs. By the Wits of the Age*. London: Printed for William Leake, 1660.

Sullivan, Mary Susan. *Plays & Masques at Court*. New Haven: Yale University Press, 1926.

Whitworth, Charles, ed. *The Comedy of Errors*. Oxford: Oxford University Press, 2002.

Zurcher, Andrew. "Consideration, contract and the end of *The Comedy of Errors*." In P. Raffield and G. Watt, eds. *Shakespeare and the Law*. Oxford: Hart Publishing, 2008.

9 *Love's Labour's Lost*

A record of the speeches and proceedings at the 1594–5 Gray's Inn Christmas revels has come down to us in the *Gesta Grayorum* pamphlet. We conduct an RCP analysis of the *Gesta* and *Love's Labour's Lost* (Appendices C and D), and conclude that not only was the play intended for performance at these revels but cancelled, but that Francis Bacon also contributed to it. Thomas Dekker and Thomas Heywood are implicated as later revisers.

9.1 The *Gesta Grayorum*

The first known account of the 1594–5 Gray's Inn Christmas revels was printed in 1688 by William Canning in a 68-page pamphlet entitled 'Gesta Grayorum / OR, THE / HISTORY / Of the High and mighty PRINCE, / HENRY / Prince of Purpoole [...]'. It sold at a price of one shilling at his shop in the Temple Cloisters, London, and reports that on 12 December 1594, Mr Henry Helmes of Norfolk was elected as Prince of Purpoole, the Lord of Misrule, to govern his mock state until Shrovetide, three days before the start of Lent on 6 February. To assist in government, he had his own Privy Council, Officers of State, Gentlemen-Pensioners, and a Guard and Captain for the defence of the realm. Over 60 members of Gray's Inn took part, some being assigned more than one role. For example, Forrest was both one of the 'Gentlemen for Entertainment' as well as the 'Chief Ranger and Master of the Game', while Damporte doubled as 'Lord Chief Baron of the Common Pleas' and 'Lord Warden of the four Ports' (*Gesta* 1914, 6–8).

On 14 December 1594, an invitation was dispatched to the Inner Temple to send an "ambassador" to take part in the revelry. They responded on 18 December with "we yield with all Good Will". The revels began on 20 December, ran until 5 January, were suspended until 1 February while the Prince pretended to visit Russia, and were suspended again until Shrovetide when Henry Helmes took a masque to Whitehall. The whole cost of the event, which was "rather to be performed by witty Inventions, than chargeable Expences" (*Gesta* 1914, 2), was met by the gentlemen of Gray's Inn (see Figure 9.1). There were

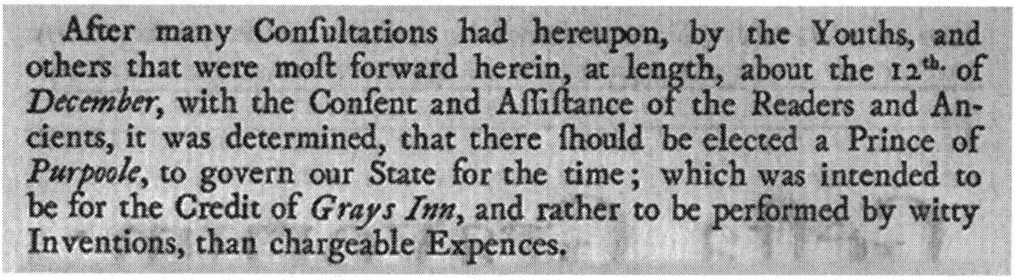
After many Conſultations had hereupon, by the Youths, and others that were moſt forward herein, at length, about the 12th. of *December*, with the Conſent and Aſſiſtance of the Readers and Ancients, it was determined, that there ſhould be elected a Prince of *Purpoole*, to govern our State for the time; which was intended to be for the Credit of *Grays Inn*, and rather to be performed by witty Inventions, than chargeable Expences.

Figure 9.1 The revels were "Rather to be performed by witty Inventions, than chargeable Expences". *Gesta Grayorum* (1688; reprinted 1914, 2).

also donations from well-wishers, for example, Lord Burleigh was generous enough to contribute ten pounds and a "Purse of fine rich Needlework" (*Gesta* 1914, 2).

The order of events is set out in Table 9.1.

As revealed in Section 5.3, Francis Bacon was elected a Treasurer in the year leading up to the revels, a position which would have allowed him to take part in their organization. There is evidence

Table 9.1 Schedule of events at the 1594–5 Gray's Inn Christmas revels

Date	*Event*
20th December	Prince crowned, Prince's Champion issues challenge, dancing of measures[a]
28th December	*The Comedy of Errors* performed with invited nobles[b]
29th December	Court hearing for the Sorcerer[c]
3rd January	Device demonstrating Amity of Graius and Templarius with invited nobles, 24 Knights of the Helmet created, reading of Articles of the Order, speeches of six Privy Counsellors, more dancing[d]
4th January	Prince's procession with Inner Temple members to Lord Mayor's house[e]
6th January	Masque and dancing with invited nobles, letter from Russian Ambassador, reading of letters of Intelligence[f]
10th January	Reading of letter from Bridewell harbour[g]
11th January	Prince 'departs' for Russia[h]
28th January	Prince's 'return' from Russia announced[i]
1st February	Prince returns on Thames, letter read out from his ship, dancing[j]
2nd February	Masque of Proteus, cancelled Grand Night, and scaffolding removed[k]

[a](*Gesta* 1914, 9).
[b](*Gesta* 1914, 20).
[c](*Gesta* 1914, 22).
[d](*Gesta* 1914, 25).
[e](*Gesta* 1914, 42).
[f](*Gesta* 1914, 43).
[g](*Gesta* 1914, 49).
[h](*Gesta* 1914, 53).
[i](*Gesta* 1914, 53).
[j](*Gesta* 1914, 54).
[k](*Gesta* 1914, 53, 57).

that whoever wrote the *GG* was also a member of Gray's Inn and actually took part in the proceedings. For example, there are two occasions when the commentator slips out of his objective mask and lapses into "we".

> Upon the 1st of *February*, the Prince and his Train were met at *Black-wall*; from whence they came upon the River of *Thames*, in a very gallant Shew. Being come so near his own Country, he left his Navy of Ships, as not fit for so short a Cut, and the matter not being very great or dangerous, and he and his Retinue took to them fifteen Barges, bravely furnished with Standards, Pendants, Flags and Streamers: There was also in every Barge, Musick and Trumpets; and in some, Ordnance and Shot. Being thus gallantly appointed, we came on our Way by the Stairs at *Greenwich*. (*Gesta* 1914, 54)

At Greenwich, letters were dispatched to Sir Thomas Heneage, excusing the Prince of Purpoole from attending Queen Elizabeth. The prince and his company passed the Tower of London, before visiting St. Paul's School where a Latin oration was read out. The *GG* continues, "Then we marched on our Way, as before, by *Ludgate*, and through *Fleet-street*" (*Gesta* 1914, 57).

More than a month earlier, the ambassador of the Inner Temple had been 'insulted' by the Night of Errors on 28 December when he was unable to see any part of the *CE* performance due to the overflow of people onto the stage. However, on the night of 3 January, "there was a most honourable Presence of Great and Noble Personages", including Lord Burleigh and the Lord Keeper, where a Masque of Amity was presented to show affection to the supposedly disgruntled ambassador of the Inner Temple. Following the masque, the Ambassador and 24 of his retinue were awarded the honour of the Order of the Knighthood of the Helmet. James Spedding, the Victorian editor of Francis Bacon's *Works* awards Bacon a hand in the composition of the script for the Articles of the Order (*Gesta* 1914, 27–31):

> These articles present in a strain of playful satire so elegant an illustration of the fashions and humours of those days, that I shall transcribe them at length; the rather as [sic] forming part of an entertainment in the preparation of which Bacon certainly had a hand, though not, I think, in the execution of this part of it. (Spedding 1861–74, I.329)

Following the Articles of the Order on 3 January, the speeches of the six Privy Councillors and the Prince's response were given (Gesta 1914,

32–42). James Spedding also attributes these to Bacon. The six Privy Councillors advise the Prince of Purpoole on the following:

1 The Exercise of War.
2 The Study of Philosophy.
3 Eternization and Fame by Buildings and Foundations.
4 Absoluteness of State and Treasure.
5 Virtue and a Gracious Government.
6 Pastimes and Sports.

Spedding judges that

> All of these councillors speak with Bacon's tongue and out of Bacon's brain; but the second and fifth speak out of his heart and judgment also. The propositions of the latter contain an enumeration of those very reforms in state and government which throughout his life he was mostly anxious to see realized. In those of the former may be traced, faintly but unmistakably, a first hint of his great project for the restoration of the dominion of knowledge, – a first draft of 'Solomon's House,' – a rudiment of that history of universal nature, which was to have formed the third part of the 'Instauratio'. (Spedding 1861–74, I.342)

In other words, on 3 January 1594–5 when the six Counsellors' speeches were delivered, it seems that Bacon's aim was to attempt to canvas support for his projects. As Alan Stewart and Harriet Knight observe, with many notable guests from Elizabeth's court in attendance, not least the queen's main adviser Lord Burleigh, "For Bacon, this was an especially rich opportunity" (Stewart and Knight 2012, I.586). James Spedding further notes (1870, xxi) that the Northumberland Manuscripts (c.1597) collection (Burgoyne 1902)[1] has "Orations at Graie's Inne revels" listed on its heavily soiled front sheet, although they are not contained in the volume, and he remarks that it would be "a correct description" of the speeches of the six Councillors.[2]

There is little dissent among scholars about Bacon's connection to these speeches. In *The Lives of the Lord Chancellors* Lord John Campbell states that "On high-days and holidays he assisted with great glee in all the festivities of the Inn" (Campbell 1851, II.280), Brian Vickers has included the six Counsellors' speeches in *Francis Bacon The Major Works* (Vickers 2002, 52–60), and *The Oxford Francis Bacon* has included 'Orations at Graies Inne revels (1594–5)' in their *Early Writings* edition (Stewart and Knight 2012, I).

However, in order to bring further evidence to bear on the claims about Bacon's contribution to the revels entertainments, and his role as compiler of the *GG*, the new method of RCP is now applied. The first task is to identify which phrases and collocations were rare before the date of the target (c.1595). In November 2012, when the relevant EEBO searches were carried out, there were 3521 searchable texts available in the database dated before 1595. To allow a significant number of informative returns, a locution is recorded as 'rare' if less than 11/3521(0.312%) records are produced. With the rarity of a locution established, a record is made of the authors who use it both before and after 1595, as well as the work it appears in, together with the date of that work. An example of a table of such results is given in Appendix G for *Pericles*, Act 1, in which 'rare' is set at 0.226%, and only authors whose usage precedes the target date are shown. If a work is dated before the *GG* (1595) then the pamphlet possibly borrows from it, and if it is dated after then there is a possible borrowing from the *GG*. For each frequently occurring author (at least three rare collocations) an RCP is constructed for that candidate which consists of a table of rare locutions shared with the target text. Appendices A–F show examples of such profiles that have been assembled for various works.

Francis Bacon has 27 different works in the EEBO database with publication dates 1597–1669 (see Table B.6, Appendix B). Only two authors register three or more rare returns for the *GG*. These are Richard Knowles, who has three correspondences published after 1595, although he was not a member of Gray's Inn, and Francis Bacon, who has ten matches from EEBO (one before 1595 and nine after) and a further nine obtained from a Google search (two before 1595 and seven after), all checked for rarity in EEBO. These RCP results are presented in Appendix C. With evidence of mutual borrowing, these tables can be reliably interpreted as suggesting that Francis Bacon contributed to the *GG*. If we examine the Commentary, that is, the descriptive text between the scripted entertainments, a wider claim can be made that Bacon not only supplied some of the devices but also wrote the *GG*. Francis Bacon has two matches from the opening Commentary of the *GG* (Table C.1, Nos 1, 2), both dated after 1595. However, there is also a passage from the Commentary that has not been subjected to a rarity test but is nevertheless striking; see Figure 9.2 (*Gesta* 1914, 68). This has similarities to a speech in *The Merchant of Venice*.[3]

Bacon employs this 'greater lessens the smaller figure' in *A Brief Discourse touching the Happy Union of the Kingdom of England and Scotland* (1603), where he makes use of the same two examples of light and water to illustrate it:

> The second condition [of perfect mixture] is that the greater draws the less. So we see when two lights do meet, the greater doth darken and drown the less. And when a small river runs into a greater, it loseth both the name and stream. (Spedding 1861–74, III.98)

> Thus on *Shrove-Tueſday*, at the Court, were our Sports and Revels ended: So that our *Chriſtmas* would not leave us, till ſuch time as *Lent* was ready to entertain us, which hath always been accounted a time moſt apt, and wholly dedicated to Repentance. But now our Principality is determined; which, although it ſhined very bright in ours, and others Darkneſs; yet, at the Royal Preſence of Her Majeſty, it appeared as an obſcured Shadow: In this, not unlike unto the Morning-ſtar, which looketh very chearfully in the World, ſo long as the Sun looketh not on it: Or, as the great Rivers, that triumph in the Multitude of their Waters, until they come unto the Sea. *Sic vinci, ſic mori pulchrum.*

Figure 9.2 'Greater lessens the smaller' figure at the close of the commentary. *Sic vinci, sic mori pulchrum* [to be conquered is a beautiful death]. *Gesta Grayorum* (1688; reprinted 1914, 68).

The figure appears again in his revised 1625 essay 'Of Deformity' using the same example as the *GG* of the Sun overpowering starlight with "the stars of natural inclination are sometimes obscured by the sun of discipline and virtue" (Bacon 1625, sig. Kk3^{v}). Even though mutual borrowing from the Commentary is not clearly established, the complexity of this construction and Bacon's repetitive use contribute to the evidence for Francis Bacon's compilation of the *GG*.

9.2 *Love's Labour's Lost*

The accurate determination of limits for certain topical allusions in *Love's Labour's Lost* (*LLL*) has proved to be problematic. The [Privy] Council Register for 1604 records "A Play of Loues Labours Lost" being performed before the king at court by the King's Men "Betwin Newers Day and Twelfe Day" under the name of "Shaxberd" (Dasent *et al.* 1890–1964, 204). The first quarto of *LLL* is dated 1598, with no entry in the Stationers Register, and bears the title-page hook line "As it was presented before her Highness this last Christmas". Since the Elizabethan New Year began on 25 March, then 1598 could mean any time from 25 March 1598 to 24 March 1599, so the "last Christmas" could have been either the 1597–8 or the 1598–9 season. To complicate matters, the title page also declares that it was "Newly corrected and augmented" which invites discussion about sales propaganda and the existence of an earlier version (Woodhuysen 1998, Appendix 1). We also have Robert Tofte's unhappy recollection of attending a performance, as recorded in his sonnet sequence *Alba: The Month's Mind of a Melancholy Lover* (1598): "Love's Labour's Lost, I once did see a play, / Yclepéd[4] so, so called to my pain". This suggests that he saw it sometime before the end of 1598 (Tofte 1880, 105). On this evidence alone, the play was in performance around Christmas 1597–8.[5]

LLL was not the only production to refer to the French court of Navarre in the 1590s. Christopher Marlowe's *Massacre at Paris* (1593) also exploited this location and might well have provided the inspiration. There is no doubt that the choice of characters was taken from the religious wars involving the Protestant Henri Bourbon, King of Navarre, and members of the Catholic League (Charlton 1918, 388; Hibbard 2008, 49). In July 1593, after being installed as Henry IV, Henri Bourbon adopted the Catholic faith to dissolve opposition. Queen Elizabeth was unimpressed, and their relationship suffered until an assassination attempt was made on Henri towards the end of 1594. The queen's disposition towards Henri Bourbon would certainly have influenced the Privy Council's assessment of whether or not *LLL* was suitable for production, and after the end of 1594 it would once again have become feasible. Charles Whitworth notes that *CE* also refers to the armed resistance of the Catholic League to Henri of Navarre who "might have been considered heir to the French throne between the years 1589 and 1594, when he was finally crowned" (2002, 133n). In *CE*, when Antipholus of Syracuse asks his servant what part of Nell's body resembles France he responds:

> In her forehead [audacity], armed and reverted [returned to former possessor] making war against her hair [heir]. (*CE* 3.2.104–10)

This observation appears to associate both *CE* and *LLL* with the French wars.

The controversy in print between Thomas Nashe and Gabriel Harvey, especially Gabriel Harvey's *Pierce's Supererogation* (1593), appears to have inspired several lines in *LLL*. The quarrel has been seen as "a solid foundation, the first to be offered to theory builders" (David 1956, xxxiv–xxxvii), while Arthur Quiller-Couch and John Dover Wilson seem confident that when Armado addresses Moth as "my tender juvenal" (1.2.8), the allusion is to Thomas Nashe, the pamphleteer whom Thomas Meres later referred to as "gallant young Juvenal" in his *Wits Treasurie* (1598) (1923, xx–xxii). Henry Chichester Hart uncovers several points of connection between the controversy and certain lines in the play (1930, xiv–xv);[6] however, George Hibbard sceptically enquires:

> What has this [Harvey-Nashe controversy] to do with *Love's Labour's Lost*, a play written for a theatre audience in the mid-1590s, not for a group of scholars spending their days in the British Museum in the 1920s? (2008, 55)

Aside from his uncorroborated assumption that the play was not conceived for academic circles, the implication is that *LLL* only contained allusions that a general audience could understand. However, the following puzzling exchange from the 1598 quarto seems even less penetrable than the Nashe reference, and the fact of its inclusion in the play is sufficient to counter the objection:

COSTARD. [...] for thou art not so long by the head as *honorificabilitudinitatibus* [...]
MOTH. [...] What is "a, b" spelt backward with a horn on his head? [...] Ba, most silly sheep with a horn [...] The last of the five vowels, if you repeat them, or the fifth, if I.
HOLOFERNES. I will repeat them: a, e, I –
MOTH. The sheep. The other two concludes it – o, u. (*LLL* 5.1.40–53)

It is worth noting that "honorificabiletudine", a variation of Costard's word, also appears on the cover-sheet of the Northumberland Manuscript collection (Burgoyne 1902).

George Hibbard further suggests that

> An even more precise dating would be possible if only it could be shown conclusively that Shakespeare was indebted to the Gray's Inn revels of Christmas 1594–5 for the idea of the Masque of Muscovites in 5.2 of his comedy. (2008, 4)

There are five rare locutions that the *GG* shares with *LL* (three are given in Table C.4).[7] These correspondences, the last four of which are in both the 1598 quarto and the 1623 *FF* versions, will now be discussed.

9.3 Parallels Between *GG* and *LLL*

Parallel 1

In *LLL*, when the "blackamoors" musically herald the arrival of the four academy members dressed as Muscovites, it echoes the Emperor of Muscovy in *GG* who enters to a trumpet fanfare and discusses an "Army of Negro-Tartars" (David 1956, xxvii). The *FF* version (but not the quarto) also has "like Muscovites or Russians" (5.2.121), and the *GG* mirrors this by mentioning the "Emperor of Russia and Moscovy" (Table D.1, No. 5; *Gesta* 1914, 44).

Parallel 2

On 1 February, the Prince of Purpoole complains of seasickness on returning from his mock journey to Moscow (Table D1, No. 6; Table C.4, No.3; Table D.7, No.3):

> I found, that my Desire [to entertain the queen at Greenwich] was greater than the Ability of my Body; which, by length of my Journey

> [from Russia] and my Sicknesse at Sea, is so weakened, as it were very dangerous for me to adventure it. (*Gesta* 1914, 54–55)

This quote is echoed in *LLL*:

PRINCESS. Amazed, my Lord? Why looks your highness sad?
ROSALINE. Help hold his brows, he'll swoon. Why look you pale?
Seasick, I think, coming from Muscovy. (5.2.391–3)

Parallel 3

As Henry Chichester Hart has pointed out, there is also a correspondence concerning the difficulties facing the four academy members (Hart 1930, xii; Table D.1, No. 2; Table D.7, No. 2):

BEROWNE: Oh, these barren tasks too hard to keep,
Not to see ladies, study, fast, not sleep. (1.1.49–50)

This quote resembles the sixth Counsellor's speech in the *GG*:

> What! nothing but tasks, nothing but working-days? No feasting, no music, no dancing, no triumphs, no comedies, no love, no ladies? (*Gesta* 1914, 41)

Aware of Parallels 1, 2, and 3, but without access to a test of their rarity, Henry Woodhuysen claims "there are few if any verbal links" (1998, 64) between the *GG* and *LLL*. However, two new parallels will now be introduced here, Parallels 4 and 5.

Parallel 4

Robert White points out, without developing the observation, that "it [*GG*] has various elaborate edicts couched in the legal terms of 'Items' that we find in *Love's Labour's Lost*" (1996, 150). An investigation reveals a similarity between the play and the Articles of the Knights of the Order that were read out at the revels. One of these Articles is as follows (see Figure 9.3):

> *Item*, No Knight of this Order shall be inquisitive towards any Lady or Gentlewoman, whether her beauty be *English* or *Italian*, or whether, with Care taking, she have added half a Foot to her Stature; but shall take all to the best. Neither shall any Knight of the aforesaid Order presume to affirm, that Faces were better twenty Years ago, than they are at this present time, except such Knight have passed three Climacterical Years. (*Gesta* 1914, 28)

'*Item*, No Knight of this Order ſhall be inquiſitive towards any La-
'dy or Gentlewoman, whether her Beauty be *Engliſh* or *Italian*, or
'whether, with Care taking, ſhe have added half a Foot to her Sta-
'ture; but ſhall take all to the beſt. Neither ſhall any Knight of the
'aforeſaid Order preſume to affirm, that Faces were better twenty
'Years ago, than they are at this preſent time, except ſuch Knight
'have paſſed three Climacterical Years.

Figure 9.3 Edict from 'The Articles of the Order'. *Gesta Grayorum* (1688; reprinted 1914, 28).

In *LLL* (1.1.128–30), Longaville reads out the following edict:

> *Item*, Yf any man be seene to talke with a woman within the tearme of three yeares, hee shall indure such publique shame as the rest of the Court can possible deuise. (Shakespeare 1598, sig. A3^{v})

Later, in Act 2 the queen decides that "Till painefull studie shall out-weare three yeares, / No woman may approach his silent Court" (Shakespeare 1598, sig. B4; 2.1.234). Both the play and the *Gesta* frame this as a legal 'Item' in which there is a demand not to see a woman for three years. Francis Bacon already has two matches with the Articles of the Knights of the Order proceedings (Table C.1, No. 3; Table C.2, No.1), so this parallel also hints at his contribution.

Parallel 5

Ferdinand opens the play with the following speech (Table D.1, No.1; Table C.4 No.1; Table D.7, No.1):

> Navarre shall be the wonder of the world;
> Our court shall be a little academie,
> Still and contemplative in living art. (1.1.12–14)

The phrase "wonder of the world" is used to describe the 'living art' or the ethics of the Stoics, which involved unveiling the secrets of the universe.[8] At the 1594–5 revels, Francis Bacon's second Counsellor's speech 'Advising the Study of Philosophy' applies the same epithet to the Prince:

> when all miracles and wonders shall cease, by reason that you shall have discovered their natural causes, yourself [the Prince of Purpoole] shall be the only miracle and wonder of the world. (*Gesta* 1914, 35)

These five rare parallels between the *GG* and *LLL* are sufficient to establish a connection between them and support the notion that the play was at least adapted with the 1594–5 Gray's Inn Christmas revels in mind.

9.4 A Play Designed Around the Revels

If *LLL* had been intended for performance at the revels, then it might have been ear-marked for one of the Grand Nights that was cancelled:

> On the next Morning [7 January] His Highnesse [the Prince of Purpoole] took his Journey towards Russia, with the Ambassador [...] there he remained until Candlemas (2 February); at which time [...] his Excellency returned home again; in which the Purpose of the Gentlemen was much disappointed by the Readers and Ancients of the House; by reason of the Term [c.23 January]: so that very good Inventions, which were to be performed in publick at his Entertainment into the House again, and two grand Nights which were intended at his Triumphal Return, wherewith his reign had been conceitedly determined, were by the aforesaid Readers and Governors made frustrate, for the Want of Room in the Hall, the Scaffolds [theatre galleries] being taken away, and forbidden to be built up again (as would have been necessary for the good Discharge of such a Matter) thought convenient. (*Gesta* 1914, 53)[9]

In fact, from 1565–1605, Candlemas, or the Feast of the Purification of Our Lady, was often reserved for the performance of a play at the Inns of Court (Dugdale 1780, 24; Walker 1897, I.352, I.374; Inderwick 1896, II.23). By this time, the audience would have already learned about the Prince of Purpoole's "Sicknesse at Sea", the second Counsellor's description of him as a "wonder of the world", and the edict about not seeing ladies for three years, all of which would have obtained recognition when the play referred to them.

Given that Francis Bacon wrote the six Counsellors' speeches, these provide him with two matches with *LLL* (Table D.1, Nos. 1 and 2). He also has two correspondences after it from his published work located through EEBO (Table D.1, Nos. 3 and 4). The Google searches add three matches before the play from his private wastebook (Table D.2, Nos. 1, 3, and 5) and three after it from his published work (Table D.2, Nos. 2, 4, and 6). He has two matches with the Articles of the Order in the *GG* (Table C.1, No. 3; Table C.2, No. 1), which acquires significance from the fact that Parallel 4 from the Articles is also a match with *LLL*. So, if Bacon wrote the Articles then he must have contrived them to mirror the play. This gives Bacon 10 matches with LLL: 3 before, 5 after, and 2 from revels speeches.

While the *CE* possesses a significant legal theme (contract law), *LLL* contains references to the revels proceedings. Even without consideration of Parallels 4 and 5, Frances Yates concludes that "The play seems to have been designed for an audience which knew of the Gray's Inn revels" (1989, 162). However, with the five rare locutions from Thomas Nashe that all precede the revels (Table D.5), the evidence directs us more to the conclusion that an existing Nashe manuscript was chosen and the revels script constructed to plant memories in the audience that *LLL* would have resonated with on Candlemas day. Since Francis Bacon was deeply embroiled in the writing of these revels the wider conclusion that he contributed to *LLL* seems credible.

As for other possible contributors, Thomas Dekker has nine correspondences dating from 1600 to 1628 (after the revels), so he is a good candidate for a later revision. Thomas Heywood is also a possible reviser, with nine matches dating from 1600 to 1648 (after the revels), though not as rare as Dekker's. So, if Shakspere was the sole author of this play one would have to ask how rare locutions from Bacon, Dekker, Heywood, and Nashe manage to appear in it and why neither Shakspere nor the Lord Chamberlain's Men exhibit any connection to the 1594–5 Gray's Inn Christmas revels. On the other hand, if Shakspere acquired it from the Inns of Court sometime after the revels then the facts can be made to conspire.

Notes

1 The fire-damaged MS, which was discovered in August 1867, has been dated to c.1597, and contains scribal copies of some of Bacon's writings. The cover sheet is soiled, but the names Francis Bacon and William Shakespeare can be seen many times in a forest of several other enigmatic scribblings.

2 Three of the Counsellors' speeches and one by the prince occur elsewhere: *Inner Temple Petyt* MS. 583, 43, f.294; cited by Chambers (1945, IV.56).

3 Note the following: "*Ner.* When the moone shone we did not see the candle / *Por.* So doth the greater glory dim the lesse, / A substitute shines brightly as a King, / Untill a King be by, and then his state / Empties it selfe, as doth an inland brooke / Into the maine of waters: musique hark" (*The Merchant of Venice*, 5.1.92–7).

4 'Yclepéd' means 'named'; *Love's Labour's Lost* has "Judas I am, yclipéd Maccabeus" (5.2.591).

5 Other supposed allusions include those to George Chapman's *The Blind Beggar of Alexandria* (1596) and his *An Humourous Day's Mirth* (1597), see Woodhuysen (1998, 75–76). Robert Wilson's *The Cobbler's Prophecy* was registered on 8 June 1594 but could well have been written at least six years earlier, and in it the god Mercury visits Ralph the Cobbler. It has been suggested that this was the inspiration for the closing line "The words of Mercury are harsh after the songs of Apollo" (5.2.918–9). There is also Thomas Meres's mention of *LLL* in his *Palladis Tamia* (1598), and the 1592–3 visitation of the plague is perhaps referenced with "Lord have mercy on us" (5.2.419).

6 For example, Gabriel Harvey's *Pierce's Supererogation or A New Praise of the Old Ass* labels Thomas Nashe "a young man of the greenest spring, as beardless in judgement as in face, and as Pennilesse in wit as in purse", with the suggestion to Nashe that his next title should be "*Pennyworth of Discretion*". In *LLL*, Costard the clown calls the page-boy Moth "thou halfpenny purse of wit, thou pigeon-egg of discretion" (5.1.68).

7 The *FF* version has 2,900 more words than the 1598 quarto and results in four additional rare locutions. Three of these are also indicated in Appendix D with "plodders" being the fourth.

8 In 1922, Professor J. S. Reid of Gonville and Caius College, Cambridge, commented, "The whole scene contains, I think reminiscences of certain features of the post-Aristotelian, especially the Stoic, philosophy, as expressed by Latin writers. The Stoic division of philosophy into three portions, viz., φυσιχή, λογιχή, ηθιχή [physical, logical, ethical] was known in every school [...] this ηθιχή [ethical] is defined [...] in the Latin writers as *ars vitae* or *ars vivendi* [living art] (as in Cic.[ero] *De Fin*, 1, 42 and *Acad.* 2, 23). Of these three portions of philosophy the Stoics made the third [living art] overwhelmingly important, so that sometimes *philosophia* was defined itself as *ars vitae* (so in Cic.[ero] *de Fin*, 3, 4 and in Sen.[eca] *Ep.* [istles] 95, 8). Again the Stoics laid great stress on the moral value of contemplation of the universe" (Reid 1922, 226–27).

9 This point was made in the barrister Nigel Cockburn's excellent book *The Bacon–Shakespeare Question* (Cockburn 1998, 141), copies of which reside with The Francis Bacon Society, London.

Bibliography

Bacon, Francis. *The Essayes or Covnsels Civill and Morall.* London: Printed by Iohn Haviland, 1625.

Burgoyne, Frank J., ed. *Northumberland Manuscripts. Collotype Facsimile and Type Transcript of an Elizabethan Manuscript Preserved at Alnwick Castle, Northumberland.* London, New York, and Bombay: Longmans, Green & Co., 1902.

Campbell, John. *The Lives of the Lord Chancellors and Keepers of the Great Seal of England.* 7 vols. Philadelphia: Blanchard and Lea, 1851.

Chambers, Edmund K. *The Elizabethan Stage.* 4 vols. Oxford: Clarendon Press, 1945.

Charlton, H. B. "The date of love's labour's lost." *Modern Language Review* 13 (1918): 387–400.

Cockburn, Nigel. *The Bacon–Shakespeare Question.* London: The Francis Bacon Society, 1998.

Dasent, John R., Atkinson, E. G., Lyle, J. V., Monger, R. F., and Penfold, P. A., eds. *Acts of the Privy Council of England (1542–1631).* 46 vols. London: HMSO, 1890–1964.

David, R. W., ed. *Love's Labour's Lost.* The Arden Shakespeare. London: Methuen, 1956.

Dugdale, William. *The History and Antiquities of the Four Inns of Court.* London: Printed for G. Kearsly, 1780.

Gesta Grayorum. *The History of the High and Mighty Prince Henry.* London: W. Canning, 1688. Reprinted by the Malone Society, Oxford: Oxford University Press, 1914.

Hart, H. C., ed. *Love's Labour's Lost*. Second edition. 1913; reprinted, London: Methuen, 1930.

Hibbard, G. R., ed. *Love's Labour's Lost*. Oxford: Oxford University Press, 2008.

Inderwick, Frederick. A, ed. *A Calendar of the Inner Temple Records*. 3 vols. London: Inner Temple, 1896.

Quiller-Couch, Arthur, and John Dover Wilson, eds. *Love's Labour's Lost*. Cambridge: Cambridge University Press, 1923.

Reid, J. S. "Shakespeare's 'Living Art.'" *The Philological Quarterly* 1 (July 1922): 226–7.

Shakespeare, William [?]. *A Pleasant Conceited Comedie called, Loue's Labors Lost*. London: Imprinted by W. W. for Cuthbert Burby, 1598. STC: 22294.

Spedding, James. *The Letters and Life of Francis Bacon*. 7 vols. London: Longman, Green, Longman, and Roberts, 1861–74.

Spedding, James, ed. *A Conference of Pleasure, Composed for Some Festive Occasion About the Year 1592 by Francis Bacon*. London: Printed by Whittingham and Wilkins, 1870.

Stewart, Alan, and Harriet Knight. *The Oxford Francis Bacon: Early Writings 1584–1586*. 1 vols. Oxford: Oxford University Press, 2012.

Tofte, Robert. *Alba: The Month's Mind of a Melancholy Lover*. London: Matthew Lownes, 1598. Reprinted by Rev Alexander B. Grosart. Manchester: Charles E. Simms, 1880.

Vickers, Brian, ed. *Francis Bacon: The Major Works*. Oxford: Oxford University Press, 2002.

Walker, James Douglas. *The Records of the Honorable Society of Lincoln's Inn: The Black Books of Lincoln's Inn 1422–1586*. The Black Books. 4 vols. London: Lincoln's Inn, 1897.

White, Robert Sommerville. *Natural Law in English Renaissance Literature*. Cambridge: Cambridge University Press, 1996.

Whitworth, Charles, ed. *The Comedy of Errors*. Oxford: Oxford University Press, 2002.

Woodhuysen, H. R. *Love's Labour's Lost*. London: Thomas Nelson and Sons Ltd, 1998.

Yates, Frances. *The French Academies of the 16th Century*. London: Routledge, 1947. Republished 1989.

10 *Twelfth Night*

A comprehensive review of the dating evidence for *Twelfth Night* is carried out. Counterarguments are given against Hotson's view that its first known performance was at Whitehall in January 1601, and it is shown that there is far greater evidence for the play having being written for enactment to the Middle Temple law students on Candlemas Day 1602. It is also established that there is no evidence that a professional company such as the Lord Chamberlain's Men gave this performance. Internal evidence is also given in support of an earlier version being presented at the 1597–8 Middle Temple revels. Having established a strong Inns of Court connection, an RCP analysis of the play lends evidence to identifying its contributors, and Francis Bacon is suggested.

10.1 Dating *Twelfth Night*'s Topical Allusions

Horace Howard Furness once wrote that "Where external evidence corroborates internal evidence, the latter is worthy of all respect" (1901, XIII.x). It might well have been a caution against Edmond Malone's treatment of *Twelfth Night* (*TN*) because, despite citing several examples of supposed topical allusions, Malone erroneously estimated the earliest date of Shakespeare's *Twelfth Night or What You Will* as being 1607 (1821, II.441–45). His unrestrained speculation extended to taking John Marston's *What You Will*, entered in the Stationers Register in 1607, as the inspiration for *TN*'s alternative title; Viola's "Then westward hoe!" (3.1.136) as a glance at Thomas Dekker's *Westward Hoe*, printed in 1607; and references to the Shah of Persia as pointing to the play *Travells of the Three English Brothers*, written in 1607. In 1821, Malone had no external evidence to support his construction and, even though his notions were in mutual agreement, his internal evidence was not "worthy of all respect". An example such as this teaches us that empirical knowledge, being conjectural in character, is never final but is continuously in a process of evolution as new evidence prompts us to revise our established expectations.

The main topical allusions in *TN*, that is, the version that has come down to us in the *FF* (1623), are as follows: the Wright–Molyneux map, the Barentz expedition to Novaya Zemlya, the Sir Anthony Shirley voyages to Persia, the Robert Jones song "Farewell dear heart", and the visit to the English court of Duke Don Virginio Orsino. Each of these will be examined in detail before providing a counter to the case that the first performance of *TN* occurred in January 1601 at Whitehall.

Commenting on Malvolio's absurd attempts to impress Olivia, Maria reports that "he does smile his face into more lines than is in the new map with the augmentation of the Indies" (3.2.74–76). In 1867, Charles Knight reproduced what he thought was Shakespeare's 'new map' (1867, II.172), entitled *Insulae Moluccae*, from the English translation of van Linschoten's *Voyages into ye Easte & West Indies*, showing the islands of Malacca and Borneo.[1] However, Charles Coote argues that the map was by no means new as it exhibits no information that was less than 30 years old at the time of publication (1877–9, 88–99). Apart from the Salomen Islands and New Guinea, it gives no more information than other maps in van Linschoten's *Voyages*, and there is no noticeable "augmentation of the Indies". In contrast, the Wright-Molyneux world map,[2] published around 1599, has more rhumb lines[3] than any of the Linschoten maps and, unlike the map reproduced by Charles Knight, displays the entire East Indies (Elam 2008, 74). Produced by Emmerie Molyneux of Lambeth, the world map includes Northern Novaya Zemlya [north of Russia] which had recently been visited by the Dutchman William Barentz on his third voyage in 1596. Details of this newly chartered territory would have reached England a short time after arriving in Holland in 1598.

Related to this is Fabian's warning to Malvolio in *TN* that "you are now sailed into the north of my lady's opinion, where you will hang like an icicle on a Dutchman's beard" (3.2.24–26). In 1596–7, the expedition led by William Barentz became stranded by ice at Novaya Zemlya. The party abandoned ship and constructed a makeshift house, where they stayed for ten months before navigating the 1,700 miles home in two small boats. The first account of events was written in Dutch by an officer Gerrit de Veer in 1598, who travelled with Barentz, and whose work was translated into English the same year (Beke 1876).[4] Taken together, these allusions can be dated to 1600. The Barentz voyage will be revisited in Section 10.2 to show why it was of particular interest to the Middle Temple.

There are two speeches in *TN* that appear to refer to the Anthony Shirley travel narratives of 1600–1601 (Sherley 1600): "I will not give my part of this sport for a pension of thousands to be paid from the Sophy" (2.5.180–81) and "They say he has been a fencer to the Sophy" (3.4.283–84). Edmund Malone saw them as an allusion to Sir Robert Shirley's employment with the Sophy (or Shah) of Persia partly on the basis of a related play *The Travells of Three English Brothers* (Thomas, Robert, and Anthony Shirley) that was shown in 1607 (Malone 1821, II.444–5). However, from the end of 1599 to April 1601, his sibling,

Sir Anthony Shirley, had also been employed by the Sophy, travelling to Moscow, Prague, and Rome to encourage Christian merchants to trade in Persia (Holden 1954, 137). Two travel narratives, one published in September 1600 and the other registered in November 1601, record the events in detail,[5] although Sir Anthony's intentions were already known by this time from a letter dated 2 June 1598 (Chew 1937, 243; Lothian and Craik 2000, xxx). John Lothian and Thomas Craik suggest that the first of these allusions is particularly significant since it is not demanded by the context (2000, xxxi). Recognition of these references by a contemporary audience evidently relied on the publication of these travel narratives, and so these allusions point to the end of 1600.

The songs in the works of Shakespeare are of particular interest for discussing dating (Warren and Wells 1994, Appendix). In *TN*, we have 'Farewell dear heart', which appears in the following musical exchange between Sir Toby and Feste:

SIR TOBY: Farewell, dear heart, since I must needs be gone.
MARIA: Nay, good Sir Toby.
CLOWN: His eyes do show his days are almost done.
MALVOLIO: Is't even so?
SIR TOBY: But I will never die.
CLOWN: Sir Toby, there you lie.
MALVOLIO: This is much credit to you.
SIR TOBY: Shall I bid him go?
CLOWN: What and if you do?
SIR TOBY: Shall I bid him go, and spare not?
CLOWN: Oh no, no, no, no, you dare not. (*Twelfth Night* 2.3.102)

As pointed out by James Halliwell-Phillipps (1883, 164–65), it first appears in *The First Booke of Songes & Ayres* by Robert Jones from 1600, where Cantus XII is given as

> Farewel dear loue since y^u wilt needs be gon,
> mine eies do shew my life is almost done,
> nay I will neuer die, so long as I can spie,
> there be many mo though y^t she do go there be many mo I feare not,
> why then let her goe I care not.

In "To the Reader" Robert Jones confesses that

> I was not unwilling to embrace the conceits of such gentlemen as were earnest to have me apparel these ditties for them; which though they intended for their private recreation, never meaning they should come into the light, were yet content upon intreaty to make incouragements of this my first adventure,

which suggests that the lyrics were not widely known before their publication in 1600.[6] Although the melody used in *TN* is unknown, Lothian and Craik take the *TN* lyrics as sufficient evidence to conclude that they are

> so closely based on the song first extant in Robert Jones's *First Booke of Songes and Ayres* (published in 1600) as to suggest that the song was new and popular and that for this very reason Shakespeare gave it an incongruous context and made the appropriate alterations: by 1601 he could have satisfied himself of the song's popularity. (Lothian and Craik 2000, xxx)

This suggests a *terminus a quo*, at least for this particular dating allusion, of 1601.

There is a character in *TN* whose name appears to be taken from real events. On 3 January 1601, Don Virginio Orsino, Duke of Bracciano, arrived in London with the intention of gaining access to the court of Queen Elizabeth (Hotson 1955, 184). When Don Virginio was just four, his father, Paolo Giordano, a Venetian general in their war against the Turks, had strangled the boy's mother in a jealous rage. Paolo married again but died when Don Virginio was 13 years old, leaving him to be brought up by Duke Ferdinand of Tuscany in Florence along with his cousin Maria de Medici (Hotson 1955, 31). In April 1859, Orsino married the grand-niece of Pope Sixtus V, Flavia Peretti, a move that was unpopular in Spain (Hotson 1955, 38).

In London, Orsino and Elizabeth had good reasons to seek each other out. They both shared a dislike of Pope Clement VIII who had Spanish sympathies, Orsino was close to Maria who in late 1600 had married Henry IV of France, a former English ally, and Ferdinand was opposed to Spain's war in Italy. While Elizabeth was hoping that the rich Duke Ferdinand would make a financial contribution towards England's war with Spain (Hotson 1955, 59), Ferdinand was keen to forge an alliance with England to strengthen Tuscany (Hotson 1955, 47).

On Tuesday 6 January 1601, Twelfth Day, there was a state dinner at Whitehall, with a supper and a play arranged for the evening. The main guest was Grigory Ivanovich Mikulin, the portly Russian Ambassador, who had been invited to ratify the Anglo–Russian treaty. At midday he dined with Elizabeth in the Great Chamber, Queen's side, while Don Virginio Orsino was afforded the lesser honour of dining in the adjacent Council Chamber. However, unlike Orsino, Mikulin did not attend the supper and play, and it is clear that as the day wore on, it was Orsino who became the main focus of attention. In a letter to his wife Duchess Flavia, dated 18 January, Duke Orsino reveals that "a comedy was performed" (Elam 2008, 93–94), and its specification still survives in the Duke of Northumberland's library, in which the preparations for "Twelfth day the 6 of January 1600" are as follows:

> To Confer with my Lord Admirall and the Master of the Revells for takeing order generally with the players to make choyse of play that shalbe best furnished with rich apparel, have great variety and change of Musicke and daunces, and of a Subiect that may be most pleasing to her Majestie. (Hotson 1955, 178–80)

Inspired by the fact that Orsino is also the name of the love-struck duke in *TN*, John Leslie Hotson enquired "Could any subject be more pleasing to her Majesty than a romance of a Duke Orsino's hopeless love for a beautiful and unpredictable Lady Olivia?" He argues that 6 January 1600 at Whitehall was the first performance of *TN*, resting his case on three main points:

a Shakespeare called his courtly comedy Twelfth Night: that is, January 6.
b His company acted at Court on Twelfth Night, January 6, 1600/1.
c Queen Elizabeth entertained a duke named Orsino on this very day (Hotson 1955, 13).[7]

John Draper was convinced enough by Hotson's argument to declare that *TN* was "the Queen's Twelfth Night entertainment to regale the living Duke Orsino" (1950, 259). Taking points (b) and (c) we now expose the weakness of the case.

Point (b)

Hotson claims that the request for "Musicke" in the specification, and the presence of Shakespeare's company, the Lord Chamberlain's Men, point to the play *TN*, which contained songs. However, the specification of the comedy states "To Confer with my Lord Admirall and the Master of the Revells [...] to make choyce of a play", which suggests that it was the Lord Admiral's company that played the "musical comedy". There is also an argument for the company being the Children of the Chapel.[8] Either of these possibilities makes the play less likely to have been *TN*.

Point (c)

Arguments have previously been made in the literature against the play being written to contain references to Duke Don Virginio Orsino's impending visit by focussing on the short notice given. On 4 December

1600, Ralph Winwood, Principal Secretary of State and temporary ambassador at the French court of Henry IV, wrote from Lyons to Sir Henry Neville in London requesting entry into court:

> I have been intreated by a Gentleman who doth accompany Don Virginio into England, (whereof in my letter of the 20th November I advertised) to address them by some letter to some one, who wold vouchsafe to make them have the sight of the Court, and access to her majestie. (*Memorials* 1725, I.280–81)

Sir Ralph wrote a further letter on 8 December, and in a response dated 28 December, Sir Henry confirms that "Your two letters of the fourth and eighth of this month [December] came both at once to my Hands upon Christmas-Day" (*Memorials* 1725, I.286). This means that 25 December 1600 was the earliest that the English court could have known with certainty about Orsino's intended arrival. With this in mind, Musgrove comments, "[Hotson's] dating implies that it [the play] was written, rehearsed, and produced in twelve days" (1969, 1), while Lothian and Craik maintain that "it is most unlikely that Shakespeare could have composed it and the actors rehearsed it between 25 December 1600 (when the date of Orsino's visit became known) and 6 January 1601" (2000, xxix). However, Elam (2008, 94) does not see the tight schedule as an obstacle, pointing out that it "does not exclude the possibility that the duke's name in the [pre-existing] comedy was simply changed to Orsino for the occasion".

If an existing *Twelfth Night* play had been changed to incorporate Orsino's name, then there must have been at least 15 modifications. It might have been prudent to obtain Orsino's approval before his public portrayal at court, but Don Virginio's letters do not mention that he was given a play manuscript to inspect; in fact, according to John Draper (1950, 113):

> My colleague, Professor J.P. Brawner, and Professor G.V.N.G. Orsini of the University of Florence (a descendant of the Duke), have been unable to find in the Florentine archives any material that suggests a connection between this embassy and the play.

Leslie Hotson does not consider the possibility that representing the main guest at the Whitehall performance as a character in *TN*, one whom Elizabeth was eager to impress, would have been fraught with diplomatic danger. For example, in *TN* Antonio refers to Duke Orsino as "Orsino, noble sir" (5.1.67), which apparently was "a blunder deserving heavy chastisement" (Draper 1950, 115), while it has been noted that the play inconsistently refers to Orsino as a Duke (1.2.25) and a Count (1.3.104), the latter being of lower standing than the former (Lothian and Craik 2000, xix, xxii). John Draper (1950, 132) also comments on Orsino's fruitless wooing of Olivia:

> according to all the canons of propriety, Olivia, after a proper mourning and a proper pause to express her maidenly coyness, should have jumped at the chance; and [the *TN* character] Orsino was socially chagrined and publicly snubbed when she did not.

In fact, Barry Adams regards the character as "no more than a laughable victim of his own fashionable sentimentality" (1978, 59), a point reiterated by Norman Brittin (1956, 212) who perceives that:

> Orsino looks rather foolish as he querulously ejaculates: You uncivil lady / To whose ingrate and unauspicious altars / My soul the faithfull'st off'rings have breath'd out / That e'er devotion tender'd! What shall I do? (5.1.110–13)

Sidney Musgrove (1969, 1–2) tends to concur, pointing out that "it is doubtful whether a touchy ducal visitor would have been pleased with a portrait of himself as a sentimental lover". However, it is left to the German literary historian Georg Gottfried Gervinus (Furness 1901, XIII.379) to provide the soundest analysis, perceiving the onstage character of Duke Orsino as one who:

> rather speculated in thought over his fruitless passion, than felt it actually in his heart; as if his love were rather a production of his fancy than a genuine feeling.

As if insulting Duke Orsino's rank were not humiliation enough, would Queen Elizabeth really wish her esteemed guest, the very man who might untie Duke Ferdinand's purse strings, to witness his depiction as an emotionally-disconnected fool? A letter from Sir Henry Neville to Sir Ralph Winwood dated 29 January 1600 informs us that "Don Virginio Orsino hath been here, and very graciously and honourably entertained by her Majesty" (*Memorials* 1725, I.292). So, from the fact that Orsino emerged without offence, one could argue that the play cannot have been *TN*. Warren and Wells (1994, 4–5) have suggested a more realistic scenario: "it is likelier that the ducal visitor and the festive occasion suggested the name of Shakespeare's duke and the title of his play, which was probably written later that year [1601]".

10.2 *Twelfth Night* and the Middle Temple

Twelfth Night would have had far less potential to corrupt foreign affairs had it been written instead for the Middle Temple. The evidence is now explored for this position by considering possible allusions in *TN* to the 1597–8 Middle Temple revels and by showing how a play with this title with its subplot of misrule would have been historically significant for the Middle Temple when performed on Candlemas day [2 February].

In 1845, the antiquarian Joseph Hunter revealed that in May 1828 he visited the British Museum where he stumbled upon an innocent-looking catalogue reference in the Harleian manuscripts "5353. – A small paper-Book of various Collections, dated 1601–3" (Hunter 1845, I.365). One item on the list was given as "3 A Diary, beginning January 1, 1601 [1602], to February 24, ditto"[9] in which "I found the following entry, containing information perfectly new concerning one of the most favourite of the [Shakespeare] comedies" (Hunter 1845, I.367):

Following the clue "my cousin in Kent" (Bruce 1868, 19), Hunter managed to identify the author as John Manningham of East Malling and the Middle Temple (Hunter 1845, 374). In 1831, John Payne Collier also claimed credit for discovering the *TN* entry by recording,

> I was fortunate to meet with it [the diary] among the Harleian MSS. in the [British] Museum [… and] excepting by the maker of the Catalogue of the Harleian MSS. (where it is numbered 5353), it seems to have remained in that collection entirely unexamined. (Collier 1831, I.320, I.327)

> **FEBR. 1601. [1602]**

> Feb.2. At our feast wee had a play called Mid "Twelue night, or What you Will," much like the Commedy of Errores, or Menechmi in Plautus, but most like and neere to that in Italian called Inganni. A good practise in it to make the Steward beleeve his Lady widdowe was in love with him, by counterfeyting a letter, as from his Lady, in generall termes, telling him what shee liked best in him, and prescribing his gesture in smiling, his apparaile &c., and then when he came to practise, making him belieue they tooke him to be mad.
> (Bruce 1868, 18)

Whoever found it first, there is no doubt that Collier takes priority in publishing the diary's *TN* entry, while Hunter was the first to identify the diary's author.[10] Diana Price (2012, 41) has noted that John Manningham shows no awareness of Shakspere being the author of the play even though his diary exhibits familiarity with Ben Jonson, Edmund Spenser, and John Marston as poets. However, a further observation can be made. On 13 March 1601 [1602], Manningham recorded his Burbidge–Shakespeare anecdote about a lady who had designs on Burbidge one night when he played Richard III. Overhearing the plot, Shakspere got to her chamber first and declared himself William the Conqueror (Bruce 1868, 39). Here was a golden opportunity for Manningham to embroider his account with a startling association, and declare this to be the very man who had authored their revels play less than six weeks earlier. However, he recorded no such connection.

There are several lines in *TN* that seem to be direct references to the Middle Temple or, at the very least, the Inns of Court. When Malvolio is imprisoned for his inappropriate wooing of Olivia, he complains about the darkness of his cell. Feste responds with "Why, it hath bay windows transparent as barricades, and clerestories towards the south-north as lustrous as ebony" (4.2.40–41). The point of the jest is to temporarily return the audience to their real environment, one that has more than one bay window as well as high windows [clerestories] in the north and south walls. Tudor halls were rectangular and were usually designed as either a 'single oriel' or 'double oriel' hall. For the former, at the higher end or dais end, a bay window (or oriel) was set in one of the long walls opposite a doorway in the other. The large bay window was intended to illuminate the high table positioned at the upper end of the space where the dignitaries sat. However, if the entrance to the hall was through the 'screens' at the lower end, then the doorway of the single-oriel design might be replaced by a second bay window directly opposite the first one. This produced the 'double oriel' hall, with Middle Temple Hall and Trinity College in Cambridge being examples (Akrigg 1958, 422–24). Figures 10.1 and 10.2 allow a comparison between Middle Temple Hall[11] and Whitehall.[12] The former has more than one bay window (*TN* says "windows", see A and B in Figure 10.1) as well as high windows set in the north and south walls, as required by Feste's witticism. The Whitehall of 1602 had only one bay window (see the curved window in Figure 10.2), with clerestories on the west and east walls. Unlike Whitehall, this qualifies Middle Temple Hall as an appropriate candidate for the "real environment".

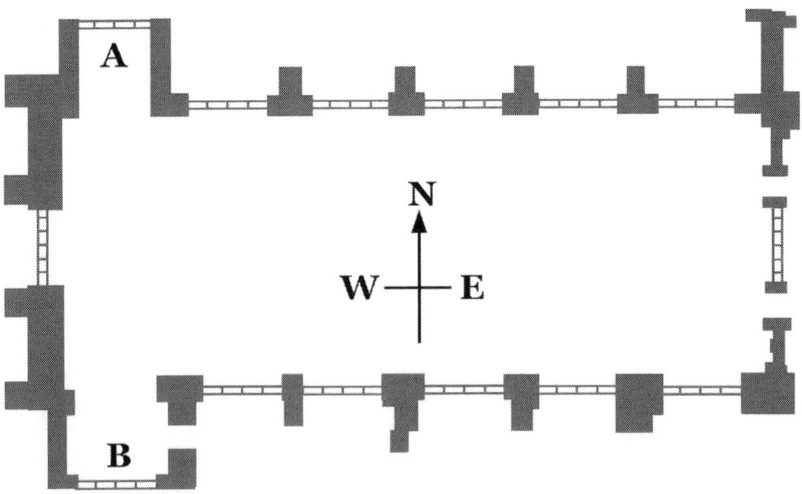

Figure 10.1 Middle Temple Hall floor plan.[13]

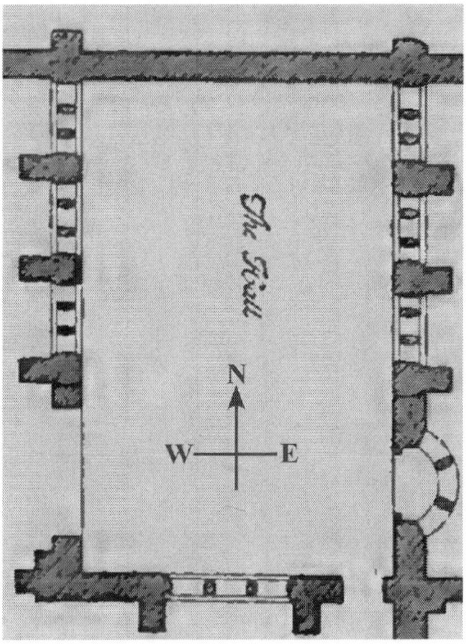

Figure 10.2 The ground plot of the ruins of Whitehall, 14 June 1718. *Survey of London* (1930, XIII.48).[14]

Andrew Gurr (1980, 164) has pointed out that:

> Playwrights such as Beaumont in *The Knight of the Burning Pestle* bring players disguised as audience on stage to comment on the play they are seeing, confusing the illusion/reality borderline with a sophistication rarely matched in any drama at the time. *Twelfth Night* is crammed with jokes about the stage illusion. At III.iv.131–2, for instance, Fabian watches Malvolio making a gull of himself and says, 'If this were played upon a stage now, I could condemn it as an improbable fiction'.

In Section10.1, two connected allusions were discussed from *TN*: the 1599–1600 publication of the Wright–Molyneux map, and the 1596–7 Barentz voyage through the north-east passage. It appears that the Middle Temple had a particular reason to be interested in these events. In 1592, Emmerie Molyneux manufactured a pair of globes, one terrestrial and one celestial, which were each two feet and one inch in diameter [0.622 m]. In 1889, it was reported that the Middle Temple library had possession of both an original celestial globe and an emended version of the terrestrial one bearing the altered date 1603, though details of their date of acquisition is wanting.[15] The 1603 globe was revised by Jodocus Hondius (Wallis 1955, 304), and

> The purpose of the revision was the incorporation of Barents's discoveries made on his third voyage in 1596 [...] In place of the [1592]

> archipelago, Novaya Zemlya is drawn as a long crescent-shaped island stretching from north to south. (Wallis 1951, 281)

The wooden house where Barentz spent the winter is shown, but his other discoveries, Bear Island and Spitsbergen, are omitted as are discoveries made by others from 1592 to 1603. According to Helen Wallis, this exhibits "the importance attributed to the knowledge of the North-east Passage revealed by his third voyage" (Wallis 1951, 281–82).[16] So, even though the globe revision occurred in 1603 after the 1602 performance of *TN*—irrespective of whether or not the Middle Temple had possession of these globes in 1592 on first publication (and this is not known)—then this would suggest that the Barentz voyage and the new Wright–Molyneux map were major talking points for those interested in travel around the time of the *TN* performance.[17]

10.3 Middle Temple Characters

Anthony Arlidge has argued that the names of two characters in *TN*, Curio and Fabian, appear to have been derived from typical Inns of Court gentlemen (2000, 92–95). In the *Scourge of Villanie* (1598), John Marston, a member of the Middle Temple, comments on the dancing at Inns of Court revels in a piece entitled *Ad rithmum*, or "the rhythm of music":

> Come all as easie, as spruce Curio will / In some court hall to show his capring [dancing] skill [...] Be not so fearful (pretty soules) to meete, / As Flaccus is the Sergeants face to greete. (Halliwell-Phillips 1856, III.269)

Reference to a "Sergeant" identifies the "court hall" as being an Inns of Court venue rather than a royal one.[18] When Everard Guilpin of Gray's Inn published his poem *Skialetheia* (1598), he included several references to the 1597–8 Christmas revels at the Middle Temple. Richard Martin, who is referred to in these revels as "Seignor *Martino*" (*Le Prince d'Amour* 1660, 79), was elected on 24 December 1597 as the mock Prince d'Amour, reigning until Candlemas [2 February] at which point he resigned. In Guilpin's second satire, Martin seems to make an appearance as "S. *Martins*":

> I had thought the last mask which thou caperedst in / Had catechiz'd thee from this errors sinne, / taught thee S. *Martins* stuffe from true gold lace, / And know a perfect from a painted face.

In the third satire, the Prince d'Amour is explicitly mentioned, the interest in travel narratives at the Middle Temple is highlighted, and Fabian makes an appearance:

> With them in ranck *La volte Publius* / Who's grown a reueller ridiculous [...] H'ath been a player to a Christmas Prince [...] I know

> some of their humorous neere of kin, / Which scorne to speake to one which hath not bin / In one of these last voyages [...] But then a simple reueller, thou art more / Thou hast some doings with the prince d'Amour / And playd a noble mans part in a play: / Now out vpon thee Fabian.

No other Shakespeare play contains the characters Curio and Fabian. Daniel Carroll (1975, 63) sees the appearance of Fabian as evidence for an early version of *TN*. It was reported on 14 January 1596–7, that 12 days earlier in the parish of Kelvedon in the Archdeaconry of Essex, "Johannem Fabian [... did] behave himself very dissolutely and wantonly [...] in taking upon him to be a lord of misrule or Christmas lorde". Whether or not this made news at the Middle Temple in 1597 is unclear, although the "lord of misrule" would have aroused interest, but

> The Fabian incident (Christmas 1596/7) might serve as a *terminus a quo* for some original version [of *TN*], which may supposed to have existed and date variously, with one of the two comedies performed at the Middle Temple between Christmas 1597 and Candlemas 1598 being likely prospects. (Carroll 1975, 65–66)[19]

Henk Gras has conducted a study of the correspondences between *TN* and the 1597–8 Middle Temple revels, particularly between the behaviour of Malvolio in *TN* and the accusations levelled at Carolus Asinius Bestia during his mock arraignment at the revels. *Twelfth Night* opens with Orsino's speech, "If music be the food of love, play on; Give me excess of it" (1.1.1–2), in which he ends with "O spirit of love! [...] / But [love] falls into abatement and low price, / Even in a minute: so full of shapes is fancy / That it alone is high fantastical" (1.1.9–15). His love for Olivia is unrequited: "And my desires, like fell and cruel hounds, / E'er since pursue me" (1.2.23–24). At the arraignment of Carolus Asinius Bestia, the charge is given to the jury, with the reminder that the Prince d'Amour has

> by sweet laws so rightly instructed us in the steps of true Love, and by admirable discipline so carefully preserved us from all distempers of irregular Fancies, as we, and none but we may justly say, We live secure from the events of Folly, strengthened from the dangers of despair, and complete in the fruits and effects of true Love. (*Le Prince D'Amour* 1660, 54; Gras 1989, 554)

In reference to the steward Malvolio confronting Sir Toby for causing a disturbance at night (2.3.87), Gras (1989, 551) suggests that "the spoilsport attitude of Malvolio could have been recognized as the anti-festive behaviour of the Temple Benchers". John Manningham, in a diary entry dated 4 November 1602, records that "Barker told certain gent. in the buttery that one of the benchers had sometime come downe for a lesse noyse" (Bruce 1868, 77). When the Clerk of the Crown at the revels reads out the indictment against "Carolus Asinius Bestia, a discontented lover", his "Preamble" to the jury says "Wheras before we were controulable at the nod of every doting Bencher [...] all well disposed minds [are drawn into] a resolution to maintain this triumphant State of Love against those vile Vipers of disdain that would fret it" (*Le Prince D'Amour* 1660, 54).

However, there appear to be further associations between *TN* and the 1597–8 Middle Temple Christmas revels. When Malvolio reads the cryptic letter that Sir Toby has planted in Olivia's garden he reaches the unlikely conclusion that "my lady [Olivia] loves me" (2.5.83). He imagines himself "three months married to her" and "calling my officers about me, in my branched velvet gown". Item 17 of "Offences inquirable by the Jury" at Bestia's mock trial reads "If any man ignorantly misinterpret his Mistresses looks, words, tokens, and thereupon willingly grow discontent, he is to pay Fine and ransome, and further to live in Captivity during her pleasure". In addition, there is Item 24:

> If any man presume of Love that is not likely, or follow with fresh suite when his Mistris is out of view; he shall not have the benefit of the Statute of Wildfowle, but may be taken in a dayner. (*Le Prince D'Amour* 1660, 58).

Thereafter, Malvolio is unusually forward with Olivia. Maria warns Olivia of his strange behaviour, reporting that he "does nothing but smile". Malvolio approaches Olivia, wearing inappropriate "cross-gartering" and "yellow [stockings] in the legs", incorrectly believing that this, together with his smiling, will leave a favourable impression on her. Olivia asks him "Why dost thou smile so [...]?" and requests that Malvolio leaves her with "Wilt thou go to bed, Malvolio?" When he misinterprets it as amorous intent, his response is "To bed! Ay, sweetheart, and I'll come to thee". A startled Maria then enquires "Why appear you with this ridiculous boldness before my lady?" (3.4.40). This passage of action has features in common with Item 30 of "The Charge given by the Chief Justice to the Jury" in Bestia's trial:

> If any man having his face of an ill aspect, or clothes of an ill fashion, shall over loudly present himself to the offence of any ladies eyes; or having an harsh voice shall speak over boldly in any Ladies ears, or with a violent breath shall offer himself too familiarly to any Ladies mouth, this is also high Treason. (*Le Prince D'Amour* 1660, 66)

In Scene 4.2, Malvolio is imprisoned in "hideous darkness" where the Clown admonishes him with "talkest thou nothing but of ladies?" We can compare this with the end of the revels trial, when Bestia is sentenced to be "close prisoner to the most loathsome Dungeon in the Fort of Fancy, there to remain fasting from Favors, and feeding on Malancholy" until he delivers "an Oration in praise of Love".

There are also legal references. A mention of a woodcock both in the Clown's speech to Malvolio (4.2.61) and Item 27 of "Offences inquirable by the Jury" (*Le Prince D'Amour* 1660, 59) seems to glance at "Andrew Woodcock's case". Feste's question to Malvolio "What is the opinion of Pythagoras concerning Wilde-fowle?" (4.2.52) appears in Item 24 as "the Statute of Wildfowle" (*Le Prince D'Amour* 1660, 58). According to Henk Gras, "All these points indicate that Shakespeare may have explored the revels of The Prince of Love [1597–8] when writing a comedy for performance in the Middle Temple" (1989, 554)

There are also two previously unknown correspondences which can be introduced here. When Maria exits in *Twelfth Night* we find "Good night, Penthisilea" (2.3.175) in response to her suggestion of forging Olivia's hand in a letter to Malvolio, and in 'The Sentence against Iealousie' at the 1597–8 Middle Temple revels, the penalty is a journey to the "Kingdome of the Amazones", a land commanded by "Penthesilea the Queen of that Country, where there are only women and want of men" (*Le Prince D'Amour* 1660, 577).[20] The play refers to a "fustian riddle" (2.5.111), and at the revels, the Clerk of the Council delivers an improvised "Fustian answer" to the Prince's "Tufftaffata Speech" (*Le Prince D'Amour* 1660, 37). These allusions reinforce the idea that some version of the play was enacted at the 1597–8 revels.

Earlier, the topical references to the Sir Anthony Shirley travel narratives of 1600–1601 were discussed. Anthony Arlidge has pointed out that at the time of the 1602 *TN* performance at the Middle Temple, the Treasurer was John Shurley of Isfield (Arlidge 2000, 56–59), his tenure running from 22 May 1601 to 14 May 1602 (Hopwood 1903, I.413, I.421). His nephew, also called John Shurley, married Jane Sherley (or Shirley) of Wiston in 1595, whose brothers were Sir Anthony and Sir Robert of the Sophy expeditions. So the *TN* references to these voyages, especially the financial reference to a "pension of thousands to be paid from the Sophy", might well have been for his benefit and would have been particularly meaningful to Middle Temple members.[21]

10.4 Misrule at the Middle Temple

The notion of misrule in *TN* will now be explored, and the argument will be developed that the history of disorder at the Middle Temple would have made Candlemas, the performance day of *TN* in 1602, highly appropriate. A theme of revelry runs throughout the play:

SIR ANDREW: I delight in masques and revels sometimes together. (1.3.111–12)

It has previously been noted that

> The subplot shows a prolonged season of misrule, or 'uncivil rule', in Olivia's household, with Sir Toby turning night into day; there are drinking, dancing, and singing, scenes of mock wooing, a mock sword fight, and the gulling of an unpopular member of the household, with Feste mumming it as a priest and attempting a mock exorcism in the manner of the Feast of Fools. (Salingar 1958, 118)

Albert Labriola is more specific, casting "Sir Toby as the Lord of Misrule and Feste as the Clown and fool" (Labriola 1975, 5). The Lord of Misrule, with variant titles, was a mock ruler who was temporarily elected over summer or Christmas to oversee revels intended to empower subordinates and mock authority. There is evidence of an "abbess of misrule" in 1284 at Godstow nunnery in Oxford (Elliott *et al.* 2004, II.621–22), and in 1583 there was revelry amongst the parishioners:

> First, all the wilde-heds of the Parish, conuenting together, chuse them a Graund-Captain (of all mischeefe) whome they inoble with the title of my Lord of Mis-rule, and him they crowne with great solemnitie, and adopt for their king. This king anointed, chuseth forth twentie, fortie, threescore or a hundred lustie Guttes like to him self to waighte upon his lordly Maiestie, and to guarde his noble person. (Stubbes 1583, sig. M2^{r})

Armed with pipes and drums, bells and handkerchiefs:

> they go to the Church (I say) & into the Church (though the Minister be at praier or preaching) dancing & swinging their handkerchiefs ouer their heds. (Stubbes 1583, M2^{v})

In *TN*, Sir Toby Belch enquires of Sir Andrew Aguecheek:

> SIR TOBY: Why dost thou not go to church in a galliard and come home on a coranto? My very walk should be a jig. (1.3.125–27)

The first two dances were certainly used at the Middle Temple revels in the time of Henry VIII.[22] It appears that the Church was chosen not only because it had "taken place of the pagan fane which dances once honoured" but also because to disrespect its authority was "excitingly impudent" (Barber 1980, 30).[23]

Returning to the parishioners we find that:

> Another sorte of fantasticall fooles bring to these hel-hounds (the Lord of mis-rule and his complices) some bread, some good-ale,

some new-cheese, some olde, some custards & fine cakes, some one thing, some another. (Stubbes 1583, sig. M3r)

In *TN*, a merrymaking Sir Toby sings "Farewell dear heart", then rebukes Malvolio for interrupting him:

SIR TOBY: Dost thou think, because thou art virtuous, there shall be no more cakes and ale? (2.3.12–13)

There is evidence that a Christmas Prince was appointed in the royal court. Henry VIII was entertained by a Lord of Misrule wherever he stayed over Christmas:

These Lords beginning their rule on Alhollon Eve, continued the same till the morrow after the feast of Purification, commonly called Candlemas day. (Stowe 1598, 72)

However, Edmund Chambers reminds us that Elizabeth discontinued the tradition:

I do not find that Elizabeth, like her father and brother, ever appointed a Lord of Misrule, although there is some trace of an election of a King of the Bean on the last and greatest day of all, Twelfth Night. (Chambers 1945, I.19)

The universities were also partial to disordered festive rule. At Merton College, Oxford, a "king of beans" (*Rex fabarum*) appeared during Christmas 1485–6, and various other Oxford colleges elected a Lord or Prince of Misrule well into the seventeenth century (Elliott *et al.*, 2004, II.612–13). The earliest recorded Christmas Lord at Cambridge appeared at Christ's College in the 1539–40 Christmas season, and in 1544–5 at St. John's College the Lord took responsibility for organizing plays. Such appointments were unopposed by the authorities so long as the vice-chancellor gave prior approval (Nelson and Elliott 2010, II.731).

At the Inns of Court law schools, a Prince of Purpoole was elected at Gray's Inn, a Prince of Sophy at the Inner Temple, a Lord Lieutenant or Prince de la Grange at Lincoln's Inn, and a Prince d'Amour at the Middle Temple. However, only the identities of three of these mock rulers are known during Shakspere's lifetime: two at Gray's Inn and one at the Middle Temple. At the Middle Temple revels 1597–8, it is clear when the reign of their Prince d'Amour ended:

Upon Candlemas night, the Prince wearied with the weight of government, made a voluntary resignation. (*Le Prince D'Amour* 1660, 89)

The minutes of the Middle Temple parliament for 25 November 1584 suggest that on Candlemas night the students frequently appointed their own rebel prince:

> No outcries in the night shall be made, nor chambers broken open, as by the Lord of Candlemas night or such like disorder, on pain of putting out of commons. (Hopwood 1903, I.272)

It was a practice that continued because on 6 February 1590 we learn that

> Divers gentlemen put out of commons for misorder on Candlemas night, have petitioned to be restored and pay a fine of 10l [£10]. (Hopwood 1903, I.311)

While again on 11 February 1592,

> In spite of the orders against a Lord of Misrule on Candlemas night, divers gentlemen of the House on last Candlemas night joined with Mr. Amerideth and Mr. Lower, who were expelled in 33 Eliz [Parliament 5 Feb 1591] for breaking the said orders, and broke open chamber doors and abused many gentlemen of the House. (Hopwood 1903, I.326)

It seems that one of the culprits was Richard Martin who, although expelled for his exploits, was reinstated in time to be elected as the Prince d'Amour for the 1597–8 revels.

So while the Middle Temple revels had a formally elected Prince d'Amour with scripted speeches and skits, the students installed their own unofficial Lord of Candlemas to terrorize the fraternity on Candlemas night. The Middle Temple imposed fines and expulsions to arrest the practice, and by the time of the 1602 revels we find no mention of it in the records. Alan Nelson has declared that "Its very title [*Twelfth Night*] conflicts with its Middle Temple performance at Candlemas" (2011, 306). However, our argument shows that a play called *Twelfth Night*, which bore a title traditionally associated with misrule, would have been ideal for the Middle Temple students at Candlemas, a night historically associated with their own brief tyrant. It is noteworthy that the theme of love in *TN* was also the theme of the 1597–8 and 1635–6 Middle Temple revels, which supports its use for the 1601–2 Christmas season.

10.5 The Acting Company

Without providing any evidence, Edmund Chambers opines that the two comedies at the 1597–8 Middle Temple revels and the 1602 *TN* performance were "probably supplied by professional actors" (Chambers 1945, I.222). Previously, James Halliwell-Phillips had seemed rather dogmatic about this idea:

> There is no doubt that the comedy [*TN*] was performed by the Lord Chamberlain's Company, and very little that Shakespeare himself was one of the actors who was engaged. (Halliwell–Phillips 1883, 171)

However, as shown in Tables 8.1 and 8.2, precedent favours Inns of Court players. In the period 1585–1605, only payments to musicians are regularly indicated for all four inns (Nelson and Elliott 2010, I.108–37, III.880–92). For example, for the Christmas when *TN* was performed, the minutes of the Middle Temple Parliament dated 27 November 1601 for the 1601–2 season state:

> The feast of Christmas shall be solemnly, not grandly, kept. Commons shall be continued until next term. A cartload of coals, 40s. for the minstrels, and 5l. as a favour, are allowed to those who remain. (Hopwood 1903, I.418)

The intriguing "favour" appears to have been for food and beverage [commons] rather than a play. There is evidence that if a payment for a play had been made it would have been appropriate to record it in the Middle Temple Parliament minutes. For example, on 3 February 1510, the day after Candlemas, we read,

> It was agreed that 35s. shall be allowed to Welles, the Steward for the time of Christmas last past, for apparels at the same time, and 6s. 8d. for reward given to the players, which they received from John Fitz James, junior, then Treasurer. (Hopwood 1903, I.30)

On the other hand, when the Palgraves Players performed at the Middle Temple on Candlemas 1616 the Parliament Book neglected to mention it.[24] So, although the Middle Temple Parliament Book is not a consistent record of professional plays enacted there, the fact remains that the claim that a professional company gave the 1602 performance is in want of corroboration. Considering the extent to which *TN* is suffused with Middle Temple allusions, it seems not to fit the profile of a touring play that a professional company would have brought.

It is clear that the Middle Temple players were capable of acting in their own productions around 1602. At court on 6 January 1598, they performed the 'Masque of Nine Passions' (Nelson and Elliott 2010, II.747). Also, in a letter from Sir John Popham to Sir Robert Cecil dated

8 February 1601 [1602], just six days after the *TN* performance, the Lord Chief Justice declared that:

> I haue so dealt with some of the Benchers off the mydle Temple as I haue brought that the house wylbe wylling to Beare CC markes towardes the Charg off what ys wysshed to be donne to her maiesties good lyking and if the yong gentylmen wylbe drawen in to performe what ys off their partes I hope yt wylbe effected. (Nelson and Elliott 2010, I.135)

So, the Middle Temple had a playing company capable of performing before the queen at the time *TN* was enacted in February 1602.

10.6 A Middle Temple Play

A review of the dating evidence for *TN* carried out in this chapter suggests that it was played in the 1601–2 season, not a year earlier, as John Leslie Hotson claims. This is supported by Sir Anthony Shirley travel narratives, "Farewell dear heart" from Jones's *The First Booke of Songes*, and the appearance of Duke Orsino at Whitehall on 6 January 1601, an event that seems to have inspired the choice of name for one of the *TN* characters. Alan Nelson remarks that

> While the strong claim that *Twelfth Night* was a Middle Temple play in some foundational or original sense cannot (I think) be sustained, some evidence can be marshalled in support of Arlidge's more limited claim that Inns of Court gentlemen might have cooperated in the play's performance. (Nelson 2011, 306–7)

Relying on examples from 1616 and 1619, he continues:

> for some Inns of Court entertainments were performed by a mixture of amateurs and professionals.

However, the play seems to have been written with a Middle Temple audience in mind, with likely references to the hall in which it was played; a pair of Molyneux globes in the Middle Temple; the Treasurer John Shurley; the Inns of Court gentlemen Curio and Fabian; several reasonable allusions to the 1597–8 Middle Temple revels; and a subplot of disorder and revelry, which, since Elizabeth had not continued the tradition of installing a Christmas Lord of Misrule, would have been more suitable for an Inns of Court audience than a royal one. There is also good reason why a play called *Twelfth Night*, with its associations of disorder and revelry, would have been historically appropriate for a performance at Candlemas to Middle Temple revellers. In addition, the suggestion that an earlier version of *Twelfth Night* was played as one of the Comedies at the 1597–8 Middle Temple revels is supported by allusions to Malvolio's humiliation in the mock Bestia trial at these revels.

There is no evidence that a professional company participated in the performance of *TN* at the Middle Temple in 1602, and apart from Lincoln's Inn in the period 1564–80 (see Table 8.1), the first evidence of external involvement appears in the 1605–6 season, when the Inner Temple is known to have employed a professional company.[25] The Inns of Court had a long tradition of using their own performers, so without documentary evidence that professional players enacted *Twelfth Night*, the default position must be that Inns of Court members performed it.

10.7 An RCP Analysis of *Twelfth Night*

With the notion that *TN* was designed for performance at the Middle Temple, perhaps as early as the 1597–8 Middle Temple revels, and noting the external evidence that it was enacted at the 1601–2 revels, we now turn to an RCP analysis of the play to attempt to identify its contributors (Appendix E). From Tables E.3 and E.4, all four of George Chapman's and all four of Thomas Heywood's rare matches occur after 1602, which at best indicate their borrowing from the play, and since neither dramatist was a member of any of the Inns of Court, they seem not to be appropriate candidates for contribution, at least to these two possible versions. From Table E.5, Ben Jonson has three rare matches before 1602 and one after. This gives a hint of contribution, but, like Heywood, not being a member of the Inns of Court, it is difficult to see how Jonson might have been permitted to have a hand in either of the possible revels versions. In fact, this might serve as evidence that he edited it later in the *FF* (1623).

The case seems weighted more in favour of Inns of Court writers, and this consideration then places Francis Bacon squarely in the frame. Table E.1 gives his returns from the EEBO database, resulting in two matches before 1602, while Table E.2 shows the returns from Google searches of his work, thereby locating two before 1602 and two after. With a total of four matches before 1602 (the play borrowed from Bacon) and two after (Bacon borrowed from the play), this produces a good case for Bacon having a hand in *TN*. Particularly noteworthy is the play's "*Deliculo surgere*, thou knowest" (Table E.2, No. 2), the earliest known example appearing in William Lily's *A short introduction to grammar* (1549) as "Diluculò surgere saluberrimum est". This is the form that Bacon chose to record in his *Promus* (c.1592–4) wastebook (see Figure 10.3), which was the second known occurrence after William Lily.[27] Its third known appearance was in *TN*.

So, the suggestion here is that not only was *TN* designed to contain allusions to the Middle Temple, but also Francis Bacon, the producer of the Inns of Court players, had a hand in it.

Figure 10.3 *"Diluculo surgere saluberrimum est"*. Francis Bacon, *Promus of Formularies and Elegancies* (1592–4, British Library, Harley 7017, f.112).[26]

Notes

1 The full English title is *Jan Huyghen van Linschoten his Discours of Voyages into ye Easte & West Indies*, published in Amsterdam in 1596. An English translation was printed in London by John Wolfe in 1598 and was published by the Hakluyt Society in 1885. Charles Coote identifies the map location as "folio 328 of Linschoten" by which he means the English edition. The map did not appear in the original Dutch version nor in any of the subsequent German and Latin editions (see Coote 1877–9, 88–99).

2 It was published occasionally in Volume 2 (1599) and generally in Volume 3 (1600) of Hakluyt's 'Principal Navigations', see Wallis (1951, 288n).

3 A rhumb line spirals down from the North Pole on the globe, crossing all lines of longitude at the same angle and appears as a straight line on Wright's map. The map follows the principles of projection set out in *Certaine Errors of Navigation* (1599) by the noted mathematician Edward Wright.

4 De Veer's dedication is dated 29 April 1598. Latin, German, and French translations also appeared in 1598, and an Italian version in 1599. An English translation was entered in the Stationer's Register on 13 June 1598, with a title that describes how the ship was "beset in Iyce" (Lothian and Craik 2000, xxxii).

5 *A True Report of Sir Anthony Shierlies Iourney* (1600) states that Sir Anthony went "to Casbine in Persia: At which place he met with the great Sophie", events reported by "two Gentlemen who haue followed him in the same the whole time of his trauaile, & are lately sent by him with Letters into Englande. September 1600". There followed *A new and large discourse of the trauels of Sir Anthony Sherley Knight* (1601) written by "*William Parry Gentleman, who accompanied Sir Anthony in his Trauells*".

6 The lyrics of Cantus XII later appeared in Richard Johnson's *The Golden Garland of Princely Pleasures and Delicate Delights* (1620) under the title "Coridons farewell to Phillis". Vincent (1906, xiii) claims that this title was an "old ballard [...] printed in 1590", but without a source citation it is unverifiable.

7 In a letter dated 3 February 1600 [1602] from John Chamberlain to Dudley Carleton, he notes that "[Orsino] shold haue ben [feasted] by the Lord Treasurer, and by Grayes Ynne that made preparation of shewes to entertain him, but he made such haste away that they were disappointed" (Nelson and Elliott 2010, II.685).

8 Orsino reported that "there was acted a mingled comedy, with pieces of music and dances" (Hotson 1955, 202). The Accounts of the Revels at Court name three companies that played on Twelfth day at night 1601 [1602] before the queen at Whitehall: the "servauntes to the lord Chamberleyne", "the Lord Admyrall" company, and "the Children of the Chappell". The last named

were rewarded: "for a play presented before her Matie on Shrouesondaye at night x^{li}. and for a showe wth musycke and speciall songes prepared for ye purpose on Twelfth day at night c^{s}. in all [...] xv^{li}" (Cunningham 1842, xxxiii).

9 The book measures less than six inches by four, contains 133 leaves, and is written in a minute hand. In addition to detailed notes on sermons attended, it contains a miscellany of rumours, aphorisms, book extracts, and personal recollections of journeys into Kent and Huntingdonshire. The diarist was evidently on good terms with Dr Henry Parry, one of Her Majesty's chaplain's, who attended her during her last days at Richmond, having included a record of the queen's failing health.

10 John Payne Collier's reputation as a forger of manuscripts, especially those at Dulwich College, justifiably raises doubts about the authenticity of the Manningham *TN* entry. Knowles *et al.* (1984) have given several reasons why the *TN* entry is genuine. Chief among these is that Manningham preferred continuity, appending the first entry of a month to the final entry of the previous month without a break in the text. If the *TN* entry was interpolated by Collier then Manningham must have left a space after the final entry of January into which Collier could have made a false entry for 2 February. However, this space would have been inconsistent with the continuity of the rest of the diary. An even stronger reason why Collier could not have forged the entry is that he met with the MS in the "British Museum [Library]", and then, as now, he must have examined the diary under strict supervision. So the opportunity for fabrication, especially considering the difficulties that replicating such minute handwriting would present, is unlikely to have arisen.

11 Middle Temple Hall was completed in 1570 but severely damaged at the screen end in the Second World War after which it was fully restored. It has five bays on both the north and south walls and a bay window on each side of the west end where the dais is situated. There is an entrance porch at the north east corner behind the oak screen and a double hammer beam roof.

12 The Whitehall of 1602 was burnt down in 1697; however, a description survives. "The building comprised six bays [not bay windows], with a projecting oriel [bay window] on the east side at the upper end [bottom of Figure 10.2], where would also be situated the dais with the great arched fireplace on the opposite [short] wall". See *Survey of London* (1930, XIII.48).

13 It measures 100 feet by 41 feet.

14 Reproduced from *Survey of London* (1930, XIII.48). The Great Hall measured 40 feet by 70 feet.

15 In 1889, Clement Markham found that a set of Molyneux globes were "in the library of the Middle Temple", but there is no evidence for how and when they were acquired (Hues and Markham 1889, xxxi–xxxii; Wallis 1951, 275–90).

16 Molyneux followed the Gerrit de Veer map of 1598 rather than the Wright–Molyneux map of 1599–1600.

17 In 1856, the Molyneux globes were situated at Oxford and Cambridge Universities and "in severall Libraries (here, and beyond seas)", see Wallis (1951, 275–76). The globes are also alluded to in detail in *The Comedy of Errors* (3.2.117–44), so the author of these references had evidently seen them.

18 The antiquarian Sir William Dugdale informs us that "the Feasts, viz. All Saints and Candlemass, are the only Feasts in the whole year made purposely for the Judges and Sergeants in this Society" (Nelson and Elliott 2010. III.780).

19 The two Comedies enacted at the 1597–8 Middle Temple revels appeared on 28 December and 2 January.

20 This is not searchable in EEBO. The mention of "Penthisilia" occurs with a rarity of 24/4233 (0.567%) before 1602. This revels occurrence is the only known use before *Twelfth Night.*

21 At the 1597–8 Middle Temple revels, the remit of the mock Lord Treasurer was "to receive all the Revenews of the Crown; as Sigh, Sonnets, Tears, Vows, Protestations, &c. and to give allowance and pensions out of them to all such as desire them" (*Le Prince d'Amour* 1660, 25).

22 Reporting on revels at the Middle Temple, Dugdale states: "Besides these solemn Revells, or measures aforesaid, they had wont to be entertained with Post Revells performed by the better sort of the young Gentlemen of the Society, with Galliards, Corrantoes, and other Dances, or else with Stage-playes: the first of these Feasts being at the beginning, and the other at the latter end of Christmas". The feasts were on "All Saints [Hallowmass Day, 1 November], and the Purification of our Lady [Candelmas Day, 2 February]" Dugdale (1780, 89, 95).

23 In 1576, churchwardens in Canterbury were asked by their superiors whether they had "suffered any Lordes of Mysrule, or Summer Lordes or Ladies, or anye disgysed persons, or others in Christmasse, or at Maygames, or any Morrice dauncers, or at any other tymes, to come unreuerently into the Church or Churchyarde, and there to daunce, or play any unseemly partes, with scoffes, ieates, wanton gestures or ribald talke, namely in the time of common prayer" (*Articles* 1576, No. 61).

24 The first record of a receipt is 27 January 1612 [1613] for a masque. We then have several musicians receipts, with the first Players' Receipt occurring in 1615 [1616]: "Receved of Mr Baldwin, for a play parformed by the Palgraves Players, on Candlmas day last 1615 [1616] the Sume of twelue poundes" (Nelson and Elliott 2010, I.162, I.189).

25 Two plays were rewarded at five pounds each at the Inner Temple in the 1605–6 season, and although the players are not recorded as professional, later similar records where an outside company is named suggest it (Nelson and Elliott 2010, I.137–38).

26 Francis Bacon, British Library, Harley 7017, f.112, dated c.1592–4. This is also cited in Pott (1883, 385), although it is incorrectly given there as "salubrium" instead of "saluberrimum est".

27 The search {deliculo surgere} indicates a rarity of 1/4233 (0.024%) before 1602.

Bibliography

Adams, Barry B. "Orsino and the Spirit of Love: Text, Syntax, and Sense in Twelfth Night." *Shakespeare Quarterly* 29 (Winter 1978): 52–59.

Akrigg, G. P. V. "Twelfth Night at the Middle Temple." *Shakespeare Quarterly* 9 (Summer 1958): 422–24.

Arlidge, Anthony. *Shakespeare and the Prince of Love, The Feast of Misrule in the Middle Temple.* London: Giles de la Mare, 2000.

Articles to be enquired of, within the Prouince of Canterburie. London: Willyam Seres, 1576.

Barber, C. L. *Shakespeare's Festive Comedy.* Princeton University Press, 1959; Eighth Paperback Printing, 1980.

Beke, Charles T., ed. "The true and perfect description of three voyages." In *The Three Voyages of William Barents to the Arctic Regions (1594, 1595, and 1596), by Gerrit de Veer.* Transl. William Phillip. Second edition. Imprinted at London for T. Pavier, 1609. Reissued London: Printed for the Hakluyt Society, 1876.

Brittin, Norman A. "The Twelfth Night of Shakespeare and of Professor Draper." *Shakespeare Quarterly* 7 (Spring 1956): 211–16.

Bruce, John, ed. *Diary of John Manningham*. London: J. B. Nichols and Sons, 1868. Printed for the Camden Society.

Carroll, D. Allen. "Fabian's Grudge against Malvolio." *Shakespeare Quarterly* 26, No. 1 (Winter 1975): 62–66.

Chambers, E. K. *The Elizabethan Stage*. 4 vols. Oxford: Clarendon Press, 1945.

Chew, Samuel Chew. *The Crescent and the Rose*. New York: Oxford University Press, 1937.

Collier, John Payne. *The History of English Dramatic Poetry to the Time of Shakespeare and Annals of the Stage*. 3 vols. London: John Murray, 1831.

Coote, Charles H. "Shakspere's 'New Map.'" In *The New Shakspere's Society Transactions 1877–9*. Series 1, No. 7. London: Trubner & Co.

Cunningham, Peter. *Extracts from the Accounts of the Revels at Court in the Reigns of Queen Elizabeth and King James I*. London: Printed for the Shakespeare Society, 1842.

Draper, John W. *The Twelfth Night of Shakespeare's Audience*. California: Stanford University Press, 1950.

Dugdale, Sir William. *The History and Antiquities of the Four Inns of Court*. London: Printed for G. Kearsly, 1780.

Elam, Keir. *Twelfth Night*. Arden Shakespeare. London: Methuen Drama, 2008.

Elliott Jr, John R, Alan H. Nelson, Alexandra F. Jonston, and Diana Wyatt, eds. *Records of Early English Drama: Oxford*. 2 vols. Toronto: University of Toronto Press, 2004.

Furness, Horace Howard. *Twelfe Night, or, What You Will*. A New Variorum Edition Shakespeare. Philadelphia: J. B. Lippincott Company, 1901.

Gras, Henk. "Twelfth Night, Every Man Out of His Humour, and the Middle Temple Revels of 1597–8." *Modern Language Review* 84 (July 1989): 545–64.

Gurr, Andrew. *The Shakespearean Stage, 1574–1642*. Cambridge: Cambridge University Press, 1980.

Halliwell–Phillipps, James O. *The Works of John Marston*. 3 vols. London: John Russell Smith, 1856.

Halliwell-Phillips, James O. *Outlines of the Life of Shakespeare*. London: Longmans, Green, and Co, 1883.

Holden, William P. *Twelfth Night or What You Will*. First edition 1922. New Haven: Yale University Press, 1954.

Hopwood, Charles H., ed. *Middle Temple Records*. 3 vols. London: Butterworth and Co., 1903.

Hotson, John Leslie. *The First Night of Twelfth Night*. London: Rupert Hart–Davis, 1955.

Hues, Robert, and Clement Markham. *Tractatus De Globis Et Eorum Usu: A Treatise Descriptive of the Globes Constructed by Emery Molyneux and Published in 1592*. Printed by the Hakluyt Society, 1889.

Hunter, Joseph. *New Illustrations of the Life, Studies, and Writings of Shakespeare*. 2 vols. London: J.B. Nichols and Son, 1845.

Knight, Charles, ed. *The Pictorial Edition of the Works of Shakespeares*. Comedies. Second edition revised. London: George Routledge & Sons, 1867.

Knowles, Richard, Robert K. Turner, and William C. McAvoy, eds. *Twelfth Night, or, What You Will*. Modern Language Association of America, 1984.

Labriola, Albert C. "Twelfth Night and the comedy of festive abuse." *Modern Language Studies* 5 (Autumn 1975): 5–20.

Le Prince d'Amour, or the Prince of Love. With a collection of several ingenious Poems and Songs. By the Wits of the Age. London: Printed for William Leake, 1660.

Lothian, J. M., and T. W. Craik. *Twelfth Night*. Arden Shakespeare. London: Thomson Learning, 2000.

Malone, Edmund. *The Plays and Poems of William Shakespeare*. 21 vols. London: Printed for F. C. and J. Rivington [etc.], 1821.

Memorials of Affairs of State in the Reigns of Queen Elizabeth and King James I. 3 vols. London: T. Ward, 1725.

Musgrove, S., ed. *Twelfth Night or What You Will*. Edinburgh: Oliver & Boyd, 1969.

Nelson, Alan H. "New light on drama, music, and dancing at the Inns of Court to 1642." In J. Archer, E. Goldring, and S. Knight, eds. *The Intellectual and Cultural World of the Early Modern Inns of Court*. Manchester: Manchester University Press, 2011.

Nelson, Alan H., and John R. Elliott Jr, eds. *Records of Early English Drama: Inns of Court*. 3 vols. Woodbridge: D. S. Brewer, 2010.

Pott, Mrs Henry. *The Promus of Formularies and Elegancies (being private notes, circ. 1594, hitherto unpublished) by Francis Bacon*. Boston: Houghton, Mifflin, & Co, 1883.

Price, Diana. *Shakespeare's Unorthodox Biography: New Evidence of an Authorship Problem*. Shakespeare-authorship.com, 2012.

Salingar, L. G. "The design of Twelfth Night." *Shakespeare Quarterly* 9 (Spring 1958): 117–39.

Sherley, Anthony. *A True Report of Sir Anthony Shierlies iourney to Venice*. London: Printed by R. Blower for I. Iaggard, 1600. STC: 22425.

Stowe, John. *Survay of London*. London: Imprinted by John Wolfe, 1598.

Stubbes, Phillip. *The Anatomie of Abuses*. London: Printed by Richard Jones, 1583.

Survey of London, St. Margaret Westminster, Part II. Montagu H. Cox and Philip Norman, eds. London: London County Council, 1930.

Vincent, Charles, ed. *Fifty Shakspere Songs*. Boston: Oliver Ditson, 1906.

Wallis, Helen M. "The first English globe: A recent discovery." *The Geographical Journal* 117 (September 1951): 275–90.

Wallis, Helen M. "Further light on the Molyneux globes." *The Geographical Journal* 121 (Sept 1955): 304–11.

Warren, Roger, and Stanley Wells. *Twelfth Night*. Oxford: Clarendon Press, 1994.

11 *The Tempest*

William Strachey's unpublished (until 1625) 'True Reportory', a secret Virginia Company report, is examined for the rare correspondences it shares with *The Tempest*. The Virginia Company's propaganda pamphlet *A true declaration* (1610b) is shown to have relied heavily on 'True Reportory', and Francis Bacon, who was a leading member of the Virginia Company, emerges as a contributor to this company pamphlet. This means that he must have inspected 'True Reportory', a confidential source for the play, before it received its first known performance in November 1611. After exploring how *The Tempest* was used as a political tool, an RCP analysis of the play, Appendix F, is invoked to show the extent of Bacon's influence.

11.1 The Virginia Colony

In December 1606, the London Virginia Council succeeded in persuading several merchant companies and noblemen to finance a new settlement in Virginia.[1] Assured of a share in the gold that the Spanish had earlier reported (Brown 1890, I.105–6), the adventurers committed enough money to dispatch three ships and 144 planters from Blackwall Stairs on the Thames across the Atlantic.[2] After being delayed for six weeks by strong winds, Captain James Newport found a long passage past the Canaries and the West Indies, and although his navigation eventually failed him, a storm fortuitously delivered him to the Virginia coastline. As the first wave of colonists sailed into Cape Henry on 26 April 1607, the tide of expectation was high, and after sailing 40 miles down the River James they pitched a three-sided fort on the north side. Unfortunately, the marshy ground proved unwholesome, and typhoid and dysentery soon struck down the new settlers (Stith 1747, 44–6). Disease, native attacks, and a divided governing body but mainly famine eventually brought them to desperation, and only Captain John Smith's ingenuity and persistence in trading for corn with the Indian chief Powhaton saved the colony from extinction.

By the time the third supply weighed anchor at Falmouth on 8 June 1609 with 600 men, the second Virginia Charter had replaced Jamestown's ineffective President and Council with a single Governor appointed by the Council in London.[3] Thomas West, who was also Baron De La Warr and Captain-General, was to be the first incumbent, but, until his arrival the following year, Sir Thomas Gates, Lieutenant-General, was to assume command. On 23 July, the nine vessels of the third supply were hit by a hurricane; the *Sea Venture*, which carried the colony's main commanders Gates, Somers, and Newport, became separated from the rest of the fleet, and the ship was wrecked at Bermuda with the unprecedented survival of the entire crew. Despite several attempts at mutiny, they managed to use the wreck of the *Sea Venture* and the abundant cedar wood at Bermuda to construct two vessels and continue for Jamestown.[4] The shipwreck was sensational news when it reached England in 1610, and, as we shall see, it became a source event for Shakespeare's *The Tempest*. In this respect, the play seems to have relied partly on published Virginia pamphlets, such as John Smith's *A true relation* (1608) and Richard Rich's *Newes from Virginia* (1610), as well as on secretary William Strachey's 20,000-word classified company report 'True Reportory', which was sent back from the Virginia Colony in July 1610. Other unpublished information about the Virginia colony also seems to have found its way into the play, facts that later appeared in Ralph Harmor's *A True Discourse* (1615) and John Smith's *The generall historie* (1624).

While the private aim of the Virginia Company was to obtain a financial return at the earliest possible opportunity, their promotional sermons and literature framed matters rather differently (Fitzmaurice 2003, 69). David Quinn describes the Counseil for Virginia's *A true declaration* (1610b)[5] as "the most distinguished piece of propaganda for the colony", and one of its aims was to quell rumours about disorder in the colony, enticing prospective adventurers [investors] with the promise of abundant riches (Quinn 1979, V.248). Evidence will be presented that it almost certainly relied on William Strachey's 'True Reportory', so that whoever compiled *A true declaration* must have had one of the sources for *The Tempest* in front of him.

It is clear that the oaths of secrecy imposed on Virginia Company members, and the attacks on players in its literature, render it unrealistic to expect a non-member such as Shakspere to have been allowed access to the Strachey report. Here, it will be argued that it is more likely that information from this document, together with other inside information, was released by one or more members of the Company to include in *The Tempest* so that English interest in the New World could be advertised at court to invited European ambassadors. In fact, the first known performance of *The Tempest* was on 1 November 1611 before King James at Whitehall by the "Kings Players" (Chambers 1945, IV.177), followed by a performance in February 1612–13 at the wedding of Princess Elizabeth and the Elector of Palatine, also by the King's Men.[6]

By examining the EEBO database for rare phrases in *A true declaration* and *The Tempest*, Appendix F, it can be shown that a good candidate for compiling the former and supplying information for the latter was the essayist and Solicitor General Sir Francis Bacon who was a leading member of the Virginia Company, and later had a hand in producing masques at Whitehall (Clarke 2014, Tables 7.3 and 8.6).

11.2 The 'True Reportory' and *The Tempest*

The notion that Strachey's 'True Reportory' is the main influence on the play was first suggested by Morton Luce (1901, Appendix 1), and was echoed in subsequent work by Charles Gayley (1917, 59–69) and Robert Cawley (1926, 688–726). In 1625, Samuel Purchas published Strachey's 20,000-word report with the date "July 15, 1610" in the heading (Purchas 1625, IV.1734–58), and since it describes no events later than Sir Thomas Gates leaving for England on that date, then the most credible hypothesis is that it travelled with Gates to England and was delivered to the Virginia Company around 1 September 1610. This position has been tested by Roger Stritmatter and Lyn Kositsky (2007, 447–72), who argue that it was written later than 1610, after Strachey arrived back in London to lodge at Black Friers around October 1611, so it was too late to contribute to the first known performance of *The Tempest* on 1 November 1611. However, Alden Vaughan (2008), Tom Reedy (2010), and the present author (Clarke 2011; 2016) have set out persuasive evidence against these objections. William Strachey later wrote a preface to the *Lawes Divine, Morall and Martiall* (1612) from his "lodging in the Black Friers" in which he refers to a work of his on Bermuda and Virginia which had "many impediments, [and] as yet must detaine such my observations in the shadow of darknesse" (Strachey 1612, sig. A2). This can only be a reference to the 'True Reportory', and surely reveals his frustration that its publication had been thwarted by the Council.[7]

In 1901, Morton Luce (1901, 162) compared *The Tempest* with 'True Reportory' and cautioned

> Before dealing with the subject of parallel passages I may perhaps remind the reader or student that such resemblances will not all of them be equally striking, and that an opinion should be based upon the extracts collectively, not individually.

Unfortunately, unless the parallels are rare it makes little difference whether or not they are considered collectively. In EEBO, the 5377 pre-1611 searchable texts have been used to conduct an RCP[8] test that allows the extent to which *The Tempest* relied on Strachey's 'True Reportory' (1610) to be calculated. Table 11.1 shows the most significant results in comparison with the Virginia Company's *A true declaration* (1610b).

Table 11.1 Rare collocation comparison of 'True Reportory' (1610; Purchas 1625, IV), A *true declaration*, and *The Tempest*

'True Reportory' (1610)	*True Declaration (1610)*	*The Tempest (1611)*
"the sharpe windes blowing Northerly". (p. 1738)		"To run vpon the sharpe winde of the North". (2.2)[a]
"as we condemne not Kent in England, for a small Towne called Plumstead, continually assaulting the dwellers there (especially newcommers) with Agues and Feuers; no more let vs lay scandall, and imputation vpon the Country of Virginia, because the little Quarter wherein we are set downe [...] appears to be vnwholesome, and subiect to many ill ayres, which accompany the like marish [marshy] places". (p. 1753)	"No man ought to judge of any Countrie by the fennes and marshes (such as is the place where James towne standeth) except we will condemne all England, for the Wilds and Hundreds of Kent". (p. 32) "our fort [...] is most part inuironed with an ebbing and flowing salt water, the owze of which sendeth forth an vnwholsome & contagious vapour". (p. 33)	"vnwholesome fen" (1.2.322)[b] "*Adr.* The ayre breathes vpon vs here most sweetly. *Seb.* As if it had Lungs, and rotten ones. *Ant.* Or, as 'twere perfum'd by a Fen". (2.1.47–49) "All the infections that the sun sucks up / From bogs, fens, flats, on Prosper fall and make him / By inch-meal a disease!" (2.2.1–2)
"euery man from thenceforth commanded to weare his weapon, [...] and euery man aduised to stand vpon his guard". (pp. 1744–5)		"tis best we stand vpon our guard; / Or that we quit this place: let's draw our weapons". (2.1.321–22)[c]

[a]This correspondence was pointed out by Gayley (1917, 230). There are 7/5377(0.130%) document returns from EEBO before 1611 for {the sharp wind(s)} but none in the context of it being a north wind. Up to 1626, only two returns satisfy this context, the first being the 'True Reportory' (1610; Purchas 1625), which was first published in *Purchas his pilgrimes* (1625), and the second being *The Tempest* (1611), which was first published in the *First Folio* (1623). The Strachey report provides the *only* match with *The Tempest,* and it was an unpublished description when the first known performance of the play was given in 1611.

[b]Francis Bacon seems to have this in mind when, in his essay 'Of Plantations', he suggests, "It hath beene a great Endangering, to the Health of some Plantations, that they haue built along the Sea, and Riuers, in marish and vnwholesome Grounds"; Bacon (1625). The search {unwholesome fen} has no returns before 1611, while {unwholesome near.15 marish} yields 3/5377(0.056%). See Clarke (2014, Section 7.4).

[c]There are 2/5377(0.037%) returns shared by the searches {stand upon his/our guard} and {weapon(s) near.30 guard} when the documents were individually inspected for context.

The rare parallels in Table 11.1, together with those that are to follow, contribute to the evidence that the Bermuda shipwreck of 1609 was a source event. They also assist the case that unpublished inside information about the Virginia colony was used in the play.

11.3 Shakspere's Inaccess to the 'True Reportory'

When Samuel Purchas informed his readers in 1625 that "M. Strachies copious discourse shall feast you with the liuely expression of others miseries" (1625, IV.1733), it became clear why the 'True Reportory' could not have been made public in 1610. The company was trying to attract new investment, and an unauthorized publication of the 'True Reportory' would have been the greatest danger to the Virginia Company.[9] In fact, there are three main reasons why Shakspere the actor could not have gained access to Strachey's report.

Point 1

There was a prohibition on information leaving the colony (Kingsbury 1906, III.i.20a; Brown 1890, 398–99; Swem 1957, 66). In a letter dated 7 July 1610 to the Virginia Company of London, Governor De La Warr writes "I administered an oath of faith, assistance, and secresy; their names were these [...] William Strachey, Esq. Secretary [and Recorder]" (Brown 1890, I.407–8). Presumably, this was the same oath that was overseen by Edward Maria Wingfield in 1607:

> You shall keepe secret all matter Comitted & reuealed vnto you [...] & you shall not deliur any thing concerning the affaires of the Counsell to any other person to bee coppied out or ingrossed, wth out first making the Gournor accquainted therwith and leaue obtayned.[10]

The secrecy with regard to letters did not go unnoticed by Spain's secret agent in the colony, Francisco Maguel. In a report dated 1 July 1610 he notes:

> [the English] have issued orders prohibiting any one from taking letters with him beyond the frontiers, and also from sending any, especially to private individuals, without their first being seen and read by the governor. (Brown 1890, I.398–99)

The restriction on information that passed out of Virginia also extended to its passage into England. When Sir Thomas Gates set out for Virginia on 10 May 1610, he carried with him sealed instructions from the Virginia Council. Item 27 demanded that:

> You must take especiall care what relačons [information] come into England and what łres [letters] are written & that all things of that nature may be boxed vp and sealed and sent to [sic] first to the Counsell here. (Swem 1957, 66)

Of course, the prohibition on information leaving Virginia would have been futile if the London Virginia Council of 1610 had not maintained it. In 1619, Council members were required to take an oath of secrecy, and order 8.70 of the "Orders and Constitutions" stated that

> He shall be bound by oath to keepe secret all matters of secrecy: And not to discover [reveal] the proceedings of the Counseil, and Comitties extraordinary, till such time as themselves shall publish the same.[11]

Point 2

The Company literature warned against players who were misrepresenting the colony on the stage and thereby discouraging investment (Whitaker 1613, sigs A2 and C2; Johnson 1612, sig. A3^{v}; Strachey 1612, sig. P4^{v}).[12] For example, as noted by Robert Cawley (1926, 700), on 21 February 1610, the Reverend William Crashaw delivered a sermon in London "before the right honourable the Lord LaWarre, Lord Governour and Captaine Generall of Virginia, and others of his Majesties Councell for that Kingdome, and the rest of the adventurers in that plantation". After declaring that the colony had "only three enemies. 1. The Divell, 2. The Papists, and 3. The Players" (Brown 1890, I.361) Crawshaw began to expand on his concerns:

> As for Plaiers: [...] nothing that is good, excellent or holy can escape them [...] they abuse Virginea [...] and such as for which, if they speedily repent not, I dare say Vengeance waits for them. (Brown 1890, I.366–67)

This informs us that Virginia Council members were warned of the danger that players posed before the 'True Reportory' was sent back to England. However, Crashaw was not the only one to deliver a caution. In the Epistle Dedicatory to Robert Johnson's New Life of Virginia (1612) we find

> the malicious and looser sort (being accompanied with the licentious vaine of stage Poets) haue whet their tongues with scornfull taunts against the action it selfe. (sig.A3^{v})

William Strachey, the secretary at the colony, edited a pamphlet entitled *Lawes Divine* (1612), which set out the rules of conduct for the colony. There is a prayer on the last page that was recited every morning and evening to the colonists, with the line,

> O Lord we pray thee fortifie us against this temptation: let Sanballat, & Tobias, Papists & players & such other Amonites & Horonits the scum and dregs of the earth [...] let such swine wallow in their mire. (sig.P4^{v})

In other words, the threat posed by players was advertised to the whole colony.

Point 3

There is no doubt that the Spanish had designs on the colony. On 30 September 1610, Don Alonso de Velasco of the Spanish Council of State urged Philip III to exploit the vulnerability of the English by sending a force to "drive out the few people that have remained there" (Brown 1890, I.418). Philip declined. So, there would also have been a political price to pay, had the 'True Reportory', which exposed the weaknesses in the colony, gone beyond the safety of the Virginia Council and fallen into Spanish hands.

So it cannot be expected that a businessman such as William Shakspere, irrespective of the number of Council members he knew, could have gained access to the 'True Reportory' before *The Tempest* was performed at Whitehall in November 1611. All of these points have recently been examined in considerable detail elsewhere (Clarke 2011, 13–27).

11.4 *The Tempest* and Virginia Company Literature

By examining other notable contemporary shipwreck events, it is clear that apart from the *Sea Venture* at Bermuda, there is no other case that possesses the requisite combination that appears in *The Tempest* of a storm dispersing a fleet on the high sea, only the flagship being shipwrecked, all hands surviving, and the rest of the fleet continuing their voyage (Clarke 2011, 14–15)[13] The play shares several noteworthy rare parallels with contemporary Virginia Company literature. For example, Prospero's sprite Ariel sets down the storm-tossed ship safely in the harbour. The fatigued crew were so overworked that some fell asleep, and the hatches were closed:

> The Marriners all vnder hatches stowed,
> Who, with a Charme ioyned to their suffred labour
> I haue left asleep. (*The Tempest* 1.2.230–320)

This circumstance is confirmed by the Boatswain's "We were dead of sleep, / And – how we know not – all clapp'd under hatches" (5.1.230–31). Silvestor Jourdain, who was on board the *Sea Venture* when it hit the storm, recalled that

> All our men, being vtterly spent, tyred, and disabled for longer labour, were euen resolued, without any hope of their liues, to shut up the hatches, and to haue committed themselues to the mercy of the sea. (1610, 4–5)[14]

Apart from the Jourdain and Hughes accounts of the 1609 Sea Venture wreck (see also Hughes 1615, sig. A4; Smith 1624, 174), there is a report of the Thomas Cavendish voyage to the South Sea in 1591, which gives "the next day the storme ceased, and most of our young Saylers, which we call men of top a yard, being wearied with their nights worke that was past, were vnder Hatches asleepe"; however, the manuscript was not published for another 16 years (Purchas 1625, IV.1205). So, in 1611, this collocation was rare.[15]

Also, the term "freshes" is used in *The Tempest*:

> for Ile not shew him
> Where the quicke Freshes are. (3.2.66–67)

This is also a rare correspondence, and it appears in John Smith's *A true relation* (1608), a Virginia Company-related publication as well as his *A Map of Virginia* (1612).[16]

Due to the storms that engulfed the island, Bermuda was known as the 'Ile of Diuels' (Jourdain 1610),[17] and the spirit Ariel appears to hint at this with

> the kings sonne Ferdinand
> With haire vp-staring (then like reeds, not haire)
> Was the first man that leapt; cride hell is empty,
> And all the Diuels are heere. (1.2.212–16)

Ariel even mentions the 'Bermoothes' or Bermuda:

> Safely in harbour
> Is the Kings shippe, in the deep Nooke, where once
> Thou calldst me vp at midnight to fetch dewe
> From the still-vext Bermoothes,
> there she's hid. (1.2.227–230)

Bermuda was only mentioned in the contemporary literature in the context of exploration, and Richard Abrams (2012, 545–47) has pointed out that Richard Rich's *Newes from Virginia* (1610), registered on 1 October 1610, demonstrates the "first recorded instance of the *ooth*-spelling in English, and Shakespeare's the second".[18]

However, the most impressive evidence of the relation between *The Tempest* and the 1609 shipwreck at Bermuda arises from Caliban's speech on edible items, which has previously been the subject of much debate (Vaughan and Vaughan 2007, 216–17):

> I' prithee, let me bring thee where Crabs grow;
> And I with my long nayles will digge thee pig-nuts;
> Show thee a Iayes nest and instruct thee how
> To snare the nimble Marmozet; I'le bring thee
> To clustring Philbirts [hazelnuts], and sometimes I'le get thee
> Young Scamels from the Rocke. (2.2.167–172)

The earliest return for the EEBO search {crabs near.40 filberts} is in a book by Ralph Harmor (1615, 23), secretary to the colony from 1611–14. Describing Virginia, he reports:

> some filberds haue I seene, Crabbes great store, lesse, but not so sower as ours, which grafted with the Siens of English aple trees, without question would beare very goode fruite, and we doubt not but to haue the Siens enough the next yeere, there being in Sir Thomas Gates his garden at Iames town, many forward apple & peare trees come vp.[19]

Sir Thomas Gates was at the colony from 24 May to 20 July 1610 and again from August 1611 to March 1614, when he transferred authority to Sir Thomas Dale. The point here, and it is one that seems to have passed unnoticed hitherto, is that the only known published use of this combination of 'Philberts' and 'crabs' from *The Tempest* appears in a contemporary Virginia Company report on the colony which appeared after the first known performance of *The Tempest*. So, whoever supplied this information about the colony for *The Tempest* knew it before Ralph Harmor's publication.

Caliban's edible items have an additional role to play in dating parts of *The Tempest*.[20] In *A Dictionary of Birds* (Newton 1893–6, 815) the suggestion is made that the *First Folio*'s compositor set the word 'scamel' erroneously by reading the first 'e' in the scrivener's copy as a 'c'.[21] He should instead have set it as 'Seamel', a rare bird endemic to Bermuda. Caliban hints that the 'scamel' is edible, only the young are taken, and it can be found on the rocks. A number of contemporary documents relating to Bermuda discuss a bird called the 'seamall' or 'cahow', which they emphasize above any other livestock in respect of the simplicity with which it could be captured for consumption (Hughes 1615, sig. B1^{v}–B2; Hughes 1621, sig. A4^{v}; Smith 1624, sig. Z2).

William Strachey's 'True Reportory' (Purchas 1625, IV.1740–1), written in 1610, mentions a "Sea-Meawe" with "Our men found a prettie way to take them, which was by standing on the Rockes or Sands by the Sea side". In a 1625 marginal note to the description of the "Sea-Meawe", editor Samuel Purchas has added "Web-footed Fowle. They call it of the cry which it maketh a *Cohow*". However, for publication of *The Tempest*'s revelation that the young were preferred, we have to wait until Captain John Smith's *The General Historie of Virginia* (1624, sig. Z2) where we find "The Cahow is a Bird of the night, for all the day he lies hid in holes in the Rocks, where they and their young are also taken with as much ease as may be".

This was a bird whose behaviour was unknown in England until information about Bermuda reached London with the returning voyagers at the start of September 1610 (Jourdain 1610, 9),[22] and reinforces the view that *The Tempest* shipwreck alludes to the one at Bermuda in 1609.[23] As with the 'Philberds' and 'crabs', this information was unpublished in 1611, when *The Tempest* had its first known performance, but nevertheless found its way into the dialogue.

So, there are several examples of contemporary Virginia Company literature—William Strachey's 'True Reportory' (1610, first published by Purchas in 1625), Sylvestor Jourdain's *A discovery* (1610), Richard Rich's *Newes from Virginia* (1610), Ralph Harmor's, *A True Discourse* (1615), and John Smith's *The generall historie* (1624)—that seem to share rare collocations with the play. In consequence, two main points can be made:

1 The 1609 *Sea Venture* shipwreck at Bermuda was a source event for *The Tempest.*
2 Unpublished information about the colony had been inserted into the play before its first known performance in 1611.

The suggestion here is that this could only have been achieved with the assistance of one or more Virginia Company members.

11.5 'True Reportory' and *A True Declaration*

A true declaration (1610b) was a propaganda pamphlet issued by the London Virginia Company to quell rumours of disorder in the colony and attract investment. Several documents appear to have influenced it: William Strachey's 'True Reportory' (Purchas 1625, IV.1734–58), Sylvester Jourdain's *A discovery* (1610), and a letter dated 7 July 1610 from the Council of Virginia to the Virginia Company of London signed by Lord de la Warr and others (Brown 1890, 402–13). Charles Gayley (1917, 52, 230) points out with respect to *A discovery* (1610) that "[*A true declaration*'s compiler] embodies from it some five phrases not found in his other sources", while Tom Reedy (2010, 540) shows that the pamphlet follows the Lord de la Warr letter more closely than other texts when reporting the condition of the colony.[24] However, *A true declaration*'s main influence was 'True Reportory', which was first published in 1625 and, according to our best information, arrived in England on 1 September 1610. It contains a detailed account of the July 1609 shipwreck at Bermuda, the survival of the entire crew, the mutinies on the island, and the building of two cedar-wood pinnaces which they used to reach Jamestown in May 1610. The 'True Reportory' differs from *A true declaration* in that it openly discusses the disease and hostility of the environment. William Strachey's account was deemed so sensitive that it was withheld from publication until 1625 when it appeared in Samuel Purchas's *Purchas his pilgrimes*. Nevertheless, several favourable extracts appear in *A true declaration*.

For example, with respect to the *Sea Venture* crew's attempt to save themselves during the storm, the 'True Reportory' informs us "how mutually willing they were, yet by labour to keepe each other from drowning, albeit each one drowned whilest he laboured" (Purchas 1625, IV.1736). *A true declaration* recasts this as "those which laboured to keepe others from drowning were halfe drowned themselues in labouring" (Counseil for Virginia 1610b, sig. D1^{v}). Tom Reedy declares this tightening of Strachey's antimetabole to be "almost incontrovertible text evidence that the Virginia Company writer follows Strachey" (Reedy 2010, 539).

One passage in the 'True Reportory' (Purchas 1625, IV.1750) relating to rumours about the poor quality of the country is shown here, with the selections that appear in *A true declaration* (Counseil of Virginia 1610b, 31) added in italic:

> Then *let no rumour of the* pouerty of the *Country (as if in the wombe thereof* there *lay not those elementall seedes,* which could produce many fair births *of plenty, and increase*, and better hopes, then any land vnder the heauen to which the Sunne is no neerer a neighbour) I say, let no imposture rumour, nor any fame of some one, or a few more changeable actions, interposing by the way, or at home, *waue any mans faire purposes* hitherward, *or wrest them to a declining and falling off from the businesse.*[25]

There is yet another unique correspondence between the 'True Reportory' (Purchas 1625, 1753) and *A true declaration* (Counseil of Virginia 1601b, sig. E2^{v}) of some 70 words relating to the health of the colonists. The relevant passage from the 'True Reportory' is given here, with the version in *A true declaration* again added in italic:

> *for* of foure *hundred and odde* men, *which were seated at the Fals*, the last yeere when the Fleete came in with fresh and yong able spirits, *under the government of Captain Francis West, and of one*

> *hundred to the Seawards (on the South side of our River) in the Country of the Nansamundes, under the charge of Captaine John Martin, there did not so much as one man miscarry*, and but very few or none fall sicke, whereas *at James Towne, the same time, and the same monthes, one hundred sickned, & halfe the number died.*

In deciding which account came first, it should be clear that the author of *A true declaration* has simply edited down the accounts given in the 'True Reportory'. Given that the Strachey report was first published with the date "July 15, 1610" in the heading and that *A true declaration* was registered at Stationers' Hall on 8 November 1610, there is good evidence here that the latter's author had the 'True Reportory' in front of him when he compiled it.

The unattributed *A true declaration* is a work of about 10,800 words, and in the opinion of Morton Luce it "was penned with considerable literary skill" (Luce 1901, 167). It is written from the point of view of one main author, "And though it bee not for a theoreticall Schollar, to circumscribe the dominions of Princes, yet a few proofes from antiquity, shall suffice to controwle ignorant or presumptuous follie" (Counseil for Virginia 1610b, sig. C2). The compiler also declares that he has been privy to "the secrets of the iudiciall councell of Virginia" (sig. A3^{v}).

Three main candidates have been advanced as its principal originator. Andrew Fitzmaurice has suggested that it was "probably written by Dudley Digges" (2003, 177), while the American classical scholar Charles Mills Gayley thought it was "probably, Sir Edwyn Sandys" (1917, 52). Although Leslie Hotson chose "Sir Edwyn Sandys or Sir Dudley Digges" (1937, 225), David James found a different candidate:

> I have no doubt it was the Solicitor–General [Sir Francis Bacon], incomparably the greatest advocate and orator of the age [...] To read over the first book of *The Advancement of Learning* is to see the same style, ordonnance [sic], and learning at work as show themselves in the *Declarations* [*True and Sincere Declaration* and *A true declaration*]. (James 1967, 97–98)

All three were prominent Virginia Council members with previous publications.[26] As far as rhetorical figures are concerned, samples of Bacon's work exhibit a better match with *A true declaration* than equal-size samples of Digges and Sandy's work. More significantly, using EEBO, Bacon's corpus shares six rare collocations with the pamphlet, whereas those of Sandy and Digges share none (Clarke 2014, Tables 8.3 and 8.5, respectively). On this evidence, Bacon seems to have contributed to *A true declaration*, which means that he must have had access to the 'True Reportory', one of the sources for *The Tempest*. This is not to argue that Bacon originated the play, only that he seems to have been in an ideal position to influence its content.

Francis Bacon's interest in the Virginia Company is well documented. Having been held back by Queen Elizabeth and her chief adviser Robert Cecil, after King James came to power he rose to become Solicitor–General (1607), Attorney–General (1613), and Lord Chancellor (1618). He formed a strong interest in the New World, and in February 1607, two months after the first planters had left the Thames for Virginia, he made a speech in Parliament pointing out that "the solitude of Virginia was crying out for inhabitants".[27] In 1609, he composed a tract entitled "Certain considerations touching the plantations in Ireland",[28] and in the same year the Second Virginia Charter named him as one of 52 Council members, only three of whom were neither a knight nor a Lord. Michael Keirnan states that the Charter "may have been prepared in part by Bacon in his capacity as Solicitor General" (2000, 244), an assertion that seems to have originated with the American colonial historian Alexander Brown (1890, 207). Several years later, after completing *The Historie of Travaile into Virginia Britannia*, William Strachey sent the "Lord High Chancellor of England" Sir Francis Bacon a manuscript copy with the following dedication:

> Your Lordship ever approving himself a most noble fautor [supporter] of the Virginia Plantation, being from the beginning (with other lords and earles) of the principal counsell applyed to propagate and guide yt. (Strachey 1849)[29]

11.6 *The Tempest* as a Political Tool

There is evidence that *The Tempest* was used to impress invited foreign ambassadors at court. The king had an active role in the Virginia colony, putting his signature to three Virginia Charters in 1606, 1609, and 1611. Samuel Lucas (1850, 1) notes that:

> The attention of King James was so favourably directed to the advantages attending the plantation of colonies, in consequence of certain experiments of his in the Highlands [...] that he readily harkened to the applications which were made to him.

However, his interest in the colonies was more than just a sociological experiment. He also realized their political advantage. David Nuzum (1959, 20) has suggested that William Strachey's 'True Reportory' was purposely lent to Shakspere by the Company "as part of a concerted scheme of propaganda to support the London Company in its enterprise". The present work argues against Shakspere's access, but the notion that the play was used as a political tool seems well founded. About 18 months after the first known performance of *The Tempest* at Whitehall, a masque was devised precisely for this purpose. On the evening of 15 February 1612–13 at the wedding of Princess Elizabeth of England to Frederick V, Elector Palatine of the Rhine in Germany, a masque credited to George Chapman (1614) was given by Middle Temple and Lincoln's Inn:

> It proclaimed the English interest in America, and prophesied for the married pair honour and riches such as they believed would come from the great gold mines of Virginia. (Sullivan 1913, 73, 67–81)

After mentioning Virginian priests and princes, it refers to "a rich Island lying in the South-Sea":

> In which Island (beeing yet in command of the Virginian continent.) A troupe of the noblest Virginians inhabiting, attended hether the God of Riches, all triumphantly shyning in a Mine of gould. (Chapman 1614, sig. D2^{v})[30]

The intention seems to have been to present the invited ambassadors at the masque with an impression of the riches available to the English in the New World, and riches meant political power. So, when *The Tempest* was played at Whitehall in November 1611 and also at the Elizabeth–Palatine marriage celebrations in February 1612–13,[31] it seems to have been intended as a message to the invited ambassadors about England's new financial strength.

David Nuzum (1959, 19–20) has also declared that

> Their giving a public dramatist [Shakspere] access to a confidential report ['True Reportory'] so dangerous that they were even then seeking by royal charter to suppress such intelligence implies that no mere chance placed this material in Shakespeare's hands; and indeed the Company would hardly [have] permitted him to use it but for some excellent reason; and no one but the Council of the Company could have put it into his hands.

However, not only does it seem unrealistic that Shakspere would have had access to it, but there is evidence that not even the secretary of the Virginia Company had seen it. On 14 December 1610, just over three months after the Strachey report had reached the Virginia Company, the company secretary Richard Martin dispatched a letter to William Strachey in Virginia with the *Hercules* asking questions that the

'True Reportory' had already answered (Culliford 1965, 123–25). Had Martin seen the 'True Reportory', there would have been no need to write it.

This leaves the question as to how material from a sensitive company document such as 'True Reportory' found its way into *The Tempest,* which few Virginia Company members could have inspected. Shakspere could not have seen it, but the evidence suggests that Francis Bacon did. Furthermore, Bacon is known to have been a producer of masques and devices, having later been commended in print for producing two masques at Whitehall (see Section 5.5):

> 20 February 1612–13: Elizabeth–Palatine marriage celebrations, jointly played by Gray's Inn and Inner Temple players, writing credited to Francis Beaumont. (Beaumont 1613, sig. B)
>
> 6 January 1613–14: Earl of Somerset–Lady Frances Howard marriage celebrations, played by Gray's Inn members, writing credited to George Chapman. (Chapman 1614)

The first of these was about 18 months after *The Tempest* was played at Whitehall in November 1611, at a time when Bacon was also a close adviser to King James. We shall now examine the evidence for Bacon's influence on the play, first by taking a few examples of how his own views on colonization correspond with Virginia Company pamphlets, and then by looking at rare collocations that his corpus shares with *The Tempest.*

11.7 Francis Bacon's Rare Parallels with *The Tempest*

When *A True and Sincere Declaration* (1610a) appeared,[32] it gave the three "Principall and Maine Endes" of the plantation as "Religious, Noble, and Feaseable" (Counseil for Virginia 1610a, sig. C1). These relate to the propagation of Christianity, reducing an expanding English population, and the return of commodities. It concludes with the hope that God might:

> nourish this graine of seed, that it may spread till all people of the earth admire the greatnesse, and sucke the shades and fruite thereof. (sig. D2)[33]

This is comparable with Bacon's

> The Kingdome of heauen is compared not to any great kernel, or nut; but to a graine of Musterd, which is one of the least of grains, but hath in it a propertie and spirit hastily to get vp and spread. (Bacon 1612, sig. Q3^{v})

As for the justification for colonization, William Symond's sermon *Virginia Brittania* in April 1609, which was addressed to the "Aduenturers and Planters for Virginia", had relied entirely on biblical precedent:

> Goe teach (saith he [Christ]) all nations, and baptize them in the name of the Father, the Sonne, and the Holy Ghost. (1609, sig. C)

However, *A true declaration* did not see this as sufficient reason:

> To preach the Gospell to a nation conquered, and to set their soules at liberty, when we haue brought their bodies to slauerie; It may be a matter sacred in the Preachers, but I know not how iustifiable in the rulers. Who for their meere ambition, doe set vpon it, the glosse of religion. (Counseil for Virginia 1610b, sig. B2^{v})

In fact, this was precisely Bacon's position which he expressed in a letter to Sir George Villiers (1616) "To make no extirpation of the natives under pretence of planting religion: God surely will no way be pleased with such sacrifices" (Spedding 1861–74, VI.21).

As for *The Tempest*, it has several notable rare parallels with Bacon's work (Appendix F, Tables F.1 and F.2). The strongest post-dates the play. *The Tempest* has

> That now he was
> The Iuy which had hid my princely Trunck,
> And suckt my verdure [health] out on't. (1.2.86–87)

In *The historie of the reigne of King Henry the Seuenth* (1629), which Bacon completed in October 1621, we find "But it was ordained, that this Winding-Iuie of a PLANTAGANET, should kill the true *Tree* it selfe"; see Figure 11.1 (Table F.1, No. 1).

The idea of self-deception by repetition of a fabricated tale appears in the play as follows; see Figure 11.2 (Table F.1, No. 2):

> Like one
> Who hauing into truth, by telling of it,
> Made such a synner of his memorie
> To credite his owne lie, he did beleeue
> He was indeed the Duke, out o' th' Substitution
> And executing th' outward face of Roialtie
> With all prerogatiue". (1.2.99–105)

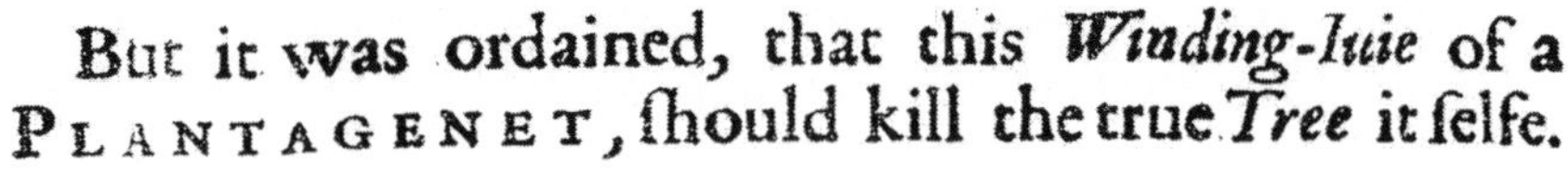
But it was ordained, that this *Winding-Iuie* of a PLANTAGENET, ſhould kill the true *Tree* it ſelfe.

Figure 11.1 Correspondence with *The Tempest*'s "The Iuy which had hid my princely Trunck". Francis Bacon, *The historie of the reigne of King Henry the Seuenth* (1629, 176).

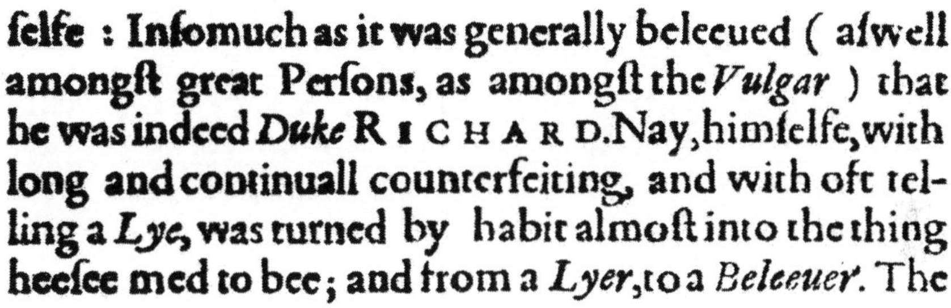
ſelfe : Inſomuch as it was generally beleeued (aſwell amongſt great Perſons, as amongſt the *Vulgar*) that he was indeed *Duke* RICHARD.Nay,himſelfe,with long and continuall counterfeiting, and with oft telling a *Lye*, was turned by habit almoſt into the thing heeſee med to bee; and from a *Lyer*,to a *Beleeuer*. The

Figure 11.2 Correspondence with *The Tempest*'s "he did beleeue He was indeed the Duke". Francis Bacon, *The historie of the reigne of King Henry the Seuenth* (1629, 111).

Only Francis Bacon, again in *The historie of the reigne of King Henry the Seuenth* (1629), has anything resembling this when discussing the imposter Perkin Warbeck:

> Insomuch as it was generally beleeued (aswell amongst great Persons, as amongst the *Vulgar*) that he was indeed *Duke* RICHARD. Nay, himselfe, with long and continuall countefeiting, and with oft telling a *Lye*, was turned by habit almost into the thing heesee med [he seemed] to bee; and from a *Lyer*, to a *Beleeuer*". (Spedding *et al.* 1857–82, XI.210)[34]

Arthur Quiller–Couch and John Dover–Wilson (1921, 91) see these lines from *The Tempest* ("Like one ...") as counterfeit coining metaphors, and Bacon also made use of a similar device in *King Henry the Seuenth* "To counterfeit the dead image of a King in his coyne, is an high Offence by all Lawes: But to counterfeit the liuing image of a King in his Person, exceedeth all Falsification" (Spedding *et al.* 1857–82, XI.219).

A further close connection between Bacon's work and the play can be examined. The idea of a person playing the role of a screen to protect a great man appears in the play as "To haue no schreene between this part he plaid, / And him he plaid it for" (*The Tempest* 1.2.107–8). In Francis Bacon's essay "Of Envy" (1625), this role is played by "inferior Officers" who are kept in their positions "For by that meanes, there be so many Skreenes betweene him [a great person] and Enuy"; see Figure 11.3 (Table F.1, No 3).

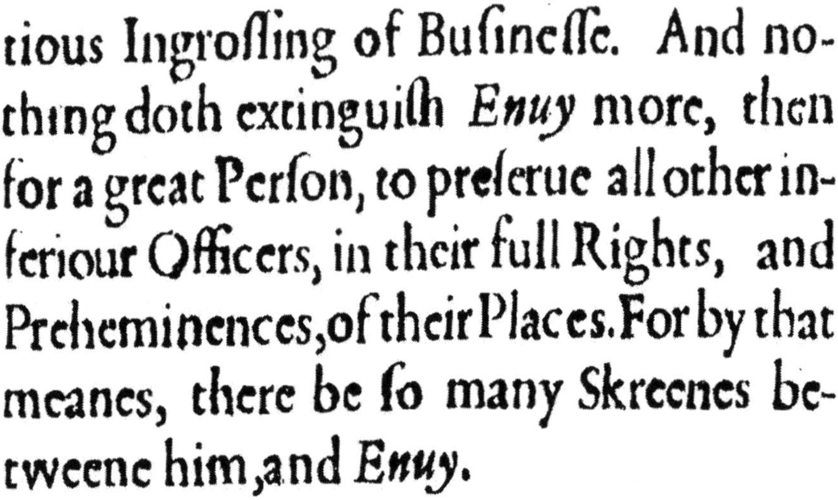
tious Ingroſſing of Buſineſſe. And nothing doth extinguiſh *Enuy* more, then for a great Perſon, to preſerue all other inferiour Officers, in their full Rights, and Preheminences, of their Places. For by that meanes, there be ſo many Skreenes betweene him, and *Enuy*.

Figure 11.3 Correspondence with *The Tempest*'s "schreene between this part he plaid / And him he plaid it for". Francis Bacon, *The Essayes* (1625, 46).

Finally, a rare correspondence emerges from the following lines:

> Thy bankes with pioned, and twilled brims
> Which spungie *Aprill*, at thy hest betrims;
> To make cold Nymphs chast crownes. (*The Tempest* 4.1.71–73)

Despite several EEBO searches no results occur before 1611. However, noting Shakespeare's "Nymphs chast crownes", there is Rembert Dodoens's *A niewwe herball* (1578, 244–45) with "his flowers and leaues are much smaller [than the usual female piony], and the stalkes shorter, the whiche some call Mayden or Virgin Peonie" as well as "Pionie floureth at the beginning of May, and deliuereth his seed in June". However, only two examples have been located that mention 'piony' in April: one is in *The Tempest*, and the other is in Bacon's essay "Of Gardens" (1625) in which we find "In *Aprill* follow, The Double white Violet; [list of flowers] The Tulippa; The Double Piony" (Bacon 1625, 267).[35] This is located through a Google search (Table F.2. No.3).

Since these rare examples occur in Bacon's work after 1611, this serves as good evidence that he borrowed from the play, but to argue a contribution there also needs to be examples of the play borrowing from Bacon. In that case, we have a state of mutual borrowing which is so unlikely (unless there is an open dispute in print between two authors) that it should instead be interpreted as making a contribution to *The Tempest*. There are three such rare returns. The play's "print of goodnesse" (1.2.352) when searched in EEBO with {print of good(ness)} yields only two cases before 1611. One is "nor geue any printe of good life" in John Jewel's *A replie vnto M. Hardinges answeare* (1565), and the second is Bacon's "hath the print of Goode" in *The two books* (Table F.1, No.5). Another locution is "The Mistris which I serue, quickens what's dead" (3.1.6), which yields three returns for Bacon (Table F.1, No.8). The earliest is his "Secrecie in Sutes is a great meanes of obtaining, for voicing them to bee in forwardnes may discourage some kind of suters, but doth quicken and awake others" in his essay "Of Sutes" (1597). So here we present 12 rare Bacon parallels, 3 before the play and 9 after.[36]

In summary, the argument developed here is that in 1611, unpublished intelligence about the Virginia colony appeared in *The Tempest*, information that Shakspere was unlikely to have had access to. This was in addition to facts that had already appeared in Virginia Company publications. This suggests that one or more Virginia colony specialists contributed material about the colony for the play. With rare parallels both before and after the first known performance of *The Tempest*, and with his access to 'True Reportory' (one of the play's sources) through his work on the Virginia Company's *A true declaration*, there is a strong case here that one of these company members who contributed to *The Tempest* was Francis Bacon.

Notes

1 The voyages sent to Virginia were partly funded by merchant companies such as the Clothworkers Company, the Fishmongers Company, and the Stationer's Company.
2 The ships were the *Susan Constant*, *Godspeed*, and *The Discovery*.
3 In his essay 'Of Plantations' Sir Francis Bacon writes "For Gouernment, let it be in the Hands of one, assisted with some Counsell" (1625, 202).
4 On 10 May 1610.
5 It was entered for publication at Stationers' Hall on 8 November 1610 by Sir Thomas Smith, Sir Maurice Barkley, Sir George Coppin, and Master Richard Martin; see Brown (1890, I.427).
6 "Item paid to John Heminges upon the Cowncells warrant dated att Whitehall xxo die Maij 1613" lists 14 plays performed at the wedding, including *Much Adoe abowte Nothinge*, *The Tempest*, *The Winter's Tale*, and *The Moore of Venice*; see Chambers (1930, II.343).
7 The manuscript for *The Historie of Travaile into Virginia*, which Strachey wrote in 1612 but failed to publish, covered only Virginia. Its first publication was by the Hakluyt Society in 1849.
8 Search date February 2013, see Clarke (2014, Section 7.4).
9 For a detailed discussion of the so-called Strachey 'B' manuscript publicized by Ivor Noël Hume in 2001, see the footnotes in Clarke (2014, Section 7.5). The conclusion of the present author is that it is a poor early

nineteenth-century transcription of the 'True Reportory' from Purchas (1625) rather than a contemporary copy; see Hume (2001).

10 This oath dating from 1607 was administered "by the Governor and counsell after Mr Secretarie Dauison death to Edward Sharples" in the winter 1623; see Kingsbury (1906, III.6–4).

11 On the Second Virginia Charter of 1609, "members of the council were still required to take a special oath administered by one of the high officers of state, and refusal to give the oath could mean disqualification for the office"; see Craven (1957, 5).

12 All three were published under the authority of the Virginia Council.

13 The Counseil for Virginia's *A true declaration* (1610, 17) mentions "the storme that separated the admirall from the fleete".

14 Lewes Hughes, a preacher on Bermuda, sent a letter to England in 1615, reiterating Jourdain's account "they so tired and out of hope, as they resolued to shut vp the hatches, and commit themselues to the mercy of God". In Hughes (1615, sig, A4).

15 An EEBO interrogation of the 5,377 records that constitute the pre-1611 searchable texts for {tired/asleep/sleeping near.20 hatches} produces no accounts relating to sleeping under hatches in the context of a ship in a storm.

16 There are only 2/5377(0.037%) returned uses before 1611, these being "April, when the great freshes do come" in Bernardino de Escalante, *A discourse of the nauigation* [China] (1579) and "the freshes by reason of the Rockes haue left markes of the inundations", Smith (1608).

17 Thomas Dekker refers to "a voiage to the yland of Hogs and Diuels, (the Barmudas)" in his play *If it be not good, the Diuel is in it* (1612).

18 Rich uses the spelling "Bermoothawes" on the title page of *Newes from Virginia*. Abrams (2012) seems not to have been aware that over 100 years earlier, Morton Luce (1901, Appendix A, 159) had already identified the "Bermoothawes" spelling in Rich's pamphlet.

19 An investigation of EEBO using the search string {crab(s) near.40 filberds/filberts/filbirts/philbirts/philberts} registers no returns before 1611. While Harmor has the earliest occurrence, the next return appears in Shakespeare's *The Tempest* in the *First Folio* (1623).

20 One should not fall into the error here of assuming that a topical allusion dates the entire play text. It only dates the topical allusion.

21 "These four comedies (*The Tempest*, *Two Gentlemen*, *Merry Wives*, and *Measure for Measure*), together with *Winter's Tale* are generally accepted as set from scribal copies prepared by Ralph Crane" (Donno 2003, 166).

22 Jourdain says "no man was euer heard, to make for the place, but as against their wils".

23 I am grateful to Lyn Kositsky for pointing out the following reference about an earlier reported bird known as an 'Alcatrazzi'. Unfortunately, it falls short as a candidate for Caliban's 'scamel' as it is inedible: "These younge ones are so fatte and wel fedde that they can not bee eaten. And are taken for none other intent but only to make grease for candels to burne in the nyght" (d'Anghiera 1555, 191).

24 The author of *A true declaration* admits using "the letters of the Lord La Ware" in compiling the document Counseil for Virginia (1610b, sig. A3^{v}).

25 The compiler of *A true declaration* states that these are "the words and phrase of that noble Gouernour, the Lo. Laware, as it is warranted to mee by the copie of his Letters sent to the Virginian Councell".

26 The members of the central Virginia Council are listed on Lord de la Warr's commission into Virginia dated 28 February 1609–10. It bears the following

signatures: Southampton, Pembroke, Philip Montgomerie, Theophilus Howard, Edward Cecill, William Waad, Walter Cope, Edward Conoway, Thomas Smith, Baptist Hicks, Dudlie Diggs, Robert Mansill, Christopher Brook, and William Romney (Brown 1890, I.384).

27 "The allusion to Virginia is not in the printed speech but is to be found in the Journals" (Gardiner 1895, 333n).

28 This date is James Spedding's estimate (1861–74, IV.116). The Oxford Francis Bacon dates it to 1606 (Kiernan 2000, XV.239).

29 Bacon became Lord Chancellor in January 1618, a date that serves as the *terminus post quem* for the dedication.

30 The masque has the phrase "flintie-hearted" in the 'Presentment', which appears in Shakespeare's *Venus and Adonis* as "O! pity, 'gan she cry, flint-hearted boy". An EEBO search on {flint/flinty hearted} with spelling variations yields 1/3340(0.030%) returns before 1593, so it was rare at the time of use.

31 The Accounts of the Treasurer of the Chamber lists a payment to John Heminge dated "1613, May 20" for playing *The Tempest* at the wedding, see MS Rawl. A. 239, Bodleian Library, Oxford.

32 It was entered in the *Stationers' Register* on 14 December 1609.

33 This originates from Mark 40:30–32, Geneva Bible.

34 For a detailed discussion, see Clarke (2014, Table 7.1, No. 18 & footnote).

35 This is not keyed text, so it is unavailable to an automated EEBO search.

36 For a 13th, "in some passion" that follows the play, see Clarke (2014; Table 7.1, No. 70).

Bibliography

Abrams, Richard. "Newes from Virginia (1610): Source for Prospero's epilogue." *Notes and Queries* 257, No. 4 (December 2012): 545–47.

d'Anghiera, Pietro Martire. *The Decades of the Newe World or West India.* Translated from Latin into English by Rycharde Eden. London, 1555. STC: 647.

Bacon, Francis. *The Essaies of Sr Francis Bacon Knight.* London: Printed by Iohn Beale, 1612.

Bacon, Francis. *The Essayes or Covnsels Civill and Morall.* London: Printed by Iohn Haviland, 1625.

Beaumont, Francis. *The Masqve of the Inner Temple and Grayes Inne.* London: Imprinted by F[elix] K[ingston] for George Norton, 1613.

Brown, Alexander. *Genesis of the United States.* 2 vols. Cambridge and Boston: Houghton, Mifflin, and Co., 1890.

Cawley, Robert R. "Shakspere's Use of the Voyages in *The Tempest.*" *Proceedings of the Modern Language Association of America* 21 (1926): 688–726.

Chambers, Edmund K. *William Shakespeare: A Study of the Facts and Problems.* 2 vols. Oxford: Clarendon Press, 1930.

Chambers, Edmund K. *The Elizabethan Stage.* 4 vols. Oxford: Clarendon Press, 1945.

Chapman, George. *The Memorable Masqve of the Two Honovrable Hovses or Innes of Court; the Middle Temple and Lyncolnes Inne.* London: George Norton, 1614.

Clarke, Barry R. "The Virginia Company and *The Tempest.*" *Journal of Drama Studies* 5 (July 2011): 13–27.

Clarke, Barry R. "A linguistic analysis of Francis Bacon's contribution to three Shakespeare plays: *The Comedy of Errors*, *Love's Labour's Lost*, and *The Tempest*." PhD thesis, Brunel University, U.K. 2014.

Clarke, Barry R. "The Virginia Company's role in *The Tempest*." In Petar Penda, ed. *The Whirlwind of Passion: New Critical Perspectives on William Shakespeare*. Cambridge: Cambridge Scholars Publishing, 2016.

Counseil for Virginia. *A True and Sincere Declaration of the Purpose and Ends of the Plantation begun in Virginia. Set Forth by the Authority of the Gouernors and Councellors Established for that Plantation*. London: Printed for I. Stepney, 1610a.

Counseil for Virginia. *A True Declaration of the Estate of the Colonie in Virginia with a Confutation of Such Scandalous Reports as Haue Tended to the Disgrace of so Worthy an Enterprise*. London: Printed for William Barret, 1610b.

Craven, F. W. *The Virginia Company of London*. Williamsburg, VA: Virginia's 350th Anniversary Celebration Corp., 1957.

Culliford, G. *William Strachey, 1572–1621*. Charlottesville: University Press of Virginia, 1965.

Dekker, Thomas. *If it be Not Good, the Diuel is in it*. London: Printed [by Thomas Creede] for I[ohn] T[rundle], 1612.

Dodoens, Rembert. *A Niewwe Herbal, or Historie of Plantes*. London: Gerard Dewes, 1578. STC: 6984.

Donno, Elizabeth Story. *Twelfth Night, or, What You Will*. Cambridge: Cambridge University Press, 2003.

Fitzmaurice, Andrew. *Humanism and America*. Cambridge: Cambridge University Press, 2003.

Gardiner, Samuel R. *History of England*. London: Longmans, Green, 1895.

Gayley, Charles M. *Shakespeare and the Founders of Liberty in America*. New York: Macmillan, 1917.

Harmor, Ralph. *A True Discourse of the Present State of Virginia and the Successe of the Affaires there Till the 18 of Iune 1614*. London: Printed by Iohn Beale for William Welby, 1615.

Hotson, John L. I, *William Shakespeare*. London: Jonathan Cape, 1937.

Hughes, Lewes. *A Letter Sent into England from the Summer Ilands*. London: Printed by I. B[eale] for William Welby, 1615.

Hughes, Lewes. *A Plaine and True Relation of the Goodnes of God towards the Sommer Ilands*. London: Printed by Edward All-de, 1621.

Hume, Ivor Noël. "William Strachey's unrecorded first draft of his sea venture saga." *Avalon Chronicles* 6 (2001): 57–88.

James, David G. *The Dream of Prospero*. Oxford: Clarendon Press, 1967.

Johnson, Robert. *The New Life of Virginea*. London: Printed by Felix Kyngston for William Welby, 1612. STC: 14700.

Jourdain, Sylvestor. *A Discovery of the Barmudas, Otherwise Called the Ile of Deuels*. London: Printed by Iohn Windet, 1610.

Keirnan, Michael ed. *The Essayes or Counsels, Civill and Morall*. Vol. XV. 15 vols. The Oxford Francis Bacon. 1985; reissued Oxford University Press, 2000.

Kingsbury, Susan M. *Records of the Virginia Company*. Washington: Government Printing Office, 1906.

Lucas, Samuel. *Charters of the Old English Colonies in America*. London: John W. Parker, 1850.

Luce, Morton, ed. *The Tempest*. London: Methuen, 1901.

Newton, A. *A Dictionary of Birds*. London: Adam and Charles Black, 1893–6.

Nuzum, David. "The London company and *The Tempest*." *West Virginia Philological Papers* 12 (1959): 12–23.

Purchas, Samuel. *Purchas His Pilgrims*. 5 vols. London: W. Stansby, 1625.

Quiller–Couch, Arthur, and John Dover Wilson. *The Tempest*. First edition. Cambridge: Cambridge University Press, 1921.

Quinn David B, ed. *New American World: A Documentary History of North America to 1612*. 5 vols. New York: Arno Press, 1979.

Reedy, Tom. "Dating William Strachey's true reportory." *Review of English Studies* 61 (2010): 529–52.

Rich, Richard. *Newes from Virginia*. London: Printed by Edward Allde, 1610.

Smith, John. *A True Relation*. London: I. Tappe, 1608.

Smith, John. *A Map of Virginia*. Oxford: William Hale, 1612.

Smith, John. *The General Historie of Virginia, New England, and the Summer Isles*. London: Printed by I[ohn] D[awson] and I[ohn] H[aviland] for Michael Sparkes, 1624.

Spedding, James. *The Letters and Life of Francis Bacon*. 7 vols. London: Longman, Green, Longman, and Roberts, 1861–74.

Spedding, James, Robert Leslie Ellis, and Douglas Denon Heath. *The Works of Francis Bacon*. 15 vols. Boston: Houghton, Mifflin, and Company, 1857–82.

Stith, William. *The History of the First Discovery and Settlement of Virginia*. Williamsburg: Printed by W. Parks, 1747.

Strachey, William. *For the Colonie in Virginea Britannia. Lawes Diuine, Morall and Martiall*. London: Printed at London for Walter Burre, 1612.

Strachey, William. *The Historie of Travaile into Virginia Britannia*. London: Printed for the Hakluyt Society, 1849.

Stritmatter, Roger, and Lynn Kositsky. "Shakespeare and the voyagers revisited." *Review of English Studies* 58 (2007): 447–72.

Sullivan, Mary S. "Court masques of James I." Unpublished doctoral thesis. University of Nebraska, 1913.

Swem, Earl G, ed. "The three charters of the Virginia company of London." In *Jamestown 30th Anniversary Historical Booklets 1–4*. Williamsburg, VA: Virginia 350th Anniversary Celebration Corporation, 1957.

Symonds, William. *A Sermon Preached at White-chappel, in the Presence of Many, Honourable and Worshipfull, the Aduenturers and Planters for Virginia. 25 April 1609*. London: Printed by I. Windet for Eleazer Edgar and William Welby, 1609.

Vaughan, Alden. "William Strachey's true reportory." *Shakespeare Quarterly* 59 (Fall 2008): 243–73.

Vaughan, Virginia M., and Alden T. Vaughan, ed. *The Tempest*, Arden Shakespeare. Thomson Learning, 2007.

Whitaker, Alexander. *Good Newes from Virginia*. London: Imprinted by Felix Kyngston for William Welby, 1613.

Part III

Attribution Methods

12 A History of Authorship Attribution

A survey is taken of various early attribution methods such as reliance on intuition, hapax legomena, and mean sentence length. Counts that are performed, such as those on specific word usage, are found to depend on the genre of the piece. Methods that rely on counts of authorial habit often rest on the unjustifiable assumption of a single contributor.

12.1 A Body of Text

About 2.6 million years ago, our ancestors, *Homo habilis*, began to fashion stones into meat-cleaving tools to assist in their scavenging of animal carcasses that more skilful predators had abandoned. It took another 800,000 years for *Homo erectus* to develop their own hunting skills, a transition that coincided with the creation of spears and hand axes to incapacitate their quarry. When slivers of sharpened flint were attached to strong wooden shafts, weapons were produced that could be given flight and force. This made the superior speed of the prey less of an advantage. The introduction of copper-smelting with tin in 5,000 BC by the Vinča culture in Serbia resulted in a bronze metal that led to much improved weapons and armour.[1] A further improvement occurred around 2,200 BC when techniques for smelting iron ore were developed. Here, the addition of carbon resulted in steel that represented an increase in metallic hardness and strength.[2]

The choice of tool was determined by the task in hand. Sharp-edged tools were used for cutting, rounded-stone tools for grinding, and heavy non-brittle tools were tasked with hammering. The history of authorship attribution is itself an account of the development of tools, ones which have been specifically designed to expose the contents of a textual carcass long since abandoned. Some of these tools have a greater penetration than others, and methods of increasing precision have had to be devised to improve the accuracy of separation of a body of text into its component contributors.

12.2 External and Internal Evidence

The kind of evidence that is external relates to the environment in which the work was created. Examples of this type include an author having a history of earlier attributions, or particular views, or particular institutional affiliations, or receiving credit in contemporary records, such as letters, diaries, or the *Stationers' Register.* By consulting original documents, an historical context for the work can be constructed, the accuracy of which depends on both the quality and quantity of connections (Love 2002, 51).

The Stationers' Company of London holds a register of copyright claims from 1554 to 2000 (Arber 1875–7). In the Renaissance, not every published work was registered and not every registered work was published. For example, Shakespeare's *As You Like It* was registered on 4 August 1600 but was not published until the *First Folio* (1623). Nevertheless, the register often contains more information than appears on the title page of the work, sometimes associating the named author with other contemporary figures. An important resource for play attribution from the 1590s is the diary of Philip Henslowe who owned the Rose Theatre at Southwark, south of the river Thames. Henslowe was a pawn broker, moneylender (usurer), and theatre impresario, and from 19 February 1591–2 to 5 November 1597 his dramatic records give the titles of the plays that were performed at the Rose, their daily receipts, and his payments to dramatists. One notable entry occurs for 3 March 1591–2, where Shakespeare's "harey the vj" is recorded as being acted by Lord Strange's Men, a performance which took "iij^{ll} xvj^{s} 8^{d}" in gate receipts (Foakes 2002, F7, 13). The error of using external evidence alone can be shown from the example of *The Batchelars Banquet*, a pamphlet that had been attributed to Thomas Dekker in a sale catalogue from 1800. Frank Percy Wilson, an expert on Dekker, subsequently showed their linguistic styles to be inconsistent (Lake 1975, 5).

Internal evidence is taken from the text itself and can consist of biography, ideas, and style. It is clear that in an analysis of style, internal evidence relies on external evidence:

> canonical studies by means of internal evidence cannot reasonably be undertaken by anyone who wantonly mistrusts external evidence: for without some unquestioned attributions no other attributions can be questioned. (Lake 1975, 4–5)

In other words, the texts against which the target text is compared must be reliably attributed.

12.3 Non-Scientific Practice

Three cases will suffice as an illustration of non-scientific procedure.

> One must not despise slander, no matter how false it may be. Some people know how to increase it, and on their account it is well to

> be on one's guard against such actions. You'd find in them all many things to harass; but if the advantages are in the majority – that's the thing to look at. Property covereth a multitude of woes. (Kock 1888, III.27–28)[3]

This is a translation of a fragment of an early play *The Boiotian Girl* that was discovered by Dr Theodorus Kock in work by the Attic poet Menander (343–292BCE). The satirical author Marcus Terentius Varro (116–27BCE), who had been commended as "the most learned of the Romans",[4] had attributed it to Plautus (d.184BCE), and in Book III of *Attic Nights*, after noting that Aquilius had been a candidate, Aulus Gallius (d.180CE) agreed, asserting that "nor will any other habitual reader of Plautus doubt it". Gallius had only 14 lines of the work in front of him and relied entirely on his own intuition. There was no attempt at collation with known works by Aquilius, no analysis of metre, and no consideration of dramatic structure, although since Plautus borrowed from Greek New Comedy the last point would not have been decisive (Love 2002, 16).

For the second case, David Erdman (1966, 45–68) has discussed the unusual case of an article on literary forgery published by an anonymous author. Following his work on identifying contributors to the *Morning Post*,[5] Professor Erdman was in no doubt that the author of a certain anonymous article was Samuel Taylor Coleridge. The second week of January 1800 saw the publication of the third volume of a three-volume set entitled *Copies of Original Letters from the French Army in Egypt [...] Intercepted by the British Fleet in the Mediterranean*.[6] This particular volume purported to present the letters of Napoleon Bonaparte and his associates, dating from the autumn of 1799 on the occasion of the military leader's departure from Egypt. On Monday 3 February 1800, an anonymous article appeared in the *Morning Post* on this topic, discussing the authenticity of the intercepted letters presented in the volume:

> Any work which claims to be held authentic, must have had witnesses, and competent witnesses; this is external evidence. Or it may be its own competent witness; this is called internal evidence. Or its authenticity may be deduced from indirect testimony, such as the absence of all contradiction[7].

The author of the article focused on the third point, noting that the unidentified editors[8] of the three volumes claimed that the letters in the third volume were intercepted at different times by the Turkish and English ships of war. However, this assertion could not been verified as no vessel or commander of a vessel had been named. So there was no external evidence. One 'Bonaparte letter', on page 21 of the third volume, refers to Chieks in Egypt "who are timorous, unacquainted with arms, and, like all other priests, know how to inspire the people with fanaticism". The trouble was, a Chiek was an Arab chief who was well acquainted with arms and had no connection to the priesthood. Realizing that the letter exhibited an error that would not have been expected from Bonaparte, the *Morning Post* article declared that "a very ignorant and very impudent forger" had been at work (Erdman 1978, III.145–52).

David Erdman set himself the task of discovering the author of the *Post*'s article. Having studied Coleridge's articles in the *Morning Post*,[9] he could point to three examples of the poet's use of a particular metaphor in support of his claim that there was a recognizable style.[10]

> The first, of political adaptability: 'What a rare fluidity must a man's Principles possess, that can be emptied so rapidly from one mould into another, and assume, with such equal facility, the shape of each!' The second, of Pitt: 'parental ambition [was] his mould – he was cast rather than grew.' The third, of the French Constitution: it was absurd to think 'that a constitution could receive its final and faultless shape at one cast; that the passions of [...] the French, should run at once into the mould, like melted ores, and harden in a few hours into perfection.' The third and second examples are from known works; the first is from a new discovery. The reasoning in each seems of the same fluidity and mould. (Erdman 1966, 60)

Words such as 'sequaciousness', 'weather-wisdom', 'fugacious', 'unadding', and 'humanness' in the *Post* article were also recognized as having been used by Coleridge elsewhere (Love 2002, 108). Here, the investigator's accumulated internal evidence was accepted by scholarly consensus as sufficient to establish Coleridge's attribution, even though Professor Erdman had no means to test the rarity of his parallels. For all he knew, there might have been other authors who had used this same set of words which both Coleridge and the article's independent author might have used as a common source.

Our third case relates to an alleged newly-discovered Shakespeare play. For *Double Falsehood, or the Distrest Lovers* (1728), we have only Lewis Theobald's personal testimony to rely on for the evidence that his eighteenth-century text was based on Shakespeare and Fletcher's *Cardenio*. Despite no contemporary copy surviving, manuscript or printed, in March 2010, the Arden Shakespeare admitted the play into the Shakespeare canon.

In none of these three cases is there a well-defined procedure that might be followed by another investigator, and neither are there any criteria by which a judgement might be given concerning what constitutes a contribution.

12.4 Biographical Delusions

There is no doubt that a writer must draw on his own experience, either direct or second-hand, to obtain the material to fashion a work. However, what is unknown in this process is the extent to which the creator has conflated personalities and events from experience in order to arrive at the fictional result. In studying the text of a drama or novel, one is not necessarily dealing with autobiographical allusions. It could easily be part of an account of someone else's condition. Harold Love (2002, 87) advises us that

> one would have to proceed with great caution in attempting to profile a dramatist through his or her characters (which has not stopped many attempts). Such a matching of profiles would not establish the matter on its own but would be a useful adjunct to other arguments.

Proponents of alternative single-author theories of the Shakespeare canon have invested enormous effort in constructing an argument for a particular candidate that revolves around a certain set of points of connection with a play. Not the slightest attention is given to the fact that this can also be carried out with more or less equal weight for another candidate whose life events intersect with a different set of facts. A biographical investigation of this kind can only gain force if one refuses to acknowledge similar constructions for other candidates, so that by viewing the case out of context, the favoured candidate seems to be the only possibility. The fact that constructions for other candidates appear equally credible points to the lack of discrimination in the practice. To illustrate the futility of the exercise, in 1601, there was a dispute that went to the Star Chamber between Sir Thomas Posthumus Hoby (1566–1640) and William Eure, both of Gray's Inn. Hoby was a Puritan who made it his business to root out Popish recusants, and, in doing so, he succeeded in enraging his Yorkshire neighbours. It seems that by way of revenge, a party of visitors led by William Eure stayed at his house and disturbed Hoby's family by playing cards, disrupting prayers, and generally engaging in riotous behaviour. In *Twelfth Night*, Sir Toby Belch, Sir Andrew Aguecheek, and Feste are singing loudly in Olivia's house while the rest of the house are taking their night-time rest. The steward Malvolio descends the stairs to complain:

> MALVOLIO: My masters are you mad? Or what are you? Have you no wit, manners, nor honestie, but to gabble like Tinkers at this time of night? Do yee make an Alehouse of my Ladies house [...]? (*Twelfth Night* 2.3.87–90)

Maria waits until Malvolio is out of earshot, then exposes him as a Puritan:

TOBY: Possesse us, possesse us, tell us something of him.
MARIA: Marrie sir, sometimes he is a kinde of Puritane. (2.3.138–39)

Sir Dunbar Plunket Barton (1853–1937), who served as Solicitor-General for Ireland, suggests that Shakespeare was alluding to the above-mentioned incident with Sir Thomas Posthumus Hoby disguised as Sir Toby in the play by role reversal:[11]

> Sir Toby Belch and his fellows are represented as keeping late and disorderly hours in Olivia's house, and as making the Puritan steward Malvolio the target of their pranks. The coincidence of date, the common features of the baiting of a Puritan and of the disturbance of a Lady's household, and of the jingling similarity between the names 'Hoby' and 'Toby' lend colour to the suggestion. (Barton 1929, 62–63)

Whether or not this is true, on this evidence alone, no one could justifiably claim that Sir Thomas Posthumus Hoby wrote *Twelfth Night*, or even contributed this scene about himself. It should be clear from this example, that using the interpretation of an event in a play to identify its unknown author is biographical delusion. By refusing to admit any fact that might falsify a favourite candidate, those who make such claims have arranged matters so that they can never be wrong.

There is a further argument against single-author theories. The evidence obtained so far from various forms of attribution study point to many hands in the plays. From the RCP method alone, we have Robert Greene, Christopher Marlowe, and Anthony Munday for *3 Henry VI* (see Section 6.6), while Francis Bacon, Thomas Dekker, Thomas Heywood, and Thomas Nashe are highlighted in *Love's Labour's Lost* (see Section 9.4). Neither can Bacon's strong presence in *The Tempest* be easily overlooked (see Section 11.7). Stylometric methods, despite their shortcomings, surely register a noteworthy approximation to the truth when it is mainly one hand that permeates the work. So there are several authors who are responsible for the Shakespeare canon. Anyone who holds a single-author theory, whether for Shakspere or some other personality, would have to be in denial in the face of such evidence. The only conclusion possible is that single-author theories can only be sustained by employing a selective blindness which amounts to a descent into religious dogmatism.

12.5 The Introduction of Counting Methods

12.5.1 Hapax Legomenon

This term refers to a word that appears in an author's corpus once only. It is a rare word in that author's canon, but the mistake has often been made of generalizing this fact and assuming that it is also a rare word in English texts of that era. As will be demonstrated, hapax can be commonplace. For example, 'prejudicial' appears once only in Shakespeare for *3 Henry VI* (1.1.144), but a search of Chadwyck–Healey's EEBO database reveals that prior to 1614 it appears 600 times in the extant searchable published literature. In fact, it was so well used that it dates as far back as William Caxton's *Here endeth the book named the dictes* (1477), with "I haue meruayll of them that saye thinges preiudicial where silence were more prouffitable". Extensions of the hapax term are 'dis-legomenon', 'tris-legomenon', and 'tetra-legomenon', which, respectively, refer to two, three, and four occurrences of a word in a canon.

Walter Percy Workman, the headmaster of Kingswood School in Bath, UK, was a man who believed that St. Paul wrote the Pastoral Epistles.[12] In the *Expository Times* of 1 January 1896, he published a paper arguing that hapax were not a useful indicator of common authorship, after learning that hapax had been used to show that St. Paul did not write *The Pastoral Epistles*. First, he presented his opponents' position by showing that the numbers of hapax per page in *The Pastoral Epistles* (1 Timothy, 2 Timothy, and Titus), which are framed as letters from Paul of Tarsus, were twice the values for the undisputed Epistles of St. Paul (1 & 2 Corinthians, Galatians, Philemon Philippians, Romans, and 1 Thessalonians). According to his opponents, this was evidence of different authorship. Workman then presented the hapax per page counts for each Shakespeare play and found the range to be 3.4–10.4, a result that demonstrated that if an author could have such a large variation, then hapax was inappropriate as an authorial marker. His point was that the variation of hapax counts between the pastoral and undisputed Epistles was insufficient evidence to oppose the attribution of *The Pastoral Epistles* to St. Paul. Such a variation might occur naturally in an author's canon and would not necessarily indicate different authorship.

Nevertheless, Walter Workman (1896, 418) thought the rarity of locutions could be informative:

> The general tendency of a writer, as he advances in knowledge of a language, and mastery over its possibilities, is to use more unusual words and more involved constructions.

However, and this was something that Workman neglected to point out, the definition of 'unusual' in the context of written work would have to involve the entire extant literature of the period and not just the corpus of a single author.

In relation to the Shakespeare hapax, Joseph Rudman (1998, 356) has asked "How many words were copied over from his source material such as Holinshed's *Chronicles* or North's *Plutarch*?" It is a vital question for it might well be the case that a particular word is a hapax in the Shakespeare canon, and only a single dramatist out of 20 leading dramatists shares its use. However, no conclusion should be reached until the possibility of borrowing from earlier sources has been minimized by a 'rarity' check of the contemporary literature. Such a check has the effect of tightening the exclusivity of connection between an unattributed target text and the corpus of a particular author. This is precisely the focus of the new RCP method in Chapter 14.

Table 12.1 demonstrates that although hapax are by definition rare in a canon, they can also be commonplace words in relation to a database of contemporary literature. Shown are 12 randomly selected hapax from the plays of Shakespeare together with the play it originates from. The frequency against each word is the number of texts in the EEBO database that contain that word.[13] It is clear from this table that the fact that a word is a hapax does not make it an appropriate authorial marker.

So any candidate for contribution who shares Shakespeare hapax cannot be concluded to be a contributor until a suitable check has been carried out. This would examine how common it is for other writers of the period to share a similar number of Shakespeare hapax. Without such a check, the evidence for the proposed contributor is presented out of context.

12.5.2 Sentence Length

In the early 1880s, Lucius Sherman (1892, 349) took up the question as to whether "the sentence length average was constant in a given author for different works and periods of production". With the assistance of some of his students, he examined texts of at least 300 sentences, and

Table 12.1 Frequency of randomly selected hapax from Shakespeare in EEBO database

Word	*Play*[14]	*Frequency*	*Word*	*Play*	*Frequency*
Adventured	*Cym.*	483	Imported	*Tim.*	175
Commissioners	*H5*	471	Inconveniences	*H5*	917
Confidently	*AWW*	455	Prejudicial	*3H6*	598
Distasted	*Tro.*	55	Purposing	*1H6*	538
Hollanders	*3H6*	100	Remonstrance	*MM*	48
Implacable	*TN*	141	Tenures	*Ham.*	77

found that Thomas De Quincey's (1785–1859) *California* (1852) and *China* (1857) did not vary in mean sentence length from his earlier *Confessions of an English Opium-Eater* (1822). Neither did he find any variation for Thomas Carlyle (1795–1881) between his articles for the *Edinburgh Review* (1827) and his *History of Frederich II of Prussia* (1858). The mean number of words per sentence was also tabulated for many other writers including Francis Bacon (28 words), John Dryden (45 words), Thomas Macauley (23 words), and John Milton (60 words). Additional stylistic features were quantified, such as the 'mean number of predications per sentence' and the 'percentage of simple sentences'. This convinced him that the invariance of sentence length, predication average, and simple sentence percentage were valid authorial markers.

However, over 20 years later, Robert Moritz (1903, 229–53) pointed out a number of inaccuracies in the so-called 'Sherman principle'. Firstly, it would not be possible to compare a prose essay with a dramatic piece, even if the drama were in prose, because the mean sentence length for the drama would turn out to be smaller. To illustrate this Moritz selected two works by Goethe: his prose drama *Goetz von Berlichingen* (1773) and his prose essays *Bildhauerkunst* (1755). For the latter, he calculated the mean number of words taken over 100 sentences and for five 100-sentence blocks, then took the mean of his five results. He repeated this for the prose drama, with the length of each of his five blocks raised to 500 words each. The prose drama had a mean of 8.5 words per sentence, while the prose essays resulted in 31.5. Encouraged, Moritz turned to two prose compositions by Schiller: the tragedy *Die Rauber* (1781) and the extended essay *Geschichte des dreißigjährigen Kriegs* (1802). Again the mean sentence length for the drama was shorter than that for the essay, 11.5 words against 27.3. Two prose works by Swift were also tested: the drama *Polite Conversation* (1738) and the essay *Four Last Years of Queen Anne* (1769); the first gave 12.4, and the second gave 54.8. For Dryden it was 16.9 drama to 42.3 prose. Moritz pointed out that Sherman had even conducted a similar study of his own, examining prose from both Shakespeare's and Bacon's works. Sherman had taken 5,002 prose sentences from Shakespeare, and 2,041 from Bacon's *Essays* and *New Atlantis*, to calculate a mean of 12.39 for the drama and 32.59 for the essays (Moritz 1903, 235). So, mean sentence length for prose drama is less than for prose essays and, in methods involving a count of habitual authorial behaviour, this variation needs to be accounted for when attempting to identify an author.

Moritz also selected two compositions by the same author that were quite different in nature. For example, Henry Longfellow's play *The Spanish Student* (1843) gave 10.2 against his prose romance *Hyperion* (1839) which yielded 23.8. Walter Scott's drama *Auchindrane* had 21.2 against his *Life of Napoleon* 47.9. Pairs of works by Thomas Carlyle, Bayard Taylor, James Lowell, and Oliver Holmes exhibited a similar variation with genre. The deciding test consisted in a survey of 15 works by Goethe ranging across many different genres: drama, romance, allegory, criticism, biography, science, and correspondence. The resulting range of mean sentence length was 5.0–34.7. Moritz had demonstrated that

> the sentence-length of a work depends both upon the writer's sentence-instinct and upon the particular form of composition into which his thought is cast. (Moritz 1903, 243)

He also reasoned that as sentence length decreases, fewer predications will be present, and more simple sentences will appear (Moritz 1903, 244). So, for a given author, 'mean sentence length', 'mean number of predications per sentence', and 'percentage of simple sentences' depend on genre, when authorial habit is being measured.

It should be made clear that if this kind of study has any application to a text of unknown attribution, one would need to be sure that there is only a single contributor. As soon as a plurality of hands has engaged with it then the segment-based count becomes that of an unidentifiable compound of authors. It is astonishing that in modern times, stylometric practitioners still take certain scenes of a Shakespeare play—usually those that have not been otherwise attributed—and claim them to be a pure representation of Shakspere of Stratford's writing. First, there is considerable doubt as to the extent to which revision has corrupted the word counts. Second, as pointed out in Chapter 4, the *First Folio* (1623) is not a reliable record of contribution, and so there is a need to test the extent of Shakspere of Stratford's involvement. However, if one wished to set up a scientific test to examine Shakspere's contribution to a Shakespeare play, he has no independent letters or prose works with which to make a comparison. In other words, the extent of his contribution is untestable. The only occasion for which his contribution might be placed within approximate limits would be after exhaustive tests for other contributors have mapped out the regions of a target text that they have supplied. His possible contribution would then be narrowed by elimination. Even then, and this is what makes it approximate, there might be parts contributed by other untestable hands. So, rather than boldly assert Shakspere's ownership of unattributed scenes, the correct approach would be to accept that until comprehensive tests for other hands have been carried out, any claim about the extent of his contribution is uncorroborated conjecture.

Notes

1 Bronze is usually composed of 88% copper and 12% tin.

2 The earliest evidence of steel manufacture dates from 1,800 BC at Kırşehir Province, Turkey.

3 Menander fragments 88–92 of *Boiotis* [The Boiotian Girl]. For an English translation, see Allison (1921, 323).
4 Marcus Fabius Quintilian, *Institutio Oratoria*, X, 1.95.
5 *The Morning Post* was published in London from 1772 to 1937.
6 The first pamphlet appeared on 27 November 1798 and the second on 8 March 1799 according to dated frontispieces.
7 More accurately, its inauthenticity may be surmised from the presence of contradiction.
8 Who turned out to be William Gifford and George Canning.
9 Coleridge wrote for *The Morning Post* and its evening sister paper the *Courier* between 1798 and 1818; see Love (2002, 56–57).
10 *The Morning Post*, 12 December 1799, 19 March 1800, and 4 November 1802.
11 Those drawn to puzzles will note that 'Sir T P Hoby' contains the letters 'Toby' in the correct sequence.
12 The current 'scholarly' consensus is that they were written one or two generations after St. Paul's death; see Marshall and Towner (1999).
13 The search was conducted on 31 December 2012 using the spelling variations provided in EEBO, and a database of 5,764 keyed records, with the number of searchable texts available before 1614.
14 *Cym* is *Cymbeline*, *H5* is *Henry V*, *AWW* is *All's Well That Ends Well*, *Tro* is *Troilus and Cressida*, *3H6* is *3 Henry VI*, and *TN* is *Twelfth Night*.

Bibliography

Allison, Francis G., transl. *Menander, the Principle Fragments*. London: William Heinemann, 1921.

Arber, Edward, ed. *A Transcript of the Registers of the Company of Stationers of London 1554–1640 A.D.* 5 vols. London: Private print, 1875–7.

Barton, Dunbar Plunket. *Links Between Shakespeare and the Law*. London: Faber and Gwyer, 1929.

Erdman, David. "The signature of style." In D. Erdman, and E. Fogel, eds. *Evidence for Authorship: Essays on Problems of Attribution*. Ithaca: Cornell University Press, 1966.

Erdman, David, ed. *The Collected Works of Samuel Taylor Coleridge: Essays on His Times I*. 3 vols. Princeton, NJ: Princeton University Press, 1978.

Foakes, Reginald A., ed. *Henslowe's Diary*. Second edition. Cambridge University Press, 2002.

Kock, Theodorus. *Comicorum Atticorum Fragmenta*. 3 vols. Leipzig: B. G. Tuebner, 1888.

Lake, David. *The Canon of Thomas Middleton's Plays*. Cambridge: Cambridge University Press, 1975.

Love, Harold. *Attributing Authorship: An Introduction*. Cambridge: Cambridge University Press, 2002.

Marshall, I. Howard, and Philip H. Towner. *A Critical and Exegetical Commentary on the Pastoral Epistles*. International Critical Commentary. Edinburgh: T&T Clark, 1999.

Moritz, Robert. "On the variation and functional relation of certain sentence-constants in standard literature." In F. M. Fling, ed. *University Studies of the University of Nebraska*. 3 vols. Lincoln, NE: University of Nebraska, July 1903, 229–53.

Rudman, Joseph. "The state of authorship attribution studies: Some problems and solutions" *Computers and the Humanities* 31, No. 4 (1998): 351–65.

Sherman, Lucius. "Development of form in English Literature." In *On Certain Facts and Principles in the Development of Form in Literature*. Paper 8. Papers from the University Studies Series. The University of Nebraska. (1892). Accessed online 27 December 2017, http://digitalcommons.unl.edu/univstudiespapers/8

Workman, Walter. P. "The hapax legomena of St. Paul." *Expository Times*. 1 January 1896.

13 Modern Attribution Methods

A technical exposition of modern stylometric and phrase-matching techniques is developed. The Zeta and Delta methods of stylometry are examined in detail to highlight the weakness of the single-contributor assumption. Examination of a modern phrase-matching application to *Pericles*, Act 1, shows that, in proposing George Wilkins, it makes use of commonplace phrases and collocations. A new RCP analysis of Act 1 improves on these methods and shows that Thomas Dekker is a stronger candidate for contribution than George Wilkins.

13.1 Critique of Modern Methods

Stylometric techniques involve what their name implies: style measurement or a count of style. A segment of text is taken and a certain linguistic feature is counted, such as a predetermined set of words, word endings, or the positions of stressed syllables.[1] This is repeated for several segments of text to obtain a set of counts. The counts are then compared with prepared counts obtained from the canons of known authors to ascertain the closest match. Given an unattributed text, the assumption that underpins all such methods is that the section of text under examination is uniform in a single author's hand and that the enumerated features of that text are an exclusive characteristic of this putative author.

MacDonald Jackson (2017, 49–59) has framed the procedure as a race in which only one candidate can emerge victorious, and since the methods are designed to locate only one contributor to a section of text this seems an appropriate characterization. In order to justify the method, practitioners place excess weight on the notion of 'collaboration' with the implication that while it might be true that different contributors worked on a text, they did so contemporaneously. This allows them to work with cooperation and exclusivity on their allocated scenes to avoid corrupting the integrity of the count of any particular segment with multiple hands. One cannot help wondering if this assumption of independent contribution is nothing more than a modern projection onto the past, unwittingly contrived to defend the limitations of stylometry. The trouble is, there is no vehicle by which the twenty-first century can reach any knowledge about the full extent of 'revision', that is, the uncoordinated application of multiple hands to a segment. There is nothing to prevent a later contributor from expanding, then amending, an earlier text for consistency of style.[2] An unknown compound of several contributors would then possess a set of counts that might fortuitously fall in the vicinity of those recorded for some known single author's canon resulting in a misattribution. This wider and more realistic assumption of 'revision' is a serious impediment to stylometric methods, and it creates the demand for a more forensic procedure in which the identity of several hands in a text can be processed without mutual interference.

If one focusses instead on phrases and collocations in a target text, they can be examined independently of each other, without the expedient assumption of uncorrupted text in a single hand. However, the studies that have been carried out focus entirely on a small set of known dramatists so that if some lesser-known writer has made a contribution to the target text then there is no prospect of detection. A more potent objection is that the phrases and collocations are not estimated for rarity so that many of them are commonplace. The implications of a commonplace phrase are not usually elucidated, but the crucial point is this. Let us take a target text A of unknown provenance and a select database of the plays of 20 popular Renaissance dramatists {B, C, D, ...}. For a particular phrase in A, let only dramatist B share it. If B's use is later than A's, then there is a suggestion that B borrowed the phrase from A. With no other dramatist involved the case seems persuasive. However, suppose there are several other texts of prose, poetry, or prose-drama, with an earlier use of this phrase than A or B, none of whose authors are in the select database. What is to prevent A and B from having borrowed from one of these undetected writers, or even from different ones? Without checking the possibility of such an influence, the exclusivity of the borrowing connection between A and B is compromised. For this reason, care must be taken to check that the phrases and collocations under examination are rare in relation to the extant literature of the period in view.[3] To this end, the database should include all writers of the period with extant works, for this then empowers us with a more accurate estimate of the exclusivity of phrase matching between A and B and the subsequent claim for borrowing. Of course, there is no 'perfect' method of estimating rarity, but the use of a contemporary searchable database, even an incomplete one such as EEBO,[4] presents the best data that is presently available.

A second objection relates to the direction of influence of a correspondence. It is not enough to point to a number of matched phrases between A and B. Care must be taken to estimate whether B's use pre-dates or post-dates the target A, for then a clearer picture emerges of the direction of possible borrowing. If there is borrowing in both directions—mutual borrowing—one has a case for a contribution to the target text.

Taking these points into account, from 2012–13 the present author developed the method of RCP, details of which are set out in Chapter 14. One advantage over present methods is that it is not obstructed by the presence of multiple hands in a section of text. In addition, the entire searchable database of writers in EEBO is admitted for possible sources so that by recording only rare phrases (in relation to the extant literature of the period) the charge of commonplace cannot be sustained. As Joseph Rudman (1998, 360) points out:

> Many studies have compared a single style marker (or some small number of markers) to a fingerprint – an authentication method considered infallible. However, one whorl or loop is not sufficient for a positive identification [...] A better analogy would be to DNA matching. The autoradiogram with its multiple markers does not claim infallibility but does claim probabilities approaching certainty.

It should be clear that the more markers that a known author's canon shares with an unattributed piece, the stronger is the claim for contribution. However, a marker must be rare; otherwise the method fails to converge on particular authors.

13.2 The Zeta Test

In the first decade of the twenty-first century, John Burrows (2005) introduced the Zeta test, which essentially takes a segment of text and counts the number of occurrences of a preselected set of words. To illustrate, let us consider the following scenario. Each Sunday afternoon a museum receives a coach party of 60 elderly ladies from various local towns. The museum 'knows' that only one of a possible ten towns—Aytown, Beetown, Ceetown, and so on—each with a population of 500 elderly ladies, will visit with a coach trip, but it never knows in advance which town intends to turn up. Nevertheless, the museum has a way of identifying the town without approaching the members of the coach party. Having been meticulous in researching the wardrobe habits of each town's inhabitants, a list of 50 different dress labels (manufacturers) has been compiled that the ladies might wear. An expert is employed who is highly skilled at identifying dress labels at a glance. When a coach party arrives, a log is to be compiled on the labels worn by the ladies that should reveal their town of origin. However, for such an identification to succeed, research data on the dress habits of each of the ten towns must be compiled in advance for comparison.

13.2.1 Data Preparation

Let us start with a particular town, say Aytown. A list X of 20 favoured Aytown dress labels and a list Y of 20 non-Aytown labels is produced as follows. The population of 500 elderly ladies in Aytown is divided into equal segments, say 10 segments of 50 ladies. Each of 60 dress labels (D1, D2, D3, and so on) is assigned an X score and a Y score, each being the sum of two fractions. For the X score, we add the fraction of Aytown segments in which that label is worn, a number from 0 to 1, to the fraction of non-Aytown segments in which it is not worn, also a number from 0 to 1. This gives a total number 0–2, which is an indicator of Aytown bias towards that dress label.

The following example should clarify the calculation of the X score. Let there be 10 Aytown segments and 9 × 10 = 90 non-Aytown segments for the nine remaining towns: Beetown, Ceetown, Deetown, and so on. Suppose a dress label D1 is worn in three of the ten Aytown segments, then the proportion is 0.3. Let D1 also be worn in 18 of the non-Aytown segments, so that it is not worn in 72/90 = 0.8 of them. The X score is the sum of these, that is, 0.3 + 0.8 = 1.1. The closer the X score is to 2, the stronger that label serves as an Aytown marker, and to be a strong marker it needs to be well worn in Aytown and not so elsewhere. After this Aytown calculation has been carried out for each of the 60 dress labels, the top 20 scoring labels are selected for the list X.

For the Y score, we add the fraction of Aytown segments in which D1 is not worn, to the fraction of non-Aytown segments in which it is. In our example, label D1 is not worn in 7/10 = 0.7 of the Aytown segments but is worn in 18/90 = 0.2 of the non-Aytown segments. The total Y score for D1 is 0.7 + 0.2 = 0.9. The procedure is much simplified by noting that the X and Y scores must total 2. Again, for list Y, the closer the sum is to 2, the better it serves as a non-Aytown marker. The top 20 scores for Y give the list Y. We now have two lists: a list X of labels that strongly indicate Aytown preference and a list Y that strongly contraindicates Aytown. This is the preparation that is required for testing whether or not the coach party is from Aytown. Similar X and Y lists must then be obtained for the nine remaining towns.

13.2.2 Graphical Representation

To finalize our preparation, we now construct an 'Aytown marker graph' where each of the 10 Aytown and the 90 non-Aytown segments, with 50 ladies to each segment, is given a position on a graph plot. For this, each segment needs to be given two values (x, y), where the value x is the number of labels from list X that occur, given as a fraction of the number of different labels worn by the ladies in that segment. The value y is similarly obtained.[5] Since the Aytown segments have high x values and low y, they congregate to the lower right as crosses in Figure 13.1, while the non-Aytown segments have low x and high y, and are grouped around the upper left as circles. Similar graphs are constructed for the remaining nine towns, and all ten graphs are to be used for comparison with the coach passenger dress-label log.

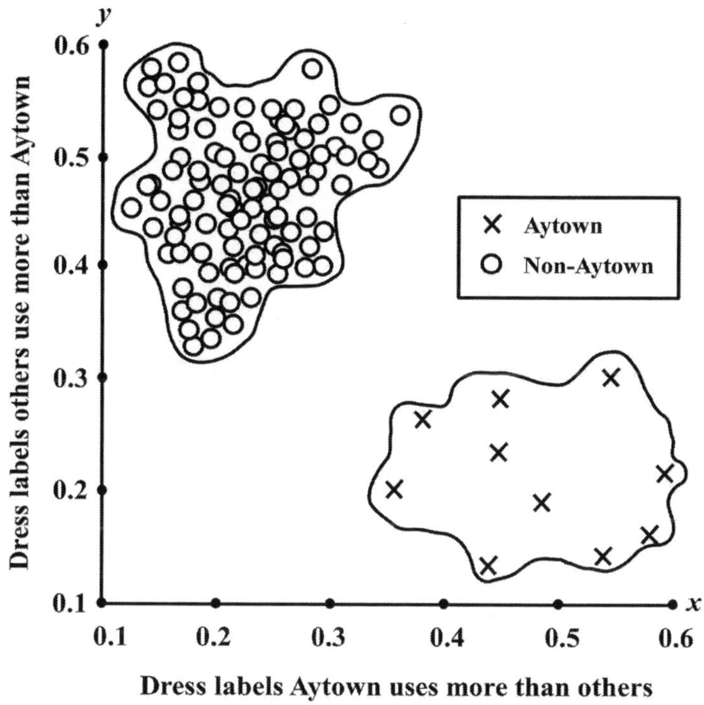

Figure 13.1 Marker and non-marker dress labels for Aytown.

13.2.3 Finding the Best Match

So now the coach party arrives and the museum's Head of Dress-label Recognition identifies at a glance all the dress labels the ladies in the coach party are wearing. The 60 visiting ladies are divided into three segments of 20 each, and each segment is given a pair of (x, y) values which depends on the town for which one is testing. For an Aytown test, the assigned x value is the number of different labels from the Aytown list X as a fraction of the number of different labels worn in the coach-party segment under calculation, and the y value is similarly calculated from the Aytown list Y. Once these three (x, y) pairs have been obtained, the segments, represented as grey diamonds, are placed on the Aytown graph plot for comparison (see Figure 13.2). A similar check is performed for the other nine towns using their specific X and Y lists. In this way, the town with the best correspondence is identified. It turns out that the three coach party segments have the best fit to the positive marker region for Aytown (see Figure 13.2). The Head of Dress-label Recognition concludes that this is a coach party from Aytown, and with a glow of self-satisfaction sends in his invoice.

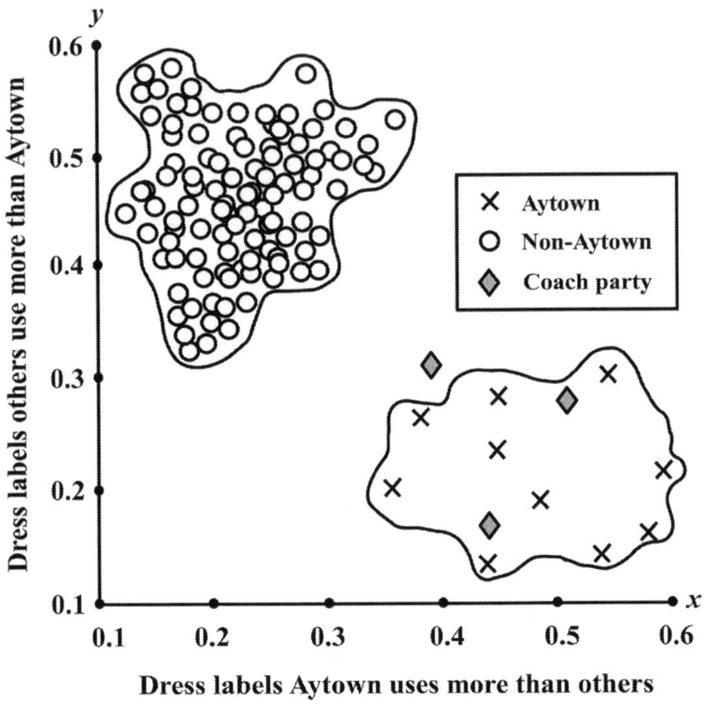

Figure 13.2 Placing the three coach party segments on the Aytown plot.

13.2.4 Limitations of the Method

However, a problem now arises. As stated, the assumption has been made that the coach party of elderly ladies is all from the same town, and as a consequence the calculated data is for a coach party of single-town origin. However, the museum is later informed that on this particular occasion the coach has picked up 15 passengers from Beetown, 18 from Ceetown, and 27 from Deetown to make up the 60 passengers, and they have been thoroughly mixed when divided into the three segments of 20 each. What has happened is that the subsequent combination of dress labels worn by the ladies is such that the group imitates the combination that a coach load entirely from Aytown might have worn (see Figure 13.2). We now have a false result, and it arises from a test that is only designed for a single-town coach party. The museum has applied this test without knowing in advance how many different towns and in what proportion they have made up the visiting coach party that day.

13.2.5 Application to 3 Henry VI

A similar procedure is applied to the Zeta-test play attribution. In order to ascertain whether or not a given target text is a Shakespeare play, one first needs to prepare two marker-words lists X and Y for the Shakespeare corpus. To run *3 Henry VI* through this process, John Burrows has used a database of 27 core Shakespeare plays—analogous to Aytown—and 109 plays by others—analogous to non-Aytown—each of which was assumed to be attributable to a single identifiable originator.[6] Each author's corpus was divided into segments of 2,000 lexical words, disregarding speech, act, and scene boundaries, resulting in 291 Shakespeare (X) and 1,009 non-Shakespeare segments (Y).[7] A set of 1,000 marker words was now prepared, analogous to the dress labels. These are separated into two equal groups, a list X of Shakespeare markers and a list Y of non-Shakespeare ones. For X, the 500 words that most frequently appear in the Shakespeare segments and not in those of other plays are obtained, and for Y they chose the 500 words that are least prevalent in the Shakespeare plays, but most often occur in the non-Shakespeare work.[8] Care is taken to ensure that the lowest-rated Shakespeare segment still has more characteristic Shakespeare words than the highest-rated non-Shakespeare segment, and vice versa.[9]

As part of the preparation, the method is tested on a Shakespeare play that has been set aside for the purpose, and which has not been used to select any of the marker words.[10] For example the 13 segments, each of 2,000 words, from *Coriolanus* provide the test case. Similar to the dress labels, each segment is assigned a point on a graph where the horizontal x-axis gives the number of Shakespeare-markers as a fraction of the total number of different words, and the vertical y-axis provides the number of non-Shakespeare markers as a fraction of the same total number of different words. Even though a word might be repeated in a segment, only its first appearance is registered. The Shakespeare segments are expected to congregate to the lower right and the non-Shakespeare ones to the upper left. The result for the test run on *Coriolanus* is shown in Figure 13.3. Here, the segments of the play fall mainly amongst the Shakespeare segments. Also, as part of the preparation, a non-Shakespeare play might be tested, making sure that it is excluded from the non-Shakespeare segments from which the marker words are collected. The effect of the dubious single-author assumption is clear to see in Figure 13.3 as there is no clear separation of the Shakespeare and non-Shakespeare regions.

Now, the dubious assumption in which trust is placed is that there are 27 plays in the Shakespeare canon, or scenes taken from the 27 plays, which have only one contributor, namely, William Shakspere of Stratford. Given the doubt as to the extent of Shakspere's writing in virtue of his untestability, and the absence of a method that might detect multiple hands, this is a highly dubious conjecture.

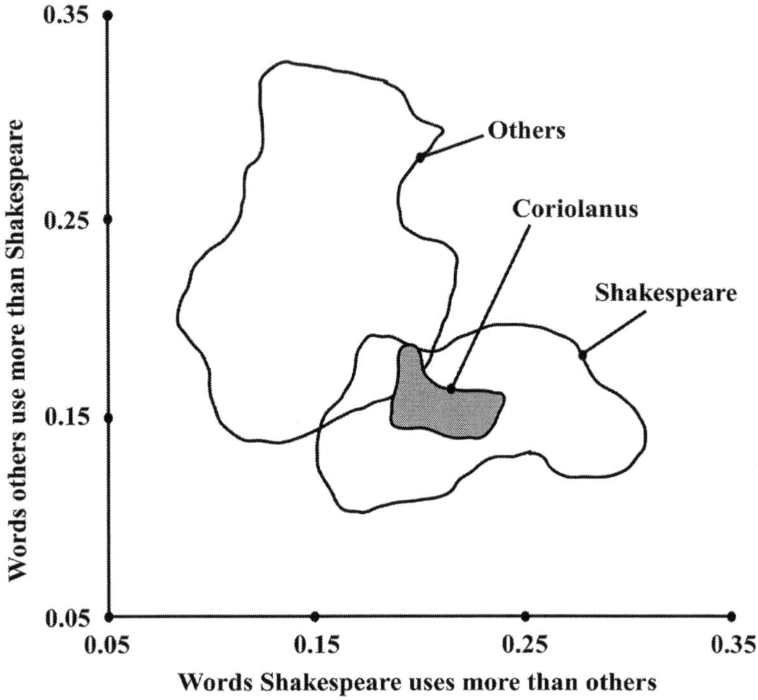

Figure 13.3 Zeta test based on lexical words found in the Shakespeare canon. Regions of 2,000-word segments in Shakespeare, *Coriolanus*, and others are represented. The number of Shakespeare marker words in a given segment is expressed as a fraction of the total number of different words in that segment (Craig and Kinney 2009, Figure 2.2).

The Zeta test has been applied to *3 Henry VI* to discover whether or not Greene or Marlowe, or one of several others, exclusively had a hand in it. The two main versions of *3 Henry VI* are the Octavo version *The true Tragedie of Richard duke of Yorke, and the death of good King Henrie the Sixt* (1595), and the larger *First Folio* text *The third Part of Henry Sixt with the death of the Duke of YORKE* (1623). The former is a mutilated text containing "conspicuous passages of nonsense" (Martin 2001, 105), while the latter has nearly a 1,000 extra lines. This suggested to Randall Martin, editor of The Oxford Shakespeare edition, that the Octavo version was a memorial reconstruction by actors (2001, 106–7). John Burrows and Hugh Craig (2017, Table 11.1, 195) divide the *First Folio* version into Shakespeare and non-Shakespeare scenes, which are treated separately.[11] Again, this step is not to be recommended.

13.2.6 Test Against Robert Greene's Canon

First, a test against Robert Greene's body of work is carried out where the preparation is directed towards obtaining a pair of X and Y word lists: Greene and non-Greene marker words. Then for each 2,000-word segment of *The third Part of Henry Sixt*, a count is made of the Greene markers that occur as a fraction of the total number of different words in that segment. This numbering appears along the horizontal axis of Figure 13.4. For the count of non-Greene markers in each segment, the vertical axis is similarly labelled. The supposed Shakespeare (that is, Shakspere from Stratford) segments are shown as circles, and the non-Shakespeare are depicted as triangles. Both types of segments in the play all appear towards the non-Greene region. For Greene to be indicated, the Shakespeare circles would need to be near the non-Greene region and the non-Shakespeare triangles around the Greene region. The triangles are not around the Greene region, and so Burrows and Craig reject Robert Greene as a contributor to *3 Henry VI*.

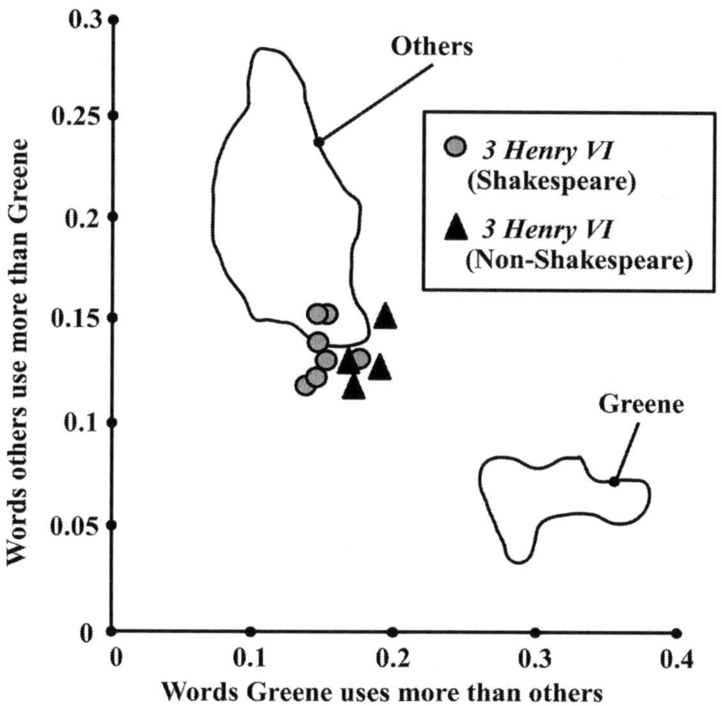

Figure 13.4 Zeta test of lexical words: a plot of Greene and non-Greene 2,000-word segments and the location on that plot of Shakespeare and non-Shakespeare segments in *3 Henry VI* (Burrows and Craig 2017, Figure 11.3, 205).

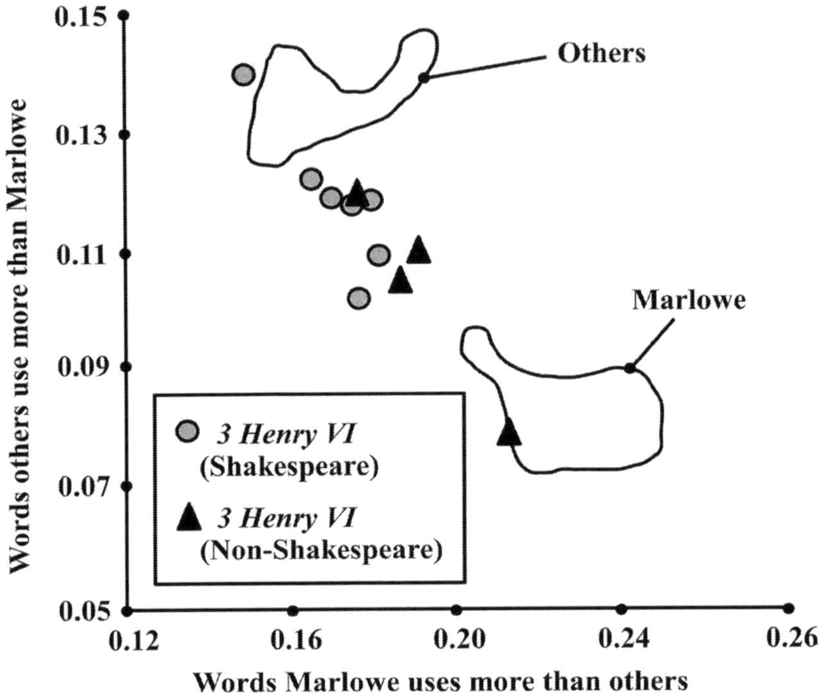

Figure 13.5 Zeta test of lexical words: a plot of Marlowe and non-Marlowe 2,000-word segments and the location on that plot of Shakespeare and non-Shakespeare segments in *3 Henry VI* (Burrows and Craig 2017, Figure 11.5, 206).

13.2.7 Test Against Marlowe's Canon

A similar test is performed using Marlowe's seven plays, so an alternative pair of X and Y word lists is prepared: Marlowe and non-Marlowe marker words.[12] Then each segment of the Shakespeare and non-Shakespeare segments in *The Third Part of Henry Sixt* is examined for the fraction of Marlowe markers (horizontal axis) and the fraction of non-Marlowe words it contains (vertical axis). The result is represented in Figure 13.5 for both the Shakespeare and non-Shakespeare segments from *3 Henry VI*. Here, for Marlowe to be implicated, the circles must be in the 'Others' region and the triangles in the 'Marlowe' region. However, only one of the triangles is near the Marlowe region, the other three being located in between, so the result should be marked down as inconclusive.[13]

Commenting on the overlapping of Shakespeare and non-Shakespeare regions, circles and triangles, Craig and Kinney (2009, 25) suggest that

> we are dealing with writers who are at liberty to imitate each other, to try new styles, and to write differently for a particular occasion or genre [...] It is no wonder that success in discrimination is not complete.

If this is suspected, then an accompanying test that can indicate borrowing from earlier works is needed to justify this claim.

John Burrows and Hugh Craig (2017, 197) are clear about the crucial assumption that their test rests on:

> We assume, for instance, that sections of the play were written by one writer at a time, rather than by a team [... and] that if revision by a different writer, or corruption in the process of transmission, took place, it did not fundamentally alter the underlying authorial style.

They even admit that "we are unsure of what may have intervened between those texts and their authorial originals" (Burrows and Craig 2017, 196), a confession that clearly exposes the limitations of the test for the tasks assigned to it. Contrary to Burrows and Craig, it is suggested here that revision *does* "fundamentally alter the underlying authorial style".

13.3 The Delta Test

The Delta test, in the form that John Burrows (2002) developed it, relies on a database of 58 plays that are assumed to be single-authored and well-attributed. First, the 500 most common words over the whole database are counted. Then we take one of the plays P_j, where $j = 1, 2, \ldots, 58$, and calculate the relative frequency f_{ij} of each of the 500 words w_i, where $i = 1, 2, \ldots, 500$, that is, we quantify its occurrence in the play P_j as a fraction of the total word count in that play, using only the 500 preselected words. A mean score for that word μ_i is then calculated over the 58 plays. For example, suppose in play P_1, the total word count taken over the 500 preselected words is 6000. Let 'cabbage' be word number 27, w_{27}, and suppose it appears 15 times in P_1. Then its relative frequency, $f_{27,1}$, is 15/6000 = 0.0025. The mean score for 'cabbage' accrues from adding together its 58 relative frequencies, one for each play, and dividing by 58. Let us suppose that this comes out as $\mu_{27} = 0.0018$. Next, for each word w_i in the play P_j, a value z_{ij} is calculated as the difference between the relative frequency and the mean for that word, normalized by dividing by the standard deviation σ_i, so that $z_{ij} = \left(f_{ij} - \mu_i\right) / \sigma_i$.[14] This procedure increases the effect of the lowest scoring words. Returning to our example, we can calculate a standard deviation σ_{27} for 'cabbage' from its frequency distribution across the 58 plays. Let us take this to be $\sigma_{27} = 0.04$. Then for P_1, our 'cabbage' calculation of $z_{27,1}$ becomes $z_{27,1} = \left(0.0025 - 0.0018\right) / 0.04 = 0.0175$. Finally, for a comparison of two plays, P_1 and P_2, say, the Burrows' Delta value Δ_B is calculated as follows. For each word denoted by i, the z-values z_{ij} from the two plays are subtracted and the magnitude $|z_{i1} - z_{i2}|$ is taken. Finally, the sum of these positive differences is obtained over all n = 500 words as $\Delta_B = \sum_{i=1}^{n} |z_{i1} - z_{i2}|$. The lower the Delta score, the smaller is the distance measurement Δ_B between the two plays, and the closer is their correspondence. A Burrows' Delta Δ_B is calculated in this way for each play ranged against the target text, and the smallest Delta score is then taken as an indicator of the most likely author of the target.

The problem is that for *3 Henry VI*, Marlowe's *Edward II* emerges as the play with the lowest Delta score for both the Shakespeare—Delta score 0.829—and the non-Shakespeare scenes—Delta score 0.787 (Burrows and Craig 2017, Tables 11.5 and 11.6, 201–2). In other words, *Edward II* resembles both types of scene on the Delta test, undermining the discriminatory motive of the test.

13.3.1 Limitations of the Zeta and Delta Tests

The lack of clarity in the results from both the Delta and Zeta tests for *3 Henry VI* suggests that it has been misapplied. Maciej Eder (2011, 101) goes so far as to declare the assumption "naïve" that "texts in a corpus are purely 'individual' in terms of being written solely by one author and not influenced by other writers".

Craig and Kinney ask "how can we be sure that some of the distinctive Shakespearean phrasings are not in fact common expressions from his own time?" (2009, 15). Neither the Delta nor Zeta test, as presented, takes account of this possibility.

Neither can the scene divisions of *3 Henry VI* into Shakespeare and non-Shakespeare be justified. With several Shakespeare plays already shown to be the work of several hands, a play from the canon must be assumed from the outset of testing to have a compound of contributors, who might not have worked contemporaneously, which any applied test must be designed to separate. Neither the Delta nor Zeta test with their single-contributor assumption is equipped to achieve this. It is absurd then to assume that Shakspere of Stratford wrote any part of a Shakespeare play that has not yet undergone such separation, especially when the extent of his contribution is not available to test. The synonymous use of 'Shakespeare' with Shakspere is unjustified.

John Burrows (2012, 373) suggests that "An improved capacity to test shorter samples at high levels of accuracy would be of more immediate value than further small improvements in treating longer tests". The new method of RCP, which will be examined in detail in Chapter 14, was designed in 2013 to achieve exactly that.

13.4 Phrases and Collocations

Gabriel Egan (2017, 61) makes the point that if a researcher uses a database of texts it must be available for others to check. He cites the case of Donald Foster who used his own SHAXICON database, and Brian Vickers who placed his trust in a plagiarism-detection software called Pl@giarism.[15] In 2008, the latter constructed a database of 75 plays that were thought to have been performed before 1596. No one else appears to have had access to it in order to check the results.

A further point concerns methodology. Brian Vickers has searched for trigrams (and longer n-grams) that appear in both *Arden of Faversham* and in works by Thomas Kyd. He then checked to see if they appeared in works by other authors in his database. If they were unique to the play and Kyd's canon, he took this as evidence of Kyd's authorship. He reported finding 76 such triples, together with longer n-grams such as 'and faine would have', 'Ile none of that', 'there is no credit in', and 'thou wert wont to' (Egan 2017, 62).[16] The question arises: why was this not carried out for other authors not in his database? The possibility should have been eliminated that these other authors might also have matches with the play. If they occur before the play then they might have been sources for the n-grams, and the convergence towards exclusivity of the Kyd and *Arden of Faversham* matches is then compromised.

In relation to Brian Vickers's 'unique' matches between the Additions to *The Spanish Tragedy* and the Shakespeare works,[17] Gabriel Egan (2017, 66) makes precisely this point that a search of the EEBO-TCP database should have been carried out for non-dramatic works:

> Vickers should have looked beyond the drama since if a phrase is simply the common currency in the period [...] then finding it in the Additions to *The Spanish Tragedy* and Shakespeare's works has no significance for authorship attribution. This is what Muriel St Clare Byrne meant by the necessity of performing a 'negative check'.

This is exactly the difficulty that haunts the use of hapax legomena, see Section 12.5. MacDonald Jackson (2017, 49) has subsequently demonstrated that

> *Arden of Faversham* yields a great many more unique matches with both *1 Henry VI* and *The Taming of the Shrew* than with any of Kyd's canonical plays. In that two-horse race, Shakespeare beats Kyd.

If 'Shakespeare' is tasked by MacDonald Jackson to denote 'in the Shakespeare canon' then the ground is safe, but if instead he means 'Shakspere of Stratford' then this is an untestable claim. It is a mistake to assume that an attribution method must necessarily be a test for an originator as "Mere similarities between play X and the canon of playwright A, even though striking, cannot alone establish a probability that playwright A wrote play X" (Jackson 2017, 59). In portraying attribution testing as a horse race with only one winner, MacDonald Jackson is holding exactly this assumption, that there can only be one author of the target text under examination, and methods such as the Zeta and Delta tests are redundant without this assumption. No attribution test can ever claim to have found the single-originator of a block of text since its originator might not exist in the database that the text is being compared against.[18] For this reason, an attribution test can never be more than a test of contribution, and one should allow the possibility that a segment of text has more than one contributor.

When MacDonald Jackson introduced a counting method involving a collection of phrases and collocations from the 'Literature Online' database, which contained almost all of early English drama as well as the most celebrated poetry and some prose, he was clear that his technique

> is most readily applied to cases where (a) there is a small number of candidates for the authorship of a scene or passage, and (b) each of these candidates was the sole author of several plays. (Jackson 2008, 193)

In citing the case of William Rowley's *All's Lost by Lust,* he set up a control test which pitched works by Massinger, Middleton, Heywood, and Rowley against a long speech in the play. The result was that his method correctly identified Rowley. However, the Rowley play is fairly certain to be by one main hand, and a test of this kind is only suitable to detect a single contributor so long as actor, editorial, scribal, or dramatist intervention has not significantly corrupted it. For MacDonald Jackson's method to work there must only be one main contributor. What if there is a diversity of contributors to the segment under test whose proportions conspire in such a way to imitate another particular dramatist? How can one be sure for a text of *unknown provenance* that this is not the case?

13.4.1 A Cure for a Cuckold

The 1661 quarto of *A Cure for a Cuckold* is attributed to John Webster and William Rowley. The idea that Thomas Heywood had contributed was introduced by H. D. Gray in 1927; in fact, F. L. Lucas (1927, III.10–18) had previously given (5.5.1–131) to Webster, (5.1.132–352) to Heywood, and (5.1.353–522) to Rowley. So MacDonald Jackson searched the works of these three playwrights in 'Literature Online' for phrases and collocations obtained from these portions. Only five Heywood plays were searched in order to bring the number of words in each

Table 13.1 Phrasal linkages in *A Cure for a Cuckold*, 5.1 (Jackson 2008, 195)

	Webster	*Heywood*	*Rowley*
5.1.1–131	8	30	4
5.1.132–352	31	7	8
5.1.353–522	3	3	11

corpus approximately into correspondence. A search return was logged only if it appeared in the work of exactly one of these three candidates, that is, if it had exclusivity among the three. A repeated return for a particular phrase or collocation was ignored. For example, 'more near', 'Pray, your name', 'I do entreat you', and 'gives him dead' all produced returns. The results are shown in Table 13.1.

From his search data Jackson concluded that "Heywood had indeed contributed to *A Cure for a Cuckold*" (2008, 195). However, there is no information here as to whether Thomas Heywood's returns occurred before or after the assumed date of the play, an issue commonly referred to as 'direction of influence'. Neither is there any indication as to the rarity of the phrase or collocation in relation to the contemporary literature, a point that has already been addressed with hapax legomena (see Section 12.5). Without investigating a phrase's earlier use by others, the convergence towards exclusivity between Heywood and the author(s) of *Cuckold* cannot be estimated. Heywood could easily have borrowed from other earlier texts in which that phrase can be found.

13.4.2 Pericles

In 1609, '*THE LATE, / And much admired Play, / Pericles, Prince of Tyre*' appeared in a quarto edition, with 'William Shakespeare' on the title page.[19] It is the only version that has reached us, those that follow being reprints. It is generally agreed to be a corrupt copy. The first recorded attendance at the play occurred between May 1606 and July 1608, when Zorzi Giustinian, the Venetian Ambassador to England, took a party to see it, most likely at the Globe. This was reported by Giustinian's interpreter Odoardo Guatz who during a witch-hunt against Protestantism was interrogated ten years later about the leisure habits of the men he served:

> The Ambassador Giustinian went with the French ambassador and his wife to a play called Pericles, which cost Giustinian more than 20 crowns. He also took the Secretary of Florence. (Hinds 1908, 592–600)[20]

The George Wilkins novel *The Painful Adventures of Pericles Prince of Tyre* (1605), some of which is in blank verse, appears connected to the Shakespeare play since not only does it mirror parts of the play verbatim, but it mentions in its opening Argument that it was "by the King's Maiestie's Players excellently presented".[21]

The first to assign the first two acts of *Pericles* to George Wilkins was Nicolaus Delius (1868) on the basis of similarities with Wilkins's *The miseries of inforst mariage* (1607). The Reverend Fleay agreed but added that "the second author was, I think, unquestionably William Rowley" (1874, 201). Adding tone to the scenario, Harry Baker (1908, 112–14) suggested that in 1607 Wilkins wrote "a complete drama on Pericles", and that the reason he wrote the novel a year later was because he "disposed of his drama to Shakspere's company". Not wishing that Shakspere should take all the credit (and the name 'William Shakespeare' *did* appear on the play's title page) Baker suggests that Wilkins brought out the novel in advance of the play *Pericles*. Since a survey of the shifting opinions of scholars with time is not the prime focus of this treatise, attention will be directed back towards attribution methods in relation to *Pericles*.[22]

Unfortunately, Wilkins has only one single-attribution play *The miseries* (1607) and no dramatic verse in the 'Literature Online' database, so in order to produce a fair comparison, the Shakespeare corpus is reduced to *The Tempest*, which although substantially shorter than the Wilkins play, apparently serves as compensation in having more "of its subject matter in common" with *Pericles* (Jackson 2008, 203). MacDonald Jackson's test aims to find phrases and collocations from *Pericles* that appear in the selected sample of one author but not the other.

> The whole of *Pericles* was worked through line by line, with every significant content word and collocation being checked in all attested spellings and combinations of spellings [...] Our concern is with *Pericles* phrases and collocations that occur in either Shakespeare's *The Tempest* or Wilkin's *The Miseries of Enforced Marriage*, but not in both of those plays. (Jackson 2008, 204)

While Acts 1 and 2 have 304 Wilkins hits and 102 Shakespeare, Acts 3–5 have 177 for the former and 274 for the latter.

The trouble is, as Dr Jackson suspected, some of his listed correspondences are commonplace (Jackson 2008, 208). This can be seen in Table 13.2, where some of the *Pericles*, Act 1, items in his list have been checked by the present author against the Early English Books Online database. Here, the number of returns in the fourth column arises from the 6,624 documents that are searchable before the date 1609.

There are others on the boundary between rarity and commonplace that have more favourable alternative contributors. For example, in

Table 13.2 Phrases and collocations from *Pericles*, Act 1, checked for rarity

Locution	*Pericles*	*Search*	*No. returns*
1	"to the judgment of the eye" (1.0.42)[a]	{judgment fby.4 eye}	24/6624(0.362%)
2	"for death remember'd should be like a mirror" (1.1.46)	{should be like}	over 100/6624(>1.510%)
3	"on sweetest flowers yet they poison breed" (1.1.34)	{sweetest flowers}	45/6624(0.679%)
4	"which I fear" (1.1.44)	{which I fear}	99/6624(1.495%)
5	"but I must tell you" (1.1.79)	{but I must tell you}	23/6624(0.347%)

[a] Line numbers from Suzanne Gossett, ed., *Pericles*, The Arden Shakespeare (Bloomsbury, 2016).

Locution 1 "to the judgment of the eye" we find that Thomas Dekker's "Would stay the iudgment of the curiost eye" in *Patient Grisill* (1603) precedes Wilkin's use in *Miseries* (1607). Also, a search for Locution 5 "but I must tell you" returns two of Nashe's plays *Blurt master constable* (1602) and *The honest whore* (1604) as well as one of Marlowe's *D. Faustus* (publ. 1603) which again all precede Wilkin's *Miseries* (1607).

Even when a return is rare, there might be a more favourable alternative author match. For example, "bad child worse father" searched as {bad fby.2 worse} has 4/6624(0.060%) returns before 1609, but Thomas Nashe with *Summers last will and testament* (1592, published 1600) precedes George Wilkin's use of it in *Miseries* (1607).

Table 13.3 shows the results of the present author's RCP analysis of *Pericles*, Act 1, being a summary of the full log that appears in Appendix G. A rare return before the play date 1609 is shown with a '•', while one that is registered after 1609 appears as '○'. All collocations occur in less than 0.1% of records that exist before the assumed play date 1609, except those marked with '*', which are also contained in less than 0.27% of records. Where two authors make use of the same locution the order of use is indicated.

Since all his correspondences precede *Pericles*, we could not, on the basis of Table 13.3, reliably declare that George Wilkins was anything more than just a source for *Pericles*, Act 1. In fact, with rare returns both before and after 1609, the best candidate for contribution appears to be Thomas Dekker. Michael Drayton's repeated use of locutions is also of interest.

So, unless a locution can be shown to be rare in relation to a contemporary database of texts (such as EEBO), then the charge of 'commonplace' can always be made. What this implies is that although two texts (one attributed and one unattributed) might share a locution, the possibility has not been minimized that each might have obtained it from an earlier

Table 13.3 Rare phrase and collocation correspondences from *Pericles*, Act 1: Author key: RG Robert Greene, TN Thomas Nashe, GW George Wilkins, TD Thomas Dekker, PM Philip Massinger, TH Thomas Heywood, MD Michael Drayton. The black circles indicate matches before the target date; the white ones show matches afterwards. Priority is indicated by '1st' and '2nd'.

Coll. No.	*RG*	*TN*	*GW*	*TD*	*PM*	*TH*	*MD*
2	•						
5		•(1st)	•(2nd)				
8*			•				
10					••		
11						○	
12							•
14				•(1st)			•••(2nd)○○
15							••
16				•			
17			•				
18	•					○	
19				•			
21	•						
23			•				
24*	•						
28				○(1st)		○(2nd)	
29						•	
30					○		
31*		•(1st)		••○(2nd)			
33		•					
34		•					
35					○		

source, which need not even be a common one. Attention must also be paid to the possibility of mutual borrowing, where a candidate for contribution has sufficient rare matches to indicate both directions of influence. This is the crucial feature in arguing for a contribution. These issues have been addressed in the new RCP method presented in the next chapter.

Notes

1 For example, a count might be made of the number of preselected words in a 2,000-word block that are most often used in a known author's canon.
2 There are two versions of *3 Henry VI*, namely, *The true Tragedie of Richard duke of Yorke* (1595) and *The third Part of Henry Sixt* (1623), where phrases from the former have been amended in the latter.
3 A measure of rarity might involve the proportion of returned records containing the searched phrase or collocation before the assumed target text

date. The numerical assignment of this proportion is a matter of definition, but less than 0.1% should suffice. At any rate, the value can be adjusted arbitrarily, so that an increase in value will result in more returns, while a decrease will produce less.

4 Which is only 46% searchable to April 2017.

5 As counted on the day that the data was collected. For simplicity, any bias of label choice due to weather, say, has been ignored.

6 The list is given in Craig and Kinney (2009, Appendix A).

7 A 'lexical word' has semantic content, such as 'gentle' and 'brave'.

8 Examples of Shakespeare words are 'gentle', 'answer', and 'beseech', and for non-Shakespeare we have 'yes', 'brave', 'sure', and 'hopes'; see Craig and Kinney (2009, 18).

9 For Shakespeare X markers, the highest scoring is 'gentle' which appears in 0.69 of the Shakespeare segments and fails to appears in 0.55 of the others, giving it a total score of 1.24. The lowest scoring is 'heaven', with values of $0.71 + 0.32 = 1.03$.

10 In other words, marker words have been obtained from only 26 of the 27 Shakespeare plays.

11 Shakespeare scenes are 1.3, 1.4, 2.1, 2.2, 2.4, 2.5, 2.6, 3.1, 3.2, 4.1, 5.1, 5.3, 5.4, 5.5, 5.6, 5.7, and the rest that are non-Shakespeare are 1.1, 1.2, 2.3, 3.3, 4.2, 4.3, 4.4, 4.5, 4.6, 4.7, 4.8, 5.2.

12 This assumes that there is no contention as to what properly belongs to Marlowe in these works.

13 For the Zeta test on the *First Folio* version, two other variables were added "frequencies of pairings of common grammatical words like *she* and *when*, and sequences of three lexical words" (Burrows and Craig 2017, 197). Consecutive words such as these are called n-grams, a couple being a bi-gram, and a triple being a tri-gram. The variant spellings are standardized, and the plays taking part are limited to the date range 1580–99, resulting in 17 Shakespeare and 63 non-Shakespeare plays.

14 This is a standard transformation in statistics when changing from a normal distribution in a random variable X, with mean μ and standard deviation σ, to a standard normal distribution Z, with mean zero and standard deviation unity.

15 Vickers used it to collaborate with Marcus Dahl in investigating *Arden of Faversham* to identify three-word phrases (trigrams).

16 Gabriel Egan claims that 'Ile none of that' also appears in Robert Yarrington's *Two Lamentable Tragedies* (1594), while 'thou wert wont to' is in John Lyly's *Love's Metamorphosis* (1590). Presumably, these works were not in Vickers's database.

17 Vickers reported finding 116 such matches.

18 How can any test cover the possibility that an unfinished manuscript by an unknown unpublished author might have been acquired by a reputable dramatist and revised? In this case, only the reviser's marks would be identifiable.

19 It was entered in the *Stationers' Register* on 20 May 1608 to Edward Blount.

20 This was an interrogation in London of the interpreter Odoardo Guatz (Guazzo) on 18 April 1617, recorded in the "Appendix: Miscellaneous 1616" (Hinds 1908). In fact, the object of the enquiry was Ambassador Antonio Foscarini who was acquitted 15 months later.

21 The Wilkins novel takes about one-third of the text verbatim from Lawrence Twine's novella *The Pattern of Painful Adventures* (registered 1576); see Hoeniger (1997, xvi).

22 For example, a comprehensive account of *Pericles* can be found in Vickers (2002, 291–332).

Bibliography

Baker, Harry T. "The relation of Shakspere's Pericles to George Wilkin's novel, The pain-full aduentures of Pericles, Prince of Tyre" *Journal of the Modern Language Association of America* 23, No. 1 (1908): 100–118.

Burrows, John. "'Delta' – A measure of stylistic difference and a guide to likely authorship" *Literary and Linguistic Computing* 17, No. 3 (2002): 131–47.

Burrows, John. "Who wrote Shamela? Verifying the authorship of a parodic test" *Literary and Linguistic Computing* 20, No. 4 (2005): 437–50.

Burrows, John. "A second opinion on 'Shakespeare and authorship studies in the twenty-first century'" *Shakespeare Quarterly* 63, (Fall 2012): 355–92.

Burrows, John, and Hugh Craig. "The Joker in the pack? Marlowe, Kyd, and the Co-authorship of *Henry VI, Part 3*." In Gary Taylor and Gabriel Egan, eds. *The New Oxford Shakespeare Authorship Companion*. Oxford: Oxford University Press, 2017.

Craig, Hugh, and Arthur Kinney, eds. *Shakespeare, Computers, and the Mystery of Authorship*. Cambridge: Cambridge University Press, 2009.

Delius, Nicolaus. "Über Shakespeare's Pericles, Prince of Tyre" *Shakespeare Jahrbuch* 3 (1868): 175–204.

Eder, Maciej. "Style markers in authorship attribution, a cross-language study of the authorial fingerprint" *Studies in Polish Linguistics* 6 (2011): 99–114.

Egan, Gabriel. "The limitations of Vickers's trigram tests." In Gary Taylor and Gabriel Egan, eds. *The New Oxford Shakespeare Authorship Companion*. Oxford: Oxford University Press, 2017.

Fleay, Frederick Gard. "On the play of *Pericles*" *Transactions of the New Shakspere Society* 1 (1874): 195–209.

Hinds, Allen B., ed. *Calendar of State Papers Relating to English Affairs in the Archives of Venice, Volume 14, 1615–1617*. London: His Majesty's Stationery Office, 1908.

Hoeniger, F. David. *Pericles*. The Arden Shakespeare. Second edition. London: Bloomsbury, 1997.

Jackson, MacDonald P. *Defining Shakespeare, Pericles as Test Case*. Oxford: Oxford University Press, 2008.

Jackson, MacDonald P. "One horse races." In Gary Taylor and Gabriel Egan, eds. *The New Oxford Shakespeare Authorship Companion*. Oxford: Oxford University Press, 2017.

Lucas, F. Lee, ed. *The Complete Works of John Webster*. 4 vols. London: Chatto and Windus, 1927.

Martin, Randall. *Henry VI, Part 3*. The Oxford Shakespeare. Oxford University Press, 2001.

Rudman, Joseph. "The state of authorship attribution studies: Some problems and solutions" *Computers and the Humanities* 31, No. 4 (1998): 351–65.

Vickers, Brian. *Shakespeare, Co-Author: A Historic Study of Five Collaborative Plays*. Oxford: Oxford University Press, 2002.

Wilkins, George. *The Painfull Aduentures of Pericles Prince of Tyre*. London: Printed by T. P. for Nat: Butter, 1605.

Wilkins, George. *The Miseries of Inforst Mariage*. London: Printed for George Vincent, 1607.

14 The New Method of Rare Collocation Profiling

Details of the new RCP are given, and its advantages over present stylometric and phrase-matching methods are pointed out. Justification is provided for the non-equalization of corpus size, with evidence from the tests showing that at least seven EEBO plays for a given author are sufficient to begin to form a judgement as to contribution. A test case, the long poem *A Funerall Elegye* (1612), is discussed to further suggest that Shakspere had works under his name that were not his.

14.1 The EEBO Search Engine

AUTHORSHIP: A set of linked activities (authemes) which are sometimes performed by a single person but will often be performed collaboratively or by several persons in succession. —Harold Love (2002, 39)

Chadwyck-Healey's Early English Books Online (EEBO) database contains digitized page images of over 130,000 titles, which amounts to almost every book, pamphlet, or broadside published from 1473 to 1700.[1] Since 1999, the Text Creation Partnership (TCP), which is based at the University of Michigan, has worked to transcribe the digital images into fully searchable text in two phases.[2] The EEBO-TCP Phase I from 2000 to 2009 succeeded in producing 25,363 texts, and Phase II from 2010 to 2015 made a further contribution. To April 2017, a total of 60,237 fully searchable texts covering 1473–1700 have been prepared.

The input screen for the search engine is shown schematically in Figure 14.1. Whatever keywords are entered into the 'KEYWORD(s)' box, the 'Check for variants' feature below it allows a checkbox selection of spelling variants. Proximity operators such as 'NEAR' and 'FBY' (followed by) used in the 'KEYWORD(s)' allow the specification of a certain distance between keywords. For example, {head NEAR.3 time} will return all examples where there are up to three word-steps from the word 'head' to the word 'time' in either direction. The search {head FBY.3 time} ensures that the word 'time' is after the word 'head', with up to three word-steps from one to the other. The truncation operator '*' gives flexibility in returned word endings. For example, {fon*} will return examples of 'font', 'fond', 'fondly', 'fondest', and so on. The wildcard operator '?' gives variation in

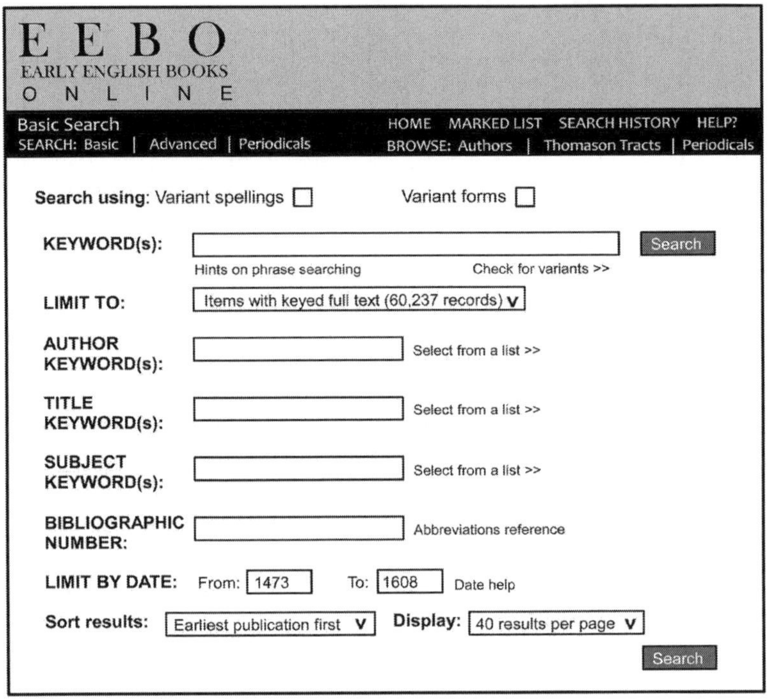

Figure 14.1 Schematic representation of input screen for Chadwyck-Healey's EEBO-TCP search engine.

a character position in a word, returning words with one or no character in that position. For example, {hono?r} yields 'honor' and 'honour'. These last two functions are incompatible with the variant spelling feature.

14.2 The RCP Method

The following method was developed by the present author during PhD research conducted from 2010 to 2013 at Brunel University, UK. If one focusses on phrases and collocations in a target text, they can be examined independently of each other, without the expedient assumption of collaboration, that is, a pre-arranged exclusive allocation of segments to the text's contributors. Such an assumption is necessary for the application of stylometric methods to be justified, but the influence of later revision and the consequent corruption of the single-author ideal cannot be known in advance. Also, the stylometric studies that have been carried out focus entirely on a small set of known dramatists; so, if some lesser-known writer has made a contribution there is no opportunity for identification. Where collections of phrases and collocations are obtained, they are not usually estimated for rarity, so that the convergence to an exclusivity of correspondence is compromised by the failure to check the extent of borrowing from earlier sources. For this reason, care must be taken to ensure that the phrases and collocations under examination are rare in relation to the entire extant literature of the period in view.[3] This then empowers us with greater confidence in the exclusivity of the matches.

The method broadly consists of the following procedure.

1 A text of unknown attribution (target text) is systematically examined line by line, identifying possible rare phrases and collocations. Although an attempt is made to be exhaustive, the choice is undoubtedly exposed to the human error of omission, and although for a text such as *The Tempest* over 1,000 searches might be made (with only rare collocations logged), it is acknowledged that some informative searches might have been inadvertently overlooked. However, since it is not known in advance which authors are to be returned by the searches, there can be no bias towards any particular author by such exclusions. In any case, researchers are at liberty to append new correspondences at a later date in order to improve the accuracy of the profiling.[4]

2 Chadwyck-Healey's Early English Books Online (EEBO) database is used to conduct a search on each suspected phrase or collocation in order to identify its degree of 'rarity' before the assumed date of the play. In relation to the estimation of 'rarity', while it is true that to April 2017 only 46% of the extant texts are searchable, and the database is therefore incomplete, it must surely leave us in profit to use the best data currently available, rather than suspend all endeavours until the full database of digital images has been transcribed.

3 The phrase or collocation is entered in the 'KEYWORD' box, the variant spellings are chosen from the 'check for variants' beneath it, the 'sort results' (bottom of graphic) is set to 'Earliest publication first', and the 'display' is set to '40 results per page'. The 'SEARCH' button is then engaged.

4 The returns are listed down the screen in order of ascending date, and a count is made of the number of returns before the assumed year of the target text. If sufficiently rare (e.g. the number of returns divided by the number searchable before the target date is less than, say, 0.17%) then that phrase is accepted, and details of all the authors who used it before the assumed play date are recorded. An example of this logging procedure is given in Appendix G for *Pericles*, Act 1, where the footnotes present the possible sources. A list is also made of those authors who used it after the target date (not shown in Appendix G). Only the first use is recorded for any author, and repeated editions of a text are ignored for the count. Typically, over 1,000 searches might be made for an average-length Shakespeare play.

5 The definition of rarity is arbitrary, and the test can be carried out at varying levels. The greater the percentage of returns admitted before

the target date, the greater will be the information available; however, this must be balanced against the increased effort required in recording the additional data. For *Pericles*, 'rare' was pitched at less than 0.226% of the searchable database before the target date (see Appendix G).

6 On occasion, when a particular context must be met by a search string, all returned records are individually inspected. This is a time-consuming procedure which involves opening up every document returned to examine the collocation's environment.

7 On completing the searches, a rare-collocation profile (RCP) is constructed for each author who logs at least three rare returns (see Appendices A–F), showing the number of correspondences for that author before the target date (where the target might have borrowed from the author) and the number after that date (where the author might have borrowed from the target). This accounts for direction of influence. The criterion used here for strong mutual borrowing is that two rare returns must occur for a candidate, both before or after the assumed target date. A complex locution could suffice instead of two weaker ones (e.g. see John Ford's parallels in Section 14.5). However, there need not even be an absolute criterion for contribution. A relative criterion would suffice where it is declared that with the evidence presently available, candidate A emerges as the best candidate for contribution, and candidate B as the second best, and so on.

8 EEBO can sometimes misattribute returned texts so that the works of those authors for whom a profile is constructed must be independently checked to ensure a reasonably accurate single-authorship attribution. Returned texts with shared authorship are problematic and are rejected. In any case, it is recognized that the concept of a single author is only an approximation, but nevertheless the texts upon which our confidence is based surely direct us closer to the truth than no data at all.

9 Mutual borrowing is considered to be unlikely unless two authors are known to have engaged each other in print (e.g. the Harvey–Nashe controversy). So the greater the indication of mutual borrowing, the greater is the weight placed on the conjecture that the profiled author is a contributor to the target text.

10 It is possible that the assumed date of the target text might be inaccurate. For example, if the date were in error five years either way, the estimate of rarity would still be reasonable. However, the decision as to which locutions were borrowed from the target and vice versa would be in need of revision. Consequently, the conclusion as to whether or not mutual borrowing has occurred—a candidate has sufficient rare returns to demonstrate both directions of influence—will be dependent on the assumed target date. In that case, statements of the following form apply: 'For a target date of 1612, John Smith exhibits mutual borrowing'.

For an author whose number of works in EEBO is insufficient to register sufficient returns, nothing can be decided. At the time the test is conducted, the evidence either exists for a candidate, or it does not, and if it does not then the returned conclusion about that author must be 'undetermined'. No attempt is made to follow stylometry and 'equalize' corpora. As in a court of law, all the extant evidence is used. The logged locutions by their very nature are infrequent, and there is no evidence from the RCP analyses so far conducted that complex phrases and collocations are genre or epoch dependent nor that the number of returns for an author is proportional to the extant corpus size.[5] The advantage of RCP over present methods is that, being forensic in nature, it is not obstructed by the presence of multiple hands in a section of text. The selection of particular phrases does not demand a segment of text uniform in one hand. Also, the demand for rarity means that no phrase used can be dismissed as commonplace in relation to the extant literature of the period. The convergence of the correspondence between the unattributed target and a known writer narrows as the rarity and number of matchings in both directions increases. Once several rare phrases from the target have been associated in a state of mutual borrowing with a particular author in EEBO, the method becomes informative.

14.3 Non-Equalization of Author Corpora

It seems absurd that in identifying rare collocations in a target text, the method of stylometry in equalizing corpora should be imitated in that information that might serve as evidence should be rejected. It would be rather like the judge in a court case deciding that since the defence can produce only one witness then this is also the prosecution's entitlement, even if the rejected prosecution witnesses are in possession of persuasive evidence. This is exactly what happens when one imposes the condition that the corpora of authors in EEBO should be equalized with the target text, by selecting a common genre, a common time period, and a common total word count. For example, in discussing the first two acts of *Pericles*, MacDonald Jackson uses the only play attributed to George Wilkins (*The miseries of inforst mariage*) and is thereby forced to use only one (*The Tempest*) from the Shakespeare canon (see Section 13.4.2). It is a practice that dispenses with vital data.

While in stylometry, frequently occurring words might be genre and date dependent, in RCP it is the rarity of a collocation and its consequent inner complexity that renders it independent of genre and date. In *The Tempest*, for "The Mistris which I serue, quickens what's dead" (3.1.6), Francis Bacon has three returns for the search {quickens near.4 dead/life/alive} from work dated 1597, 1607, and 1620 (Table F.1, No. 8). Clearly, time has not restricted his use of it. Neither has genre left its mark because if we consider its sources, 'Of Suitors' (1597) is an essay about law and 'The Article of the General Naturalization of the Scottish Nation' (1607) is a speech about politics. In the comedy *Twelfth Night* (c.1602), "From the rude seas enrag'd" (5.1.76) (Table E.6, No. 5) also occurs in the history play *The tragedie of King Richard the second* (1597) when searched as {rude sea(s)}. For the comedy *Love's Labour's Lost* (c.1594), "prickes me on" (1.1.256) (Table D.6, No. 1) reappears in *The history of Henrie the Fourth* (1598). These locutions are evidently not genre specific, and there is no evidence from the RCP tests so far conducted that any allowance for varying genre or date need be made.

One accusation that has been levelled against the RCP method concerning the lack of equalization maintains that without comparing corpora of equal size, an unfair advantage is afforded to those with the greatest presence in the database. There are two arguments against this, the first *a priori* and the second *a posteriori*, both of which will now be developed.

14.3.1 A Priori Argument

There is a vital assumption that has been overlooked in the objections to a lack of equalization. It is that the style of an author is already predetermined before any test is carried out. The application of the test does not occasion the coincidence of style, it only allows its exposure. If the style has sufficient cognitive complexity, and the test is designed to pick up that level of construction, then with sufficient data available for a particular candidate, the test will either root out the affinity with the target or pass over the lack of it. Unlike stylometric word counts, the focus on obtaining a set of individual rare collocations, most of which possess a coherence that points to an ordered mind, allows a window into the mental organization and cognitive preference of different personalities. The size of the available corpus of an author has no causal influence on the type of personality exhibited. A large corpus can reinforce the conclusion that an author has a concurrent style to the target, but will leave uncorroborated a candidate with no returned concurrence. A small corpus might still yield sufficient returns to suggest a concurrent author (see the test on John Ford's *A Funerall Elegye* in Section 4.1), but if it does not, then nothing can be decided until more textual data is available. One needs to be ready to accept the conclusion 'undetermined' if insufficient evidence is available for a possible candidate.

14.3.2 A Posteriori Argument

The evidence obtained from the RCP tests so far carried out shows that a large corpus size in EEBO for a particular author has no major influence on an appearance in the results and that an EEBO corpus of at least seven works can be sufficient to make a reasonable case for contribution. An RCP analysis of *3 Henry VI* is given in Chapter 6. Bacon only has one return for this play out of his 27 searchable works in EEBO, whereas Marlowe has eight from seven works. Here, Bacon's superior corpus size has not been an advantage. For *A Funerall Elegye* (1612), although the Shakespeare corpus in EEBO contains the 36 plays in the *First Folio* (1623) only five matches occur, whereas John Ford, who only has nine works, registers 16 correspondences; see Table 4.2 (Clarke 2014, Tables 4.3 & 4.4). Bacon again appears only once. If the critics of RCP are to be consistent, for the analysis of *The Tempest* they must maintain that Ben Jonson's 22 works in EEBO, Thomas Heywood's 24, and Thomas Middleton's 24 present an ideal opportunity for them to obtain a comparable number of returns to Bacon's 9 from 27 works, but these three dramatists only manage a total of five returns between them (Clarke 2014, Table 7.2). For the Virginia Company's *A true declaration* (1610), Richard Braithwaite has 34 texts and Thomas Taylor has 43, both much larger than Bacon's 27, but they only register three rare matches each from EEBO, while Bacon has six (Clarke 2014, Table 8.5). There are also other authors in EEBO with large corpora. For example, Robert Greene has 32 verifiable works in EEBO, yet in four of the Shakespeare plays and in the three pamphlets tested so far,[6] the number of his returns is insignificant. This suggests that the size of corpus in EEBO has no effect on a predetermined style but only influences the extent to which this style (if it is present) is exposed. The 27 works that Francis Bacon has in EEBO only present an advantage to the *judgement* of the researcher, and cannot induce a notable correspondence to a target text with which *a priori* he has no concurrence of style. A large corpus only serves to amplify the detected homogeneity or non-homogeneity of a predetermined style with that of a target text. In contrast, a small corpus has the disadvantage that its insufficiency might permit any *a priori* homogeneity with the target text to pass unnoticed.

14.4 The Running Track[7]

Those who object to the lack of equalization in the RCP method are saturated in the methods of stylometry. Here, a select number of horses are entered into a race by special invitation only, while other thoroughbred writers such as those from the Inns of Court are deemed unworthy of a run-out. The race is designed to result in a single winner because for these test practitioners, each text segment under examination can only have one contributor. To preside over a fair race, devotees equalize corpora for genre, date, and word count, so that once each horse has been given an equal handicap, it is the one that demonstrates the greatest stamina over the course before him that crosses the line first. As already pointed out, the assumption of a single contributor to a text segment in a target of unknown provenance cannot be justified. A better approach would be to assume several contributors and construct a suitable method that might identify them. It then ceases to be a race with only one winner and transforms into a test of suitability for the particular course set, which several horses might be capable of completing if they possess a sufficient measure of the requisite characteristics.[8]

The question is, given a set of authors $\{A_1, A_2, A_3, \ldots\}$ that have *a priori* contributed to a target text, is there enough evidence in terms of observed rare collocation sharing to allow each author at least two matches both before and after the assumed date of the text. To be awarded the prize of 'contributor', all runners over the course must aspire to this state of mutual borrowing, so there might be several winners. Unfortunately for RCP, this is not always the case, and for those who have insufficient data in EEBO, their failure to register allows no decision about their claim. In contrast, a stylometric method, in a desperate endeavour to include a favoured runner in the starting line-up, crops its corpus to suit that of the smallest contestant, rejecting vital evidence. The RCP method makes no attempt to slim down an obese horse to fit into the starting gate. It is quite content to allow all comers to run, content in the knowledge that above a certain limit,[9] the size of the creature has no significant bearing on the nature of the outcome. Either the animal will have the requisite stamina to last the course or it will fall short. For those too slight to complete it, nothing can be decided; however, the beast is quite at liberty to enlarge its body of work and trot out again at a later date. Unfortunately, those that are amply proportioned but still fall short are the least likely to prove suitable for the course should further evidence later arise.

For Francis Bacon, additional searches from Google have been added to enlarge his corpus. However, this is no attempt to drag a dead horse over the finishing line. As stated earlier, the absence of returns from a large corpus, although indeterminate, could just as well be interpreted as contraindicating contribution (as it does for Bacon with *3 Henry VI* and *A Funerall Elegye*), and the addition of Google searches merely serves to enhance the clarity of judgement.

14.5 A Test Case: A Funerall Elegye (1612)

In 1989, the forensic linguist Donald Foster argued that *A Funerall Elegye* (1612), which was published under the unidentified initials "W.S.", was a Shakespeare poem (W. S. 1612). Its subsequent inclusion in the Norton, Riverside, and Longman Shakespeare collections signalled its acceptance into the canon; however, its attribution to Shakespeare was challenged, most notably by Gilles Monsarrat (2002) and Brian Vickers (2002), who both argued for the dramatist John Ford (1586–1639); see Section 4.1. Unfortunately, in 2002, their database was limited, and so an accurate assessment of the rarity of certain stylistic traits in relation to the published literature of the era was unobtainable.

There is significant external evidence in favour of John Ford's attribution. The *Elegye* relates to the murder of William Peter from Devonshire in January 1612. Ford was born in Ilsington, Devonshire, not far from William Peter. They both attended Exeter College, Oxford, and they were both there in the period 1601–1602, sharing the same tutor, Simon Baskerville. Memorial poems were Ford's province. He wrote them on the death of the Earl of Devonshire, Sir Thomas Overbury, Ben Jonson, and John Fletcher. As with the *Elegye*, they set out the subject's virtues, attacked his enemies, and assured his eternal fame (Vickers 2002, xxvi–xxvii). In support of Foster's case, Ian Lancashire (1997, 171) points out that George Eld, who printed *Shake-speare's sonnets* (1609), was also the printer of *A Funerall Elegye*. However, it seems to have passed unnoticed that he was also the printer of John Ford's *Honor triumphant* (1606b).

Less than three weeks after the murder, a poem was entered in the *Stationers' Register* "A funeral Elegye In memory of the late virtuous master WILLIAM PEETER". With no bookseller's name on the title page, it had the appearance of a private publication and might well have been "printed in fewer than a dozen copies" (Foster 1997, 115–16). Foster compared the *Elegye* with all known writing of the period by authors with the initials "W.S." and reached the conclusion that it belonged to the work of Shakespeare. However, in 2002, Brian Vickers opposed the introduction of the *Elegye* into the Shakespeare canon, arguing instead for the dramatist John Ford. In the same year, Gilles Monsarrat (2002) carried out collocation searches on the *Elegye* but, like Dr Vickers, did not have the depth of database such as Chadwyck-Healey's EEBO to test the rarity of his phrases.

In the RCP test that was applied to the poem, the rarity was set at a return of less than 0.2% of the searchable texts, that is, less than 11/5471 available records before 1612. It turns out that only two canons yield more than three rare returns: the Shakespeare corpus and that of John Ford. Although John Ford has nine searchable works in the EEBO database, and the Shakespeare canon has 40,[10] Ford registers 16 returns to Shakespeare's 5 (see Figure 14.2). Furthermore, almost all of Ford's returns (15 of them) post-date the *Elegye*, and rest above the 1612 line in Figure 14.2, while all of Shakespeare's (five of them) precede it. This almost prohibits a conclusion, as the result mainly points to Ford borrowing from the poem and the poem borrowing from Shakespeare. However, in order to indicate mutual borrowing, which is so rare that it instead argues a contribution, the demand is made that an author requires rare matches both before and after the date of the target text. The single rare return by Ford that precedes the long poem is "And set thee as a President to Men" (W. S. 1612, sig. B2^{v}) which, as Gilles Monsarrat (2002, 189)

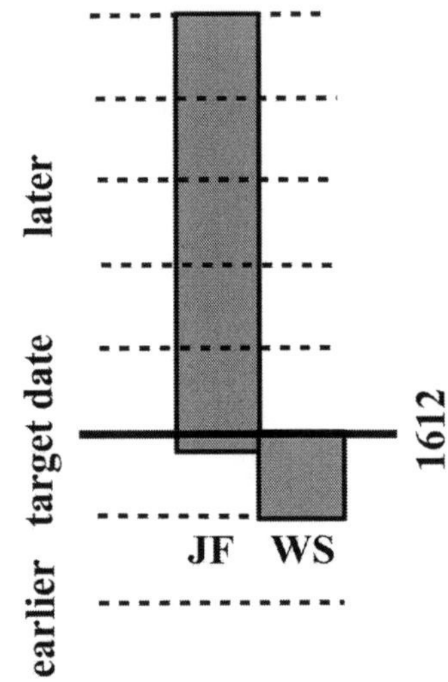

Figure 14.2 The number of rare correspondences between John Ford (JF) and the Shakespeare canon (WS). W. S., *A Funerall Elegye* (1612).

points out, also appears in Ford's *Fames memorial* (1606a). In fact, it can *only* be found in Ford's work. Fortunately, it is complex enough to stand as strong evidence of the poem borrowing from Ford, and this favours his mutual borrowing and contribution. So the conclusion reached is that *A Funerall Elegye* (1612) is John Ford's poem but that significant borrowings from the Shakespeare canon appear. Given that the poem was signed 'W.S.', and it was a tribute to the murdered William Peter, was Ford concerned about retribution from the assailant and so contrived to pass it off as a Shakespeare work? It is an interesting scenario.

14.6 Summary of RCP Conclusions

To date, the RCP method has been applied to five full Shakespeare plays: *The Comedy of Errors*, *3 Henry VI*, *Love's Labour's Lost*, *The Tempest*, *Twelfth Night*, and Act 1 of a sixth play *Pericles*. An investigation has also been carried out on the long poem *A Funerall Elegye* (1612), the Virginia Company propaganda pamphlet *A true declaration* (1610), and an account of the 1594–5 Gray's Inn revels *Gesta Grayorum* (1688). Reduced tests have also been performed, for example, on selected locutions in *Vertue's Common-wealth* (1603), and on the full *Groats-worth of Witte* (1592) letter.

Of the Shakespeare plays, Francis Bacon makes an appearance most significantly in *The Tempest*, followed by *Love's Labour's Lost*, and *Twelfth Night*, while his detectable influence on *Gesta Grayorum* is almost beyond doubt. Thomas Heywood is a good candidate for a post-1594 revision of *The Comedy of Errors*, while John Ford has more evidence than the Shakespeare canon of a correspondence with *A Funerall Elegye*. The rare matches that Thomas Nashe has with *Love's Labour's Lost*, all of which precede the Gray's Inn revels (1594–5), hint at his prior influence on the play. The RCP method has also been used to conclude that Robert Greene, Christopher Marlowe, and Anthony Munday have left their signature on *3 Henry VI*, and that it was Greene himself who wrote the *Groats-worth* letter.

Notes

1 Chadwyck-Healey is the humanities publishing arm of ProQuest, based in Ann Arbor, Michigan, which sells research materials to universities and libraries around the world.
2 The Text Creation Partnership (TCP) is a collaboration between main two groups: (1) ProQuest's Early English Books Online (EEBO), Gale Cengage's Eighteenth-Century Collections Online, and Readex's Evans Early American Imprints (who collectively own millions of page images in over 125,000 volumes); and (2) 150 libraries worldwide who jointly fund and own the fully searchable text files that have been created.
3 The measure of rarity used involves the proportion of returned records containing the searched phrase or collocation before the assumed target text date. The value of this proportion is a matter of definition, but less than 0.17% should suffice for most plays. At any rate, the value can be increased to admit more returns and the variation of the numbers of correspondences for the possible contributors can be observed. The disadvantage of increasing this percentage is the consequent increase in the workload of logging returns.
4 David Lake states that "not only must resemblances be pointed out, but the non-occurrence of the feature(s) in question must be demonstrated in many other texts of the same period": Lake (1975, 7).
5 Since the individual locutions carry a greater cognitive complexity than simple words and reflect the personality of the author, two independent thinking minds cannot be expected to express themselves the same way, no matter how much they write.
6 *Gesta Grayorum* (c.1594–5, published 1688), *A Funerall Elegye* (1612), and *A true declaration* (1610).
7 This refers to Macdonald P. Jackson's characterization of stylometry as a 'one-horse race' (Jackson 2017, 49–59).
8 Here 'stamina' refers to the registration of sufficient rare returns from EEBO both before and after the assumed target text date.
9 As previously stated, evidence from running the tests shows that an author with at least seven play-length texts in the EEBO database is sufficient to begin to form a judgement.
10 This consists of the 36 *First Folio* plays, the *Sonnets*, *Venus and Adonis*, *Lucrece*, and the *Pericles* quarto.

Bibliography

Clarke, Barry R. "A linguistic analysis of Francis Bacon's contribution to three Shakespeare plays: *A Comedy of Errors*, *Love's Labour's Lost*, and *The Tempest*." PhD thesis, Brunel University, UK. 2014.

Ford, John. *Fames Memoriall, or the Earle of Deuonshire Deceased*. Printed at the private press of Lee Priory, 1606a. STC: 11158.

Ford, John. *Honor Triumphant*. London: Printed by [G. Eld] for Francis Burton, 1606b. STC: 11160.

Foster, Donald W. *Elegy by W. S.: A Study in Attribution*. Newark, DE: University of Delaware Press, 1989.

Foster, Donald W. "A funeral elegy: W[illiam] S[hakespeare]'s 'Best-speaking witnesses.'" In Leeds Barroll, ed. *Shakespeare Studies*. 25 vols. 1997, 115–40.

Jackson, MacDonald P., "One horse races." In Gary Taylor and Gabriel Egan, eds. *The New Oxford Shakespeare Authorship Companion*. Oxford: Oxford University Press, 2017.

Lake, David. *The Canon of Thomas Middleton's Plays*. Cambridge: Cambridge University Press, 1975.

Lancashire, Ian. "Empirically determining Shakespeare's idiolect" *Shakespeare Studies* 25 (1997): 171–85.

Love, Harold. *Attributing Authorship: An Introduction*. Cambridge: Cambridge University Press, 2002.

Monsarrat, Gilles. D. "A funeral elegy: Ford, W.S., and Shakespeare" *The Review of English Studies* 53, (2002): 186–203.

Shakespeare, William [?]. *Shake-Speare's Sonnets*. London: Printed by George Eld for T. T., 1609. STC: 22353.

Vickers, Brian. *'Counterfeiting' Shakespeare*. Cambridge: Cambridge University Press, 2002.

W. S. [?] *A Fvnerall Elegye. In Memory of the Late Vertous Maister William Peter of Whipton Neere Excester*. London: Imprinted by G. Eld, 1612.

Epilogue

Unidentified Plays at Inns of Court Revels

Since Francis Bacon was a producer of the Inns of Court players, the investigation into his connection to the Shakespeare canon finds a natural entrance by focussing on plays that might have passed through these schools of law. Regarding such plays, Margaret Knapp and Michal Kobialka (2001) have not only suggested *Twelfth Night* (Chapter 10) but several others: *Troilus and Cressida* (Elton 2000), *Timon of Athens* (Bradbrook 1966), and *Measure for Measure*.[1] This is in addition to *The Comedy of Errors* (Chapter 8) and *Love's Labour's Lost* (Chapter 9), which have already received detailed attention in the present work. With Shakspere being excluded from the Inns of Court in the 1590s, these plays are an excellent place to excavate associations between some of the Shakespeare plays and Inns of Court writers who contributed to the lawyers' revels. There is still the suggestion of an unidentified play at the 1594–5 Gray's Inn revels because, as the *Gesta Grayorum* (1688, 53) inform us,

> so that very good Inventions, which were to be performed in publick at his [the Prince] Entertainment into the House again, and two grand Nights [...] were by the aforesaid Readers and Governors made frustrate.

A 'grand Night' usually meant a play. One of them appears to have been *Love's Labour's Lost*, but what was the other? Also, the 1597–8 *Prince d'Amour* revels at the Middle Temple had two unidentified comedies (*Le Prince d'Amour* 1660, sigs G2^{r} & G3^{r}).[2] There is evidence that one was a reduced version of *Twelfth Night*, but again what was the other? So there is much scope here for new research.

The Mysterious Brian Melbancke

There is an intriguing case surrounding one Brian Melbancke and his publication *Philotimus* (Melbancke 1583). For the EEBO search {[adjective] and voluble} or {voluble and [adjective]} in relation to *The Comedy of Errors*, he has the earliest return with "very fine and voluble" (Table B.2, No. 2).[3] This is a rare locution that Bacon also shares, with "voluble and sharpe". For the construction "He is the ground of my defeatures" (2.1.98–99) from *CE* (Table B.5, No. 3), when an EEBO search for {defeature(s)} is carried out, he is not only the earliest rare return but the only return before 1594.[4] The word "defeatures" also appears in *Venus and Adonis* (1593), which means that Melbancke is the *only* possible EEBO source for this word in the poem. In *Vertues Common-wealth* (1603), with which Bacon has been associated in Chapter 7, we find "brain-sicke multitude" (Crosse 1603, sig. Q^r), while Bacon has "mutinous brain-sick soldier" in a Queen's Day device from 1595, see Section 7.2. Melbancke turns up again with "brain-sick youth".[5] Now, the title page of *Philotimus* (1583), the pamphlet in which all of these correspondences occur, declares the work to be "Compiled by BRIAN MELBANCKE / Student at Graies Inne". However, there is no record of a Melbancke or Milbancke registered at Gray's Inn at that time nor was there a George Wastnes (or Wastneys) who included an effusive commendatory preface about Melbancke (Foster 1889, 550). There is a further dedication "TO THE VVORSHIPFVL / and my very frends, the Gentlemen / Students in the Innes of Court and Chauncerie, / and the vniuersitie of Cambridge", which suggests that in 1583 our subject was both a member of the Inns of Court and a former Cambridge University student but not under the name Melbancke. It is a mystery that invites interpretation, but I recommend a suspension of judgement until a thorough stylistic analysis of *Philotimus* (1583) has been undertaken.[6]

Ideologies

The main aim of the present work is to challenge the 'thinking in a vacuum' that has hitherto paralyzed debates between competing single-author theorists, and instead bring facts to the discussion based on a new method of textual analysis in order to move the investigation forward. It should be clear from all that has been said so far that the idea that William Shakspere of Stratford was the single author of the *First Folio* plays, or even a contributor, is a notion in search of evidence.[7] The *First Folio* is an unreliable document for attribution and this now needs to be accepted. In fact, the time is now ripe for all single-author theorists to abandon their narrow ideological perspective and take a wider view of the scenery that surrounds them: Shakspere's claim to contribution is untestable, the claim for single authorship by an alternative candidate is untestable, and there are many hands of revision in the Shakespeare work.[8]

The greatest impediment to progress is an attitude that has corrupted all ages of human investigation, that is, the dogmatic insistence that all evidence must be rejected that is inconsistent with one's own views, that Nature must conform to one's will. While it is true that powerful religious authorities in centuries past have been its main advocates, it is nevertheless a child of science who stamps his feet and stubbornly refuses to accept a 'no' from the external world. Left unopposed by the authority of the senses, an infant of this kind comes to believe that the world is under his control. Real advancement can never result from such disconnected isolation. If our knowledge is to mature we must freely admit our errors and adjust our conjectures to embrace contrary and contextual evidence. If we are interested in what is true rather than what we would like to be true, then our judgement must be allowed access to the external world.[9] Otherwise, the whole enterprise produces nothing but an entrenched belief system in the service of the will. While the denial of all evidence that intrudes on our constructions can maintain a comforting private sanctuary, the avoidance of a critical test that necessitates its defence can never lead to the real truth of the matter.

Notes

1 For a discussion of Bacon's parallels with *Measure for Measure* see Melsome (1945, 34–73).
2 "*Wednesday* night [29 December] there was a comedy" and "Upon *Munday* at nighty [sic] [2 January] there happened a comedy".
3 The combined search rarity is 5/3340(0.150%) before 1594. *Philotimus* includes a dedication to "Phillip, Earle of Arundell".
4 The rarity is 1/3440(0.029%) before 1594.
5 Only 10/4464(0.224%) before 1603 are in the context of it being an adjective for a person or persons.
6 In case evidence eventually emerges from a test of style for Francis Bacon as a contributor to *Philotimus*, he was quite capable of inventing pseudonyms. His manuscript fragment *Valerius Terminus, Of the Interpretation of Nature* (1603) appears under the pen name Valerius Terminus with the promise of annotations by the fictional Hermes Stella (Spedding *et al.* 1863, VI.25–76). The MS resides in the British Library, Harley MS 6463, f.1^{v}. A contemporary early draft copy in a student notebook has been reported by Serjeantson (2013).
7 The declaration that Shakspere is in want of contributor evidence is not the same as the claim that he made no contribution.
8 "Ideologues are people who pretend they know how 'to make the world a better place' before they've taken care of their own chaos within", Norman Doidge, Foreword in Peterson (2018, xiv).
9 In an interview with John Freeman in 1959, broadcast as 'Face to Face' on BBC television (4 March 1959), Bertrand Russell cautions "Never let yourself be diverted either by what you wish to believe, or by what you think would have beneficent social effects if it were believed. But look only, and solely, at what are the facts".

Bibliography

Bradbrook, Murie C. "The *Comedy of Timon*: A revelling play of the Inner Temple." *Renaissance Drama* 9 (1966): 83–103.

Crosse, Henry. *Vertues Common-wealth: Or the Highway to Honovr*. London: Printed for Iohn Newbery, 1603. [Huntingdon Library].

Elton, William R. *Shakepeare's Troilus and Cressida and the Inns of Court revels*. Aldershot: Ashgate, 2000.

Foster, Joseph, ed. *The Register of Admissions to Gray's Inn, 1521–1889*. London: Hansard Publishing Union, 1889.

Gesta Grayorum: or the History of the High and Mighty Prince, Henry. London: Printed for W. Canning, 1688.

Knapp, Margaret, and Michal Kobialka. "Shakespeare and the prince of Purpoole: The 1594 production of *The Comedy of Errors* at Gray's Inn Hall." In Robert Miola, ed. *The Comedy of Errors: Critical Essays*. New York: Routledge, 2001.

Melbancke, Briane. *Philotimus. THE WARRE betwixt Nature and Fortune*. London: Printed by Roger Warde, 1583. STC: 17801.

Melsome, William S. *The Bacon-Shakespeare Anatomy*. London: George Lapworth & Company Ltd, 1945.

Peterson, Jordan B. *12 Rules for Life: An Antidote to Chaos*. London: Allen Lane, 2018.

Le Prince d'Amour, or the Prince of Love. With a Collection of Several Ingenious Poems and Songs. By the Wits of the Age. London: Printed for William Leake, 1660.

Serjeantson, Richard. "The philosophy of Francis Bacon in early Jacobean Oxford. With an edition of an unknown manuscript of the 'Valerius Terminus'." *The Historical Journal* 56, No. 4 (December 2013): 1087–106.

Spedding, James, ed. *The Works of Francis Bacon*. 15 vols. Boston: Taggard and Thompson, 1863.

Appendix A
RCP results for *3 Henry VI*

Tables of rare returns for Robert Greene, Christopher Marlowe, Anthony Munday, and Thomas Lodge are given.

In what follows, both *The true Tragedie of Richard duke of Yorke* (1595) and *The third Part of Henry Sixt* (1623) are systematically and manually examined by word, phrase, and collocation.[1] These are also to be referred to as the *Octavo* 'O' and *First Folio* 'F1' versions, respectively. With the assumed date of the play as c.1592, there are 4,156 texts in Chadwyck-Healey's Early English Books Online (EEBO) database available for search before that date.[2] During the examination, a phrase or collocation that is suspected of being unusual is typed into the search engine, and the number of texts that contain that locution before the assumed date is noted. If this is less than 16 (0.385% of the 4,156 texts) then the phrase is recorded as rare. The authors who share the use of that locution are then also recorded. Robert Greene died in September 1592, so, although the publication date of his work might be later, all his work must have been written before that date, and so all of his returns are included in the rarity count. Christopher Marlowe died in May 1593, so a similar inclusion is made for his publications.[3] A given locution in Table A.1 may be assumed to occur in both the *First Folio* (with its line numbers) and the Octavo version, unless it indicates 'F1' for *First Folio* only, or 'O' for Octavio only. The results are freely reproducible by anyone with access to EEBO in a university library. What follows is not the log of rare matches (an example of a log for the first act of *Pericles* is given in Appendix G) but the Rare Collocation Profiling (RCP) tables for each significant author, derived from the log.

In 1590, Thomas Lodge worked with Robert Greene on *A Looking Glass for London and England* (pub. 1594), and there is "Dark cloudie death" (2.6.62) from *3 Henry VI* (both versions) that appears in this work.[4] The dramatist with the next highest number of returns after the authors tabulated below is George Peele with three cases: "vnpeople" (1.1.126) in *The loue of King Dauid* (1599), "Chearfull Colours" (5.1.58) in *The araygnement of Paris* (1594), and "mangled body" (5.2.7) in *The battell of Alcazar* (1594), all at less than 0.12% rarity.

Table A.1 RCP results from EEBO for Robert Greene when searching *3 Henry VI*. 'F1' indicates *First Folio* only and 'O' indicate Octavo only

No.	*Locution in 3 Henry VI*	*EEBO search*	*Greene work*	*Rarity*
1	"Vow by Heauen(s)" (1.1.24)	{vow by heaven(s)}	*Orlando Furioso* (1594)[a]	2/4156(0.048%)
2	"With Purple Faulchion [sword] painted to the Hilt, In blood of those who had encountred him" (1.4.12)[b]	{painted near.5 blood}	*Euphues his censure to Philautus* (1587)	7/4156(0.168%)
3	"Thou hast slaine the flower of Europe" [F1] (2.1.70-1)	{flower of Europe}	*Alcida Greenes metamorphosis* (1617)	1/4156(0.024%)
4	"Ne'er may he liue to see a Sun-shine day" (2.1.186)	{sunshine day}	*Greenes neuer too late* (1590)	5/4156(0.012%)
5	"To let thy tongue detect thy base-borne heart"(2.2.143) [F1]	{base born} [context: 'base born' + noun][c]	*Orlando Furioso* (1594)	3/4156(0.072%)
6	"Thy Brothers blood the thirsty earth hath drunk" (2.3.15) [F1]	{thirsty earth}	*The Scottish historie of James the fourth* (1598)	5/4156(0.012%)
7	"Thy tough Commixtures melts" (2.6.6)	{commixture(s)}	*Farewell to folly* (1591)	13/4156(0.313%)
8	"This is the quondam King" (3.1.23)	{quondam king}	*Farewell to folly* (1591)	3/4156(0.072%)
9	"I pawne mine honour and my credit" [O][d]	{pawn my/mine honour}	*Orlando Furioso* (1594)[e]	1/4156(0.024%)
10	"Ile wear the willow garland for his sake" (3.3.228)	{willow garland}	*Ciceronis amor* (1589)	6/4156(0.144%)
11	"Whose armes gaue shelter to the Princeley Eagle" (5.2.12)	{princely eagle}	*Menaphon Camillas* (1589)	3/4156(0.072%)
12	"And kept low Shrubs from Winters pow'rfull Winde" (5.2.15) [F1]	{low shrubs} [context: exposed to wind]	*Planetomachia* (1585)[f]	9/4156(0.217%)
13	"Went all afoote in Summers scalding heate" (5.7.18)	{scalding heat(e)}	*Alcida Greenes metamorphosis* (1617)	9/4156(0.217%)

[a]Henslowe's Diary records an enactment at the Rose Theatre in February 1592.
[b]*The True Tragedy* has "With purple Faulchen painted to the hilts, In blood of those whom he had slaughtered".
[c]When a context is given in square brackets, the returns are individually inspected to ensure it satisfies the given context.
[d]The *First Folio* has "I pawne my Credit, and mine Honor" (3.3.116).
[e]Robert Greene has "I will pawne my honor to his gage".
[f]Here Greene has "Low shrubbes withstand great tempests" but also in *Greenes vision* (1592) is "strongest gustes offend lesse the low shrubs than the tall Cedars". Later, but without mentioning wind "But low shrubs wither at the Cedars roote" William Shakespeare, *Lucrece* (1594).

Table A.2 RCP results from EEBO for Christopher Marlowe when searching *3 Henry VI*

No.	*Locution in 3 Henry VI*	*EEBO search*	*Marlowe work*	*Rarity*
1	"Not separated with the racking Clouds" (2.1.27) [F1][a]	{racking cloud(s)}	*Tamberlaine the Great* (1590)	1/4156(0.024%)
2	"And spight of spight, needs must I rest a while" (2.3.5) [F1][b]	{spight of spite}	*Doctor Faustus* (1616)	5/4156(0.120%)
3	"Smile gentle heauen" (2.3.6)[c]	{gentle heauen(s)}	*Edward the second* (1594)[d]	1/4156(0.024%)
4	"Ill blowes the winde that profits no body" (2.5.55)	{blows the wind}	*Edward the second* (1594)	5/4156(0.120%)
5	"Whose top branch ouer-peer'd Ioues spreading Tree"[e] (5.2.14)	{Joves fby.3 tree}	*Edward the second* (1594)	3/4156(0.072%)
6	"Yonder stands the thornie Wood" (5.4.67)	{thorny wood} [context: metaphor for 'army of men']	*Tamberlaine the Great* (1590)	2/4156(0.048%)
7	"Which now mistrust no parcell of my feare" (5.6.38) [F1]	{parcel of my}	*Tamberlaine the Great* (1590)[f]	14/4156(0.337%)
8	"And made our Footstoole of Security" (5.7.14)	{footstool fby.2 security}	*Massacre at Paris* (1594)[g]	10/4156(0.241%)

[a]Octavo has "by a racking cloude".
[b]Octavo has "And force perforce needs must I rest myself".
[c]Octavo has "heauens".
[d]"the gentle heauens haue not to do in this" Christopher Marlowe, *The troublesome raigne and lamentable death of Edward the second* (1594). STC: 17437.
[e]Note "from Ioues brode tree" Ovid, *The .xv. books* (1567), STC: 18956.
[f]Marlowe has "parcel of my Empery" and "parcel of my funeral".
[g]Marlowe has "And makes his footstool on securitie".

Table A.3 RCP results from EEBO for Anthony Munday when searching *3 Henry VI*

No.	*Locution in 3 Henry VI*	*EEBO search*	*Munday work*	*Rarity*
1	"But I haue reasons strong and forceable" (1.2.3)	{strong fby.2 forceable} [context: second word 'and']	*Zelauto* (1580)	5/4156(0.120%)
2	"And much effuse of blood" (2.6.28)	{effuse of blood}	*The English Romayne lyfe* (1582)	1/4156(0.024%)
3	"You catch a clap" [O]	{catch a clap}	*The paine of pleasure* (1583)	2/4156(0.048%)
4	"Brought him to the door of death" (3.3.105)	{door of death}	*The death of Robert, Earle of Huntington* (1601)	10/4156(0.241%)
5	"Twere a pity to sunder them" (4.1.24)	{to sunder them}	*The first book of Amadis of Gaule* (1590)	4/4156(0.096%)
6	"Belike she minds to play the Amazon"[a] (4.1.106)	{play the Amazon}	*The death of Robert, Earle of Huntington* (1601)	1/4156(0.024%)
7	"Se wee, well couer'd with the Nights black mantle" (4.2.22) [F1]	{black mantle}	*Palmerin D'Oliua* (1588)	3/4156(0.072%)
8	"Though Fortunes malice ouerthrow my State" (4.3.46) [F1] "auoiding Fortunes malice" (4.6.28) [F1]	{fortunes malice}	*The first book of Amadis of Gaule* (1590)	1/4156(0.024%)
9	"About thy coal-black hayre" (5.1.54) [F1]	{coal black}	*Palmerin of England* (1602)	1/4156(0.024%)
10	"The Night-crow cry'de, aboding lucklesse time" (5.6.45)	{luckless time}	*The first book of Amadis of Gaule* (1590)	2/4156(0.048%)
11	"O may such purple teares be alway shed"[b] (5.6.64)	{purple tears}	*The death of Robert, Earle of Huntington* (1601)	0/4156(unique)[c]

[a]Appears in Octavo but EEBO did not return it possibly due to the italic font for 'Amazon'.
[b]Also in William Shakespeare, *Venus and Adonis* (1593).
[c]Here 'unique' means that the target text registers the first use of the locution.

Table A.4 RCP results from EEBO for Thomas Lodge when searching *3 Henry VI*

No.	*Locution in 3 Henry VI*	*EEBO search*	*Lodge work*	*Rarity*
1	"Rageing windes blowes vp a storme of teares" [O]	{storm of tears}	*Rosalynde* (1592)	0/4156(unique)
2	"Her teares will pierce into a marble heart"[a] (3.1.38) [F1]	{marble heart} [context: pierce it]	*Scillaes metamorphosis* (1589)	1/4156(0.024%)
3	"is the wind in that doore?"[b] [O]	{the wind in that door}	*A looking glasse* (1594)	9/4156(0.217%)
4	"Vnfained friend" (3.3.202)	{unfeigned friend}	*The vvounds of ciuill vvar* (1594)	15/4156(0.361%)
5	"Thor art no Atlas for so great a weigh [as the kingdom]" (5.1.36)	{Atlas near.5 weight}	*Scillaes metamorphosis* (1589)	3/4156(0.072%)
6	"And this word [Loue] which Gray-beards call Diuine"[c] (5.6.81)	{grey beards}	*The vvounds of ciuill vvar* (1594)	2/4156(0.048%)

[a]Lodge has "my moanings are like water drops, That neede an age to pearce her marble heart".
[b]Also appears in William Shakespeare, *The historie of Henrie the Fourth vvith the battell at Shrewsburie* (1598), that is, *1 Henry IV* (4.3).
[c]Octavo has "greybeards/graybeards" with 2/4156 returns, but the Octavo text is not returned by EEBO.

Notes

1 That the test was conducted manually rather than using an unbiased algorithm might raise an objection as to the bias towards this or that candidate. However, the choice of searches is not determined by any particular author. The authors sharing the search string are unknown until the search result is returned. Also, any collocation searches that have been missed can be appended later. After repeated revisions, the table should tend to a meticulous state that no present computer algorithm could obtain.
2 This was the state of EEBO on 4 April 2017.
3 Although only documents before 1592 determine the rarity, the search was conducted between the dates 1473–1690.
4 With no returns before 1592.

Appendix B
RCP results for *The Comedy of Errors*

Tables of rare returns for Francis Bacon, Thomas Heywood, Thomas Nashe, and the Shakespeare canon are given for *The Comedy of Errors*. A list of Bacon's works in the EEBO database is also provided.

This section gives the results of a RCP search with the EEBO database and Google search engine on *The Comedy of Errors* (c.1594).[1] Every discernible phrase and collocation in the play is checked with the search engine of the Early English Books Online (EEBO) database to assess its rarity.[2] The ones that are sufficiently rare are recorded. The authors who used these rare phrases in common with the play are also logged and a DNA-type profile constructed for each author in the form of a table. See Table B.6 for a list of Bacon's searchable works in EEBO.

While the EEBO database is used to test the rarity of a locution, a candidate for contribution need not have all their work in EEBO. For example, letters and speeches found elsewhere can be introduced for matching. The main aim is to decide if sufficient evidence exists from any source to argue for a candidate's contribution. For any author with insufficient textual material, nothing can be decided and any claim to their contribution is untestable. It turns out that Francis Bacon has speeches and letters that do not appear in EEBO, and Google searches which have been checked for rarity with EEBO can be carried out to extend the rare matches with *CE*. These are logged in Table B.2.

There is evidence here of borrowing from *CE* by Francis Bacon, but only No. 2 in Table B.2, being earlier than 1595, exhibits a borrowing of the play from Bacon. This hint of mutual borrowing argues a contribution to the play by Bacon, but without further pre-1594 evidence it is not a particularly strong argument. If there was a later revision, say for the 1604 performance, then Bacon has two rare matches before this new play date and the argument for his contribution is then stronger.

All Heywood's rare correspondences occur after 1595, indicating a borrowing from the play, and so if he contributed to this play it must

Table B.1 RCP results from EEBO for Francis Bacon when searching *The Comedy of Errors*

No.	*Locution*	*EEBO search*	*Bacon's work*	*Rarity*
1	"doomed to die" (1.1.153)	(i) {doomed to die} (ii) {doomed to}	"doomed to perpetuall imprisonment" *The wisedome of the ancients* (1619)[a]	(i) 0/3340(unique) (ii) 2/3340(0.060%)
2	"creepe in crannies" (2.2.31)	{in crannies}	"So as the Species doe passe [...] in Crannies, or Chinks, as to the Sound" *Sylua syluarum* (1627)	0/3340(unique)
3	"by fine and recoverie" (2.2.74–75)	{fine and recovery}	"be cut off by fine and recovery" *Maxims of the Law* (1596)[b]	1/3340(0.030%)
4	"The folded meaning of your words deceit" (3.2.36)	(i) {folded near.5 meaning} (ii) {folding up} [context: obscure meaning of words]	"conducing as well to the folding vp, and keeping of things vnder a veil" as well as "And the second (out of the foulds of Poeticall fables) laies open those deep Philosophicall mysteries" *The wisedome of the ancients* (1619)[c]	(i) 0/3340(unique) (ii) 0/3340(unique)
5	"In food, in sport, and life-preseruing rest / To be disturb'd, would mad or man, or beast" (5.184–86)	(i) {sport near.6 sleep} (ii) {exercise near.6 sleep} (iii) {sport near.6 rest} (iv) {exercise near.6 rest}	"To be free minded, and chearefully disposed at howers of meate, and of sleepe, and of exercise, is the best precept of long lasting" *Essayes* (1597)[d]	(i) 0/3340(unique) (ii) 2/3340(0.060%) (iii) 0/3340(unique) (iv) 0/3340(unique)

[a]Translated into English by Sir Gorges Knight (1619), STC: 1130. Sir Gorges was employed by Bacon at this time, so it is a fair assumption that Bacon supervised the translation. Also Anon, *The taming of the shrew* (1594), STC: 23667.
[b]Bacon (1803, IV.115).
[c]Translated into English by Sir Gorges Knight (1619), STC: 1130.
[d]'Of Regiment of Health' Bacon (1597, 9).

Table B.2 RCP results from Google for Francis Bacon when searching *The Comedy of Errors*

No.	*Locution*	*EEBO search*	*Bacon's work*	*Rarity*
1	"hauing so good a meane" (1.2.18)	{so good a mean}	"and where I have so good a mean as Mr. Matthew" letter to Earl of Bristol (1623)[a]	1/3340(0.030%)
2	"voluble and sharpe discourse" (2.1.93)	(i) {voluble and [adjective]} (ii) {[adjective] and voluble}	"No wise speech but easy and voluble" *Promus* wastebook (1592–4)[b]	(i) 3/3340(0.090%) (ii) 2/3340(0.060%)
3	"present satisfaction" (4.1.5)	{present satisfaction}	In 'Valerius Terminus' (1603)	1/3340(0.030%)

[a]Montagu (1850, III.149).
[b]British Library, Harley 7017, f.85, cited in Pott (1883, 117).
[c]British Library, Harley 6462; "Valerius Terminus" (1603), see Spedding *et al.* (1863, VI.25–76).

Table B.3 RCP results from EEBO for Thomas Heywood when searching *The Comedy of Errors*

No.	*Locution*	*EEBO search*	*Heywood's work*	*Rarity*
1	"quit the penalty" (1.1.22)	{quit the penalty}	*The English traueller* (1633)	0/3340(unique)
2	"Ile limit thee" (1.1.149)	{limit thee}	"I limit thee my sight" *A woman kilde* (1607)	0/3340(unique)
3	"doomed to die" (1.1.153)	(i) {doomed to die} (ii) {doomed to}	"doomd to die" *A woman kilde* (1607)	(i) 0/3340(unique) (ii) 2/3340(0.060%)
4	"present satisfaction" (4.1.5)	{present satisfaction}	*Gynaikeion* (1624)[a]	1/3340(0.030%)
5	"stigmatically" (4.2.22)	{stigmatical}	*Gynaikeion* (1624)[b]	4/3340(0.120%)
6	"not a ragge of monie" (4.4.87)	{rag of money}	*The royall king* (1637)	2/3340(0.060%)
7	"loathesome abject scorn" (4.4.104)	{abject scorn}	*The iron age* (1632)	1/3340(0.030%)
8	"A liuing dead man" (5.1.241)	{living dead}	*The first and seconde partes of King Edward the Fourth* (1600)	0/3340(unique)
9	"time's deformed hand" (5.1.298)	{hand of time}	*The iron age* (1632)	0/3340(unique)

[a]Bacon precedes Heywood in its use.
[b]Also used by Henry Crosse, *Vertues Common-wealth* (1603). STC: 6070.5.

Table B.4 RCP results from EEBO for Thomas Nashe when searching *The Comedy of Errors*

No.	*Locution*	*EEBO search*	*Nashe's work*	*Rarity*
1	"put the finger in the eie and weep" (2.2.207)	{finger in the eye}	"and then he puts his finger in his eie, and cries" *Pierce Penilesse* (1592)	3/3340(0.090%)
2	"stigmatically" (4.2.22)	{stigmatical}	*Haue with you to Saffron-walden* (1596)[a]	4/3340(0.120%)
3	"not a ragge of monie" (4.4.87)	{rag of money}	*The apologie of Pierce penilesse* (1592)[b]	2/3340(0.060%)
4	"a huge infectious troope / Of pale distemperatures" (5.1.81–82)	{pale near.5 distemperature(s)}	"discerne the distemperature of their pale clients" *The terrors of the night* (1594)	1/3340(0.030%)

[a]Its second earliest use is by Robert Greene, Menaphon (1589). STC: 12272.
[b]Nashe precedes the use by Thomas Heywood.

Table B.5 RCP results from EEBO for Shakespeare canon when searching *The Comedy of Errors*

No.	*Locution*	*EEBO search*	*Shakespeare work*	*Rarity*
1	"doome of death" (1.1.2)	{doom of death}	*Titus Andronicus* (1594) *Henry the fifth* (1600)	5/3340(0.150%)
2	"makes you to keep unwed" (2.1.26)	{unwed}	*The passionate pilgrime* (1599)	8/3340(0.240%)
3	"He is the ground of my defeatures" (2.1.98–99)	{defeature(s)}	*Venus and Adonis* (1593)	1/3340(0.030%)

have been as a later revision, possibly for the 1604 performance. At this date he would also have a revised play borrowing from him. If there was no later revision (before the *First Folio* editing), then he is only a borrower from the 1594 play.

With three rare locutions before 1595 there is evidence here that the play borrowed from Nashe. No. 2 is evidence that Nashe borrowed from the play, so with weak mutual borrowing, Nashe has a hint of a claim to contribution.

Table B.6 Searchable texts by Francis Bacon in EEBO database[a]

Date	*Title*	*Short title*
1597	*Essayes Religious meditations*	STC: 1137
1599	*A letter written out of England to an English gentleman remaining at Padua*	STC: 10017
1601	*A declaration of the practises & treasons attempted and committed by Robert late Earle of Essex*	STC: 1133
1603	*A briefe discourse, touching the happie vnion of the kingdomes of England, and Scotland*	STC: 1117
1604	*Certaine considerations touching the better pacification, and edification of the Church of England*	STC: 1120
1604	*Sir Francis Bacon his apologie, in certaine imputations concerning the late Earle of Essex*	STC: 1111
1605	*The two bookes of Francis Bacon. Of the proficience and aduancement of learning, diuine and humane To the King*	STC: 1164
1614	*A declaration of the demeanor and cariage of Sir Walter Raleigh*	STC: 20652.5
1619	*The wisedome of the ancients, written in Latine by the Right Honorourable Sir Francis Bacon Knight, Baron of Verulam, and Lord Chancelor of England. Done into English by Sir Arthur Gorges Knight*	STC: 1130
1625	*Apophthegmes new and old*	STC: 1115
1625	*The translation of certaine psalmes into English verse*	STC: 1174
1627	*Sylua syluarum: or A naturall historie In ten centuries.*	STC: 1168
1629	*The historie of the reigne of King Henry the Seuenth*	STC: 1161
1641	*Cases of treason*	Wing: B274
1641	*The confession of faith*	Wing: B280
1641	*Three speeches of the Right Honorable, Sir Francis Bacon Knight [...] Concerning the post-nati naturalization of the Scotch in England union of the lawes of the kingdomes of England and Scotland*	Wing: B337
1642	*An essay of a king*	Wing: B282
1642	*The learned reading of Sir Francis Bacon [...] upon the statute of uses*	Wing: B301
1642	*Ordinances [...] for the better and more regular administration of iustice in the Chancery*	Wing: B316
1648	*The remaines*	Wing: B318
1651	*A true and historical relation of the poysoning of Sir Thomas Overbury*	Wing: T2487
1657	*Resuscitatio, or, Bringing into publick light severall pieces of the works, civil, historical, philosophical, & theological*	Wing: B319
1658	*New Atlantis a work unfinished*	Wing: B307
1661	*A letter of advice written by Sr. Francis Bacon to the Duke of Buckingham*	Wing: B302
1662	*A charge given [...] at a sessions holden for the verge [...] declaring the latitude of the jurisdiction thereof*	Wing: B276
1662	*True peace*	Wing: B339
1669	*Baconiana, or, Certain genuine remains*	Wing: B269

[a]Accessed November 2012.

Notes

1 For the full RCP search results see Clarke (2014, Section 6.5). Search date May 2013.

2 To qualify as a rare locution, the number of returns was set at less than 6/3340(0.180%) of the searchable documents before 1594, the assumed date of the play. If a locution satisfied this condition it was recorded, and the authors who used it both before and after this date were noted.

Selected Bibliography

Bacon, Francis. *Essayes. Religious Meditations.* London: Printed for Humfrey Hooper, 1597. STC: 1137.

Bacon, Francis. "Maxims of the law." In *The Works of Francis Bacon*, 10 vols. London: Printed for J. Johnson and Company, 1803.

Clarke, Barry R. "A linguistic analysis of Francis Bacon's contribution to three Shakespeare plays: *A Comedy of Errors*, *Love's Labour's Lost*, and *The Tempest*." PhD thesis, Brunel University, UK. 2014.

Montagu, Basil, ed. *The Works of Francis Bacon*, 3 vols. Philadelphia: A. Hart, 1850.

Pott, Mrs Henry. *The Promus of Formularies and Elegancies*. Boston: Houghton, Mifflin, & Co, 1883.

Spedding, James, Robert Leslie Ellis, and Douglas Denon Heath, eds. *The Works of Francis Bacon*. 15 vols. Boston: Taggard and Thompson, 1863.

Appendix C
RCP results for *Gesta Grayorum*

Tables of rare returns for Francis Bacon and Richard Knowles are given, the only candidates with at least three rare correspondences.

This section gives the results of a Rare Collocation Profiling (RCP) search with the Early English Books Online (EEBO) database and Google search engine on the *Gesta Grayorum* (c.1595). Every discernible phrase and collocation in the pamphlet is checked with the search engine of the EEBO database to assess its rarity.[1] The ones that are sufficiently rare are recorded. The authors who used these rare phrases in common with it are also recorded—the logging table is given by Clarke (2014, Table 5.2)[2]—and a DNA-type profile constructed for each author in the form of a table. While the EEBO database is used to test the rarity of a locution, a candidate for contribution need not have all their work in EEBO. For example, letters and speeches found elsewhere can be introduced for matching. The main aim is to decide if sufficient evidence exists to argue for a candidate's contribution. For any author with insufficient textual material, nothing can be decided, and any claim to their contribution is untestable. See Table B.6 in Appendix B for a list of Bacon's searchable works in EEBO.

Since Francis Bacon has speeches and letters than do not appear in EEBO then Google searches can be carried out to obtain further matches. Since *a priori*, the matching or non-matching of Bacon's style to the *Gesta* is predetermined, enlarging the number of Bacon texts available for comparison does not provide a greater weight to his claim for contribution. The subsequent absence of matches could just as well add a greater weight to his lack of contribution. In other words, Bacon could either pass or fail the contribution test, and the number of texts will not affect the outcome, only the weight attached to it. A search of his letters and speeches has been made using the Google search engine, then rarity-checked with EEBO, and the result is shown in Table C.2.

We also examine the three rare matches that occur for Richard Knowles, all from his work *The general historie* (1603).

Table C.1 RCP results from EEBO for Francis Bacon when searching the *Gesta Grayorum*

No.	*Locution*	*EEBO search*	*Bacon's work*	*Rarity*
1	"And there took his place in his Throne, under a rich cloth of state" (Commentary: p. 9)	{a rich cloth}	"he was set upon a Low Throne richly adorned, and a rich cloth of State over his head" *Sylua syluarum* (1627)[a]	1/3521(0.028%)
2	"to be deeply bound to their Merits" (Commentary: p. 11)	{deeply bound to}	"so deeply bound to her Maiestie" *A declaration* (1601)[b]	6/3521(0.170%)
3	"make any narrow Observation of His Excellency's Nature and Fashions" (Articles of the Knights of the Order: p. 30)	{narrow observation(s)}	"as men of narrowe obseruation may concyue them" *The two bookes* (1605)[c]	0/3521(unique)
4	"quench appetite" (1st Counsellor's speech: p. 33)	{quench appetite}	"But rather, they [Waters of Parnassus] quench Appetite, and Desires" letter to Earl of Essex (1594–5)[d]	0/3521(unique)
5	"Alexander the Great wrote to Aristotle, upon publishing of the Physicks, that he esteemed more of excellent Men in Knowledge, than in Empire" (2nd Counsellor's speech: p. 34)	(i) {knowledge near.8 empire} ∩ {Aristotle near.10 Alexander} (ii) {Aristotle greeting}	"in his [Alexander's] letter to Aristotle after hee had set forth his Bookes of Nature [...] himselfe esteemed it more to excell other men in learning & knowledge, than in power and Empire" *The two bookes* (1605)[e]	(i) 1/3521(0.028%) (ii) 2/3521(0.057%)
6	"two Lakes adjoining, the one of fresh water, and the other of salt" (2nd Counsellor's speech: p. 35)	{lakes near.10 fresh} ∩ {lakes near.10 salt}	"We haue great Lakes, both Salt and Fresh" *Sylua syluarum* (1627)[f]	1/3521(0.028%)

(Continued)

No.	*Locution*	*EEBO search*	*Bacon's work*	*Rarity*
7	"your Coin be stamped with your own Image" (3rd Counsellor's speech: p. 39)	{be stamped with} [context: 'coin' and 'image' mentioned]	"Coyns of Gold to be stamped with his own Image" 'The charge against William Talbot' (1614)[g]	0/3521(unique)
8	"Constantine the Great was wont to call with Envy the Emperor Trajan, Wallflower, because his Name was upon so many Buildings" (3rd Counsellor's speech: p. 36)	(i) {wallflower} [context: relating to Trajan] (ii) {Constantine near.10 Trajan} [context: relating to wallflower]	"For Traiane erected many famous monuments and buildings, insomuch as Constantine the Great, in emulation was woont to call him Parietaria, Wall flower, because his name was vppon so many walles" *The two bookes* (1605)[h]	(i) 0/3521(unique) (ii) 0/3521(unique)

[a]Francis Bacon, "New Atlantis", *Sylua syluarum* (1627). STC: 1168. Only 4/7607 occurred before 1626.

[b]Francis Bacon, *A declaration* (1601). STC: 1133. Only 8/4149(0.193%) occurred before 1601.

[c]"as men of narrowe obseruation may concyue them" in Francis Bacon, *The Two Bookes* (1605, sig. Ff2), STC: 1164. This is the first use after the *Gesta*.

[d]"But rather, they [Waters of Parnassus] quench Appetite, and Desires", letter to Earl of Essex, in Francis Bacon, *Resuscitatio* (1657, sig. Mmm), Wing: B319. In a marginal note, Dr William Rawley, Bacon's Chaplain, writes "I am enduced by the Stile, and other Characters, to own them, to be his [Bacon's]". James Spedding (1861–74, I.345) dates this letter to the turn of 1594–5. Also "And such Humours as are Light, and Cholericke, which quench Appetite most" in Francis Bacon, *Sylua Syluarum* (1627, p. 117), STC: 1168, a posthumous publication.

[e]Francis Bacon, *The Two Bookes* (1605, sigs K^{v}–K2), STC: 1164. Only 3/4628(0.086%) matches occurred before 1605.

[f]"We haue great Lakes, both Salt and Fresh;" from "New Atlantis" in Francis Bacon, *Sylua syluarum* (1627, 33). STC: 1168. Only 7/7726(0.091%) matches occurred before 1627.

[g]"Coyns of Gold to be stamped with his own Image" in Francis Bacon, *Resuscitatio* (1657), Wing: B319. This was the charge against William Talbot in 1614. Bacon has the first use after the *Gesta*.

[h]Bacon has the first use after the *Gesta*. "For Traiane erected many famous monuments and buildings, insomuch as Constantine the Great, in emulation was woont to call him Parietaria, Wall flower, because his name was vppon so many walles" in Francis Bacon, *The two bookes* (1605, sig. I3^{v}). STC: 1164. EEBO failed to return this entry since the 'e' at the end of 'traiane' had been incorrectly keyed as a 'c' to make 'traianc'.

There is ample evidence here of borrowing from the *Gesta* by Francis Bacon. Some matches, such as No.7 in Table C.1 and Nos. 2, 4, and 5 in Table C.2, are the first use after the *Gesta*'s. Locution No. 4 in Table C.1, and Nos. 1 and 3 in Table C.2, are earlier than 1595, and exhibit a borrowing of the pamphlet from Bacon. This mutual borrowing of rare correspondences argues his contribution. Richard Knowles, who was not a member of Gray's Inn, shows some evidence of borrowing but none of being borrowed from, and so there is insufficient evidence of his contribution (see Table C.3).

Table C.2 RCP results from Google for Francis Bacon when searching the *Gesta Grayorum*

No.	*Locution*	*EEBO search*	*Bacon's work*	*Rarity*
1	"selling of Smoak" (Articles of the Knights of the Order: p. 30)[a]	{sell(ing) smoke} [context: incident in court]	"*Fumos vendere* [To sell smoke]" *Promus* (1592–4)[b]	3/3521(0.085%)
2	"set them the right way to the wrong place" (Prince's opening speech: p. 32)	{right way to the} [context: ... wrong place]	"thereby set themselves in the right way to the wrong place" 'Valerius Terminus, or Of the Interpretation of Nature' (1603)[c]	0/3521(unique)
3	"[Augustus Caesar] I found the City of Brick, but I leave it of Marble" (3rd Counsellor's speech: p. 36)	{city of brick} [context: left it marble]	"as Augustus said, that he had received the city of brick, and lefte it of marble" 'Mr Bacon's discourse in the Praise of his Sovereign' (1592)[d]	0/3521(unique)
4	"with an humor of Innovation and Alteration" (4th Counsellor's speech: p. 37)	{humour of innovation}	"so far are we from any humour of innovation of encroachment" 'Speech touching purveyors' (1604)[e]	0/3521(unique)
5	"Fame is too light" (5th Counsellor's speech: p. 39)	{fame fby.4 light} [context: light of weight]	"Generall fame is light" *The two bookes* (1605)[f]	0/3521(unique)
6	"all suits and vexations, all causeless delays" (5th Counsellor's speech: p. 40)	{vexation(s) near.10 delay(s)}	"abuses of laws by delays, covins, vexations, and corruptions in informers" 'Maxims of the Law' (1596–7)[g]	1/3521(0.028%)
7	"to add Beams of honour" (King at Arms reading letter: p. 45)	{beam(s) of honour}	"it was your grace to illustrate me with beams of honour" 'Letter to King James' (1621)[h]	1/3521(0.028%)
8	"Bulwarke of Christendom" (Russian ambassador's speech: p. 46)	{bulwark of christendom}	"hitherto been the bulwark of Christendom against the approaches of the Turk" 'Draught of a Proclamation for a Parliament' (October 1620)[i]	1/3521(0.028%)

(*Continued*)

No.	Locution	EEBO search	Bacon's work	Rarity
9	"that there be such Sparks of Dissention and Mischief; but if there be, We will make haste to quench them" (Prince's speech: p. 52)	i {sparks of dissention} [context: relating to undesirable behaviour] ii {sparks near.15 quench(ed)(es)(ing)}	"for the quenching of the sparks of troubles and discords in foreign parts" 'Draught of a Proclamation for a Parliament' (October 1620)[j]	i 0/3521 (unique) ii 1/3521 (0.028%)

[a]The Roman Emperor Alexander Severus discovered that his secretary was using his position to promise poor men that he would prosecute their suits, receiving their gifts for no intended return. Severus tied his secretary to a post and choked him with smoke, declaring that "they which sell smoke should so perish with smoke", cited in Pierre de La Primaudaye, *The French Academie* (1586, 411). STC: 15233. Robert Greene repeated the story in *Farewell to folly* (1591).

[b]British Library, Harley 7017, f.85, cited in Pott (1883, 116).

[c]"thereby set themselves in the right way to the wrong place" in Francis Bacon, "Valerius Terminus, or Of the Interpretation of Nature" (1603), in Spedding *et al.* (1863, VI.25–76). British Library, Harley MS 6462. This is not in the searchable EEBO database.

[d]British Library, Harley MS 6797, art.5; James Spedding (1861–74, I.119) dates this to 1592.

[e]Spedding (1861–74, III.183) dates this to 1604, the earliest use after the *Gesta*, and reports taking it from a manuscript copy which has corrections in Bacon's hand, British Library, Harley MS 6769, f.170.

[f]Bacon has the second use after the *Gesta*. It appears to originate with Virgil "one euylie goddesse callyd fame or renomee whiche is more lighte than ony other thynge", Virgil, *Here fynysheth the boke yf [sic] Eneydos* (1490, sig. 43^{v}). STC: 24796.

[g]"Maxims of the Law" in Bacon (1803). The *Oxford Francis Bacon*, Vol. 2, dates this to 1596–7.

[h]Spedding (1861–74, VII.168) estimates the date to be 1621. There are 3/6742(0.044%) occurrences before 1621.

[i]Spedding (1861–74, VII.125). Has a rarity of 4/6574(0.061%) before 1620.

[j]Spedding (1861–74, VII.124).

Table C.3 RCP results from EEBO for Richard Knowles when searching the *Gesta Grayorum*

No.	Locution	EEBO search	Knowles's work	Rarity
1	"memorable Slaughter" (Russian ambassador's speech: p. 46)	{memorable slaughter}	*The generall historie* (1603)	0/3521(unique)
2	"Bulwarke of Christendom" (Russian ambassador's speech: p. 46)	{bulwark of christendom}	*The generall historie* (1603)[a]	1/3521(0.028%)
3	"gallantly Appointed" (Commentary: p. 55)	{gallantly appointed}	*The generall historie* (1603)[b]	2/3521(0.057%)

[a]First known use was Johannes Sleidanus, *A famous chronicle* (1560). STC: 19848A.

[b]The first known appearance is in Raphael Holinshed, *The firste [laste] volume* (1577). STC: 13568b.

Table C.4 RCP results from EEBO for *Love's Labour's Lost* when searching the *Gesta Grayorum*

No.	*Locution*	*EEBO search*	*LLL lines*	*Rarity*
1	"by reason that you shall have discovered their natural causes, your self shall be left the only Miracle and Wonder of the World" (2nd Counsellor's speech: p. 35)	{wonder of the world} [context: a person deciphering Nature]	"Nauar shall be the wonder of the world"[a]	2/3521(0.057%)
2	"What! Nothing but Tasks, nothing but Working-days? No Feasting, no Musick, no Dancing, no Triumphs, no Comedies, no Love, no Ladies?" (6th Counsellor's speech: p. 41)	(i) {tasks near.20 feast(s)(ing)} (ii) {tasks near.20 love} (iii) {tasks near.20 ladies} [context: deprivation of pleasure]	"O these barraine raskes, too hard to keepe, / Not to see Ladyes, study, fast, not sleepe"[b]	i 0/3521(unique) ii 0/3521(unique) iii 0/3521(unique)
3	"I found, my Desire was greater than the Ability of my Body; which by my Journey, and my sickness at Sea, is so weakened" (Prince's letter to Sir Thomas on return from Russia: pp. 54–55)	(i) {seasick(e) near.80 russia} (ii) {"sea sick(e)" near.80 russia} (iii) {"sickness" near.80 russia} (iv) {seasick(e) near.80 muscovy} (v) {"sea sick(e)" near.80 muscovy} (vi) {"sickness(e)" near.80 muscovy}	"why looke you pale? / Sea sicke I think comming from Muscouie"	i 0/3521(unique) ii 0/3521(unique) iii 0/3521(unique) iv 0/3521(unique)[c] v 2/3521(0.057%)[d] vi 0/3521(unique)

[a]The queen is a "wonder of the world" for her governance in John Lyly, *Pappe with an hatchet* (1589). STC: 17463.
[b]Both in quarto and FF.
[c]Added variation 'muscouie' to all 'muscovy' searches.
[d]William Shakespeare, *A Pleasant Conceited Comedie Called Loues Labors Lost* (1598), STC: 22294. Same line as in *FF*.

Notes

1 To qualify as a rare locution, the number of returns was set at less than 6/3340(0.180%) of the searchable documents before 1595, the assumed date of the pamphlet. If a locution satisfies this condition it is recorded and the authors who use it are noted.
2 Search date November 2012.

Selected Bibliography

Bacon, Francis. "Maxims of the Law." In *The Works of Francis Bacon*, 10 vols. London: J. Johnson, W.J. and J. Richardson and others, 1803.

Clarke, Barry R. "A linguistic analysis of Francis Bacon's contribution to three Shakespeare plays: *A Comedy of Errors*, *Love's Labour's Lost*, and *The Tempest*." PhD thesis, Brunel University, UK. 2014.

Pott, Mrs Henry, ed. *The Promus of Formularies and Elegencies.* Boston: Houghton, Mifflin & Co., 1883.

Spedding, James, ed. *The Letters and Life of Francis Bacon.* 7 vols. London: Longman, Green, Longman, and Roberts, 1861–74.

Spedding, James, Robert Leslie Ellis, and Douglas Denon Heath, eds. *The Works of Francis Bacon.* 15 vols. Boston: Taggard and Thompson, 1863.

Appendix D
RCP results for *Love's Labour's Lost*

Tables of rare returns for Francis Bacon, Thomas Dekker, Thomas Heywood, Thomas Nashe, the Shakespeare canon, and the *Gesta Grayorum* are given.

This section gives the results of a Rare Collocation Profiling (RCP) search with the Early English Books Online (EEBO) database and Google search engine on *Love's Labour's Lost* (c.1594). Every discernible phrase and collocation in the play is checked with the search engine of the EEBO database to assess its rarity.[1] The ones that are sufficiently rare are recorded. The authors who used these rare phrases in common with the play are also logged, together with the work it appears in, and a DNA-type profile constructed for each significantly returned author in the form of a table. While the EEBO database is used to test the rarity of a locution, a candidate for contribution need not have all their work in EEBO. For example, letters and speeches found elsewhere can be introduced for matching. The main aim is to decide if sufficient evidence exists to argue for a candidate's contribution. For any author with insufficient textual material, nothing can be decided and any claim to their contribution is untestable. See Table B.6 in Appendix B for a list of Bacon's searchable works in EEBO. The full logging table for *LLL* is given by Clarke (2014, Section 6.5), and shown here are the RCP results for significantly returned authors, extracted from the logging table.[2]

Bacon's letters and speeches have been searched with Google, then rarity-checked in EEBO, and the result is recorded in Table D.2.

The RCP results for Thomas Dekker, Thomas Heywood, Thomas Nashe, and the Shakespeare canon are given below.

Ben Jonson has five rare matches in the searches: "body pine(s)"; {repute near.5 estimation}, {carriage near.5 estimation}, {carriage near.5 bearing}; {trip "and" go}; {silver moon}; and {Promethean fire}. They all follow *LLL*, and although he has the first use of 'Promethean fire' after *LLL*, he follows the other major writers in their use of the others. So he is not a strong candidate for contribution.

Table D.1 RCP results from EEBO for Francis Bacon when searching *Love's Labour's Lost*

No.	*Locution*	*EEBO search*	*Bacon's work*	*Rarity*
1	"Nauar shall be the wonder of the world" (1.1.14)	{wonder of the world}	"by reason that you shall have discovered their natural causes, your self shall be left the only Miracle and Wonder of the World", *Gesta* (c.1595, 35), 2nd Counsellor's speech	2/3340(0.060%)
2	"O, these barren taskes, too hard to keepe, / Not to see Ladies, study, fast, not sleepe" (1.1.49–50)	{tasks near.20 ladies} [context: deprivation of pleasure]	"Nothing but Tasks, nothing but Working-days? No Feasting, no Musick, no Dancing, no Triumphs, no Comedies, no Love, no Ladies?" Gesta (c.1595, 41), 6th Counsellor's speech	0/3340(unique)
3	"a man of good repute, carriage, bearing, & estimation" (1.1.265–66)	(i) {repute near.5 estimation} (ii) {carriage near.5 estimation} (iii) {carriage near.5 bearing} [context: person's quality]	"But howsoeuer succeeded, by a moderate Carriage and bearing the Person of a Common-friend" *The historie of the reigne of King Henry the Seuenth* (published 1629, completed October 1621)[a]	(i) 0/3340(unique) (ii) 0/3340(unique) (iii) 0/3340(unique)
4	"I my continent of beauty" (4.1.110)	{continent of} [context: human characteristic]	"it [knowledge] is but a portion of Naturall Philosophy in the continent of Nature", *The two bookes* (1605)[b]	0/3340(unique)
5	"Like Muscovites, or Russians" (5.2.121) [not in quarto 1598]	(i) {russians near.5 muscovites} (ii) {russia near.5 muscovy}	"Emperor of Russia and Moscovy", Gesta (c.1595, 44)	(i) 4/3340(0.120%) (ii) 0/3340(unique)
6	"why looke you pale? / Sea-sicke I thinke comming from Muscouie" (5.2.393)	(i) {seasick(e) near.80 muscovy} (ii) {"sea sick(e)" near.80 muscovy}	"I found, my Desire was greater than the Ability of my Body; which by my Journey, and my sickness at Sea, is so weakened", Gesta (c.1595, 54–55)	(i) 0/3340(unique) (ii) 0/3340(unique)

[a]The rarity before 1622 is 4/6921(0.058%).

[b]Also "For as they [strumpets] are a painted continent of flatterie", Henry Crosse, *Vertues Common-wealth* (1603), STC: 6070.5. This reinforces the connection of Bacon to the *Vertues* pamphlet, although Bacon follows Crosse's use. Only 7/5268(0.133%) cases were returned before 1610.

Table D.2 RCP results from Google for Francis Bacon when searching *Love's Labour's Lost*

No.	*Locution*	*EEBO search*	*Bacon's work*	*Rarity*
1	"sweet and voluble" (2.1.76)	(i) {sweet "and" voluble} (ii) {voluble and [adjective]} (iii) {[adjective] and voluble}	"No wise speech but easy and voluble" *Promus* wastebook (1592–4)[a]	(i) 0/3340(unique) (ii) 3/3340(0.090%) (iii) 2/3340(0.060%)
2	"Follie in Fooles beares not so strong a note, As fool'ry in the Wise, when Wit doth dote" (5.2.75–76) [not in quarto]	{folly near.15 fool(s)} ∩ {folly near.15 wise}[b]	"Hence a little folly in a very wise Man [...] detracts greatly from their character and reputation" *De Augmentis Scientiarum* (1623)[c]	(114/3340) ∩ (214/3340) = 0/3340(unique)
3	"Thou now requests but Mooneshine in the water" (5.2.208)	{moonshine in the water}	"For the moonshyne in the water" *Promus* wastebook (1592–4)[d]	9/3340(0.269%)[e]
4	"I see the tricke on't" (5.2.460)	(i) {trick on it} (ii) {put(ting) trick(s) upon}	"Some build rather vpon abusing others, and as wee now say, putting trickes vpon them" *The Essaies* (1612)[e]	(i) 0/3340(unique) (ii) 0/3340(unique)
5	"You leere vpon me, do you? There's an eie / Wounds like a leaden sword" (5.2.481)	{leaden sword} [context: injure with it]	"Plumbeo jugulare gladio [to kill with a leaden sword]" *Promus* wastebook (1592–4)[f]	1/3340(0.030%)
6	"Behold the window of my heart, mine eie" (5.2.827)	{window fby.3 heart(s)}	"Your Majesty shall obtain the curious window into hearts of which the ancients speak" 'Device of an Indian Prince' (November 1595)[g]	1/3340(0.030%)

[a] British Library, Harley 7017, f.85, cited in Pott (1883, 117).

[b] Here, the intersection operator '∩' indicates shared returns between the two searches. In the present case, none were shared.

[c] Translated from Latin, but the sense should not be lost. Francis Bacon quotes a parable of Solomon from Ecclesiates 10:1, "As dead flies do cause the best ointment to stink; so doth a little Folly him that is in reputation for wisdom and honour", and explains, "Hence a little folly in a very wise Man [...] detracts greatly from their character and reputation"; see Francis Bacon, *De Augmentis Scientiarum* (1623; Chapter 2, No. XI), see Spedding *et al.* (1864, IX.246). Not in the 1598 quarto of *Love's Labour's Lost.*

[d] Pott (1883, 247).

[e] Slightly outside the rarity limit.

[f] Francis Bacon, *The essaies* (1612, sig. C), STC: 1141, which is not keyed-in text in EEBO but only in digital image (May 2013). Also in *The Tempest* (2.2.57–58) we have "Doe you put trickes vpon's with Saluages". The rarity before 1612 is 1/5471(0.018%).

[g] See Pott (1883, 264). The only precedent that indicates injury with the sword is "you had with this your leadden sweard killed God haue mercie on his sowle" in Jerónimo Orsório, *A learned and very eloquent treatie* [sic] (1568), STC: 18889, trans. from Latin by Iohn Fen.

Table D.3 RCP results from EEBO for Thomas Dekker when searching *Love's Labour's Lost*

No.	*Locution*	*EEBO search*	*Dekker's work*	*Rarity*
1	"wholesome Physicke" (1.1.228–29)	{wholesome physic}	"Plies me with wholesome Physic" *The whore of Babylon* (1607)	2/3340(0.060%)
2	"the dancing horse will tell you" (1.2.53)	{the dancing horse}	*The Owles almanacke* (1618)	0/3340(unique)
3	"A whitly wanton with a velvet brow" (3.1.193)	{velvet brow}	"by the veluet brow of darknes" *Blurt master-constable* (1602)	0/3340(unique)
4	"Trip and go my sweete, deliuer this Paper into the hands of the King" (4.2.139)	{trip "and" go}	*Shomakers' holiday* (1600)[a]	3/3340(0.090%)
5	"Nor shines the siluer Moone" (4.3.28)	{silver moon}	*The magnificent entertainment giuen to King Iames* (1604)[b]	2/3340(0.060%)
6	"Promethean fire" (4.3.327) [not in quarto 1598]	{Promethean fire}	*The Owles almanacke* (1618)[c]	0/3340(unique)
7	"White handed Mistris" (5.2.230)	{white handed}	"white-handed fate" *Britannia's honour* (1628)	0/3340(unique)
8	"To dash [spoil] it like a Christmas Comedie" (5.2.462)	{to dash it}	"first inuented the manner how to dash it out of the igniferous flint" *The Owles almanacke* (1618)[d]	0/3340(unique)
9	"Not so my Lord, a tweluemonth and a day" (5.2.816)	{twelvemonth and a day}	*The wonderfull yeare* (1603)[f]	0/3340(unique)

[a]Spedding (1861–74, I.390).
[b]Thomas Nashe has prior use in *The apologie of Pierce Pennilesse* (1592). 'Alice trip and go' was a character in Titus Maccius Plautus, *An enterlude for children to play named Iack Iugler* (1570), STC: 14837a.5.
[c]Dekker is the first dramatist to use this after *LLL*.
[d]Ben Jonson, *The characters of two royall masques* (1608) and Thomas Heywood, *The brazen age* (1613) precede him.
[e]The only major writer to use this outside *LLL*.
[f]Again the only major writer to use this outside *LLL*.

Table D.4 RCP results from EEBO for Thomas Heywood when searching *Love's Labour's Lost*

No.	*Locution*	*EEBO search*	*Heywood's work*	*Rarity*
1	"though the body pine" (1.1.25)	{body pine(s)}	"Come, patience, then; and though my body pine" *Edward IV, Part 2* (1600)[a]	1/3340(0.030%)
2	"dutie prickes me on" (1.1.256)	{pricks me on}	*A woman kilde in kindnesse* (1607)[b]	3/3340(0.090%)
3	"the meed of punishment" (1.1.257)	{the meed of}	"Whilst Bess has gold, which is the meed of bays" *The fair maid of the west, Part II* (c.1630)	5/3340(0.150%)
4	"a light wench" (1.2.117–18)	{light wench}	"you take her for a light wench" *The second part of, if you know not me* (1606)[c]	0/3340(unique)
5	"Promethean fire" (4.3.327) [not in quarto 1598]	{Promethean fire}	"Have borrowed lustre and Promethean fire" *The Golden Age* (1611)	0/3340(unique)
6	"White handed Mistris" (5.2.230)	{white handed}	"Tell us, who shall untie the virgin zone of the white-handed Psyche" *Love's Mistress or the Queens Masque* (1636)	0/3340(unique)
7	"Faith vnlesse you play the honest Troyan" (5.2.672)	{play the honest}	"Will you play the honest man" *Pleasant dialogues* (1637)	2/3340(0.060%)
8	"There stay, vntill the twelve Celestiall Signes / Haue brought about their anuall reckoning" (5.2.792–93)	{twelve celestial signs}	"By the sagitarry, which is one of the 12 celestial signs" *The Life of Merlin* (1641)	2/3340(0.060%)
9	"Change not your offer made in the heate of blood" (5.2.795)	{heat of blood}	"Forgive me, God, t'was in the heat of blood" *A woman kilde in kindnesse* (1607)[d]	3/3340(0.090%)

[a]There are only 3/4017(0.075%) examples before 1600.
[b]There are only 7/4877(0.144%) examples before 1607.
[c]There is only 1/4746(0.021%) example before 1606.
[d]There are 11/4877(0.226%) examples before 1607.

Table D.5 RCP results from EEBO for Thomas Nashe when searching *Love's Labour's Lost*

No.	*Locution*	*EEBO search*	*Nashe's work*	*Rarity*
1	"Small haue continuall plodders euer wonne, / Saue base authoritie from others Bookes" (1.1.86)	{plodders} [context: unimaginative writers]	"Grosse plodders they were all, that had some learning and reading, but no wit to make vse of it" *The vnfortunate traueller* (1594)	2/3340(0.060%)
2	"I my continent of beauty" (4.1.110)	{continent of} [context: human characteristic]	"the second continent of Delicacy, which is Lust, or Luxury" *Christs teares ouer Ierusalem* (c.1593, published 1613)	1/3340(0.030%)
3	"*facile procor gellida, quando pecas omnia sub vmbraminat*" (4.2.92)[a]	{praecor/precor/procor gellida/gelida}	"[Gabriel Harvey] verdits Pierce Pennilesse for a Grammer Schoole wit; saies his Margine is as deeplie learnd as Faust praecor gelida" *The apologie of Pierce Pennilesse* (1592)[b]	4/3340(0.120%)
4	"Trip and go my sweete, deliuer this Paper into the hands of the King" (4.2.139)	{trip "and" go}	"shalt not breath a wit, trip and goe, turne ouer" *The apologie of Pierce Pennilesse* (1592)	3/3340(0.090%)
5	"Nip not the gaudie blossomes of your Loue" (5.2.797)	{gaudy blossoms}	"be-deck it with gaudy blossoms" *Christs teares ouer Ierusalem* (c.1593, published 1613)[c]	2/3340(0.060%)

[a] Earliest return is "Vt Mantuan. [line break] Fauste, precor, gelida, quádo pec omne sub vmbra ruminat" under "Chewe the cudde" in Richard Huloet, *Huloets dictionarie* (1572), STC: 13941.

[b] It is a response to "for his margine is as deeplie learned, as *Fauste precor gelida*", which is aimed at Thomas Nashe in Gabriel Harvey, *Foure letters, and certaine sonnets especially touching Robert Greene, and other parties, by him abused* (1592), STC: 12900.5.

[c] Nashe used this about the same time as Drayton, "Thy gaudy Blossomes blemished with colde" Michael Drayton, *Idea the shepheards* (1593), STC: 7202.

Table D.6 RCP results from EEBO for the Shakespeare canon when searching *Love's Labour's Lost*

No.	*Locution*	*EEBO search*	*Shakespeare work*	*Rarity*
1	"dutie prickes me on" (1.1.256)	{pricks me on}	"honor prickes me on" *The history of Henrie the Fourth* (1598) "My dutie pricks me on" *The Two Gentlemen of Verona* (1623)	3/3340(0.090%)
2	"good luster of conceit" (4.2.86)	{luster of}	"the luster of the better" *The historie of Troylus and Cresseida* (1609)	3/3340(0.090%)
3	"pauca verba" (4.2.162)	{pauca verba} [context: inserted in English text]	"Pauca verba, Sir John" *The Merry Wives of Windsor* (1623)[a]	0/3340(unique)
4	"Nor shines the siluer Moone" (4.3.28)	{silver moon}	"the clowd that hides the siluer Moon" *Lucrece* (1594)	2/3340(0.060%)
5	"Ah you whoreson loggerhead" (4.3.202)	{loggerhead}	"Well goe thy way, thou shalt be logger head" *Romeo and Juliet* (1597)[b]	0/3340(unique)
6	"Follie in Fooles beares not so strong a note, As fool'ry in the Wise, when Wit doth dote" (5.2.75–76) [not in quarto]	{folly near.15 fool(s)} ∩ {folly near.15 wise}	"For folly that he wisely shows is fit; / But wise men, folly fall'n, quite taint their wit". *Twelfth Night* (1623)	(114/3340) ∩ (214/3340) = 0/3340(unique)
7	"Change not your offer made in the heate of blood" (5.2.795)	{heat of blood}	*The historie of Henrie the Fourth* (1598)	3/3340(0.090%)
8	"To moue wilde laughter in the throate of death?" (5.2.844)	{throat of death}	"Seeking for Richmond in the throat of death" *The Tragedy of Richard the Third* (1623)	0/3340(unique)

[a]The first quarto (1602) has "Good vrdes sir Iohn, good vrdes".
[b]Robert Greene has the first known use, "And to loggerhead your son, I giue a wandering life" in Robert Greene, *The Scottish Historie of Iames the Fourth* (1598), STC: 12308.

Table D.7 (Identical to Table C.4) RCP results from EEBO for the *Gesta Grayorum* when searching *Love's Labour's Lost*

No.	*Locution*	*EEBO search*	*LLL lines*	*Rarity*
1	"by reason that you shall have discovered their natural causes, your self shall be left the only Miracle and Wonder of the World" (2nd Counsellor's speech: p. 35)	{wonder of the world}[context: a person deciphering Nature]	"Nauar shall be the wonder of the world"[a]	2/3521(0.057%)
2	"What! Nothing but Tasks, nothing but Working-days? No Feasting, no Musick, no Dancing, no Triumphs, no Comedies, no Love, no Ladies?" (6th Counsellor's speech: p. 41)	(i) {tasks near.20 feast(s)(ing)} (ii) {tasks near.20 love} (iii) {tasks near.20 ladies} [context: deprivation of pleasure]	"O these barraine raskes, too hard to keepe, / Not to see Ladyes, study, fast, not sleepe"[b]	(i) 0/3521(unique) (ii) 0/3521(unique) (iii) 0/3521(unique)
3	"I found, my Desire was greater than the Ability of my Body; which by my Journey, and my sickness at Sea, is so weakened" (Prince's letter to Sir Thomas on return from Russia: pp. 54–55)	(i) {seasick(e) near.80 russia} (ii) {sea sick(e) near.80 russia} (iii) {sickness near.80 russia} (iv) {seasick(e) near.80 muscovy} (v) {sea sick(e) near.80 muscovy} (vi) {sickness(e) near.80 muscovy}	"why looke you pale? / Sea sicke I think comming from Muscouie"	(i) 0/3521(unique) (ii) 0/3521(unique) (iii) 0/3521(unique) (iv) 0/3521(unique)[c] (v) 2/3521(0.057%)[d] (vi) 0/3521(unique)

[a] The queen is "wonder of the world" for her governance, in John Lyly, *Pappe with an hatchet* (1589), STC: 17463.
[b] Both in quarto and FF.
[c] Added variation 'muscouie' to all 'muscovy' searches in EEBO.
[d] William Shakespeare, *A pleasant conceited comedie called, Loues labors lost* (1598), STC: 22294. Same line as in *FF*.

Notes

1 To qualify as a rare locution, the number of returns was set at less than 6/3340(0.180%) of the searchable documents before 1594, the assumed date of the play.
2 Search date May 2013.

Selected Bibliography

Clarke, Barry R. "A linguistic analysis of Francis Bacon's contribution to three Shakespeare plays: *A Comedy of Errors*, *Love's Labour's Lost*, and *The Tempest*." PhD thesis. Brunel University, UK. 2014.

Gesta Grayorum: Or the History of the High and Mighty Prince, Henry. London: Printed for W. Canning, 1688.

Pott, Mrs Henry, ed. *The Promus of Formularies and Elegencies.* Boston: Houghton, Mifflin & Co., 1883.

Spedding, James, ed. *The Letters and Life of Francis Bacon.* 7 vols. London: Longman, Green, Longman, and Roberts, 1861–74.

Spedding, James, Robert Leslie Ellis, and Douglas Denon Heath, eds. *The Works of Francis Bacon.* 15 vols. Boston: Taggard and Thompson, 1864.

Appendix E
RCP results for *Twelfth Night*

Tables of rare returns for Francis Bacon, George Chapman, Thomas Heywood, Ben Jonson, and the Shakespeare canon are given.

This section gives the results of a Rare Collocation Profiling (RCP) search with the Early English Books Online (EEBO) database and Google search engine on *Twelfth Night* (c.1602).[1] Every discernible phrase and collocation in the play is checked with the search engine of the EEBO database to assess its rarity.[2] The ones that are sufficiently rare are recorded. The authors who used these rare phrases both before and after the assumed date are logged, and a DNA-type profile is constructed for each author in the form of a table.

Table E.1 RCP results from EEBO for Francis Bacon when searching *Twelfth Night*

No.	*Locution*	*EEBO search*	*Bacon's work*	*Rarity*
1	"[our fancies] … sooner lost and worne" (2.4.39)	{lost "and" worn}	"some to reduce the ancient liberties and customs pretended to be lost and worn out" 'Speech at the trial of Earl of Essex' (1600–1601)[a]	3/4233(0.071%)[b]
2	"that that is, is" (4.2.15)	{that that is is}	"There is little friendship in the worlde […] That that is, is betweene superiour and inferiour" 'Of followers and friends' *Essayes* (1597)[c]	1/4233(0.024%)

[a]Spedding (1861–74, II.225). Spedding states that he obtained a MS report of the trial from one John Tollemach of Helmingham Hall, Suffolk, and Bacon's speech seems to have been available to the reporter at the trial (1861–74, II.218).
[b]First use is recorded as "yet were your labor lost and worne" Thomas Sternhold, *The Whole Booke of Psalmes* (1562), STC: 2430.
[c]Bacon has the first use.

Since Francis Bacon has speeches and letters that do not appear in EEBO, then Google searches can be carried out to obtain further matches. A search of his letters and speeches using Google has been rarity-checked in EEBO, and the result is logged in Table E.2.

So, from Tables E.1 and E.2, Francis Bacon has four rare matches before 1602, which is evidence of the play borrowing from him, and two after, which is evidence of him borrowing from the play. This serves as

Table E.2 RCP results from Google for Francis Bacon when searching *Twelfth Night*

No.	*Locution*	*EEBO search*	*Bacon's work*	*Rarity*
1	"shee bore a minde that enuy could not but call faire" (2.2.28)	{bore a mind}	"I ever bore a mind to serve her Majesty in some middle Place" 'Letter to Lord Burghley' (1591)[a]	3/4233(0.071%)[b]
2	"*Deliculo surgere*, thou know'st" (2.3.2)	{deliculo/ diliculo surgere}	"Diluculo surgere saluberrimum est" *Promus* wastebook (c.1592–4)[c]	1/4233(0.024%)
3	"For folly that he wisely shewes, is fit; / But wisemens folly falne, quite taint their wit" (3.1.68–69)	{wise man/ men/mens near.6 folly}	"Hence a little folly in a very wise Man [...] detracts greatly from their character and reputation" *De Augmentis Scientiarum* (1623)[d]	2/4233(0.047%)
4	"My matter hath no voice, Lady" (3.1.90)	{hath no voice}	"yet hath no voice in the parliament of England" 'Case of the Post-Nati of Scotland' (1606–7)[e]	5/4233(0.118%)

[a] Shaw (1733, I.413–14).

[b] Three returns from EEBO before 1602, the first being "he bore a minde farre estraunged to" Francesco Guicciardini, *The historie of Guicciardin*, 1579, STC: 12458a. Bacon has the second known use (not available in EEBO), followed by "She bore a mind more haughtie than" William Warner, *Albions England* (1597), STC: 25082a.

[c] Bacon's version appears to have been sourced from its first known use as "Diluculò surgere saluberrimum est, To arise betime in the morning is the most wholesome thing in the world" from 'The first Concord' of 'The Concordes of Latine Speech' in William Lily, *A short introduction to grammar* (1549), STC: 15611 (not searchable in EEBO).

[d] Translated from Latin, but the sense should not be lost. Francis Bacon quotes a parable of Solomon from Ecclesiates 10:1 "As dead flies do cause the best ointment to stink; so doth a little Folly him that is in reputation for wisdom and honour" and explains "Hence a little folly in a very wise Man [...] detracts greatly from their character and reputation"; see Francis Bacon, *De Augmentis Scientiarum* (1623; Chapter 2, No. XI), see Spedding *et al.* (1864, IX.246). This also appears in *Love's Labour's Lost*, see Table D.2, No.2 (*FF* only).

[e] Spedding *et al.* (1857–82, XV.208), also see British Library, King's MSS 17A. LVI. p. 262, corrected by Bacon.

evidence of a contribution. If there was an earlier version for the 1597–8 Middle Temple revels, Bacon would then have two before and four after, which is still evidence of a contribution.

With all Chapman's correspondences occurring after 1602 he cannot be taken as a contributor to the Inns of Court versions, only a borrower.

We note that Table E.4, No. 4 "A solemne combination shall be made" (5.1) appears in "Princes to joyne in a solemn combination" *The rat trap* (1641) which EEBO unverifiably attributes to Heywood. Either way, all Heywood's correspondences follow the play so that all that might be claimed is that he used it as a source. Ben Jonson has 22 verifiable works in the EEBO database, and Table E.5 sets out his profile.

Here with three locutions from 1600 to 1602 and one later, Jonson could only have borrowed from a 1597–8 version of the play, and he has a weak case for contribution to a 1602 version. The fact that it was

Table E.3 RCP results from EEBO for George Chapman when searching *Twelfth Night*

No.	*Locution*	*EEBO search*	*Chapman's work*	*Rarity*
1	"vnfriended" (3.3.10)	{unfriended}	"as to cast your selfe vnacquainted, vnfriended, vncommended [...]" *Two wise men* (1619)	5/4233(0.118%)[a]
2	"giues him out to be of good capacity, and breeding" (3.4.194)	{good breeding}	"not gentlemen of good breeding" Two *wise men* (1619)	3/4233(0.071%)[b]
3	"that that is, is" (4.2.15)	{that that is is}	"That, that is, is in lawyers they ingrosse all" *Monsieur D'Olive* (1606)	1/4233(0.024%)[c]
4	*"that's all one" (5.1.206)*	*{that's all one}*	*Bussy d'Ambois (1607)*	*2/4233(0.047%)[d]*

[a]First returned use is Raphael Holinshed, *The first [laste] volume of the chronicles* (1577), STC: 13568b.
[b]First return is Edward Daunce, *A briefe discourse* (1590), STC: 6291.
[c]Bacon has first use. There are only eight returns before 1690.
[d]Ben Jonson, *Euery man out of his humor* (1600), STC: 14767. It also appears in Shakespeare's *Love's Labour's Lost*, published in quarto in 1598, as well as in five other Shakespeare plays. Michel de Montaigne has it in *Essays* (1613), STC: 18042, which was first translated into English in 1603 by John Florio.

Table E.4 RCP results from EEBO for Thomas Heywood when searching *Twelfth Night*

No.	*Locution*	*EEBO search*	*Heywood's work*	*Rarity*
1	"Good night, Penthisilea" (2.3.175)	{Penthisilea}[a]	"Penthisilea Queene of Amazons" *The Iron Age* (1632)	24/4233(0.567%)[b]
2	"and his incensement" (3.4.246)	{incensement}	"We engage our own dear love 'twixt his incensement" *The Rape of Lucrece* (1608)	1/4233(0.024%)
3	"that's all one" (5.1.206)	{that's all one} [context: not 'that is']	*If you know not me* (1605) *The fayre mayde* (1607)	2/4233(0.047%)
4	"A solemne combination shall be made" (5.1.382)	{solemn combination}	"Princes to joyne in a solemn combination" *The rat trap* (1641)	0/4233(unique)

[a]Spelling variations: 'penthisilia', 'penthesilia', 'penthesilea'.
[b]Outside the limit of rarity but of interest for its connection to the 1597–8 Middle Temple revels (*Le Prince d'Amour* 1660).

Table E.5 RCP results from EEBO for Ben Jonson when searching *Twelfth Night*

No.	*Locution*	*EEBO search*	*Jonson's work*	*Rarity*
1	"She's nothing ally'd to your disorders" (2.3.97)	{not/nothing allied to}	"I am not allied to the sculler yet" *Bartholomew Fair* (performed 1614)	3/4233(0.071%)[a]
2	"what you would are out of my welkin, I might say Element, but the word is ouer-worne" (3.1.59)	{out of my/his/ our element}	"out of his element I feare" *The fountaine of selfe-loue* (1601)[b]	3/4233(0.071%)
3	"Vnder your hard construction must I sit" (3.1.119)	{hard construction}	"you feare 'twill [last Scene] be rackt by some hard Construction" *The comicall satyre of euery man out of his humour* (1600)	2/4233(0.047%)
4	"that's all one" (5.1.206)	{that's all one} [context: not 'that is']	*The comicall satyre of euery man out of his humour* (1600)	2/4233(0.047%)[c]

[a]Earliest return is "we are not allyed to throne", Thucydides, *The history* (1550), STC: 24056.
[b]This was such a characteristic locution of Jonson's that it was lampooned by Dekker "tis out of his Element", Thomas Dekker, *Satiro-mastix* (1602), STC: 6521, spoken by Horace who represents Ben Jonson.
[c]First returned use is Thomas Storer, *The Life and Death of Thomas Wolsey Cardinall* (1599), STC: 23294.

enacted at an Inns of Court weighs against him. However, if he edited the *First Folio* (1623), it would have given him an opportunity to contribute to the only version that survives.

In case anyone should interpret Table E.6 as evidence of Shakspere's contribution, the assumption cannot be made that these texts are entirely his, for that is a conjecture that is itself in need of test. Without any independent prose works or letters for Shakspere, the extent of his contribution cannot be ascertained.

Table E.6 RCP results from EEBO for the Shakespeare canon when searching *Twelfth Night*

No.	*Locution*	*EEBO search*	*Shakespeare work*	*Rarity*
1	"For folly that he wisely shewes, is fit; / But wisemens folly falne, quite taint their wit" (3.1.68–69)	{wise man/ men/mens near.6 folly}	"the Wise mans folly is anathomized" *As You Like It* (c.1599)	2/4233(0.047%)
2	"vnfriended" (3.3.10)	{unfriended}	"those infirmities she owes, vnfriended" *King Lear* (1608)	5/4233(0.118%)
3	"giues him out to be of good capacity, and breeding" (3.4.194)	{good breeding}	"may complaine of good breeding" *As You Like It* (1623)	3/4233(0.071%)
4	"they haue heere propertied me" (4.2.96)	{propertied}	"His voice was propertied" *Anthonie and Cleopatra* (1623)	0/4233(unique)
5	"From the rude seas enrag'd" (5.1.76)	{rude sea(s)}	*The tragedie of King Richard the second* (1597) *A midsommer nights dreame* (c.1595)	3/4233(0.071%)
6	"that's all one" (5.1.206)	{that's all one} [context: not 'that is']	*As You Like it* (c.1599) *Love's Labour's Lost* (c.1594) *Merry Wives of Windsor* (c.1600), *A midsommer nights dreame* (c.1595), *Taming of the Shrew* (c.1593), *Two Gentlemen of Verona* (c.1594)	2/4233(0.047%)

Notes

1 The logging table was not included in the PhD thesis and the RCP profiles of the significantly returned authors appear here for the first time. Search date February 2013. The Google returns are checked for rarity with EEBO.
2 To qualify as a rare locution, the number of returns was set at less than 6/4233(0.142%) of the searchable documents before 1602, the assumed date of the play. If a locution satisfied this condition it was recorded and the authors who used it were noted.

Selected Bibliography

Le Prince d'Amour, or the Prince of Love. With a collection of several ingenious Poems and Songs. By the Wits of the Age. London: Printed for William Leake, 1660.

Pott, Mrs Henry, ed. *The Promus of Formularies and Elegencies.* Boston: Houghton, Mifflin & Co., 1883.

Shaw, Peter, ed. *The Philosophical Works of Francis Bacon*, 3 vols. London: Printed for J. J. and P. Knapton [etc.], 1733.

Spedding, James, ed. *The Letters and Life of Francis Bacon.* 7 vols. London: Longman, Green, Longman, and Roberts, 1861–74.

Spedding, James, Robert Leslie Ellis, and Douglas Denon Heath, eds. *The Works of Francis Bacon.* 15 vols. Boston: Houghton, Mifflin, 1857–82.

Spedding, James, Robert Leslie Ellis, and Douglas Denon Heath, eds. *The Works of Francis Bacon.* 15 vols. Boston: Taggard and Thompson, 1864.

Appendix F
RCP results for *The Tempest*

Tables of rare returns for Francis Bacon are given. Thomas Heywood registers three rare returns after 1612, and Ben Jonson has three before. No other candidates emerge.

This section gives the results of a Rare Collocation Profiling (RCP) search with the Early English Books Online (EEBO) database and Google search engine on *The Tempest* (c.1611). There are 5377 searchable texts available in EEBO before 1611. Every discernible phrase and collocation in the play is checked with the search engine of the EEBO database to assess its rarity.[1] The ones that are sufficiently rare are recorded. The authors who used these rare phrases both before and after the assumed date are logged—see Clarke (2014, Table 7.1)[2]—and a DNA-type profile constructed for each author in the form of a table. These RCP tables are presented below.

There is also "in some passion" (4.1.144) which Bacon has in an apophthegm about a citizen of London, but James Spedding raises doubt as to its authenticity by listing it as 'spurious'.[3] Here there are six correspondences that follow the play and three before it, which serves as evidence of mutual borrowing and hence Bacon's contribution.

A search of Bacon's letters and speeches has been made using the Google search engine, with its returns checked for rarity in EEBO and the result is presented in Table F.2.

This gives a further three correspondences after the play, making a total of three before and nine that follow. This is strong evidence of Bacon's contribution.

The only others to register at least three rare returns are Thomas Heywood, who has three after 1612, and Ben Jonson, who has three before. Neither return constitutes evidence of mutual borrowing.[4]

Table F.1 RCP results from EEBO for Francis Bacon when searching *The Tempest*

No.	*Locution*	*EEBO search*	*Bacon's work*	*Rarity*
1	"that now he was / The Iuy which had hid my princely Trunck, / And suckt my verdure [health] out on't" (1.2.86–87)	(i) {ivy near.10 death} (ii) {ivy near.10 destroy(ing)(s)} (iii) {ivy near.10 kill} (iv) {ivy near.10 strangle(s)(ed)(ing)} (v) {ivy near.10 sucked}	"But it was ordained, that this Winding-Iuie of a PLANTAGANET, should kill the true *Tree* it selfe" *The historie of the reigne of King Henry the Seuenth* (October 1621, published 1629, 176)[a]	(i) 1/5377(0.019%)[b] (ii) 0/5377(unique) (iii) 0/5377(unique) (iv) 0/5377(unique) (v) 0/5377(unique)
2	"Like one / Who hauing into truth, by telling of it, / Made such a synner of his memorie / To credite his owne lie, he did beleeue / He was indeed the Duke, out o' th' Substitution / And executing th' outward face of Roialtie / With all prerogatiue" (1.2.99–105)	(i) {warbeck near.20 duke} [context: self-deception by repetition] (ii) {indeed fby.2 duke} [context: "he was indeed"]	"Insomuch as it was generally beleeued (aswell amongst great Persons, as amongst the *Vulgar*) that he was indeed *Duke* Richard. Nay, himselfe, with long and continuall countefeiting , and with oft telling a Lye, was turned by habit almost into the thing hee seemed to bee; and from a *Lyer* to a *Beleeuer*" *The historie of the reigne of King Henry the Seuenth* (October 1621, published 1629, 111)[c]	(i) 0/5377(unique) (ii) 0/5377(unique)
3	"To haue no schreene between this part he plaid, / And him he plaid it for" (1.2.107–8)	{screen(s)(es)(e) or skreen(s)(es)(e)} [context: person is a screen]	"For by that meanes, there be so many Skreenes betweene him [great person], and Enuy" 'Of envy' *Essayes or Counsels, Ciuill and Morall* (1625, 46)[d]	0/5377(unique)

(*Continued*)

No.	*Locution*	*EEBO search*	*Bacon's work*	*Rarity*
4	"vnwholesome fen" (1.2.322)	(i) {unwholesome fen} (ii) {unwholesome near.15 marish}	"It hath beene a great Endangering, to the Health of some Plantations, that haue built along the Sea, and Riuers, in marish and vnwholesome Grounds" 'Of Plantations' *Essayes or Counsels, Civill and Morall* (1625)[e]	(i) 0/5377(unique) (ii) 3/5377(0.056%)[f]
5	"print of goodnesse" (1.2.352)	{print of good(ness)}	"hath the print of Good" *The two bookes* (1605)	2/5377(0.037%)[g]
6	"beyond credit" (2.1.59–60)	{beyond credit}	'Considerations Touching a War with Spain' *Certain miscellany work* (1624, published 1670)	5/5377(0.093%)[h]
7	"For else his proiect dies" (2.1.299)	{his project}	"For, if his project had taken effect" *A declaration of the practises* [Earl of Essex] (1601)	10/5377(0.186%)[i]
8	"The Mistris which I serue, quickens what's dead" (3.1.6)	{quickens near.4 dead/life/ alive} [context: restoration]	"Secrecie in Sutes is a great meanes of obtaining, for voicing them to bee in forwardnes may discourage some kind of suters, but doth quicken and awake others" 'Of Suitors' *Essayes* (1597)[j]	5/5377(0.093%)
9	"Who would beleeue that there were Mountayneeres, / Dew-lapt, like Buls whose throats had hanging at 'em / Wallets of flesh?" (3.3.57–59)	{mountains/mountaineers near.20 throats} [context: hanging flesh]	"Snow-water is held vnwholesome; In so much as the people who dwell at the Foot of the Snow Mountaines, or otherwise vpon the Ascent, (especially the Women) by drinking of Snow-water, haue great Bagges hanging vnder their Throats" *Sylua syluarum* (1627)[l]	2/5377(0.037%)[k]

[a]Returned from EEBO by (iii) from Bacon's *Henry the Seuenth* (1629). Spedding *et al.* (1857–1874, VI.139) knew of this connection.
[b]"like iuie [ivy] so long it [Rome] hath embraced, that it hath eaten vp whole Monarchies", Thomas Ireland, *The oath of allegiance* (1610), STC: 14267.

[c]Returned from EEBO by (ii) from Bacon's *Henry the Seuenth* (1629).

[d]In 'Of Ambition' we find "There is also great vse of *Ambitious Men*, in being Skreenes to Princes, in Matters of Danger and Enuie", Francis Bacon, *The Essayes or Counsels* (1625), STC: 1148. Bacon has the second use of people as screens after *The Tempest*.

[e]Returned from EEBO by (ii) from Bacon's *The Essayes* (1625). 'Fen' and 'marsh' were used interchangeably in 1572: "Asia is also a meere, fenne, or marishe, nere to the ryuer Caystrus", see Huloet (1572, sig. Ciij), where "*Moore, fenne, or marishe*" is given under 'M'.

[f]First known use is "The aire of *Famagusta* is very vnwholesome, as they say, by reason of certaine marish ground adioyning it", Richard Hakluyt, *The principal nauigations* (1599–1600), STC: 12626a.

[g]Earliest return is "nor geue any printe of good life", John Jewel, *A replie vnto M. Hardinges answeare* (1565). STC: 14606.

[h]First known use is Raphael Holinshed, *The firste volume* (1577), STC: 13568b, & *The first and second volumes* (1587), STC: 13569.

[i]Bacon has the first known use of this locution which *The Tempest* later used.

[j]Also in a speech on 'The Article of Naturalization' delivered on 17 February 1607 we have "whether it [denial of naturalization] will not quicken and excite all the envious and malicious humours", Francis Bacon, *The union of the two kingdoms of Scotland and England* (1670), Wing: B340. In 'Novum Organon' (1620), Francis Bacon has "butterflies stupified and half dead with cold [... the heated pan] quickens and gives them life", Spedding (1857–82, VIII.249), translated from Latin c.1858 by an unnamed Cambridge undergraduate but checked by Spedding. In the posthumously published 'Sylva Sylvarum', written in English, he writes, "For as Butterflies quicken with Heat, which were benummed with Cold", Francis Bacon, *Sylua syluarum* (1627), STC: 1168.

[k]Francis Bacon, *Sylua syluarum* (1627, 340), STC: 1168, not recovered in an EEBO search due to a vertical rule in "Snow|Mountaines".

[l]The two precedents are "Stiria, A countrey ioyning to Austria and Carinthia in the este parte of Germanye, full of mountaynes sauing a little parte bordrying on Hungary, the people be rude, and the women haue so great throtes by the corruption of the water and ayre", Thomas Elyot, *Bibliotheca* (1542), STC: 7659.5, and "as they that haue swilled in the snowe waters from the mountaynes, call those imperfect, which haue not wyde and hanging throtes like themselues", Philippe de Mornay, *A notable treatise* (1579), STC: 18159.

Table F.2 RCP results from Google for Francis Bacon when searching *The Tempest*

No.	*Locution*	*EEBO search*	*Bacon's work*	*Rarity*
1	"Being once perfected how to graunt suits, / how to deny them: who t'advance and who / To trash for ouer-topping (79–81)" (1.2.98)	(i) {suits near.5 deny} [context: 'grant' by authority for advancement]	(i/ii) "to grant all suits were to undo yourself, or your people. To deny all suits were to see never a contented face" 'Letter to the king' (1620)[a]	(i) 0/5377(unique)[b]
		(ii) {grant near.5 suits} [context: 'deny' advancement]		(ii) 0/5377(unique)[c]
		(iii) {overtop(ping)(s)}	(iii) "There is Vse also of Ambitious Men, in Pulling downe the Greatnesse, of any Subiect that ouer-tops" 'Of Ambition' *The Essayes or Counsels* (1625)	(iii) 28/5377(0.521%)
2	"Doe you put trickes vpon's with Saluages" (2.2.58–59)	{put(ting) trick(s) upon}	"Some build rather vpon abusing others, and as wee now say, putting trickes vpon them" *The Essaies* (1612)[d]	0/5377(unique)
3	"Thy bankes with pioned, and twilled brims / Which spungie *Aprill*, at thy hest betrims; / To make cold Nymphs chast crownes" (4.1.71–73)	(i) {pioned}	"In Aprill follow [...] The Double Piony" *The Essayes or Counsels* (1625)	(i) 0/5377(unique)[f]
		(ii) {maiden piony}[e]		(ii) 0/5377(unique)[g]
		(iii) {virgin piony} [context: 'April' mentioned]		(iii) 1/5377(0.019%)[h]
		(iv) {piony near.30 April}		(iv) (0/5377)(unique)[i]
		(v) {pioned near.30 April}		(v) (0/5377)(unique)[j]

[a]Spedding (1861–74, VII.90); also Harley MS 3787, f.187.

[b]Earliest return is "to denie their suits with whom he [which beares all the sway] is displeased" in Marcus Tullius Cicero, *The familiar epistles* (1620), STC: 5305, but there is no mention of granting suits up to 1623.

[c]Earliest return is "and thy [God's] power to grant or deny suites made to thee, shall be no less than theirs [Bacchus and Ceres]" in Virgil, *Virgils Eclogues* (1628), STC: 24820, translated into English by W. L. Gent. No further mention up to 1623.

[d]The earliest known use is Francis Bacon, *The Essaies* (1612, sig. C), STC: 1141, which in December 2012 was not keyed-in text in EEBO but was presently only as a digital image.

[e]Added spelling variations 'peonie' and 'pionie' to this and following searches.

[f]A marginal note in Ovid has "*Ratis* is most properly a Lighter, made of pieces of timber, pioned together, whereon hay or other like things are dragged or drawen with horses on Riuers" in Ovid, *Ouids Metamorphosis* (1618, 53). STC: 18963.

[g]Richard Carew, *A Herrings Tale* (1598). STC: 4614. Does not mention April.

[h]Earliest is "his flowers and leaues are much smaller [than usual female piony], and the stalkes shorter, the whiche some call Mayden or Virgin Peonie" in Dodoens (1578, 244–45). This is doubtless what *The Tempest* is referring to with "Nymphes chaste crownes". Also "Pionie floureth at the beginning of May, and deliuereth his seed in June". However, neither example mentions April.

[i]Bacon has the second known use after the play in his 1625 essay 'Of Gardens' with "In Aprill follow [...] The Double Piony" in Francis Bacon, *The Essayes* (1625, 267). STC: 1148. This is not keyed text, so it is unavailable to an EEBO search. So, only the Shakespeare work and Bacon can be found to refer to the piony in April.

[j]This return is for the *First Folio*'s *The Tempest.*

Notes

1 To qualify as a rare locution, the number of returns was set at less than 6/4233(0.142%) of the searchable documents before 1602, the assumed date of the play. If a locution satisfied this condition it was recorded and the authors who used it were noted.
2 Search date December 2012.
3 Spedding *et al.* (XIII.417).
4 See Clarke (2014, Table 7.2).

Selected Bibliography

Clarke, Barry R. "A linguistic analysis of Francis Bacon's contribution to three Shakespeare plays: *A Comedy of Errors*, *Love's Labour's Lost*, and *The Tempest*." PhD thesis, Brunel University, UK. 2014.

Dodoens, Rembert. *A Niewe Herball, or Historie of Plantes.* London [Antwerp]: Printed by Gerard Dewes, 1578. STC: 6984.

Huloet, Richard. *Huloet's Dictionarie.* London: Thomae Marshij, 1572.

Spedding, James, ed. *The Letters and Life of Francis Bacon.* 7 vols. London: Longman, Green, Longman, and Roberts, 1861–74.

Spedding, James, Robert Leslie Ellis, and Douglas Denon Heath, eds. *The Works of Francis Bacon.* 14 vols. London: Longmans and Co. [etc.], 1857–74.

Spedding, James, Robert Leslie Ellis, and Douglas Denon Heath, eds. *The Works of Francis Bacon.* 15 vols. Boston: Houghton, Mifflin, 1857–82.

Spedding, James, Robert Leslie Ellis, and Douglas Denon Heath, eds. *The Works of Francis Bacon.* 15 vols. Boston: Brown and Taggard, 1860–64.

Appendix G
Full RCP analysis of *Pericles* Act 1

Date search completed: 8 June 2017
Search period: 1473–1690
No. keyed-in searchable texts in search period: 51868
Date of test document: 1609
No. keyed-in searchable texts prior to test document date: 6624
Definition of 'rare': *less than 15/6624 returns (0.226%) before date of test document*

The footnotes of the following table shows the full log of possible sources for rare locutions before the target date, which here is 1609. Documents returned for the year of the target date are ignored. Apart from certain notable authors, the list of usage of a collocation after the target date is not shown in the table footnotes, although they are recorded. When the log has been completed, the RCP for frequently recurring authors (at least three rare returns) are produced, see Table 13.3, Chapter 13 for a summary.

Table G.1 Full logging table of rare returns for *Pericles*, Act 1

Coll. No.	*Collocation (line No.)*	*EEBO search*	*Returns before 1609*
	ACT ONE		
1	"Please your eyes" (1.0.4)	{please your/thine eyes}	6/6624(0.091%)[a]
2	"Haue red it for restoratiues" (1.0.8)	{for restoratives}	1/6624(0.015%)[b]
3	"The purchase is to make men glorious" (1.0.9)	{make men glorious}	0/6624(unique)[c]
4	"So bucksome" (1.0.23)	{so bucksome}	2/6624(0.030%)[d]
5	"Bad childe, worse father" (1.0.27)	{Bad fby.2 worse} [context: bad <noun> worse <noun>]	4(78)/6624(0.060%)[e]

(*Continued*)

Coll. No.	Collocation (line No.)	EEBO search	Returns before 1609
6	"But custom what they did begin / Was with long use account no sin" (1.0.29–30)	(i) {account/ accounted 'no' sin} [disregarding repeated texts] (ii) {custom of sin} (iii) {count sin} (iv) {with long use}	(i) 11/6624(0.166%)[f] (ii) 106/6624(1.600%) (iii) 3/6624(0.045%)[g] (iv) 9/6624(0.136%)[h]
7	"As yon grimme looks do testify" (1.0.40)	{grim looks}	11/6624(0.166%)[i]
8	"The iudgment of your eye" (1.0.41)	{judgment fby.3 eye} [context: judgment of]	19(33)/6624(0.287%)[j] [outside rarity]
9	"to glad her presence" (1.1.10)	{to glad her}	2/6624(0.030%)[k]
10	"their best perfections" (1.1.12)	{best perfections}	3/6624(0.045%)[l]
11	"You Gods that made me man" (1.1.20)	{You Gods that} [context: no comma after Gods]	6(7)/6624(0.091%)[m]
12	"Death like Dragons heere affright thee hard" (1.1.30)	{affright thee}	11/6624(0.166%)[n]
13	"Semblance pale" (1.1.37)	{semblance pale}	1/6624(0.015%)[o]
14	"My frayle mortalitie" (1.1.43)	{frail mortality}	14/6624(0.211%)[p]
15	"And by those fearfull obiects" (1.1.44)	{fearful objects}	6/6624(0.091%)[q]
16	"For death remember'd should be like a mirror" (1.1.46)	(i) {should be like} (ii) {death near.8 mirror} [context: death compared with mirror]	(i) Over 100 (ii) 9(18)/6624(0.136%)[r]
17	"Faithfulness and courage" (1.1.64)	{faithfulness 'AND' courage}	4(5)/6624(0.060%)[s]
18	"By the tenor of out strict edict" (1.1.112)	{strict edict}	2/6624(0.030%)[t]
19	"Succeeding from so faire a tree / As you faire selfe" (1.1.115–16)	{so fair a tree}	0/6624(unique)[u]
20	"Foule Incest" (1.1.127)	{foul incest}	7/6624(0.106%)[v]
21	"Least my life be cropt" (1.1.142)	{be cropped}	14(15)/6624(0.211%)[w]

Coll. No.	*Collocation (line No.)*	*EEBO search*	*Returns before 1609*
22	"To trumpet foorth my infamie" (1.1.146)	{trumpet forth}	2/6624(0.030%)[x]
23	"It fits thee not to ask the reason why" (1.1.157)	{it fits thee/you}	5/6624(0.075%)[y]
24	"Hits the marke his eye doth leuell at" (1.1.164)	{mark NEAR.5 level at}	25/6624(0.377%)[z] [outside rarity]
25	"The sad companion" (1.2.2)	{sad companion}	0/6624(unique)[aa]
26	"Dull eyde melancholie" (1.2.3)	{dull eyed} [context: adjective/noun]	1(2)/6624(0.015%)[bb]
27	"Nor bootes it me to say" (1.2.20)	{boots it me}	6/6624(0.091%)[cc]
28	"Doe cut his threed of life" (1.2.106)	{thread of life}	5/6624(0.075%)[dd]
29	"Ile then discourse our woes" (1.4.18)	{discourse our woe(s)}	0/6624(unique)[ee]
30	"Wanting breathe to speak" (1.4.19)	{wanting breath}	8/6624(0.121%)[ff]
31	"So jetted and adorned" (1.4.26)	{jetted}	27/6624(0.408%)[gg] [outside rarity]
32	"Glad the sight" (1.4.28)	{glad the sight}	0/6624(unique)[hh]
33	"Delight the tast" (1.4.40)	{delight the taste}	7/6624(0.106%)[ii]
34	"Our cheeks and hollow eyes doe witnesse it" (1.4.51)	{cheeks near.3 hollow eyes}	4/6624(0.060%)[jj]
35	"And make a conquest of vnhappie mee" (1.4.68)	{unhappy me}	13/6624(0.196%)[kk]
36	"The Gods of Greece protect you" (1.4.95)	{Gods near.3 protect you}	2/6624(0.030%)[ll]
37	"Untill our Starres that frowne, lend vs a smile" (1.4.106)	{stars near.3 frown}	2/6624(0.030%)[mm]

[a]Thomas Becon, *A pleasaunt newe nosegay* (1543), STC: 1743; John Foxe, *Christ Iesus triumphant* (1579), STC: 11231; Thomas Churchyard, *A pleasaunte laborinth* (1580), STC: 5250; W. S., *The lamentable tragedie of Locrine* (1595), STC: 21528; John Day, *The trauailes of the three English brothers [play]* (1607), STC: 6417; Richard Kilby, *The burthen of a loaden conscience* (1608), STC: 14950. Wilkins was part author of *The trauailes.*

[b]"to drawe out quintesses for restoratiues", Robert Greene, *Perimedes the blacke-smith* (1588), STC: 12295. Later is Thomas Middleton, *No wit, [no] help like a womans comedy* (1657), Wing: M1985.

[c]Later is William Drummond, *A midnights trance* (1619), STC: 7252.5.

[d]Horace, *A medicinable morall* (1566), STC: 13805; Horace, *his arte of poetrie* (1567), STC: 13797.

[e]"bad logitians, worse subiects" Matthew Sutcliffe, *An ansvvere to a certaine libel supplicatorie* (1592), STC: 23450; "bad sowing worse fruites" Lambert Daneau, *A fruitfull commentarie* (1594), STC: 6227; "A bad account: worse seruants no man hath" Thomas Nashe, *A pleasant comedie, called Summers last will and testament* (1600), STC: 18376; "Bad words, worse deeds", George Wilkins, *The miseries of inforst mariage* (1607), STC: 25635.

[f]Thomas Becon, *Newes out of heauen* (1541), STC: 1739; I. S., *The pitifull estate* (1564), STC: 21504; George Wapull, *The tyde taryeth* (1576), STC: 25018; William Perkins, *A golden chaine* (1591), STC: 19657; Jean Taffin, *The amendment of life* (1595), STC: 23650; John Terry, *The trial of truth* (1600), STC: 23913; William Bradshaw, *A myld and iust defence* (1606), STC: 3522.

[g]"counte sinne after our awne imaginations" William Tyndale, *That faith* (1528), STC: 24454; "to count sinne no sinne" Edwin Sandys, *Sermons* (1585), STC: 21713; "Which makes men count sinne, Custom, not offence", George Wilkins, *The miseries of inforst marriage* (1607), STC: 25635.

[h]First use is Desiderius Erasmus, *An epystell* (1534), STC: 10489. Later is Francis Bacon, *Historie natural and experimentall, of life and death* (1638), STC: 1158.

[i]First use is Baldassarre Castiglione, *The courtyer* (1561), STC: 4778. Later is "but with thy grim lookes", William Shakespeare, *Coriolanus* (1623), STC: 22273.

[j]William Shakespeare [?], *Loues labors lost* (1598), STC: 22294; Ben Jonson, *Euery man in his humor* (1601), STC: 14766. With an additional adverb, "Would stay the iudgement of the curiost eye", Thomas Dekker, *The pleasant comodie of patient Grisill* (1603), STC: 6518; "the Iudgement of mine own eie" George Wilkins, *The miseries of inforst marriage* (1607), STC: 25656.

[k]Geoffrey Chaucer, *The works* (1542), STC: 5069; John Phillips, *An epitaph on death* (1581), STC: 19867.

[l]Walter Baley, *A discourse of the medicine* (1585), STC: 6909; Thomas Lodge, *A margarite of America* (1596), STC: 16660; Henry Lok, *Ecclesiastes* (1597), STC: 16696. Later is W. S., *A funeral elegye in memory of the late virtuous maister Peter of Whipton neere Excester* (1612), STC: 21526; Philip Massinger, *The bond-man* (1624), STC: 17632; Phillip Massinger, *The unnaturall combat* (1639), STC: 17643.

[m]Robert Crowley, *The confutation* (1548), STC: 6082; Quintus Curtius Rufus, *The history* (1553), STC: 6142; John Higgins, *The first parte of the Mirour for magistrates* (1574), STC: 13443; Richard Robinson, *The rewarde of wickednesse* (1574), STC: 21121.7; John Derricke, *The image of Irelande* (1581), STC: 6734; Thomas Howell, *His deuises* (1581), STC: 13875; William Barksted, *Mirrha* (1607), STC: 1429. Later is Thomas Heywood, *Troia Britanica* (1609), STC: 13366; Francis Beaumont, *Phylaster* (1620), STC: 1681.5 (attribution shared with Fletcher).

[n]Notables are "the deuilles shall affright thee a great deale more", Anthony Munday, *The first booke of Amadis Gaule* (1590), STC: 541; "my sad griefes doe not affright thee" Michael Drayton, *The tragicall legend of Robert* (1596), STC: 7232; William Shakespeare [?], *The first part of the contention* (1600), STC: 26100. Later is George Chapman, *The vvidovves teares* (1612), STC: 4994; John Marston, *The insatiate countesse* (1613), STC: 17476; William Shakespeare [?], *Romeo and Juliet, The second Part of Henry the Sixt* (1623), STC: 22273.

[o]"Of ashie semblance, pale and bloudlesse", William Shakespeare [?], *The first part of the contention* (1600), STC: 26100.

[p]Notables are Thomas Dekker, *Satiro-Mastix* (1602), STC: 6521; Michael Drayton, *The barrons vvars* (1603), STC: 7189; Michael Drayton, *Moyses in a map of his miracles* (1604), STC: 7209; Michael Drayton, *Poems* (1605), STC: 7216. Later is Michael Drayton, *Poly-Olbion* (1612), STC: 7226; Michael Drayton, *A chorographicall description of tracts* (1622), STC: 7228.

[q]Estienne de Maisonneufve, *The gallant, delectable and pleasaunt historie* (1578), STC: 17203; Michael Drayton, *The tragicall legend of Robert*, (1596), STC: 7232; Edmund Spenser, *The faerie queene* (1596), STC: 23082; I. D., *The most wonderfull and true storie* (1597), STC: 6170.7; Livy, *The Romane historie* (1600), STC: 16613; Michael Drayton, *Poems* (1605), STC: 7216. No later dramatists.

[r]"his brother kyng Richard, whose death he saw as in a mirror", Edward Hall, *The vnion of the two noble and ilustre famelies of Lancaster [and] Yorke* (1548), STC: 12722; "And of my death a mirror make" John Higgins, *The first parte of the Mirour for magistrates* (1574), STC: 13443; Thomas Churchyard, *A general rehearsall of warres* (1579), STC: 5235.2; George Whetstone, *The enemie to vnthryftinesse* (1586), STC: 25341.5; George Whetstone, *The English mirror* (1586), STC: 25336; Anon, *The raigne of King Edvvard the third* (1596), STC: 7501; John Norden, *The mirror of honor* (1597), STC: 18614; Gabriel Powel, *The resolued Christian* (1600), STC: 20150; "both in her life and in her death she was appointed to be the mirror of her time", Thomas Dekker, *The vvonderfull yeare* (1603), STC: 6535 (but *she* was the mirror not death).

[s]Sir Philip Sidney, *Arcadia* (1590), STC: 22539; Edward Vaughan, *A method* (1590), STC: 24597; John Dod, *A plaine and familiar exposition* (1607), STC: 6957; George Wilkins, *The painfull aduentures of Pericles* (1608), STC: 25638.5.

[t]Robert Greene, *Orpharion* (1599), STC: 12260; Marcus Junianus Justinus, *The historie of Iustine* (1606), STC: 24293. Later is Thomas Heywood, *The hierarchie of the blessed angels* (1635), STC: 13327.

[u]Later we have Dekker, here the Lady is referring to Tormiella "tis pitty / A Citizen should haue so faire a Tree / Grow in his Garden", Thomas Dekker, *A tragi-comedy: called Match mee in London* (1631), STC: 6529 (written in 1611).

[v]Robert Henryson, *Heire begynnis the traite* (1570), STC: 13166; George Gascoigne, *A hundredth sundrie flowres* (1573), STC: 11635; George Gascoigne, *The poesies* (1575), STC: 11636; John Lane, *Tom Tel-Troths message* (1600), STC: 15190; Barnabe Barnes, *The Diuils charter a tragaedie* (1607), STC: 1466; Simon Goulart, *Admirable and memorable histories* (1607), STC: 12135; Cyril Tourneur, *The reuengers tragaedie* (1697), STC: 24149.

[w]Notables are "nor no consent to be cropped" Robert Greene, *The carde of fancie* (1584), STC: 12262; "Lest you be cropt before you come to prime" William Shakespeare [?], *The tragedie of King Richard the second* (1597), STC: 22307; Anthony Munday, *Sir Iohn Oldcastle* (1600), STC: 18795 (attribution shared with Drayton, Wilson, Hathwaye). Later is William Shakespeare [?], *Troylus and Cressida* (1609), STC: 22331, Francis Beaumont, *The knight of the burning pestle* (1613), STC: 1674 (written in 1607).

[x]John Davies, *Wittes pilgrimage* (1605), STC: 6344; Samuel Daniel, *The Queenes Arcadia* (1606), STC: 6262. Later is Samuel Rowley, *The noble souldier* (1634), STC: 21416 (attribution shared with Dekker and Day).

[y]Ovid, *The heroycall epistles* (1567), STC: 18940; L. T. A., *Falshood in friendship* (1605), STC: 8; William Perkins, *A godly and learned exposition* (1606), STC: 19732; Christopher Lever, *Queene Elizabeths teares* (1607), STC: 15540; "Faith Sir, it fits you to be more aduis'd", George Wilkins, *The miseries of inforst marriage* (1607), STC: 25635. Later is "I'm sure it fits thee to be ever talking", Francis Beaumont, *The Captaine, Comedies and tragedies* (1647), Wing: B1581 (attribution shared with Fletcher).

[z]Notables are "Seeing then your thoughts leuell at a wrong marke", Robert Greene, *Ciceronis amor* (1589), STC: 12224; "It is the chiefest marke they leuell at", Christopher Marlowe, *Edward the second* (1594), STC: 17437.

[aa]John Webster, *The Thracian wonder* (1661), Wing: T1078A (attribution shared with Rowley).

[bb]"dull eyed foole", William Shakespeare [?], *The most excellent historie of the merchant of Venice* (1600), STC: 22296. "dull eyed", only: John Marston, *What you will* (1607), STC: 17487; Thomas Middleton, *A chast mayd* (1630), STC: 17877 (written 1613).

[cc]Henry Chillester, *Youthes witte* (1581), STC: 5137.5; William Warner, *Albions England* (1597), STC: 25082a; Lawrence Barker, *Christs checke* (1599), STC: 1423; Torquato Tasso, *Godfrey of Bulloigne* (1600), STC: 23698; Battista Guarini, *Il pastor fido* (1602), STC: 12415; Tho. Scott, *Foure paradoxes* (1602), STC: 22107. Later is John Davies, *The muses sacrifice* (1612), STC: 6338.

[dd]Brooke has the exact use of 'cut' with "Attropos shall cut, my fatall thread of lyfe", Arthur Brooke, *The tragicall historye of Romeus and Iuliet* (1562), STC: 1356.7; Humphrey Llwyd, *The breuiary of Britayne* (1573), STC: 16636; John Phillips, *A commemoration* (1578), STC: 19864; Thomas Watson, *The lamentations* (1587), STC: 25118.4; Anon., *A most pleasant comedie of Mucedorus* (1598), STC: 18230; Theophilus Field, *An Italians dead bodie* (1600), STC: 19154.3. Later is John Fletcher, *The faithfull shepheardesse* (1610), STC: 11068; Thomas Dekker, *A new crier of lanthorne* (1616), STC: 6487; Thomas Heywood, *Gynaikeion* (1624), STC: 13326; Francis Bacon, *Of the advancement and proficience of learning* (1640), STC: 1167.7.

[ee]Later is "wayle our fortunes, and discourse our woe", Thomas Heywood, *The foure prentises* (1615), STC: 13321 (acted about 1600).

[ff]Later is John Ford, *The chronicle of Perkin Warbeck* (1634), STC: 11157; Philip Massinger, *Three new playes* (1655), Wing: M1050.

[gg]Notables are George Gascoigne, *A steele glas* (1576), STC: 11645; "the two portals that ietted out", Thomas Dekker, *The magnificent entertainment* (1604), STC: 6510; and later is "they ietted vppe & downe", Thomas Dekker, *Lanthorne and candle-light* (1609), STC: 6486; "and thy houses ietted out", Thomas Nashe, *Christes teares* (1613), STC: 18368 but written before he died in 1601; "we haue Ietted long on the Stage", Thomas Dekker, *The blacke rod* (1630), STC: 6492.5.

[hh]Later is Ben Jonson, 'Vnder-woods', *The vvorkes* (1641), STC: 14754; Francis Beaumont, *Poems* (1653), Wing: B1602.

[ii]Pietro Martire Vermigli, *Most fruitfull [and] learned co[m]mentaries* (1564), STC: 24670; Heinrich Bullinger, *An exhortation* (1575), STC: 4055.5; Thomas Hill, *The gardeners labyrinth* (1577), STC: 13485; Pietro Martire Vermigli, *The common places* (1583), STC: 24669; Robert Cleaver, *A godlie forme* (1598), STC: 5383; Pierre de L'Estoile, *A true discourse* (1601), STC: 21802; Phillipe de Mornay, *The true knowledge* (1602), STC: 18163. Later is Francis Bacon, *Sylua syluarum* (1627), STC: 1168. Thomas Nashe, *Quarternio* (1633), STC: 18382, who must have used it before he died in 1601.

[jj]"hangynge chekes small holowe eies", Desiderius Erasmus, *De co[n]temptu mundi* (1532), STC: 10470.8; "hollowe eyes, leane chekes", Thomas Becon, *The reliques of Rome* (1563), STC: 1755; "my wane cheeks, my hollow eyes", John Lyly, *Euphues* (1580), STC: 17070; "with hollow eyes, pale cheeks", Thomas Nashe, *Pierce Penilesse* (1592), STC: 18373.

[kk]Notables are John Lyly, *Mother Bombie* (1594), STC: 17084; Christopher Marlowe, *The tragedie of Dido* (1594), STC: 17441; John Lyly, *The vvoman in the moone* (1597), STC: 17090; Thomas Heywood, *The first and second partes of King Edward the Fourth* (1600), STC: 13342 (perhaps shared attribution). Later is Philip Massinger, *The unnaturall combat* (1639), STC: 17643.

[ll]Augustin Marlorat, *A catholike and ecclesiasticall exposition* (1575), STC: 17406; "the gods protect you still", George Peele, *The historie of the tvvo valiant knights* (1599), STC: 5450a. Later is "The Gods protect you", William Shakespeare [?], *The Tragedie of Cymbeline* (1623), STC: 22272; "the gods protect you", Francis Beaumont, *Comedies and tragedies* (1647), Wing: B1581; "The Gods of Rome protect you all", John Webster, *Appius and Virginia* (1654), Wing: W1215.

[mm]Richard Johnson, *The most famous history* (1596), STC: 14677; Robert Albott, *Englands Parnassus* (1600), STC: 378. Later is "though his Stars have frown'd", James Shirley, *The doubtful heir* (1652), Wing: S3466, although Shirley would have been 13 years old in 1609.

Bonus Essays

Response to *Country Life* Magazine

15 Alleged Shakespeare Portrait

On 20 May 2015, *Country Life* magazine published an article claiming that historian Dr Mark Griffiths had discovered a portrait of William Shakespeare in the 1597 edition of *The Herball or Generall Historie of Plantes* by John Gerard (see Figure 15.1). On the title page are four figures, the fourth of which stands on a plinth dressed in Roman toga. Below him, engraved on the plinth is a rebus puzzle (see Figure 15.2), which has hitherto been taken to be a printer's mark of John Norton, who receives credit on the same page (see Figure 15.3). The meaning

Figure 15.1 Face alleged to be a Shakespeare portrait, from Gerard's *The Herball* (1597).

Figure 15.2 Rebus puzzle situated on a plinth below the alleged Shakespeare portrait, from Gerard's *The Herball* (1597).

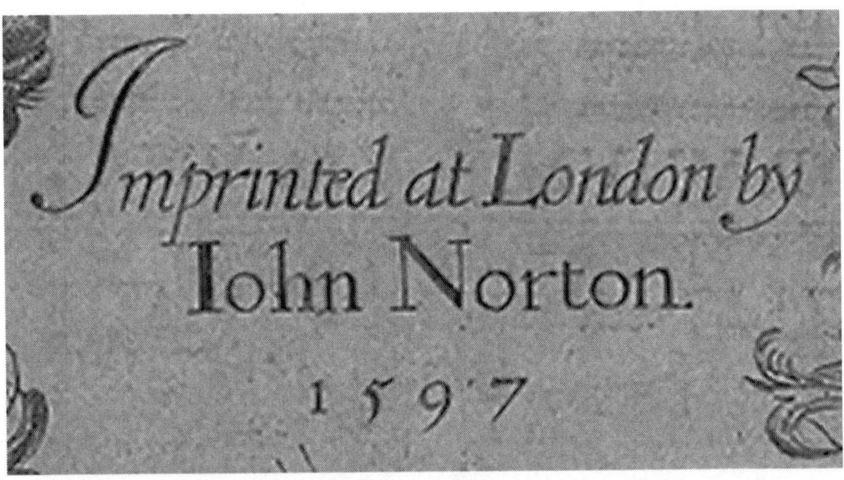

Figure 15.3 Credit to the printer 'Iohn Norton' on same page as the alleged Shakespeare portrait, from Gerard's *The Herball* (1597).

of the symbols in this rebus has so far remained obscure, but Dr Griffiths claims that rather than being a printers' mark, the rebus conceals a coded reference to William Shakespeare, who he identifies as the fourth figure.

The difficulties with Dr Griffith's rebus explanation are several. First, its non-direct, even strained, use of Latin to try to make it work: the '4' as 'quattuor', which needs to be abbreviated to 'quat.'. Adding the 'E' then makes 'quate', which means 'shake'. The need for abbreviation when other possibilities accrue (e.g. not abbreviating) immediately removes the advantage of directness from this solution. Also, there is a very clear 'N' in this rebus. Why has it been omitted from consideration? Why do the 'O' and 'R' not play a direct part in his solution? The vertical rule through the '4' makes, to Dr Griffith's mind, a spear, even though the triangular top is asymmetrical, and the bottom of the 'spear' is curiously bent to the right. It would be instructive to observe this spear in flight. A horizontally reflected 4-with-vertical-rule was often used in printers' marks, albeit without the right oblique line descending from the top of the '4', and presumably not as part of a spear (Lemoine 1997, Nos. 8, 13, 26, 28, etc). Even if Dr Griffith's explanation as 'shake' and 'spear' were the intended one, an alternative interpretation is still possible: that the rebus refers to Pallas Athena the spear shaker, Goddess of Wisdom. The generic figure on the plinth could simply be 'wise'.

The present author will now suggest an alternative solution, one which demonstrates a greater theoretical economy. Since the '4'-with-vertical-rule had previous use in printers' marks, then the most likely solution is that it *is* a printers' mark (this is not a new idea). It is certainly a credible solution since the 1597 edition of 'The herball' credits the printer as 'John Norton' (see Figure 15.3).[1] We now make full use of the 'N', 'O', 'R' and the three 'XXX' in the rebus, which, in keeping with the Roman theme, are 'tens' to make 'NORtens' (this *is* a new idea).

William Norton, who was John's uncle, had previously used a mark where the letters 'nor' were set on a barrel 'tun' to make 'nortun' (see Figure 15.4).[2] The present case also splits off the letters 'NOR' from the rest of the name.

Dr Griffiths has suggested in his *Country Life* blog that no printer could change his mark, although the Nortons had used several previous variations, and any symbol (e.g. 'XXX') that had been used by other printers had to retain its previous meaning. These are not necessary rules of rebus design.

Some explanation is required for the broken 'E'. I suggest that John Norton, who was (or was at least promoting himself as) the queen's printer, was inserting a reference to Elizabeth, and I suggest that part of the function of the oblique line descending to the right from the top of the '4' is to direct attention to that; see Figure 15.5 (Lemoine 1797, 75).

Figure 15.4 William Norton's printer's mark (McKerrow 1913, No.174) described as a 'tun with nor' (McKerrow 1913, 65).

John Norton, eſq. the queen's printer, in Latin, Greek, and Hebrew, was of the Company of Stationers, to whom he gave 1000l. to purchaſe lands, to the value of 50l. per ann. and part to be lent to poor young men of the ſaid Company. He alſo gave 150l. to the pariſh of St. Faith, under St. Paul's Church, to purchaſe 7l. 10s. yearly for ever, to be given to the poor. In 1593, he lived at the ſign of the Queen's-arms, in the houſe formerly inhabited by his couſin Bonham Norton; and, being a man of eminence, employed ſeveral others to print for him. He appears to have been the firſt who introduced Printing at Eton, in 1610."

Figure 15.5 Evidence that John Norton advertised himself as the queen's printer (Lemoine 1797, 75).

I judge that this explanation is far less strained than that given by Dr Griffiths, makes better use of all the letters, and avoids the assumption that the relatively unknown Shakspere, who in 1597 was still waiting to see his name on a play quarto, was being afforded Roman God status on a plinth in a book on gardening!

16 A Country Controversy

Introduction

On 20 May 2015, the editors of *Country Life* magazine boldly trumpeted historian Dr Mark Griffiths's claim to have found a new Shakespeare portrait in a sixteenth-century book on gardening. The case rested mainly on the interpretation of the rebus on the plinth below the figure alleged to be Shakespeare, a puzzle that has since been given a more economical treatment as a printer's mark. Not only did they judge incorrectly that this idea would float, but the boat has now been launched into even deeper water, with Dr Griffiths's further 'discovery' of a new Shakespeare playlet. This is presented under the rather appropriate title 'A Country Controversy'.

The piece in question is an entertainment delivered before Queen Elizabeth on 10 May 1591 at Theobald's, Lord Burghley's residence. It features a gardener and a molecatcher who find themselves locked in conflict about their respective claims to a jewel box found during the construction of Robert Cecil's garden (see Figure 16.1). Part of the playlet seems to represent a petition to the queen that when Lord Burghley retires from public office his second son Robert Cecil might take over his duties (Breight 1987). Flattery of the queen is used to assist the suit, so that when the Gardener declares of 'Eglantine' [the queen's flower] "the deeper it is rooted in the ground, the sweeter it smelleth in the flower, making it ever so green that the sun of Spain at the hottest cannot parch it", it could not have escaped her notice that her victory over the Spanish Armada was only three years behind them. Robert Cecil would eventually become Principal Secretary.

As Dr Griffiths informs us, "I attribute it to Shakespeare on the basis of stylistic evidence and in the light of the association that I've discovered between him, Burghley [Lord Treasurer], and Gerard [the author of 'The Herball', the aforementioned gardening book]". Unfortunately, these associations have since been placed in so much doubt that the weight now rests almost entirely on the 'stylistic evidence'. However, there is no stylistic evidence for Shakspere of Stratford as his contribution to the Shakespeare canon is at present incapable of estimation. There are

The gardiners speach

Most fortunate and faire Quene, one Whose harte Wisdome hathe layd her Crowne, and in whose handes Justice hathe left her ballance, voutsafe to heare a Contrie contryversie for y^{t} there is as great equitie in determininge poore mens unions, as of riche mens landes. The younger sonne of ye owner of this house at a litle farme of his, iii^{ee} myle hence called Pymmes, devised a plot for a garden, as me thought in a place unfytt for pleasure, beinge overgrowen wth thistles and turned up wth moles, and besides so farre from ye house y^{t} in my Cuntry capacitie a pounde had bene meeter y^{en} a paradize, what his meaning was I durst not enquire but what my labours were I dare boast of. The moles distroyed and ye plot leveled, I cast it into iiii^{or} quarters in ye first I framed a Maze, not of hissope and tyme but y^{t} wch makethe tyme itselfe to wither wth wondringe. All ye vertues, all ye greaces all ye muses wynding, and wreathinge about yor may^{tie} eache contending to be chiefe, all contented to be cherished. And this not of pothearbes but of flowers & of flowers fairest and sweetest for in so heavenly a maze, wch astonished all earthly thoughtes what did not bewtye bringe, what dyd not fortune promyse.

The Vertues were done in roses, flowers fitt for ye xii vertues having in y^{em} selfes, (as wee Gardyners have observed) above an hundred. The Graces of pawnces partie collored in one stalke, sisters never asunder but dyverselye beautified. The Muses of ix^{en} severall cullors being of sundrye natures yet all sweete all soveraigne. Theise mingled in a Maze and brought into suche shapes as Poettes and Painters have made us

Figure 16.1 Extract from 'The Gardiners speech'.[18]

simply no prose works or letter of his that may be used in a test of style against the canon. The boat has insufficient buoyancy to support the cargo. A further speech is also attributed to Shakespeare: namely *The Hermit's Speech*, "the verse address that greeted the Queen and her courtiers on their arrival at Theobald's". The evidence for both of these claims chiefly consists of a list of word and phrase parallels between the playlet and Shakespeare's accepted canon. An additional claim that Shakespeare acted in this device is pure speculation.

There are three points that will be addressed here about the argument given in *Country Life*. The first relates to the exclusivity of the phrase matches, the second to Shakspere's unlikely access to a classified letter, and the third to more plausible candidates than the Stratford man.

The History of the Playlet

There has been some doubt as to the authenticity of the documents due to the fact that it was the notorious forger John Payne Collier who first introduced them. His first action was to print the blank verse poem delivered by the Hermit to the queen on her arrival at Theobald's (Collier 1831, I.284–88). He then sent the Gardener's speech, the Molecatcher's speech, and the six-line verse concerning the jewel box to the literary historian Alexander Dyce, who declared that Collier had informed him that not only were they in the hand of George Peele, but they were also marked with a 'G.P.' signature (Dyce 1828–39, III.159–69). This was subsequently disputed by Walter Greg, who noted that the 'G.P.' signature could not be found and that the Hermit's speech was in a different hand from the rest (Greg 1925, 452–54). Support came from Peele scholar Thorleif Larsen, who compared their handwriting against Peele's autograph manuscript of *Anglorum Feriae* and thought it not in Peele's style (Larsen 1928–9). The original manuscripts are written in a secretary script and now reside in the British Library under the title 'A Speeche made before the Queen at Tybolles'.[3] Although undated, their content clearly alludes to the 1591 entertainments. Fortunately for history, a copy of the Gardener's speech also exists in the Cecil papers at Hatfield House, again undated and in secretarial script (see Figure 16.1 for an extract).[4] It seems to be a grammatically better version than the British Library manuscript (Colethorpe 1987).

Exclusivity of Phrase Matches

Dr Griffiths provides several words and phrases that appear in both the Gardener-Molecatcher playlet and the Shakespeare canon. For example, 'onions' (*Hamlet*, V.ii.218–9), 'pate' (*The Taming of the Shrew*, I.ii.12), 'paradise' (*The Comedy of Errors*, IV.iii.16), 'cunning' (*Hamlet*, II.ii.432), 'intending' (*The Two Gentlemen of Verona*, IV.iii.43–4), 'heave' (*The Rape of Lucrece*, II.412–3), and 'gird' [noun] (*1 Henry VI*, III.1.132). Running these through Chadwyck-Healey's Early English Books Online (EEBO) database allows one to find the percentage of searchable documents in which these appear before 1591, the assumed date of the playlet. With 3,397 such documents available, the results are as follows: 'onions' (5.3%), 'pate' (7.4%), 'paradise' (27.4%), 'cunning' (28.7%), 'intending' (15.4%), 'heave' (27.5%), and 'gird' [noun] (0.62%). A more complex word string, 'lord of the soil' (*2 Henry VI*, IV.x.24), results in a 0.7% return. Rarer is the Latin '*animis caelestibus irae*' (*2 Henry VI*, II.1.24), which has only 2/3397(0.09%) returns before 1591: John Harvey has one of its uses in *A discoursiue probleme* (1588).[5] A similar rarity is afforded by 'light of hearing' (*King Lear*, III.iv.90; as 'light of ear'), which appears in only 3/3397(0.09%) of searchable documents in EEBO.

The locutions, 'like a lapwing' (*Much Ado About Nothing*, III.ii.24) and 'twitteth' (*The Two Gentlemen of Verona*, IV.i.8; as 'She twits me'), have no returns before 1591. Both are used later by the dramatist George Chapman, the former in *Sir Gyles Goosecappe Knight* (1606),[6] and the latter in his translation of *Homer's Odyssey* (1615).[7] The use of 'lapwing' as a simile also appears in works by John Lyly: "wherein you resemble the Lapwing" in *Campaspe* (1584)[8] and "lapwing-like flying far from the place where I nestle" in *Mother Bombie* (1594).[9] Even Thomas Nashe found a use for it "to withdraw men (lapwing like) from his nest" in *Haue with you to Saffron-walden* (1596).[10]

Around 1597–8, Francis Bacon gave a Reading at Gray's Inn "Upon the Statute of Vses" in which the following occurs "which time they began to heave at uses" (27.5%).[11] Having been used in the sense 'to intellectually pressurize', this resembles 'that all those that be heavers at your State' from the Theobald's playlet. Virgil's rare Latin '*Tantaene animis celestibus irae*?'[12] which appears in the Gardener's speech as "*[sunt] animis caelestibus irae*" (0.09%) can be found in Bacon's then unpublished private wastebook, *The Promus of Formularies and Elegancies* (1592–4), in the form Virgil had set it down.[13]

It is fair to say that those locutions marked at greater than 1% of the EEBO searchable documents were in common use by the time they were inserted in the Shakespeare canon and are insufficiently rare to assert concordance. Unfortunately, it is a common defect of works that compare parallel words, phrases, and collocations, that no attempt is made to estimate the rarity of their use in the contemporary literature. This leaves them vulnerable to the charge of having arisen from a common source. A second issue has already been addressed, the problem of the division of attribution in the Shakespeare work, which cannot be assumed to be Shakspere's by default. Neither of these issues have been given attention by Dr Griffiths.

The Rare Word

In a passage from the Molecatcher's speech, we find

> Now, for that this Gardener twitteth me with my vocation: I could prove it a mystery not mechanical, and tell the tale of the giant's daughter which was turned to a mole because she would eat fairer bread than is made of wheat [...] and how good clerks told me that moles in fields were ill subjects in commonwealths, which are always turning up in places in which they are bred.

According to Dr Griffiths "The giant's daughter too was an actual monarch - Mary, Queen of Scots". The word 'twitteth' does not appear in the searchable database before 1591 and so is rare. Its origin is not given in the *Country Life* article, but curiously the earliest return from EEBO is in a work by William Camden (1624).

It records that in 1561, Mary Queen of Scots refused to ratify the Treaty of Edinburgh in which she was required to relinquish her claim to certain titles. This so angered Queen Elizabeth that when Mary requested safe passage from France to Scotland, the Queen of England refused. Mary's reaction is recorded by the ambassador Throgmorton in his letters (see Figure 16.2), to whom she reportedly said of Elizabeth, "Shee twitteth me, and saith, that I haue small experience" (see Figure 16.3).

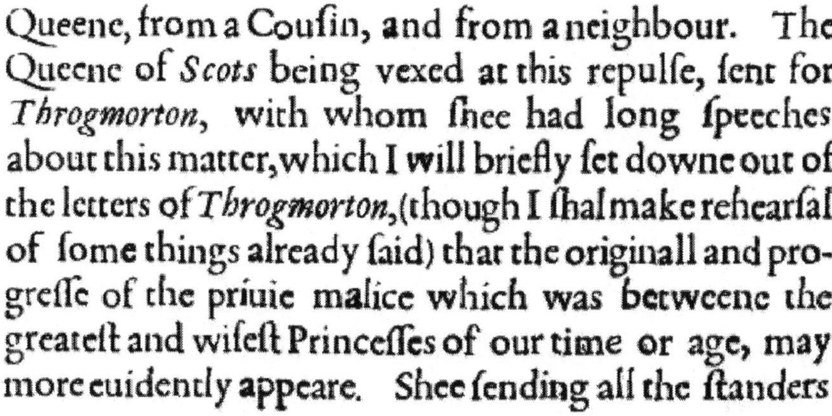
Queene, from a Couſin, and from a neighbour. The Queene of *Scots* being vexed at this repulſe, ſent for *Throgmorton*, with whom ſhee had long ſpeeches about this matter, which I will briefly ſet downe out of the letters of *Throgmorton*, (though I ſhal make rehearſal of ſome things already ſaid) that the originall and progreſſe of the priuie malice which was betweene the greateſt and wiſeſt Princeſſes of our time or age, may more euidently appeare. Shee ſending all the ſtanders

Figure 16.2 Evidence that the views of Mary Queen of Scots were obtained from the letters of Ambassador Throgmorton (Camden 1624, 4).

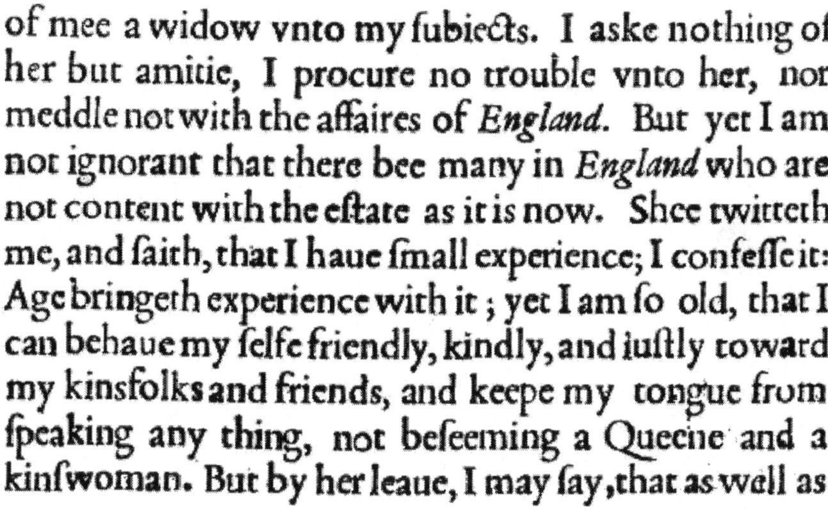
of mee a widow vnto my ſubiects. I aske nothing of her but amitie, I procure no trouble vnto her, nor meddle not with the affaires of *England*. But yet I am not ignorant that there bee many in *England* who are not content with the eſtate as it is now. Shee twitteth me, and ſaith, that I haue ſmall experience; I confeſſe it: Age bringeth experience with it; yet I am ſo old, that I can behaue my ſelfe friendly, kindly, and iuſtly toward my kinsfolks and friends, and keepe my tongue from ſpeaking any thing, not beſeeming a Queene and a kinſwoman. But by her leaue, I may ſay, that as well as

Figure 16.3 Mary Queen of Scots reports to Ambassador Thogmorton of Queen Elizabeth that "Shee twitteth me" (Camden 1624, 5).

Camden did not begin his *Annals, or Historie of Queen Elizabeth* until 1608, work that served as a basis for *The historie* (1624). Given the rarity of this word and its specific context, it appears that the author of the Molecatcher's speech had access to the ambassador's letter. In that case, one wonders how an unknown actor such as Shakespeare could have seen it.

More Plausible Candidates

The point is, there are more realistic alternatives than Shakespeare, ones who from our vantage point in time had a history of writing entertainments for the queen.

From 1594, Robert Cecil is credited with a 'Hermit's Oration' for the queen's next visit to Theobald's. Two manuscript copies survive, and both have "penned by Sir Robert Cecill" recorded on them.[14] The Hermit in this speech identifies himself as the one who petitioned the queen at Theobald's in 1591. Furthermore, the 1591 speech refers to Cecil's garden at Pymmes four miles away, which was "overgrown with thistles and turned up by moles". However, Curtis Breight (1987, 1) has disputed Cecil's claim, concluding that "there is no real evidence" that he wrote them. Nevertheless, unless Cecil delegated the writing to another and reserved the credit for himself, he seems to be a prime candidate.

Several commentators have claimed John Lyly as the speech writer. R. W. Bond thought that the box inscription was similar to some of Lyly's nonsense verses (Bond 1902, I.517–20), and by comparing elements of style, Leslie Hotson has attributed other queen's entertainments to Lyly: one at Mitcham in 1598 and another at Chiswick in 1602 (Colethorpe 1987, 4). However, G. K. Hunter declared there to be neither internal nor external evidence for Lyly's intervention.[15]

On 17 November 1592, just 18 months after the Theobald's entertainment, the Earl of Essex, who had been present at Lord Burghley's residence, presented a device before the queen. It consisted of four speeches: 'The Praise of the worthiest virtue', 'The Praise of the worthiest affection, Love', 'The Praise of the worthiest power, Knowledge', and 'The Praise of the worthiest person, Queen Elizabeth'. Two of these were published by Robert Stephens in 1734 (Spedding 1870, v–vi), and all four appeared in the Northumberland Manuscripts collection (Burgoyne 1902). All had been written by Francis Bacon who was Robert Cecil's cousin. Three years later, Bacon composed another device for Essex to present to the queen. This time the speeches featured an old Hermit, a Secretary of State, a Soldier, and an Esquire (Nichols 1823, II.371–72). The first three characters attempt to persuade Erophilus not to love the queen by presenting an argument to his Squire, the whole skit being an obvious reference to Essex's wooing of Elizabeth. The evidence for Bacon's authorship lies in an unfinished draft of a similar device in Lambeth Palace Library, written in Bacon's hand, which states that there were to be four characters, with "one dressed like an Heremite of Philosopher, representing Contemplation".[16] The actual speeches appear in another volume of the same collection with no heading, date, or docket.[17] Five days after this event, Rowland Whyte sent a letter to his friend Sir Robert Sydney identifying the person who played the Esquire as Toby Matthew, who, as Nichols later noted, "was taken into the acquaintance of that noted scholar Sir Francis Bacon of

Gray's Inn" (Nichols 1823, II.372n). It is clear from this that if Bacon was writing a speech for a Hermit in 1595 for presentation to the queen, then he is a good candidate for having done so in 1591.

In summary, the stylistic evidence that the playlet is a Shakespeare work is not specific enough. The word 'twitteth' in the context of Mary Queen of Scots points to a state letter which Shakspere as an unknown actor would have had difficulty accessing. The fact is, there were other candidates who had a stronger claim. One also wonders how a man from the lower classes with no published reputation could have found his way into Lord Burghley's favour. It was difficult enough for courtiers, so it seems unrealistic to expect Shakspere to have achieved it. It would have been easier to choose a man of noble blood who had assisted in writing one of their revels plays. The evidence for Shakespeare as author of this playlet simply does not float.

Notes

1 John Norton worked as a printer from 1621–45. He died in 1645 (McKerrow 1913, 178).
2 The mark is identified as "A tun with 'nor' and a sweet-William [...]" in the English translation of F. Guiccardini's *History of Italy* (1579), see McKerrow (1913, 65). William died in 1593, and this mark was actually used by his son Bonham Norton in 1596, a cousin of John Norton, see McKerrow (1913, 178).
3 British Library, Egerton MS 2623.
4 Cecil Papers, Hatfield House, vol. No. 140, 94.
5 STC: 12908.
6 STC: 12050.
7 STC: 13637.
8 STC: 17048a.
9 STC: 17084.
10 STC: 18369.
11 Francis Bacon, *The learned readings* (1642), Wing: B301.
12 "Is there such wrath in heavenly minds?" *Aenid* (i.15).
13 British Library, Harley 7017, f.90v; see Pott (1883, 190).
14 Lambeth Palace Library, MS 2858, f.188; Bodleian Library, Rawlinson MS D692, f.106.
15 Reported in 'Entertainments', see Breight (1982, 2).
16 Lambeth Palace Library, Gibson Papers, vol. viii, No. 274.
17 Lambeth Palace Library, Gibson Papers, vol. v, No. 18.
18 Cecil Papers, Hatfield House, vol. No. 140, 94.

Selected Bibliography

Bond, R. Warwick. *The Complete Works of John Lyly*. 3 vols. London: Clarendon Press, 1902.

Breight, Curtis C. "Entertainments of Elizabeth at Theobald's in the early 1590s." *REED Newsletter*, 12, No. 2 (1987): 1–6.

Burgoyne, Frank J., ed. *Northumberland Manuscripts. Collotype Facsimile and Type Transcript of an Elizabethan Manuscript Preserved at Alnwick Castle, Northumberland.* London, New York, and Bombay: Longmans, Green & Co., 1902.

Camden, William. *The Historie of the Life and Death of Mary Stuart Queene of Scotland.* London: Printed by Iohn Haviland for Richard Whitaker, 1624. STC: 24509a.

Colethorpe, Marion. "The Theobalds's entertainment for Queen Elizabeth I in 1591." *REED Newsletter* 12, No.1 (1987): 2–9.

Collier, John Payne. *The History of Dramatic Poetry to the Time of Shakespeare.* 3 vols. London: John Murray, 1831.

Dyce, A. *The Works of George Peele.* 3 vols. London: W. Pickering, 1828–39.

Gerard, John. *The Herball or Generall Historie of Plantes.* London: Printed by Arnold Hatfield, 1599 [1597].

Greg, Walter. W. "A Collier mystification." *Review of English Studies* 1 (1925): 452–54.

Larsen, T. "The canon of Peele's works." *Modern Philology* 26, No. 2 (1928–9): 191–99.

Lemoine, Henry, ed. *Typographical Antiquities.* London: S. Fisher, 1797.

McKerrow, Ronald B. *Printers' & Publishers' Devices in England & Scotland 1485–1640.* London: Printed for the Bibliographical Society at the Chiswick Press, 1913.

Nichols, John. *The Progresses and Public processions of Queen Elizabeth.* 3 vols. London: J. Nichols and Son, 1823.

Pott, Mrs Henry, ed. *The Promus of Formularies and Elegencies.* Boston: Houghton, Mifflin & Co., 1883.

Spedding, James, ed. *A Conference of Pleasure, Composed for Some Festive Occasion about the year 1592 by Francis Bacon.* London: Printed by Whittingham and Wilkins, 1870.

Index

Note: Boldface page numbers refer to tables; italic page numbers refer to figures.